The Lawrie Files

Game of Trust

Dr Tess Lawrie & the I Ching

Tessla Books

First published in Great Britain 2025
by Tessla Books, Bath, UK

2 4 6 8 10 9 7 5 3 1

Cover Painting courtesy of Jake Fern
Author photograph courtesy of Toufic Beyhum.

Hardback ISBN: 978-1-0682143-0-1
Paperback ISBN: 978-1-0682143-1-8

Printing by CPI Anthony Rowe
Bumper's Farm, Chippenham, Wiltshire SN14 6LH

Contents

Acronyms and Abbreviations

ADR	Adverse Drug Reactions
BIRD	British Ivermectin Recommendation Development
BMGF	Bill and Melinda Gates Foundation
CELT	Centre of Excellence for Long-acting Therapeutics
CEPI	Coalition for Epidemic Preparedness Innovations
CHD	Children's Health Defense
CIC	Community Interest Company
DHSC	Department of Health and Social Care
E-BMC Ltd	Evidence-based Medicine Consultancy Limited
EtD	Evidence to Decision
FDA	Food and Drug Administration
FLCCC	Frontline Covid-19 Care Critical Alliance
GAVI	The Vaccine Alliance (previously Global Alliance for Vaccines and Immunization).
MHRA	Medicines and Healthcare products Regulatory Agency
NIAID	National Institute of Allergy and Infectious Diseases
NICE	National Institute for Health and Care Excellence
NIH	National Institutes of Health
SAGE	Scientific Advisory Group for Emergencies
UK-CTAP	Covid-19 Therapeutics Advisory Panel
WCH	World Council for Health
WHO	World Health Organization

Foreword

I chose to co-author this book with the English rendering of Richard Wilhelm's German translation of the *I Ching (3rd Ed. 1968)*, an ancient Chinese book of wisdom, as much for the pleasure of my own study as for the education of others. Drawing from Carl Jung's acknowledgment of the *I Ching's* influence on his work, I have used this book, also called the *Book of Changes*, to enhance my understanding of incidents and events during a 13-month cycle, when I worked collaboratively with many other health advocates around the world to facilitate positive societal change.

Game of Trust, structured as a series of 64 "moves", chronicles and interrogates notable experiences in 2021. In embarking on this unusual collaboration with an old book, my primary intention was three-fold: especially for newcomers to this epic Covid-era tale of good over evil, to give an accessible roadmap of incidents and events leading to the formation of the World Council for Health and the better way movement; to provide an evidence pack for legal and lawful actions or general interest (I am often asked for this); and to reflect upon whether the *I Ching* has relevance to modern times.

Without the *I Ching* authors' eloquent and unpredictable perspective, *Game of Trust* would have been a rather dry account of events and a record of documents from the period when a dark world birthed new life. With my wise co-authors however, whose voices I have represented in italics throughout, *Game of Trust* became a novel "game of trust" in itself.

Carl Jung, who penned the foreword to the English rendering of Wilhelm's translation by Carey Baynes in 1949, wrote that *as a person with a sense of responsibility towards science, I am not in the habit of asserting something I cannot prove or at least present as acceptable to reason.*[1] Jung had used the *I Ching* for many years and it no doubt informed his theory of synchronicity. However, when it came to discussing the *I Ching*'s influence on his work and perspective, he was understandably apprehensive that Westerners would consider it merely a *collection of archaic "magic spells".*[2]

Like Jung, I am well aware of the arguments that can be brought against the *I Ching* by those unable or unwilling to think outside the formal academic or established social frameworks. This is why I conceived *Game of Trust* to be as much a conversation about right and proper conduct with the 5,000-year-old oracle, as it is a scientific experiment about the role of ancient wisdom in modern challenges.

Most scientific experiments produce reproducible findings only if the conditions are tightly controlled and variables are kept to a minimum. In contrast to the prevailing scientific method, the *I Ching* method takes into account the tiniest detail. It shares its perspective through the investigator's toss of three coins six times to form a six-line hexagram, the reading of which is interpreted by the same individual. Thus, synchronicity is the mechanism by which the *I Ching* formulates a point of view, a point of view that may resonate with the psyche and intuition of the inquirer alone.

From my inquirer's perspective, the findings throughout the process seemed remarkably significant. I postulated that the *I Ching*'s commentary may, indeed, also resonate with others familiar with events and individuals referenced in this book. Thus, whether its point of view holds general significance will be for readers to determine.

---

1   Foreword. From I Ching, by Richard Wilhelm, 3rd Ed. p.xxxiii.
2   Foreword. From I Ching, by Richard Wilhelm, 3rd Ed. p.xxxiii.

Nevertheless, at the start of this writing project, there was no way of knowing whether my novel approach to studying events and individual perspectives retrospectively would work. As I am a researcher at heart, *Game of Trust* is thus not only an experiment in the intersection of science and philosophy, but also an experiment in trust. Jung wrote, *As to the thousands of questions, doubts, and criticisms that this singular book stirs up – I cannot answer these. The I Ching does not offer itself with proofs and results; it does not vaunt itself, nor is it easy to approach. Like a part of nature, it waits until it is discovered.*[1]

There are many things that we do not yet understand, and that things change is our only certainty. Thus an ancient book called the *Book of Changes* seems an ideal tool for these rapidly changing times. In fact, the *I Ching* calls itself *a book of the future.*[2]

I hope that *Game of Trust* will inspire those always seeking *proofs and results* to reconsider the relationship between mankind and the mysterious. Carl Jung held this ancient text in the highest regard, referencing it as *the ship that is to carry us over the unknown seas.*[3] Through this "game of trust" experiment, readers may wish to contemplate whether the *I Ching* has now proven itself an ideal guide to crossing the great waters at this critical juncture in our evolution.

Dr Tess Lawrie

---

1   Foreword. From I Ching, by Richard Wilhelm, 3rd Ed. p.xxxix.
2   Foreword. From I Ching, by Richard Wilhelm, 3rd Ed. p.252.
3   Foreword. From I Ching, by Richard Wilhelm, 3rd Ed. p.xxxiii.

Preface

"Like the bird in the tree, we must be free" ~ Bob Marley

In 2017, I woke up to a devastating truth: I had been living in a system designed to keep me enslaved. No matter how hard I worked or how much we as a family accumulated, the rat race had no finish line. People suffered or died for no rhyme or reason. Life on Earth felt more like Hell.

At least two traumatic events shaped this revelation. As a young doctor in South Africa, I delivered many healthy babies, only to lose my own firstborn to meningitis, a tragedy that shattered my heart and faith in myself as both mother and physician. Years later, after painstakingly nurturing three young children, my family was thrust into another nightmare: a violent home invasion. At just two, four, and eight years of age, my children witnessed horrors no one should endure. Their father bore the physical brunt of the attack, but the scars ran through all of us. Hoping for a safer life for our family, we left South Africa in 2009.

But safety proved elusive. In the UK, the overt dangers of South Africa gave way to insidious ones. Division, inequity, and mind control permeated society, seeping into the education system and even into our children, who soon displayed signs of chronic illness and systemic conditioning. Caught up in the "breadwinner" role, my maternal influence waned, and my husband and I drifted apart in this alien, disempowering environment. In my despair, I initiated an affair, seeking an escape from the futility and pain, which culminated in my departure from the family home – an action that left four broken hearts in its wake.

One day, my estranged husband looked me in the eye and said, "You were magnificent once. What happened to you?" His words, spoken in anger, shook me to the core. What had happened to the righteous young woman who believed she could change the world? I had rather liked her too.

In the wake of separation, the gentle unfolding of my new relationship breathed life into a spark I thought I had lost. Yet I still felt trapped. Required to work harder than ever to support two households, I juggled consulting for the World Health Organization with conducting scientific reviews for various Cochrane review groups. It was during the conduct of a series of systematic reviews on the management of brain tumours that, in January 2020, I encountered Chrissy Philp, a Bath elder, philosopher and astrologer with a theory she called the "cosmic blueprint of the brain".

My first meeting with Chrissy was nothing short of transformative. To my surprise, it began not with us talking about the brain or her theory but with an ancient Chinese divination practice using a book called the *I Ching*. Shortly after I walked in the door of her glass-domed Bath penthouse, ready to hear about her brain theory, she handed me three coins and instructed me to throw them. The *I Ching* reading was startlingly stern – I had spoiled something, caused hurt, and had amends to make. The accuracy was mind-blowing. It forced me to confront my own failings, and for the first time in years, I felt a sense of clarity. I went to see my aggrieved husband the next day gifting him the sum of our material possessions.

Meanwhile, Chrissy's theories about the cosmos and the human mind fascinated and excited me. She had proved, she said, that our brains act as hardware for cosmic "software," receiving frequencies that shape our thoughts and behaviours – like a mobile phone picking up signals. Her work aligned with the idea that the universe itself might be a hologram, as concluded by the late British physicist and cosmologist Prof. Stephen Hawking. And it made perfect sense to me.

In addition, it confirmed to me something I have always felt deep down, that ancient wisdom holds the keys to navigating this chaotic reality. Everything we need has already been written, sung, danced or spoken. We just needed to read, listen, sing and share. As I immersed myself in these new and old ideas, I started to comprehend the full extent of human ignorance and exploitation and, combined with stimulating conversations with my beloved, life became very interesting indeed.

During the process of reclaiming who I am – a sovereign, joyful and spirited human being in essence, the so-called "Covid-19 pandemic" was unleashed. Many now know that it was not a real pandemic at all – it was a strategic move toward establishing a one world government contrived through a "health security" agenda. For the first time in my life, I realised we have the power to change this reality. But how? This is my story, complete with some *mys*tery.

A Message From our Mother

We are a scruffy contingent now,
Cropped and regimented by a lost tribe,
But we are the heart of Man,
And together we will rise.

Chapter 1

The Turning Point

*Thunder within the earth: the image of THE TURNING
POINT.
Thus the kings of antiquity closed the passes
At the time of solstice.
Merchants and strangers did not go about,
And the ruler
Did not travel through the provinces.[1]*

The months leading up to my debut on the Covid-19 battlefield were ominous. The so-called science surrounding the deployment of emergency Covid-19 "vaccines" was riddled with inconsistencies, and yet dissenting voices were silenced. For any health professional familiar with the literature, it should have been clear: the Covid-19 injections were neither "safe" nor "effective" by any scientific standard. Yet, I watched in frustration as fearmongering narratives spread, echoed by ignorant reporters parroting scripts from faceless authorities.

---

1   Hexagram 24, The Turning Point. The Image. From I Ching, by Richard Wilhelm, 3rd Ed.
     p.98.

A chilling uniformity of thought had descended globally, with dissent quickly fading into whispers. Raising questions about lockdowns, masks, or vaccines became dangerous territory. Esteemed doctors, scientists, and lawyers were labelled "conspiracy theorists" for daring to deviate from the narrative. Independent solutions were swiftly undermined by a coordinated campaign of disinformation and propaganda from the mouthpiece of the globalists, the British Broadcasting Corporation (BBC) and other mainstream media. Working as a consultant for the World Health Organization (WHO), I could see how evidence, and the lack of it, was being manipulated to stoke fear and enforce compliance.

The narrative promulgated by international health authorities was that the "vaccines" and only the "vaccines" could save us. The Pfizer injections had been granted conditional approval, also called emergency use authorisation (EUA), and the pressure to accept this amazingly "safe and effective" "vaccine" intensified.[1] All the while, obvious treatments for the allegedly deadly "SARS-CoV-2 virus" were undermined or ignored. In Britain, if one got ill, one's only option was to stay home until one turned blue, at which point one should call an ambulance. Banging pots and pans became an absurd weekly ritual in towns and villages, ostensibly to thank the National Health Service (NHS) staff manning relatively empty wards.

Even the sceptical were hesitant to challenge the "vaccine" narrative publicly, fearing professional and social ostracism. Dissenting groups lacked cohesion, and insidious hybrid warfare specialists sowed further division on social media. The big picture was clear to me – an anti-human agenda was at play, yet it seemed most were either afraid to acknowledge it or unable to see it.

---

[1]　The Covid-19 "vaccine" was a genetically engineered product fulfilling the criteria of a genetically modified organism (GMO). Not a traditional vaccine but rather a gene influencing product, it was also known as gene therapy. This was not disclosed to the public. From this point on, for readability, I have removed the inverted commas from the prevailing term "vaccine" when referring to these mass-produced and disseminated GMO products.

After a time of decay comes the turning point. The powerful light that has been banished returns.[1] In December 2020, a breakthrough came: an intensive care specialist, Dr Pierre Kory, testified before the U.S. Senate, presenting compelling evidence of ivermectin's effectiveness against Covid-19 symptoms. At the time, the ivermectin narrative had not yet been "contaminated" by fraudulent studies and slander. Even the WHO appeared to be taking the emerging independent studies on ivermectin seriously, having commissioned a scientific review led by Dr Andrew Hill, a research consultant from Liverpool University in the UK.

The Front Line Covid-19 Critical Care Alliance (FLCCC), a group of expert doctors led by Dr Paul Marik and Dr Pierre Kory, were among the first to review the evidence on ivermectin as a treatment for Covid-19 and found it showed strong potential to reduce Covid-19 deaths.[2] Based on evidence from 27 studies, they recommended its use globally for both prevention and treatment of the symptom complex, which involved fever, cough, brain fog, malaise, loss of taste and smell, and, as time wore on, a difficulty breathing and propensity to clot.

Used for worms and scabies in developing and Western countries alike, ivermectin is a well-established anti-parasitic medicine that has been safely used for decades. Out of patent, it costs very little to produce. The WHO includes it on their model list of essential medicines. In addition to anti-parasitic, anti-inflammatory and antiviral properties, subsequently it has also gained attention as a useful medicine in treating a variety of cancers. Despite the promising evidence presented by the FLCCC in their review, there was not yet a formal meta-analysis or pooling of data from different studies, which can increase the power of the findings and the certainty of evidence, to

---

1   Hexagram 24, The Turning Point. The Image. From I Ching, by Richard Wilhelm, 3rd Ed. p.97.
2   Kory et al, 2021. https://journals.lww.com/americantherapeutics/fulltext/2021/06000/review_of_the_emerging_evidence_demonstrating_the.4.aspx

summarise how well ivermectin worked for Covid-19 symptoms.

The WHO's appointed consultant for the ivermectin review, Dr Hill, had an academic history with extensive ties to the pharmaceutical industry; thus, it seemed unlikely that the WHO's review would yield a favourable outcome for ivermectin, given the significant financial investment, not to mention the transhumanist ideology, tied up in novel Covid-19 therapeutics and gene-based vaccines.

As an independent Research Consultant with expertise in Cochrane systematic reviews and clinical practice guideline development for the WHO, this was where I could step in, and carry out such a review in the style required for WHO recommendations and guidelines. People were dying from Covid-19 in droves, or so we were being told on the news. If I could lend my expertise to the ivermectin review, and my credibility to the cause, I might tip the balance. An effective early treatment had the potential to expose the cracks in the official Covid-19 narrative. Perhaps it might even serve as a thread to unravel the entire globalist agenda.

MOVE 1: The Ivermectin Rapid Review

The week after Christmas 2020, I burned the candle at both ends, conducting an independent systematic review of ivermectin. Taking a deep dive into the 27 studies the FLCCC had reviewed, I focused on the best-quality studies only, the randomised controlled trials (RCTs) and controlled observational studies (OCTs).

Applying my Cochrane and WHO methods experience, I produced a rapid review designed to meet the urgency of the crisis. A colleague independently verified my analyses and the conclusions were undeniable: ivermectin was safe, effective, feasible and low-cost. Compared with the unsafe experimental vaccines and high-cost novel Covid drugs being pushed on the public, its use was an obvious choice.

Confirming the FLCCC's findings, and given the overwhelming evidence showing ivermectin worked, I further suggested that place-bo-controlled trials (where patients get no active treatment for their symptoms) were ethically unjustifiable and should be terminated.

Amid intense fearmongering facilitated by the worried faces of TV news anchors, I set about sharing the findings. Entitled 'URGENT COVID-19 information: Ivermectin reduces the risk of death from COVID-19 – a rapid review and meta-analysis in sup-port of the recommendation of the Front Line COVID-19 Critical Care Alliance', I emailed key health authorities on January 4th, 2021. On the same day, the first doses of AstraZeneca's dangerous Covid-19 vaccine were officially administered, and UK's Prime Minister Boris Johnson announced a further lockdown.

Putting the full weight of my scientific credibility behind the FLCCC and ivermectin, I stated at the end of the review that I took full responsibility for the scientific integrity of the document. I also stated that I hoped policymakers would act swiftly on this critical information to save lives without delay. The full technical report (Exhibit 1)[1] and other exhibits can be found in the online repository associated with this book.

Among those to whom I sent the report were the UK Health Minister Mr Matt Hancock, and Members of Parliament (MP) Mr Jacob Rees-Mogg and Mrs Wera Hobhouse, who were the respective MPs for my home and work areas. It was also sent to members of the WHO Covid-19 evidence team via a WHO associate. Included with the submission was a brief covering letter and links to my research company website, academic identification, and record of scientific publications.

Targeting health professionals and policymakers, the urgent

---

1   Exhibit 1: Evidence-based Medicine Consultancy Ltd's Urgent Rapid Review on Ivermectin for Covid-19.

nature of the communication was made clear in the subject line of all correspondence with these officials. I also stated clearly that the report was independent, unfunded, and that I had no conflicts of interest, meaning that I was not financially invested in the outcome of the report.

After sending it out that Monday morning, the first Monday of 2021, the feeling of having started something significant was undeniable. It was a small step, barely noticeable, like dipping my toe into a pond nobody had visited or even considered the depths of. Any ripples it caused were likely to go unseen.

The return of health after illness, the return of understanding after estrangement: everything must be treated tenderly and with care in the beginning, so that the return may lead to a flowering.[1]

Without follow-up, it could easily have been a meaningless gesture. Yet, after months of impotence against the fraudulent Covid-19 agenda, taking this small step felt extremely satisfying. If nothing came of it, my next move would have to make more of an impact.

MOVE 2: Video Letter to Mr Boris Johnson

Three days passed without any engagement from the officials I had contacted. Urgent action was clearly needed, especially with the Covid vaccine rollout accelerating and the relentless TV death watch. What was being ignored by the mainstream media, but was well-known to me, were the unprecedented adverse drug reaction (ADR) reports being logged in the WHO's pharmacovigilance database, Vigibase, in collaboration with the University of Uppsala in Sweden. By mid-January 2021, just a month after the vaccines had been rolled out, there had already been over 50,000 ADR reports linked to the new vaccines. Yet neither the Uppsala University

---

1   Hexagram 24, The Turning Point. The Image. From I Ching, by Richard Wilhelm, 3rd Ed. p.98.

WHO Collaborating Centre nor the WHO made any attempt to publicise these alarming statistics. To put this in perspective, the tetanus vaccine, which had been around for decades and been given billions of times, had clocked up around 16,000 ADRs in total.

Knowing that Dr Hill and the FLCCC were set to present their case for ivermectin to the US National Institute of Health (NIH) on January 6th, I created and posted a video to the UK Prime Minister. I hoped it would help apply pressure on both sides of the Atlantic and lend additional weight to the FLCCC's ongoing efforts to help Covid patients and restore common sense.

This is what I said:

This is a letter for Mr Johnson. Dear Prime Minister, my name is Dr Tess Lawrie and I am the Director of the Evidence-based Medicine Consultancy in Bath. My business conducts industry-independent medical evidence synthesis to support international clinical practice guidelines. My biggest clients are the National Health Service and the World Health Organization.

I have recently authored a report called 'Ivermectin for preventing and treating Covid-19: A rapid review to validate the Frontline Critical Covid Care Alliance's conclusions. In connection with its findings, I sent an urgent correspondence to Mr Hancock and other members of parliament on Monday the 3rd of January. Unfortunately, I have not yet had a reply and, due to the urgent implications of the report, I am trying to reach you via this video.

The good news is that we now have solid evidence of an effective treatment for Covid-19. It is called ivermectin. Ivermectin is a very safe and effective anti-parasitic medication widely used in low- and middle-income countries to treat worms, lice and scabies in both adults and children. It has been around for decades and, not only is it on the World Health Organization's list of essential medicines, it is a Nobel prize-winning medicine, due to its increasing usefulness across a range of difference illnesses.

Between Christmas and New year, I independently reviewed 27 studies presented by the Frontline Critical Covid Care Alliance as evidence of ivermectin's effectiveness. The resulting evidence is consistent and unequivocal: ivermectin works well, both in preventing Covid-19 infections and in preventing Covid deaths, at the same doses used to treat lice and other parasitic infections.

I am very pleased to inform you that this evidence solidly substantiates the FLCCC's recommendation that ivermectin should be adopted globally and systematically for the prevention and treatment of Covid-19. Because I know there is a lot of fake news going about, I would like to assure you that you can trust the integrity of my report. I am an experienced, independent medical research consultant whose work is routinely used to underpin clinical practice guidelines. In addition, I have no conflicts of interest and have received no funding for this report. Most of all, you can trust me because I am also a medical doctor, first and foremost, with a moral duty to help people, to do no harm and to save lives. Please may we start saving lives now? Thank you very much for your help. Mr Hancock's office should have my details.

The following day, on January 8, a major incident was declared in London, with Mayor Sadiq Khan describing the Covid-19 situation as "out of control". The UK also allegedly recorded its highest daily Covid-related death toll to date – 1,325 deaths.

I opened a YouTube account in the name of the Evidence-based Medicine Limited and posted the video. This was my first foray into social media, and it felt like quite an accomplishment given my fear of public speaking and the limelight. However, my sense of personal progress was short-lived. Within a day and only about 2,000 views, the video was swiftly removed by YouTube in my first encounter with the far-reaching arm of globalist censorship, though certainly not the last. From that point on, anything I shared about ivermectin evidence was deemed unpalatable by YouTube's algorithms.

Whilst the *I Ching* was of interest to me at this time, I was not yet secure in its wisdom nor in my interpretations of it. Neither was I that amenable to the advice offered. With hindsight, it comments on the video to Johnson:

In danger like this, pause at first and wait. Otherwise you will fall into a pit in the abyss. Do not act in this way. [1] Looking back on this event through the lens of the *I Ching*, the video to the PM was indeed a risky move, one that I knew placed me in the line of danger going forward. As a consequence of this attention-gaining action, my presence had now been felt by both human powers and the AI algorithms. As I stepped into the abyss, my career, income and life as I knew it had ended. Navigating with awareness of danger would become an inevitable fact of my new life.

With respect to this particular communication, the *I Ching* further comments, *Every human being can draw in the course of his education from the inexhaustible wellspring of the divine in man's nature. But here two dangers threaten: a man may fail in his education to penetrate to the real roots of humanity and remain fixed in convention – a partial education of this sort is as bad as none – or he may suddenly collapse and neglect his self-development.* [2]

In this light, the *I Ching* cautions that those in power, like Johnson, often become trapped in the conventional systems of politics and power, forsaking their personal growth and deeper understanding of human nature. By clinging to the structures of control, they risk becoming mere tools of the system rather than evolving as

---

1   Hexagram 29, The Abysmal, line 3. From I Ching, by Richard Wilhelm, 3rd Ed. p.116-7.

2   Hexagram 48, The Well, The Judgement. From I Ching, by Richard Wilhelm, 3rd Ed. p.185-6.

true leaders with integrity. An intelligent and charismatic leader, brilliant by many accounts, one wonders whether this applies to Johnson, as my co-authors suggest.

This reminds us too not to become distracted or overwhelmed by these systems, and to instead commit to our own growth and the truth, wherever it might lead. Political and social structures come and go, they are fleeting and corruptible. True strength and wisdom come from drawing on the inexhaustible wellspring of our inner power. This is the force that transcends and endures.

MOVE 3: First BIRD meeting

I did not expect a response to the video appeal from Johnson, and indeed, I did not receive one. Perhaps he consulted with his Health Minister, Matt Hancock, or Chief Medical Adviser, Chris Whitty, or Chief Scientific Adviser, Patrick Vallance. Who knows?

To maintain the momentum, I called a meeting for 13th January 2021, naming it the British Ivermectin Recommendation Development (BIRD) meeting, following the WHO's naming convention for guideline development meetings, but replacing "WHO" with "British." BIRD would soon become a coalition of international ivermectin advocacy groups set up as a consequence of the evidence being ignored. I also prepared an Evidence to Decision (EtD) Framework document, a standard tool for WHO guideline meetings, which covers not only the effectiveness and safety of the intervention but also the values and preferences of users, equity, feasibility, acceptability, and cost considerations. Participants in guideline development are asked to vote on each of these domains (Exhibit 2).[1]

Time was pressing. With the help of my new research assistant, Dr Claire Mock-Muñoz de Luna, we sent out invitations by email to a range of esteemed academics for the virtual meeting. Our goal was

---

1   Exhibit 2: Evidence to Decision Framework of 13th January 2021.

to build a broader base of academic advocates in the UK.

However, it quickly became clear that few UK-based academics were willing to engage with Covid-19 initiatives that did not originate from government sources. As a result, we expanded our reach internationally. By the following week, we had assembled a robust group of 20 participants for the hastily arranged BIRD meeting. Aside from a handful of familiar faces, most attendees were new to me, and I was both grateful and amazed that such a high-quality group had come together on such short notice.

Amidst a sense of purpose, I recall feeling quite nervous at this first meeting, where I shared the rapid review findings, including both their implications and limitations. My aim was to educate and "hand over" the evidence on ivermectin, which I hoped would expose the unjustified vaccine rollout or at least provide people with an alternative to the genetic vaccines. Once I had sorted this out, I had in mind that I would shift my focus back to researching 5G and electromagnetic radiation, which had been a matter of private study in 2020. How naïve in hindsight!

It's astonishing to think that academics and professionals were afraid to attend an independent scientific meeting, but by 2021, such was the nature of Covid-19 'science' that several attendees clearly were and chose to remain off camera. Despite this, I was pleased to see that curiosity had drawn several distinguished professors to the meeting, such as Professor Graham Cooke of Imperial College London, and Professor Marlene Temmerman, former Director of the WHO's Department of Reproductive Health Research, who was working at Kenya's Aga Khan University at the time. The group also included experts from various fields – obstetrics and gynaecology, health economics, HIV, emergency medicine, gastroenterology, cardiology, paediatrics, and physics, as well as an independent journalist, and a politician, Mr. Richard Tice from the Reform party. It was an honour to have Dr Paul Marik and Dr Pierre Kory in attendance, upon whose efforts my rapid review was based, as well as cardiologist Dr Peter McCullough, who had authored the first scientific paper on combination treatment for Covid-19. In keeping with WHO standards, all participants had submitted 'declarations of interest' prior to the meeting.

Emeritus Prof. Jim Neilson from the University of Liverpool kindly agreed to chair the meeting. A frequent chair of similar WHO meetings and former Editor-in-Chief of the Cochrane Pregnancy and Childbirth group, his expertise and gravitas added considerable weight to our efforts.

I began by explaining the basics of ivermectin: its long history of safe use in low- and middle-income countries, its inclusion in the WHO's Model List of Essential Medicines in 2019, and its Nobel prize-winning history. I highlighted its proven antiviral and anti-inflammatory properties, which made it a promising candidate for Covid-19 treatment. It's mechanism of action was likely multi-fold. I explained how my work built upon the foundation of the FLCCC, whose initial report on ivermectin had first caught my attention and that I had seen an opportunity to strengthen their findings through a rigorous meta-analysis (pooling of data from similar studies). The meta-analysis included 11 randomised controlled trials (RCTs) and 7 observational controlled trials (OCTs) of ivermectin for prevention or treatment of Covid-19. Study sample sizes ranged from 24 to 1195 participants and studies were conducted in Argentina (2), Bangladesh (6), Egypt (3), India (2), Iran (2), Pakistan (1), Spain (1), and the USA (1). Sixteen studies were at low or moderate risk of bias and two studies were assessed as having a potentially high risk of bias pending further information from investigators. Eight were registered on clinical trial registries; most studies appeared to be self-funded, undertaken by clinicians working in the field, not by dedicated research teams. There were no apparent conflicts of interest.

For the most important review outcome, the evidence from 6 RCTs indicated that ivermectin, when used for people with Covid-19 symptoms, probably reduced deaths by an average 83% compared with no ivermectin treatment, with the risk of death being 1.3% with ivermectin versus 8.3% among people who did not get ivermectin in this analysis. This was equivalent to an average 69 fewer deaths per 1000 people in hospital with Covid-19. The effect favouring ivermectin was consistent among people in hospital with mild, moderate and severe disease, and when OCTs were included in the analysis. The evidence from RCTs further showed that ivermectin probably reduced the risk of clinical deterioration and increased the chance of improving, and was again consistent when OCTs were included in the analyses too. There was some evidence too that suggested that ivermectin may reduce hospital stay. Adverse events were rare. When evaluated for Covid-19 prevention among health care workers and Covid-19 contacts, ivermectin reduced the risk of Covid-19 infection by about 88% (4 studies, 851 participants); 34.5% got infected if they did not get ivermectin prophylactically versus 4.3% if they did.

In addition to the evidence on effectiveness and safety, I presented other considerations, such as people's values and preferences, equity, acceptability, cost, and feasibility, which are part and parcel of the WHO recommendation development framework.

Following my presentation, a lively and spirited discussion ensued. The expertise in the room was palpable, and the friendly debates between Drs Kory, Marik, and McCullough about the best clinical approach were both entertaining and validating. All three would go on to become heroes for their efforts to counter official Covid propaganda.

For the non-medics in the room, the choice was obvious. Retired physicist Dr Edmund Fordham, now a dear friend, summed it up perfectly: as a cancer survivor, he had no interest in taking an experimental Covid vaccine but saw the logic in using ivermectin, based on existing studies.

Societies of people sharing the same views are formed. But since these groups come together in full public knowledge and in harmony with the time, all selfish separatist tendencies are excluded and no mistakes are made.[1]

While a couple of participants remained non-committal, the general consensus was clear: ivermectin worked, and further placebo-controlled trials would likely be unethical. The challenge now was how to disseminate this life-saving information as widely as possible.

We discussed strategies for reaching official bodies, with publication in a high-impact journal like *The Lancet* considered to be crucial. Cochrane systematic reviews were seen as the gold standard for informing clinical guidelines, so contacting the Cochrane editors was a priority.

I suggested assembling a team of systematic reviewers for a Cochrane review, which was met with agreement. We also planned another BIRD meeting to share updated evidence and expand the group's international representation. Prof. Neilson proposed reaching out to the Cochrane editors before finalising the review to ensure it received the attention it deserved. I made a note to follow up on this the next day.

As the meeting drew to a close, I was both excited and overwhelmed. It was clear that this was not going to be an easy path. This fledgling collaboration would require much more work from me; I would not just be handing over the baby as I had hoped. I would need help. Fortunately, reinforcements had arrived, particularly in the form of the brilliant and tenacious Dr Fordham, who had thoroughly

---

1   Hexagram 24, The Turning Point, The Judgement. From I Ching, by Richard Wilhelm, 3rd Ed. p.97-8.

scrutinised the evidence and was now fully convinced.

Fordham was a retired physicist and, as mentioned, a cancer survivor. His personal experience with the healthcare industry during his battle with lymphoma had made him question the official approach to Covid-19. His enquiring mind could not accept what was being presented as the only solution.

A rare combination of clarity and fairness, Fordham's insight was invaluable and it was my great fortune that he agreed to join the Cochrane systematic review team as the consumer representative. I quickly discovered his talents extended beyond just critical thinking, he was also an excellent writer and analyst. His meticulousness and perseverance made him the perfect addition to the review team. Edmund's efforts would later become the backbone of BIRD's rebuttals and legal efforts.

You may be wondering about Dr Andrew Hill, the WHO consultant. Had I invited him to this international discussion on ivermectin? Yes, I personally invited Dr Hill to this first BIRD meeting and was disappointed that he did not come. The calibre of experts we had gathered for the meeting was powerful.

Return always calls for a decision and is an act of self-mastery. It is made easier if a man is in good company. If he can bring himself to put aside pride and follow the example of good men, good fortune results.[1] Perhaps if Hill had joined our esteemed group that day, he might have seen the value in setting aside his corporate allegiances and aligning himself with those who were genuinely trying to save lives. Nevertheless, Hill sent an apology via email the next day, and we met via Zoom. I shared the success of the meeting and invited him to join the Cochrane review team, explaining that Cochrane reviews are regarded by the WHO as the gold standard for evidence to inform guidelines. As the appointed WHO consultant, he should

---

1   Hexagram 24, The Turning Point, line 2. From I Ching, by Richard Wilhelm, 3rd Ed. p.99.

have been well aware of this, but I felt it was important to highlight it, given that our past interactions and his list of publications suggested he hadn't conducted a Cochrane review before. This became especially clear when I read the ivermectin review he published on a pre-print server just days later. It was shockingly flawed (Exhibit 3).[1] Prior to this revelation, however, Hill agreed to join our Cochrane review author team.

MOVE 4: Assembling the Cochrane Review Team

As promised to the BIRD meeting attendees, the next day I reached out to Mr Toby Lasserson, the Deputy Editor-in-Chief at the Cochrane Collaboration, requesting approval to submit a rapid Cochrane review. On board as co-authors were a strong team of British experts: Dr Andrew Bryant, a statistician from Newcastle University; Dr Therese Dowswell, a seasoned Cochrane systematic reviewer; clinicians Dr Tony Tham and Dr Scott Mitchell; Dr Edmund Fordham, physicist and consumer representative; Dr Sarah Hill, a health economist from the University of Newcastle; and Dr Andrew Hill, a Liverpool University researcher and WHO consultant. The strength and experience of our team were undeniable. With our collective expertise, we were confident that we could prepare the Cochrane review within a few weeks.

Lasserson seemed pleased that Dr Andrew Hill was involved and promptly sent us Cochrane's new rapid review template. Prof. Neilson also emailed the Cochrane editors in support of our efforts. Hill appeared enthusiastic about being part of the team, and we exchanged a fair amount of correspondence in the lead-up to the Cochrane submission on the 15th January 2021.

With renewed energy and a robust team, we got to work redoing the literature search, essentially conducting the Cochrane review

---

1   Exhibit 3. Dr Andrew Hill's original ResearchSquare pre-print of 18th January 2021.

from scratch. But before diving into the research again, we issued a press release to alert journalists and the public to the promising developments arising from the first BIRD meeting (Exhibit 4).[1] The release was predictably ignored by the mainstream media.

MOVE 5: Countering Scientific Misconduct

Taking readers back to the first week of January 2021, Dr Kory and Dr Marik were very excited to present their argument in favour of using ivermectin to the National Institute for Health (NIH) with Dr Hill, the WHO consultant. The aim of the meeting was to get ivermectin approved for use in the USA, and Kory was extremely optimistic. And why not? Dr Hill's slide presentation highlighted ivermectin treatment was associated with faster time to viral clearance, shorter duration of hospitalisation, higher rates of clinical recovery and 75% fewer Covid deaths. Dosing for five days according to Hill provided the strongest benefits. He suggested that ivermectin could be used for anyone testing positive for Covid-19, and vaccination could be used for the rest (Exhibit 5).[2]

Given Hill's supposed expert input, his position as the WHO consultant on the case, and the clinical experience of Drs Kory and Marik, the decision should have been straightforward for the NIH panel. Yet, despite the overwhelming evidence, the panel barely budged. When I next spoke with Kory and Marik, they were extremely disappointed and could not understand why the NIH had resisted. Subsequently, recognising that they could no longer justify their recommendation against ivermectin, the NIH adopted a neutral stance; however, they still refused to recommend it.

Hill had been tasked with reporting to the WHO on the dozens of new ivermectin studies months earlier. After Kory shared Hill's contact

---

1   Exhibit 4: Press Release: "Effective treatment for Covid-19 has been right under our noses".
2   Exhibit 5: Dr Andrew Hill's presentation to the US National Institute for Health.

details with me, I sent him our data spreadsheet, in the hope that this would hurry him up with a publication, and I let him know I was there to help in any way. Hill was affable, and seemed happy for the help, sending me a few queries related to assessing the risk of bias of studies. It was obvious that my ivermectin rapid review and news of the BIRD meeting had put some wind in his sails. When Dr Hill learned that my work was entirely voluntary and unfunded, he kindly offered to request £15,000 from one of his funders to support my efforts. While the gesture was generous, I declined the offer, feeling uncertain about accepting such funding. Might there be strings attached?

Then Hill surprised me. He told me he was close to publishing his review. Following our conversation, in which I invited him to join our Cochrane review team, he emailed, "Good talking to you just now – It's nice to discuss with someone who agrees, for a change! I have endured a series of criticisms and cross-examinations for the past week." His attitude gave me hope. It suggested that, despite the pressures he was under, my support and commitment to standing up for the evidence might serve as a positive influence on him.

My *I Ching* co-authors observe, *A man is in a society composed of inferior people but is connected spiritually with a strong and good friend, and this makes him turn back alone.*[1] Perhaps, like a man spiritually connected with a strong and good friend, Hill might find the courage to stand apart from the controlling forces around him?

My hopes were shattered when I read Hill's draft WHO review that weekend. At the time, it had not yet gone live on the pre-print server, but an updated version was soon submitted to *ResearchSquare* and went live on January 18th. Both versions were appalling, not only poorly written but also scientifically flawed. It was clear they had been hastily assembled, lacking the rigour one would expect from a review tied to the WHO.

---

1   Hexagram 24, The Turning Point, line 4. From I Ching, by Richard Wilhelm, 3rd Ed. p.99.

There were notable differences between the earlier and final versions, with revisions seeming deliberately crafted to undermine the evidence supporting ivermectin. It seemed improbable that all of the 42 listed authors had genuinely contributed to the work, yet the conclusions did not reflect the strength of the evidence and I wondered whether, as first author, they were his own. The inconsistencies and lack of transparency were glaring, leaving no doubt in my mind that external influences were at play.

The Hill pre-prints would subsequently attract an extensive forensic investigation by British Forensic Communications Expert, Mr Lyndon Alexander (Exhibit 6).[1] His analysis, commissioned by the French organisation Bon Sens, meticulously examined the peculiarities and inconsistencies within the Hill review. It also caught the attention of independent journalist Phil Harper, whose probing investigations would unearth the extent of conflicts of interest of Hill's associate at Liverpool University, Prof. Andrew Owen, in due course.

Despite its troubling conclusions, Hill's review presented compelling evidence of ivermectin's efficacy, showing a dose-dependent reduction in Covid-19 mortality by approximately 75%, along with a reduced risk of hospitalisation. These findings were highly significant, particularly in a climate where people with Covid symptoms were often told to stay home without treatment until they became critical. Yet, Hill's conclusions rendered the evidence practically meaningless: ivermectin should not be used, and regulators should ignore it until large randomised controlled trials (RCTs) were conducted. This recommendation should have baffled any critical thinking health professional or academic, especially given ivermectin's well-documented safety profile – safer than widely used drugs like aspirin and paracetamol.

---

1   Exhibit 6: Forensic Analysis of Dr Hill's pre-print, commissioned by Bon Sens.

Hill's pre-print, in essence, after everything he had told the FLCCC duo and me about wanting to get ivermectin approved ASAP, aligned itself with the prevailing narrative: that only vaccines could save us. Alarmed, I emailed Hill on Sunday, January 17th, immediately after reading the review. I implored him to reconsider:

"Dear Andy, Please can you retract your review asap and reframe the conclusions? More placebo-controlled RCTs are definitely not needed. Your review will do immeasurable harm. If it would help to talk you through the problems with it, please feel free to give me a call."

I had hoped the review could be retracted or corrected before it went live. My *I Ching* co-authors agree that there was still time to salvage the situation, *Slight digressions from the good cannot be avoided, but one must turn back in time, before going too far.*[1] Deviations from what is right, whether due to external pressures, personal fears, or misguided decisions, are part of being human. Yet, the *I Ching* reminds us that the critical point lies in recognising those missteps before they deepen into irreversible errors. For Hill, the pre-print publication represented such a turning point. My hope was that, even under immense pressure, he might see the need to correct course and return to a path of integrity, aligning his actions with the compelling evidence on ivermectin that he himself had highlighted.

This possibility still seemed alive when Hill proposed a virtual meeting at noon on the 18th January. However, my hopes were crushed when I awoke to find his pre-print article already published online. Was its hasty publication before peer review calculated to scupper our efforts?

The virtual meeting between Hill and me that day has since been recounted in detail, most notably in Robert F. Kennedy Jr.'s *The Real Anthony Fauci.* Within the first ten minutes of our conversation, it became clear that Hill had capitulated to external pressures. He

---

1   Hexagram 24, The Turning Point, line 1. From I Ching, by Richard Wilhelm, 3rd Ed. p.98-9.

admitted to being influenced and representing the opinion of others as well as his funders, going so far as to include an instruction in his review that regulators should not even consider the existing studies until large-scale trials had been conducted – a delay tactic that would last years.

Confirmation of my suspicions hit hard: Hill's review was not an independent scientific analysis but a weapon of sabotage. The data had been twisted, the conclusions distorted, and Hill himself manipulated in service to a much larger agenda – "vaccinating" the world's population with gene-based products.

I felt a deep sense of anger and irritation as I realised that Hill did not seem to fully comprehend the weight of his actions, nor was he willing to take responsibility for them. In the midst of my frustration, I realised I was not recording the meeting, a practice I usually followed. So I quickly pressed record. I could not allow the words I was hearing go unheard by others, especially as they suggested clear signs of scientific misconduct to me (Exhibit 7).[1]

Hill admitted to being in "a sensitive position", acknowledging that "Unitaid has a say in the paper". No-one at Unitaid was listed as an author. When I asked him to give me the name of someone at Unitaid with whom I could speak and discuss the evidence, Hill replied:

"I'll have a think about who to, to offer you with a name. But I mean, this is very difficult because I'm, you know, I've got this role where I'm supposed to produce this paper and we're in a very difficult, delicate balance. There are some people who say that we're already overstepping the mark, and this is too, um, strident because the mechanism of action doesn't support it. I know I keep going back to it."

I asked: "Who are these people, who are these people saying this?"

Hill replied: "There are... there are... I mean, when we met, I'm

---

1   Exhibit 7: Transcript of the Lawrie-Hill Meeting of 18th January 2021.

just talking about overall feedback. I'm getting from all kinds of different scientists, not just authors."

It was particularly revealing to learn that Hill was not being paid by the WHO, as one might expect, but instead by Unitaid. Even more curious was that the original version of Hill's pre-print had stated that the research grant he received was for an "unlimited" amount. I was soon to uncover that just days before our conversation, Unitaid had announced a substantial grant of about $40 million to the University of Liverpool for the establishment of a Centre for Long-Acting Therapeutics (CELT). The focus of CELT's research was to explore ways to transform inexpensive, generic medicines like hydroxychloroquine and ivermectin into injectable forms, rather than keeping them as pills.

Through the thorough investigations of independent journalist Phil Harper, I also learned that Hill's colleague, Prof. Andrew Owen, stood to gain significantly from this research. Not only would he benefit from the research grant to CELT, but he was also connected to the development of patents through his company, Tandem Nano Ltd, which focused on drug delivery technologies. Owen's biography revealed that since March 2020, he had been heavily involved in the evaluation of SARS-CoV-2 antiviral treatments. He was a member of the Trial Management Group for novel Covid drugs (the AGILE National phase I/IIa Covid-19 trial platform), and he was an advisor on the UK government's Covid-19 Therapeutics Advisory Panel (UK-CTAP). UK-CTAP would be among the so-called Covid-19 authorities maintaining Hill's non-peer-reviewed and highly flawed pre-print as proof that there was insufficient evidence on ivermectin to support its use.

My surprises for that particular day were not over, however. In my inbox, later I was to find an email from Prof. Neilson highlighting that a German group, funded privately by German Ecosystem

CEO-Sys, had registered a title that very day for a Cochrane review entitled "Ivermectin for post-exposure prophylaxis and treatment of outpatient and hospitalised Covid-19 patients" – i.e. similar to the scope of our Cochrane review!

Meanwhile, Hill struggled to maintain consistency in communicating the message of his employers. On January 19th, the very next day after publishing his pre-print undermining ivermectin's use for Covid-19, during a talk to a South African audience, he stated that if his brother were hospitalised with Covid-19, he would want him to receive ivermectin. Similarly, in an interview with the *Financial Times* that day, Hill was quoted as saying: "The purpose of this report is to forewarn people that this is coming: get prepared, get supplies, get ready to approve it, we need to be ready." This contradiction highlighted Hill's cognitive dissonance regarding the impact his unqualified pre-print would have on Covid policy worldwide. His employers would soon pressure him to delete his favourable ivermectin tweets, clearly attempting to suppress any positive messaging around this essential medicine.

Meanwhile, Dr Marik and Dr Kory from the FLCCC responded to Hill's pre-print publication in an email sent on January 21st, titled "Manuscript Concerns". Their response not only addressed Hill's mixed messages but also pointed out significant factual errors, inaccuracies, and methodological issues revealing the lack of scientific rigour in Hill's work. They kindly gave me permission to publish excerpts of their email below. The full version of their unpublished peer review of Hill's paper can be found as Exhibit 8.[1]

Dear Andrew,

Thanks so much for sharing your pre-print and also we both really enjoyed your talk with S. Africa yesterday, it was excellent, especially

---

1   Exhibit 8: Dr Pierre Kory and Dr Paul Marik's email critique sent to Dr Andrew Hill.

the Q and A. Further, we are so encouraged by your identification of a number of active prophylaxis trials, some quite large and we eagerly anticipate these trial results when available.

However, we developed some significant concerns over the current pre-print version of your manuscript, as its conclusions and interpretations were severely discordant, not only with the available data therein, but also with the tone and content of your subsequent presentation to S. Africa and numerous private comments you have shared with us during discussions of these data.

We thought it would be helpful if we performed a peer review of the manuscript as we quickly identified a number of troubling statements within the manuscript that we feel should be immediately revised lest it cause more harm than it is already causing. We hope you find the below suggested revisions helpful to you prior to your embarking further on a peer-review process with a journal.

Please see below and we kindly ask that you undertake these revisions quickly. We implore you to do this because we are highly disturbed at the evidence of what appears to be scientific misconduct.

We understand that you appear to be caught between two forces and wish you the strength in exerting your moral conscience in this situation. Many thousands of lives depend on your exercise of this courage. We are happy to chat with you about this today if you would like. Although some of the revision comments below may appear harsh, it is because we were severely troubled – but remain committed to helping you in what appears to be a terribly difficult situation.

Paul and Pierre

The friendly introduction was followed by a detailed account of the many instances of misleading and false statements in Hill's paper, ending with a plea to Hill's conscience.

Lastly, Andrew, for your sake and science's sake, we are concerned that if your scientific integrity is formally brought into question or investigation by finding that outside influences shaped your supposedly independent interpretation and conclusions (and we are already seeing questions popping up on social media), then we worry about both your past work being brought into question (i.e. many will wonder whether this is the first time you have allowed external forces to influence your scientific conclusions) and thus will begin to question prior conclusions/recommendations on various medications you have studied, as well as future ones, which would likely affect future employment opportunities. We are so sorry about this position you are in and trust we are helping give perspective and support here. Finally, we hope we are wrong about all the above but we just cannot find any other explanation for the erroneous and misleading statements in your manuscript in light of your prior presentations and shared opinions of the available data on ivermectin in COVID-19.

After receiving the email from Dr Marik and Dr Kory, Hill made small and insubstantial tweaks to the pre-print, and it was subsequently republished.

What continues to shock me is how overt and extensive the conflicts of interest were among those in positions of authority during the Covid-19 chapter. One glaring example is Prof. Andrew Owen, who not only influenced Covid policy but also profited from the influence. His involvement in CTAP, particularly in the context of his work with the Liverpool University's CELT, as well as his company patents, defied common sense. A cursory exploration of the deeply intertwined financial and academic interests of influential figures in groups like the UK's Scientific Advisory Group for Emergencies (SAGE) indicates that this would undoubtedly warrant a book of its own to unravel!

My take on Hill's role with regard to ivermectin was that he was required by his employers to acknowledge ivermectin's potential but only in a way that would not disrupt the official narrative. He was to highlight ivermectin's utility but only enough to suggest that it could be adapted or used in the future – once the long-acting ivermectin injections had been formulated perhaps. These were in development, not only through CELT but also at a French company called Medincell, which had received investment from Bill Gates to do so.[1] At some point, a profitable form of ivermectin would likely be reintroduced with a major announcement, a "miracle drug" for new "pandemics" perhaps.

Once ivermectin and other essential medicines were re-engineered into long-acting injections, they could be deployed in a manner that aligns with the global "health security" agenda.

As much as I noted Hill's complicity and sensed a lack of backbone, I also felt there was still potential for him to do the right thing. With corporate masters, it was clear that he had grown accustomed to subjugating his conscience and simply following orders. Hired by those who employ and shape "the science" to maximise their profits, his compliance had no doubt provided modest rewards and kept him employed. I had hoped that by including him in our great review team of dedicated scientists, he might be inspired to act on his conscience, especially given the dire situation mankind was in in January 2021. However, this was not to be.

To reflect once more on my co-authors' earlier point about turning back before it's too late, one is reminded that turning back requires self-awareness and courage, a willingness to face uncomfortable truths and take a stand, even when it means resisting powerful forces. In Hill's case, I saw a momentary flicker of potential, a chance for him to act in accordance with the principles of scientific honesty

---

1   Medincell's ivermectin study reports can be found at www.Lawriefiles.com

and moral responsibility, acting in honour and doing no harm. Sadly for all, that moment passed without him stepping back from the brink, and the consequences of that choice rippled far and wide.

The significance of Hill's preprint and his failure to alert the public to the corruption of "the science" surrounding Covid-19 cannot be overstated. If Hill, as the appointed WHO Consultant, had joined forces with us and spoken out, acknowledging that a safe, effective alternative to taking experimental vaccines existed, the entire narrative could have shifted. Many people would have been far less likely to be coerced into taking the dangerous injections had they known that there were other viable, low-cost options to prevent and treat Covid symptoms. Additionally, with fewer Covid-labelled deaths to count, it would have been evident to all that the "pandemic" measures were unnecessary, exposing the Covid-19 crisis as a manufactured scam.

In conclusion, Dr Andrew Hill is an example of how much harm any one of us is capable of when we do not take responsibility for our actions, when we simply follow orders. Personal accountability is a key requirement for a better world. As the scientist in charge of reviewing the evidence on ivermectin for the WHO, Hill knew ivermectin was a game-changer in those early Covid days. He told the FLCCC duo as much. He told me. His presentation to the NIH on the 6th of January shows this too. His optimistic tweets about ivermectin, which he subsequently self-censored, were eagerly welcomed and shared by Twitter followers. He was in an authoritative position in which he could have exerted influence internationally. Had Hill acted independently with integrity for the benefit of the people, he would have been honoured. Instead, he submitted to being used and kept the game-changing information to himself.

My co-authors aptly conclude, *When the time for return has come, a man should not take shelter in trivial excuses, but should look within and examine himself. And if he has done something wrong he should make a noble hearted resolve to confess his fault. No one will regret having taken this road.*[1]

The human capacity for forgiveness and compassion is as immense as its effect is liberating. However, *if a man misses the right time for return, he meets with misfortune. The misfortune has its inner cause in a wrong attitude towards the world. The misfortune coming upon him from without results from this wrong attitude. What is pictured here is blind obstinacy and the judgement that is visited upon it.*[2]

1   Hexagram 24, The Turning Point, line 5. From I Ching, by Richard Wilhelm, 3rd Ed. p.99-100.
2   Hexagram 24, The Turning Point, line 6. From I Ching, by Richard Wilhelm, 3rd Ed. p.100.

Chapter 2

Preponderance of the Small

PREPONDERANCE OF THE SMALL. Success.
Perseverance furthers.
Small things may be done; great things should not be done.
The flying bird brings the message:
It is not well to strive upwards,
It is well to remain below.
Great good fortune.[1]

If a man occupies a position of authority for which he is by nature really inadequate, extraordinary prudence is necessary.[2] Whether I was up for the job was surplus to my decision-making process when I decided to join the fray; I felt responsible to help expose the truth, and ivermectin was the key that I had been given to do so. The weight of this responsibility was both a burden and the beginning of an unexpected adventure, demanding courage beyond my insecurities, such as the

---

1   Hexagram 62, Preponderance of the Small, The Judgment. From I Ching, by Richard Wilhelm, 3rd Ed. p.240. The structure and visual representation of this hexagram gives rise to the idea that the message is brought by a bird.

2   Hexagram 62, Preponderance of the Small, The Judgment. From I Ching, by Richard Wilhelm, 3rd Ed. p.240.

fear of public speaking, and a relentless dedication to the goal. Like a fledgling taking its first tentative flights, I knew I would need to start with small, deliberate steps, trusting that each effort would bring me closer to soaring.

Shortly after the start of what would be a thirteen-month cycle, our ivermectin advocacy efforts started to yield results, drawing media and political attention while also prompting notable counteractions from those controlling the Covid-19 narrative. Merck, the multinational drug company that once owned the patent for ivermectin but was now developing novel competing Covid-19 drugs, responded with a statement on February 4th affirming its position against the use of ivermectin for Covid-19 indications. Merck claimed that its analysis of available studies found no meaningful evidence of clinical efficacy against Covid-19, and a concerning lack of safety data. Merck also reiterated that ivermectin was approved under its original brand name for treating specific parasitic infections only.

The Africa Centre for Disease Control (Africa CDC) followed suit quoting Merck verbatim and advising against the use of ivermectin for prevention and treatment of Covid-19 because there "is no conclusive clinical data to support its safety and efficacy." In actuality, this statement was more applicable to the experimental yet authorised Covid-19 drugs, like Remdesivir, and experimental yet authorised vaccines – lacing the statement with irony.

Thankfully, despite my Boris Johnson video being censored, other YouTubers, including members of the FLCCC, managed to re-upload it, which helped to increase its exposure and led to my first video interviews on ivermectin. Among the interviewers were Canadian dentist and podcaster Dr Jennifer Hibberd, and South African lawyer and journalist Shabnam Palesa Mohamed, host of The Peoples' Voice podcast. Both would become friends and allies in efforts to counter the corrupt official narrative.

The BIRD press release also garnered a spark of interest from mainstream media. A reporter by the name of David Rose emailed: "I'd like to write an article about the use of ivermectin against Covid-19 for the Daily Mail, where I am a senior writer. Please would you send me a phone number so we can have a chat?" This felt like a breakthrough. I was delighted!

MOVE 6: Fostering Media Interest

In December 2020, at a conference ironically named the World Press Freedom Conference, the scope of the Trusted News Initiative (TNI) was significantly expanded. Originally established to combat misinformation surrounding the 2020 U.S. elections, it was now tasked with orchestrating propaganda for the Covid narrative. With what emerged after the 2020 U.S. elections, it became clear that the TNI was not created to prevent election fraud but rather to obscure it.

By February 2021, Covid censorship was in full swing. Led by major media organisations such as the Associated Press, BBC, Reuters, Washington Post, European Broadcasting Union, Facebook, Financial Times, YouTube, Microsoft, and Twitter, the TNI shifted its focus to promoting the global Covid vaccine rollout and suppressing what it termed "harmful vaccine disinformation." Reporters were directed (and supplied) with narratives, while fact-checkers were recruited to enforce this agenda. This concerted effort resulted in an almost complete media blackout on ivermectin and other promising early interventions. Scientists and health professionals speaking out were discredited, cancelled and censored. Mainstream journalists were effectively prohibited from reporting on anything that deviated from the official Covid narrative. To do so required not just integrity, but considerable courage. Would Mr David Rose be that man?

Rose, being a self-professed "expert in controversy", had been burned by the truth before. In 2017, he wrote about how "global warming" data were being manipulated to influence the outcome of the Paris Agreement, and was publicly reprimanded by the Independent Press Standards Organisation. Encouragingly to my mind, he was already well-versed in stories of Covid-19 corruption. He had broken the story about the so-called VIP fast-track channel for personal protective equipment (PPE) contracts, which allowed close associates of MPs, ministers, and peers to secure contracts worth, in some cases, hundreds of millions of pounds. Many of these contracts involved the supply of defective and useless equipment from companies that had been set up hastily, with no background in the field.

I explained to him my niche expertise of evidence synthesis and guideline development, our review findings, and the struggles we had faced this past month in communicating them to health authorities. We discussed the inadequacy of the NIH's shift from opposing ivermectin to a more non-committal stance, and I offered to connect him with Dr Kory who could provide him with a firsthand account of the NIH meeting and sequelae for his story. I also shared that we had received no responses from key political figures in the UK, despite the apparent urgency to stop people dying. Towards the end of our conversation, I delicately raised my suspicions about high-level corruption surrounding ivermectin and broached the issue with Dr Hill.

Rose was unsurprised. "There's corruption everywhere you look in this story. By which I mean the whole coronavirus story. Everywhere you look, people are making big sums of money out of coronavirus and are determined to carry on doing so." It was gratifying to hear that he really 'got it'; we were on the same page I thought, more or less. I agreed to give him a newspaper exclusive to break the ivermectin story when the Cochrane review was published. This all sounded very promising.

Rose also introduced me to Conservative Party parliamentarian Mr David Davis. In a lengthy meeting via Zoom two days later, I went through the evidence and controversial aspects of the ivermectin story together again with him. This was my first close encounter with a serving "Covid-19" politician. I was hopeful that, at the very least, arming Davis with the information he needed on ivermectin would stir things up a bit and get him asking the right questions at the party head office and in parliament.

Davis listened and, to my surprise, shared his own insights. He seemed well aware that the science was being crafted and words were being scripted for the Prime Minister based on no data. Calling Prof. Neil Ferguson from Imperial College the man "who started the great Covid pandemic", Davis referred to Ferguson's infamous "500,000 deaths projection" as the flimsiest of evidence to declare a pandemic. A further unsolicited reflection was shared by him about recent rev-elations of a Christmas lockdown party at No.10 Downing Street. He was clearly disturbed by the news of what was for all intents and purposes "a total orgy", as well as the implicit duplicity of official messaging – politicians partying together while the rest of the popu-lation were made to practice "social distancing" and stay home.

Davis really seemed to get that ivermectin would be a game-changer. Both he and Rose confessed to taking vitamin D every day. "It sounds to me like when you have high levels of infection, as we do now, everyone should take ivermectin", Davis declared at the conclu-sion of the meeting.

Despite the promise of this meeting, I was left with a bad taste in my mouth. These men in their different ways yielded significant power and influence between them. Even though Davis had his own insight into and, indeed, misgivings about the official narrative, which was by his own account very problematic, he hadn't shared his significant concerns with the public to whom he was ostensibly in service.

No effective measures came about from this interaction with MP

David Davis, to my knowledge. The *I Ching* comments, *Pigs and fishes are the least intelligent of all animals and therefore the most difficult to influence. The force of inner truth must grow great indeed before its influence can extend to such creatures.*[1]

Like most politicians, perhaps Davis was not able to individually consider options in the interests of his constituency – he had to toe the party line above all else. Such *a man must always turn to his superior, from whom he can receive enlightenment.* He must pursue his *course like a horse that goes straight ahead without looking sideways at its mate [...].*[2] Close ties like this *may exist also among thieves; it is true that such a bond acts as a force but, since it is not invincible, it does not bring good fortune.*[3]

MOVE 7: Cochrane Cancels Us

In the meantime, it was up to me to inform the Cochrane Collaboration's editors of Dr Hill's removal from the review team. On January 20th, alongside the protocol submission, I wrote to Cochrane editors Toby Lasserson and Carla Soares-Weisner to inform them that Hill would no longer be part of the review team due to concerns regarding serious conflicts of interest. Among our author team, we collectively held around 120 Cochrane review titles, while Hill had none. It should have been a straightforward matter, but if my suspicions were correct, that WHO and its backers were influencing Cochrane, I feared it might be more complicated.

From the start of the outreach to the editors, it had been apparent that the ivermectin review topic was controversial for the Cochrane editors. Soares-Weisner mentioned the word "controversy" in her first correspondence without explicitly stating why. Notably, it was only after hearing that Hill would be among the authors that she and

---

1   Hexagram 61, Inner Truth, The Judgment. From I Ching, by Richard Wilhelm, 3rd Ed. p.235-6.

2   Hexagram 61, Inner Truth, line 4. From I Ching, by Richard Wilhelm, 3rd Ed. p.238.

3   Hexagram 61, Inner Truth, The Judgment. From I Ching, by Richard Wilhelm, 3rd Ed. p.235-6.

Lasserson became amenable to our submission.

Cochrane was no stranger to accusations of bias in favour of the pharmaceutical industry, so I was not entirely surprised by the response recommending a complete halt in our activities until they investigated the potential conflicts of interest. What did catch me off guard, however, was that they were not concerned about Hill's conflicts of interest; instead, they were questioning my own!

They stated that the video letter I had sent to Boris Johnson two weeks earlier had raised alarms. I was informed that my actions could potentially be seen as an intellectual or non-financial conflict of interest. Under normal circumstances, I might have agreed with them. My co-authors too indicate that, *here deviation from the rule is not a mistake.*[1] In the context of a deadly pandemic, however, how could they hold this against me?

In my defence, I emphasised that the Covid-19 emergency was an exceptional circumstance. My appeal was in line with WHO's own emergency guidelines called '*Developing global norms for sharing data and results during public health emergencies*' (Exhibit 9).[2] These guidelines state that researchers in emergency situations have a "moral obligation to share preliminary results" and must always consider the public health impact when deciding whether to withhold or share findings.

This significant and now suspiciously deleted WHO document also stated that: "There are very great risks in withholding data and results arising from analyses of that data, and these risks are to both the individual and community from which the data arises, and for nations, regions and the globe. The risks of withholding data and results must always be taken into account in the context of emergencies."

---

1   Hexagram 62, Preponderance of the Small, line 2. From I Ching, by Richard Wilhelm, 3rd Ed. p.242.

2   Exhibit 9. Developing global norms for sharing data and results during public health emergencies. A deleted WHO document.

I explained to the editors that, in line with the WHO guideline, I had weighed the consequences and found sharing the results as soon as possible to be in everyone's interest. I also highlighted that the WHO guidance cautioned journal editors that: "Journals should not hinder the sharing of data that could help mitigate the impact of such emergencies", and that "In such scenarios, journals should not penalise, and, indeed, should encourage or mandate public sharing of relevant data". The situation was dire, and a public health emergency demanded action. As my video appeal to Prime Minister Johnson had fallen on deaf ears, I was continuing with the *conscientious fulfilment* of my duty to draw attention to this clearly useful remedy. [1]

After this correspondence, however, communication from the editorial team abruptly dried up. Meanwhile, our dedicated Cochrane review team persevered with the task at hand and, by the time we had nearly completed the full review, Lasserson responded to my prompt and agreed to a Zoom meeting.

Amid the declared pandemic, Lasserson told me that my video appeal to the Prime Minister had shocked him. "I'm aware of another team doing an ivermectin review," he announced, trying not to look me in the eye. "They've been working on it for about a week or so – we'd like to give them a go at it."

Lasserson also told me that he was concerned about my stance on placebo control trials. I had stated in my rapid review that comparing ivermectin to placebo in further trials was likely to be unethical. a position grounded in basic medical ethics. Frankly, no one with Covid symptoms should have been given a placebo or nothing at all. However, I can see how my opinion would have been upsetting to those involved in expensive Covid-19 therapeutics trials, most of which included an arm where symptomatic patients received no

---

1   Hexagram 62, Preponderance of the Small, line 2. From I Ching, by Richard Wilhelm, 3rd Ed. p.242.

active treatment.

If my involvement was creating a problem for the Cochrane editors, I let Lasserson know that I was prepared to step aside, the team was robust enough without me. However, despite this proposal, our rigorous processes and experienced review team, Lasserson confirmed to me that they would not even be prepared to read our full review, which was nearing completion. Indeed, he told me that he had "looked into the evidence" and there was not enough.

What is the point of any Cochrane review then or, indeed, a team of experts, if an editor could simply eyeball a selection of studies at hand and declare whether the evidence was sufficient or not?

Feeling both annoyed and eager to advocate for our dedicated team, I tried to keep my frustration in check as I explained that it would be an extraordinary waste of resources to discard everything we had done, especially since the other team he mentioned had barely even started! But still Lasserson would not budge.

My co-authors observe of the situation: *You are sincere. And are being obstructed. A cautious halt halfway brings good fortune. Going through to the end brings misfortune.*[1]

My intention, in offering to withdraw from the review team, had been to meet Lasserson and Soares-Weisner halfway. However, it was clear to me that a decision had already been taken. It was upsetting and disheartening to see our collective effort dismissed so easily. We had all worked so hard, the work we had put in was being disregarded, and it was my fault somehow. I despaired of Lasserson too, with whom I had always had a cordial relationship – he had no idea what was at stake. Worse still, I sensed that, to save face and comply with their influencers' requests, he was planning to retrospectively solicit the German team, which Prof. Jim Neilson had flagged up in the first instance, to be their official review team. Initially, the German team's

---

1   Hexagram 6, Conflict, The Judgement. From I Ching, by Richard Wilhelm, 3rd Ed. p.28.

interest had been solely in using Cochrane's software for their privately commissioned review!

The situation here calls for extreme caution; [...] And if one were to go on, endeavouring to force his way to the goal, he would be endangered. Therefore one must be on guard and not act but continue inwardly to persevere.[1] There was no point in burning bridges with Cochrane, even though the circumstances were frustrating and the stakes high. Almost my entire income from the preceding 10 years had come from Cochrane-related activities, either preparing systematic reviews for Cochrane directly, or as part of my workstreams for the WHO in the development of WHO guidelines. As my *I Ching* co-authors suggest, the best course of action was to continue persevering inwardly. We needed to avoid playing into the hands of those pulling the strings.

At first we ought to put up with traditional ways as long as possible; otherwise we exhaust ourselves and our energy and still achieve nothing.[2] Thus, I remained courteous, and made Lasserson a final offer: even he must see that there must be some value in the drudge work already completed, that of data abstraction and risk of bias assessments. So as not to waste research, and highlighting that we had already invested 500 hours (and this was a public health emergency, was not it?), I suggested a collegial collaboration between his German team and us, offering to share our data spreadsheets with the team right away.

Lasserson was not the least interested in this generous offer. The *I Ching* notes that *the idea of conflict... in terms of character, is presented by the combination of deep cunning within and fixed determination outwardly. A person of this character will certainly be quarrelsome.*[3] I left it there. We never heard whether he conveyed this information to the German team or not. After the Zoom meeting ended, Lasserson's relief

---

1   Hexagram 62, Preponderance of the Small, line 4. From I Ching, by Richard Wilhelm, 3rd Ed. p.243.

2   Hexagram 62, Preponderance of the Small, line 1. From I Ching, by Richard Wilhelm, 3rd Ed. p.241.

3   Hexagram 6, Conflict. From I Ching, by Richard Wilhelm, 3rd Ed. p.28.

was palpable. His job was done. He had delivered the reaper's message. Our independent review on ivermectin was not negotiable. He had made sure I understood that our team's efforts were dead in the water.

I reported back to the team empty handed. They were devastated. Our statistician from Newcastle University, Dr Andy Bryant's, appeals had also fallen on deaf ears despite having a long-standing relationship with the editors as a prolific Cochrane scientist. He noted that the Cochrane editors were "fighting alleged lack of equipoise with a lack of equipoise". I've always loved the word "equipoise", which to me, for some reason, evokes images of majestic horses galloping along in slow motion! It means of course a state of balance or neutrality.

We mulled over our options, then Bryant had an idea. Why don't we contact Emeritus Cochrane Editor-in-Chief Dr David Tovey to peer review our Cochrane review once completed? If Tovey were to agree, this could mean a significant step forward and a powerful tacit endorsement of our efforts. Yes, we all agreed!

In such times a man must seek out helpers with whose aid he can carry out the task. But these helpers must be modestly sought out in the retirement to which they have withdrawn. It is not their fame nor their great names but their genuine achievements that are important. Through such modesty the right man is found, and the exceptional task is carried out in spite of all difficulties.[1]

Bryant sent the completed draft review to Dr Tovey, who was the first Editor-in-Chief of the Cochrane Collaboration (2009 to 2019), and former Editorial Director of Evidence Based Medicine at the British Medical Journal, as well as a member of the Committee for the Centre of Biomedical Research Transparency (CBRT). Fittingly, the latter declared that its mission is committed to "Ensuring that

---

1   Hexagram 62, Preponderance of the Small, line 5. From I Ching, by Richard Wilhelm, 3rd Ed. p.243.

all biomedical results – including negative/inconclusive results – are discoverable".

Tovey agreed to informally review the paper, generously making some constructive suggestions. We implemented these and acknowledged his contribution in the final peer-reviewed paper, though publication of the latter would be a while off yet!

However, our collective ego was a bit bruised. For me personally, it was particularly regrettable that my extensive experience with Cochrane since 1998 hadn't carried more weight with Lasserson and Soares-Weisner. Having worked on numerous Cochrane reviews, served as a guideline methodologist for the WHO, and earned a reputation as a respected academic, I had hoped these credentials would lend greater credibility to our team's work. Similarly, Bryant and Dowswell, both seasoned Cochrane contributors, had significant expertise to offer. Yet, despite our combined qualifications, it seemed our experience and dedication counted for little in this particular scenario. Why, we wondered together out loud, would they reject our ready review that concluded help was at hand in the the midst of an emergency? Privately, we all knew the answer.

In the years running up to Covid-19, many Cochrane reviewers like me had expressed growing concerns about the corporatisation of this once volunteer-based organisation. In particular, concerns involved the Bill and Melinda Gates Foundation (BMGF), which is an organisation created to further Mr Gates' corporate interests and influence through strategic "philanthropy". Now called The Gates Foundation, any funding directly or indirectly through Gates or Gates partners must be of concern. In 2018, the BMGF donated $1.15 million to the Cochrane Collaboration, bringing into question Cochrane's independence and objectivity.

In addition to Gates' direct and indirect funding, Cochrane was receiving funding from governments including the UK, German,

Danish, Swiss and other Ministries of Health, as well as universities like McMaster University in Canada, that have extensive corporate partnerships. It also receives commissions from the World Health Organization, whose largest single funder was Gates, through different vehicles.

Cochrane has been accused before of colluding with its financial sponsors, including the Gates Foundation, to produce reviews that favour pharmaceutical interests and promote vaccine uptake. Specific criticisms include the 2018 Cochrane review on the human papillomavirus (HPV) vaccine, which was funded by the BMGF and included an author affiliated with the US CDC, which actively promotes HPV vaccination. Researchers at The Nordic Cochrane Centre pointed out that the HPV review authors had omitted eligible trials and demonstrated reporting bias when they reached the conclusion that the HPV vaccine was safe and effective despite acknowledging that most trials were funded by vaccine manufacturers and lacked sufficient evidence of safety.[1]

At the start of the Covid-19 chapter, Cochrane faced criticism over editorial censorship and misconduct, when it held back publishing a review that found that face masks were ineffective. By withholding the review from the public for seven months while many countries mandated the use of face masks, Cochrane editors could be considered to have actively facilitated the globalist political agenda.

Furthermore, a significant flaw in the Cochrane methodology is a failure to be able to quantify financial sponsorship as a significant risk of bias. When it comes to pharmaceutical or biotechnology industry trials, the vested interests are everything. This renders big pharma RCT findings all but meaningless, and potentially many review findings too.

---

[1]   HPV vaccine safety: Cochrane launches urgent investigation into review after criticisms, The BMJ, August 2018, https://doi.org/10.1136/bmj.k3472.
    https://pharmaceutical-journal.com/article/news/cochrane-launches-urgent-investigation-of-hpv-vaccine-review

Most RCTs these days are industry funded. As a result, funding bias tends to get overlooked because the uncertainty about vested interests would render many Cochrane review findings indeterminate.

Our ivermectin review was different in this respect. Being an old, cheap generic drug, the original ivermectin trials in our review were largely unfunded, and done by clinicians in countries where ivermectin was well-known and readily available – a highly unusual situation indeed! Later, facilitated by Dr Andrew Hill's call for "larger appropriately controlled randomised trials before results are sufficient for review by regulatory authorities", Gates and the pharm industry would make sure this changed.

Meanwhile it was a sad fact to note how far The Cochrane Collaboration had moved away from its original form and intention, as a community of volunteer doctors and scientists interested in good evidence. Under its corporate handlers, and especially notable during the Covid-19 chapter, Cochrane was increasingly being used to deceive the public. Ironically, Cochrane's reputation had been built up over decades by dedicated individuals – lay volunteers, doctors and scientists of integrity – like Bryant, Dowswell and me.

We turned our backs on Cochrane and persevered. Bryant took charge, expertly re-drafting the review for a submission to *The Lancet* instead. *The Lancet*'s editor responded rapidly, suggesting we re-direct it to *The Lancet Respiratory Medicine*, which Bryant did and the editor accepted the submission. He asked me to lie low and not attract any media attention while the paper was under peer-review.

We must understand the demands of the time in order to find the necessary offset for its deficiencies and damages. In any event we must not count on great success, since the requisite strength is lacking. In this lies the importance of the message that one should not strive after lofty things but hold to lowly things.[1]

With hindsight, perhaps submitting to *The Lancet* was *striving to lofty things* still and a lesser known journal would have been more expedient. However, we knew that the article was an excellent piece of work, a fact that should be undeniable to any editor. Wherever it was published would be sure to garner the lucky journal a lot of attention and kudos.

MOVE 8: TOGETHER and PRINCIPLE Trials Add Ivermectin

BIRD's meeting and message did not go unnoticed by the secret science society. Within just two days of our first BIRD meeting, the TOGETHER Trial added the ivermectin arm, on January 15th, 2021, as a direct consequence of our press release. The trial itself had begun in June 2020 as a complex trial to investigate various existing drugs for Covid-19 treatment. Conducted in Brazil, where ivermectin is commonly used for a range of infections, the trial's ivermectin arm was added, with the first participants enrolled shortly thereafter.

However, the trial's protocol was deeply flawed. Just as those with devious intention might hobble a horse they did not want to perform well in a race, the ivermectin arm was initially underdosed – given a single dose only – a decision that immediately raised concerns about trial fixing. Due to a mountain of external criticism, they would later concede to increase the dosage to a 3-day regimen, but it had already been shown that zinc and other supplements were crucial to optimise ivermectin's effectiveness and these were not part of the protocol. Furthermore, the involvement of McMaster University and the BMGF as key players in the trial immediately raised red flags. These entities were deeply invested in new vaccine biotechnologies

---

1   Hexagram 62, Preponderance of the Small, The Judgement. From I Ching, by Richard Wilhelm, 3rd Ed. p.240.

and, as such would be prone to downplaying ivermectin's potential. The design of the trial and its setup made it glaringly clear that the findings were unlikely to favour ivermectin.

Further proof that we were treading on the tail of the tiger came a week later, when Oxford's PRINCIPLE Trial, funded by, you guessed it, the BMGF, along with FAST Grants, announced it would be adding an ivermectin arm too. FAST Grants was a Covid-19 research grant scheme supported by several globalist fronts, including BMGF, Wellcome Trust, Mastercard, and the Chan Zuckerberg Initiative. Calling the PRINCIPLE Trial a "properly-designed" trial, the Oxford PRINCIPLE Trial protocol was published in February 2021. Similarly to the TOGETHER Trial, it did not reflect the evidence already in hand from the 18 plus studies and numerous reviews already conducted.

Both trial designs overlooked the fact that ivermectin has been demonstrated to be remarkably safe for human use, that it worked best in combination with zinc and other nutritional supplements, should be given early in the course of symptoms, with food and not on an empty stomach, and that the response was dose- and duration-dependent. Decades of experience had shown that ivermectin could be administered by non-medical personnel, including individuals with limited literacy in remote rural areas, with minimal training. Most glaring, however, was the fact that the scientists from Oxford University, collaborating with Gates-funded counterparts at McMaster University, completely disregarded the ethical implications of administering placebos (i.e. giving ill people no active treatment at all). This was particularly egregious given the wealth of knowledge shared by independent scientists and doctors worldwide that there were already many ways to help people recover faster, including giving vitamin C, D and zinc.

On January 25th, *TrialSite News*, an independent scientific media based in the US, published the following article, raising some of the prevailing criticism of Oxford's move:

> The University of Oxford soon kicks "the PRINCIPLE Trial" into a higher gear now, in what they consider a pathbreaking "high-quality trial" of Ivermectin, a generic drug already evidencing significant efficacy in over two dozen clinical trials around the world, according to some researchers. The UK government also backs this pivotal study via the Department of Health and Social Care. Searching for early-onset, home-based ambulatory treatments for Covid-19, the PRINCIPLE Trial seeks to meet a gap in research in the world's richest nations to date. Nearly all of the taxpayer-financed research-based expenditures of governments in the US, UK and Europe, for example, have gone into vaccines, novel monoclonal antibodies, and novel therapeutics, with an emphasis on treating severely ill patients. Ivermectin, hailed as the "wonder drug" or "the People's medicine" for Covid-19, gains growing attention worldwide made more widely available, frankly, partly due to *TrialSite*'s consistent chronicling of these trials around the world since the original University of Monash breakthrough. The team discovered that in a lab cell culture, Ivermectin obliterates the novel coronavirus within 48 hours. Since then, *TrialSite* has covered most studies worldwide, whereas, by the summer, groups in the U.S., such as the Front Line Covid-19 Critical Care Alliance (FLCCC), commenced meta-analysis covering the dozens of Ivermectin studies around the world. According to these physician/scientists, the results reveal compelling data that Ivermectin actually reduces the Covid-19 death rate while accelerating viral clearance and transmission reduction.
>
> Enter the preeminent University of Oxford and the PRINCIPLE Trial: the globe's top investigators now seek to finally test if Ivermectin and antiviral Favipiravir, both low-cost, orally-administered,

generally available generic drugs, can be proven safe and effective in a "properly designed trial." Led by Co-Chief investigator Chris Butler, Professor of Primary Care, Nuffield Department of Primary Care, Health Services at Oxford, the study team is generally upbeat about the prospects. Still, Dr Butler notes the "gap in the data."

A critically important trial, the PRINCIPLE Trial, is also causing a stir. Groups such as the FLCCC raise the Helsinki Accords: from their vantage, they remind all about the question of ethical conduct – is it right and proper to conduct a randomised placebo-controlled trial when there is sufficient evidence that a drug can save lives? Couldn't a dose control study or well-designed observational study be run instead to both generate data and protect patients? On the other hand, that Oxford is the first major centre to embrace this important generic drug is truly game-changing and demonstrates the leadership position of that research institution again.[1]

My co-authors describe the situation with the PRINCIPLE trialists as follows: *The light of the sun as it rises over the earth is by nature clear. The higher the sun rises, the more it emerges from the dark mists, spreading the pristine purity of its rays over an ever widening area. The real nature of man is likewise originally good, but it becomes clouded by contact with earthly things and therefore needs purification before it can shine forth in its native clarity.*[2] I wrote to the lead investigator, Prof. Chris Butler, to enlighten him about BIRD's ivermectin research efforts and conclusions, though I strongly suspected he was already aware of us and them. I especially highlighted the ethical issues of giving sick people a placebo in light of the evidence in favour of ivermectin. It was not ethical. However, about my efforts with Butler specifically, the *I Ching* observes: *If one is not extremely careful,*

1   https://www.trialsitenews.com/a/bird-evidence-to-decision-framework-meeting-for-ivermectins-efficacy

2   Hexagram 35, Progress, The Image. From I Ching, by Richard Wilhelm, 3rd Ed. p.137.

Somebody may come up from behind and strike him. Misfortune.[1] At certain times extraordinary caution is absolutely necessary. [...] There are dangers lurking for which they are unprepared. Yet such dangers are not unavoidable; one can escape it if he understands that the time demands that he pay special attention to small and insignificant things.[2]

I was on my guard, well aware of the need, as an outside academic, as well as BIRD's representative, to approach the Oxford tiger carefully. Other members of our fledgling group also reached out, including Oxford astrophysicist Dr Bob Watkins. While our evidence and appeals to Butler for pragmatism and common sense were predictably dismissed, we did not force the issue. Watkins maintained intermittent collegial communication with Butler, keeping his well-connected Oxford ear to the ground, while we pressed on with our game plan.

MOVE 9: BIRD's Recommendation on Ivermectin

Perseverance furthers. [...] The flying bird brings the message[...]Great good fortune.[3] On the 20th February, the second and official BIRD meeting was held, this time with 65 participants from 15 countries. It was enormously validating that many of those present would become a significant part of the movement to counter the dystopian Covid agenda. These included FLCCC's warrior ICU physician Dr Pierre Kory, retired UK paediatrician Dr Rosamund Jones, Japanese Prof. Satoshi Omura's associate, Dr Morimasa Yagisawa, UK Mast Cell Activation Sensitivity (MCAS) expert, Dr Tina Peers, Dr Mike Yeadon, and my personal behind-the-scenes hero, Cambridge physicist, Dr Edmund Fordham. A society of like-minded people from

---

1   Hexagram 62, Preponderance of the Small, line 3. From I Ching, by Richard Wilhelm, 3rd Ed. p.242.

2   Hexagram 62, Preponderance of the Small, line 3. From I Ching, by Richard Wilhelm, 3rd Ed. p.242.

3   Hexagram 62, Preponderance of the Small, The Judgement. From I Ching, by Richard Wilhelm, 3rd Ed. p.240.

around the world was forming. A society of people who care about getting to the truth of the matter and, once there, standing up for it!

As a former Pfizer executive, Dr Yeadon was an unlikely dissident on the Covid scene. I distinctly remember our first phone call. I took the call by the window in my tiny town office on a drizzly day, watching the pigeons soaring despite the rain. Like me, Yeadon was deeply worried about the experimental Covid-19 vaccines; he said they were not safe, and urged me to inform the WHO. I assured him that I knew about the vaccines that were not vaccines and, whatever was going on, the WHO was in on it. It was a relief to speak with someone who also grasped the dire threat mankind was facing.

My co-authors capture the scenario well – we had *a dangerous abyss lying before us and a steep, inaccessible mountain rising behind us. We are surrounded by obstacles; at the same time, since the mountain has the attribute of keeping still, there is implicit a hint as to how we can extricate ourselves.*[1] Nowhere was safe and pushing forward would only lead to more obstructions. Thus, it was best not to rush off anywhere but rather to join forces with like-minded others to overcome the obstacles.

The second BIRD meeting was recorded and formal procedures were followed in line with *World Health Organization Handbook on Guideline Development*, including making panel judgements at each step of the evidence evaluation process. The BIRD Steering Group that managed the process included Dr Andrew Bryant, Dr Ketan Gajjar, Dr Scott Mitchell, Dr Claire Mock-Muñoz de Luna, Dr Tina Peers, Dr Tony Tham, and me. For the full list of participants, readers can access the full 107-page document BIRD proceedings document in the online archive as Exhibit 10.[2] The executive summary of the

---

1   Hexagram 39, Obstruction. From I Ching, by Richard Wilhelm, 3rd Ed. p.151.

2   Exhibit 10. BIRD Proceedings and Recommendations on Ivermectin for Covid-19.

BIRD Recommendation is included as Exhibit 11.[1]

As before, Emeritus Prof. Jim Neilson served as Chair. I was amused when he suggested that we might refrain from inviting the "noisy Americans" this time, noting that the lively discussion between the FLCCC duo and Dr McCullough had made his task of maintaining order during the proceedings far more challenging! Such disruptions were a rarity in the typically homogenous WHO meetings to which we were accustomed. Nonetheless, how could we exclude the FLCCC? When I spoke with Dr Pierre Kory that week and shared my dilemma, he took it in good humour. Assuring me there were no hard feelings, he promised to be on his best behaviour and suggested representing the FLCCC solo on this occasion. For the record, I also invited a WHO colleague to join as an observer but was informed that anything they did externally regarding Covid-19 required prior approval from the organisation.

For these proceedings we shared the updated version of the meta-analysis from our recently submitted publication, as well as updating the Evidence-to-Decision framework domains on values, equity, acceptability, feasibility and resource use (costs and cost-effectiveness). Notably at this time on the WHO's Vigibase website, there were 4,673 ADRs and 16 deaths linked to ivermectin since 1992; whereas for remdesivir there were 5489 ADRs and 417 deaths in one year, and for the Covid vaccines there were more than 177,052 ADRs and 1,585 deaths already – in just under 3 months since authorisation!

In case you are not familiar with remdesivir, it was the first 'antiviral' promoted as a treatment for Covid-19 by Dr Anthony Fauci and the FDA in October 2020, despite lacking evidence of its effectiveness and safety. It originally developed to treat Hepatitis C, and was subsequently investigated for Ebola and Marburg virus infection.

---

1   Exhibit 11. BIRD Proceedings and Recommendations on Ivermectin for Covid-19. Executive Summary.

As a Covid-19 treatment it would prove potentially deadly, causing kidney damage and worse, to those unfortunate enough to receive it.

In the Evidence-to-Decision framework, we did not only reference clinical trials, we referenced real world data too. In several countries, ivermectin was already being used with promising results in managing Covid-19. For example, in Peru, deaths dropped significantly after it was introduced in July 2020, though they surged again when its use was restricted months later. In India's Uttar Pradesh, the rollout of ivermectin treatment kits led to a rapid decline in deaths, with none reported on some days despite the state's massive population. Other countries like Slovakia and Zimbabwe included ivermectin in their treatment plans, and African regions that used it for other diseases saw lower Covid-19 deaths and infection rates. In nursing homes in France and the US, ivermectin seemed to help control outbreaks and reduce severe cases among elderly residents. Additionally, some studies suggested it could improve symptoms in people with extended illness, which became known as Long Covid.

The additional considerations that we presented on costs showed that ivermectin, only available as an oral formulation, was highly affordable and widely available in many countries, costing as little as $2.90 for 100 tablets. Its use as a Covid-19 treatment could reduce hospital resource burdens by shortening ICU stays and preventing severe cases, making it a potentially cost-effective alternative to more expensive strategies like mass vaccination. Unlike Covid vaccines that were costing tax-payers a fortune, requiring cold chain storage and vaccinators to administer them, oral ivermectin could be self-administered at home for both treatment and prophylaxis, further lowering costs.

Ivermectin also had the potential to improve health equity by addressing Covid-19's disproportionate impact on disadvantaged communities. Its affordability, ease of use, and long safety record made it ideal for reaching vulnerable groups such as the elderly, ethnic minorities, low-income populations, and people in low- and middle-income countries (LMICs). Unlike vaccines, ivermectin could be sent via the post to remote places without the need for refrigeration, benefiting those with limited healthcare access. Its widespread use could reduce the strain on hospitals, which we were told were bursting at the seams, and get help to many more people.

On the topic of acceptability, we highlighted that ivermectin was already included on the WHO Essential Medicine List and had a well-documented safety record, even at higher doses. Due to its safety, affordability, and potential to reduce hospital strain, all stakeholders, especially patients were likely to support ivermectin use. Given that its safety profile surpassed that of all treatments granted conditional authorisation or EUA, ivermectin use could be similarly authorised. Covid vaccines and Fauci's remdesivir had been granted EUAs based on the principle that the potential benefits outweigh the potential risks during a public health crisis. These interventions were approved despite being based on evidence of low certainty, with phrases like "may prevent" in the EUAs indicating that effectiveness was not yet fully established. Additionally, these drugs were granted EUA even though nothing was known of their long-term safety.

In contrast, ivermectin safety data were considerably more extensive than the new Covid-19-specific treatments. Therefore, in the Evidence-to-Decision framework we highlighted that, given its proven safety and potential benefits in reducing Covid-19 severity, granting EUA for ivermectin would have aligned with the same rationale used for the vaccines and other treatments. Stakeholders, including policymakers and regulatory bodies, should find it equally, if not more acceptable to approve ivermectin for emergency use, particularly given its affordability and feasibility.

In addition, ivermectin's safety and extensive record of use, with doses administered equalling one-third of the world population over 30 years, highlighted its reliability. As a cheap and generic medicine, easy to produce, with multiple manufacturers around the world, widespread use was imminently feasible. Like the review findings, these additional considerations were all in favour of ivermectin. Therefore, a recommendation in favour of ivermectin was approved by the group.

We highlighted the 2015 World Health Organization guidance on *Global norms for sharing data and results during public health emergencies* too in the final BIRD document. Though its intention, I suspect, had been to facilitate the inappropriate roll-out of inadequately trialled interventions during WHO-declared "health emergencies" and "pandemics", it supported our argument in relation to ivermectin very well. This document disappeared from the WHO website at an indeterminate date thereafter, confirming my suspicions. I could imagine the handlers on the phone to one another: "She keeps talking about this damn 'global norms' document. I thought we put that in place to get our drugs approved without hassle? We'd better take it down ASAP..."

This landmark event passed without much external fanfare, but a recording of this meeting will be archived for as long as possible on the BIRD website.[1]

The BIRD recommendation in the final BIRD Proceedings document stated the following:

The British Ivermectin Recommendation Development Panel recommends ivermectin for the prevention and treatment of Covid-19, to reduce morbidity and mortality associated with Covid-19 infection and to prevent Covid-19 infection among those at higher risk.

---

[1] The BIRD meeting recording can be found at www.Lawriefiles.com

I asked the *I Ching* for commentary on ivermectin. Was it any good from its' ancient perspective?

My co-authors liken the power of ivermectin to an energy from heaven – *The CREATIVE works sublime success.*[1] Dr Pierre Kory no doubt would be pleased to hear this, as he was the first to call ivermectin a veritable "miracle drug"!

If an inferior element has wormed its way in, it must be energetically checked at once. By consistently checking it, bad effects can be avoided[...]A pig that is still young and lean cannot rage about much, but after it has eaten its fill and become strong, its true nature comes out if it has not been previously curbed.[2] Thus, my co-authors go on to confirm that ivermectin holds great promise in its simplicity and effectiveness in curbing evil before it can take hold, especially from something that may seem insignificant to start with – like a *worm.* How witty! Indeed, ivermectin worked best when given early in those with Covid-19 symptoms. Once illness has set in, be it parasitic or another disease state, such as cancer, it becomes harder to treat and complications are more likely. Hence our recommending ivermectin for early intervention was most appropriate!

My co-authors further highlight that a preventive approach to health and wellbeing is sensible. *Human woes usually come as a result of unexpected events against which we are not forearmed. If we are prepared, they can be prevented.*[3] Much to ponder from this wisdom.

You may have noted from the BIRD proceedings document that the *Daily Mail* writer David Rose was among the attendees. We were grateful to see an article penned by him in the *Mail Online* four days later, for which I wondered whether he had paid a price; he seemed reluctant to pen anything on ivermectin thereafter. When I checked

---

1   Hexagram 1, The Creative: The Judgment. From I Ching, by Richard Wilhelm, 3rd Ed. p.4.
2   Hexagram 44, Coming to Meet, line 1. From I Ching, by Richard Wilhelm, 3rd Ed. p.172.
3   Hexagram 45, Gathering Together, The Image. From I Ching, by Richard Wilhelm, 3rd Ed. p.175.

in with him on a subsequent Zoom, he cautioned me against speaking about the vaccines, saying that no one would be able to hear anything we had to say about ivermectin otherwise.

About the circumstances of individuals such as Rose back then, the *I Ching* observes, *Keeping his hips still. Making his sacrum stiff. Dangerous. The heart suffocates. This refers to enforced quiet. The restless heart is to be subdued by forcible means.* However, *fire when it is smothered changes into acrid smoke that suffocates as it spreads[...]* Quiet induced by artificial means *will lead to very unwholesome results.*[1] My co-authors continue, *Keeping his jaws still* avoids remorse.[2] *A man in a dangerous situation, especially when he is not adequate to it, is inclined to be very free with talk and presumptuous jokes. But injudicious speech easily leads to situations that subsequently give much cause for regret. However, if a man is reserved in his speech, his words take ever more definite form, and every occasion for regret vanishes.*[3]

I suppose it was self-preservation that limited Rose's engagement with the pandemic-changing news on ivermectin. Having received my professional opinion on the Covid-19 injections, he may also have been afraid to associate with someone who was sure to be called "anti-vax" in due course. It was disappointing but, given his former experiences publishing perspectives against the approved narrative, perhaps I should have expected it.

---

1 Hexagram 52, Keeping Still, Mountain, line 3. From I Ching, by Richard Wilhelm, 3rd Ed. p.202-3.

2 Hexagram 52, line 5. From I Ching, by Richard Wilhelm, 3rd Ed. p.203.

3 Hexagram 52, line 5. From I Ching, by Richard Wilhelm, 3rd Ed. p.203.

Chapter 3

The Wanderer

THE WANDERER. Success through smallness.
Perseverance brings good fortune
To the wanderer. [1]

When a man is a wanderer and a stranger, he should not be gruff nor overbearing. He has no large circle of acquaintances, therefore he should not give himself airs. He must be cautious and reserved; in this way he protects himself from evil. If he is obliging towards others he wins success. A wanderer has no fixed abode; his home is the road. Therefore he must take care to remain upright and steadfast, so that he sojourns only in the proper places, associating only with good people. Then he has good fortune and can go his way unmolested. [2]

My co-authors' choice of *The Wanderer* as the theme for this chapter

---

1   Hexagram 56, The Wanderer. The Judgment. From I Ching, by Richard Wilhelm, 3rd Ed. p.216-7.

2   Hexagram 56, The Wanderer. The Judgment. From I Ching, by Richard Wilhelm, 3rd Ed. p.216-7.

feels fitting. In the context of what was required of me at this point in my journey, I had a long and lonely distance to travel yet, dependent on my reception by those I met along the way. Having grown up, studied, and worked as a doctor and researcher in South Africa, relocating to Britain naturally distanced me from many collegial associations. Whilst clinical work was out of the question because of my personal circumstances, establishing my own research company, Evidence-based Medicine Consultancy (E-BMC) Limited, when we arrived in our new home, enabled me to balance my other role, that of being a mother to three children navigating the aftermath of traumatic experiences in South Africa. Balancing these roles in a foreign country was challenging, but it reinforced my ability to prioritise, adapt and work hard. Persevering in spite of difficulties is one thing I excelled at, a characteristic I learnt hiking in the Drakensberg with my father as a girl. This would prove essential in countering an anti-human, globalist agenda planned decades, if not longer, in advance.

Not being part of an academic institution, a realm I have always disliked, both isolated and liberated me. Institutions, with their cold, sterile interiors or inflated historic prestige, have never appealed; I have always believed that the merit of one's work should stand on its own, judged by results rather than status and association. As such, I've always found the subtle hierarchies and unspoken rules of "boys' club" culture that permeates academia deeply unpalatable. It is a system that fosters compliance over originality, allegiance over merit and, in my opinion, kills genius. Given my disdain for institutions, I've never bothered with academic rankings or metrics. Thus, I was surprised when my new BIRD acquaintance Dr Edmund Fordham told me he had looked me up and my ranking was higher than the average Oxford professor's standing.

Being without a fixed academic or institutional abode is a fairly unusual position compared to most doctors and scientists. It afforded me the relative freedom to choose where to direct my academic energy. Thus, early in my career I made a conscious choice never to work with the pharmaceutical industry, to preserve my independence and autonomy. Though this substantially limited my earning potential, it did not bother me, as money has never driven me anywhere for its own sake.

With a clinical background favouring obstetrics and gynaecology, before Covid-19, the research work I enjoyed most focused on improving the experience of pregnancy and childbirth. Unfortunately, natural birth processes had been overridden by 'the science' mentality, transforming potential empowering maternal experiences into horrendously medicalised ones instead. My work in this area, particularly with the World Health Organization (WHO), had felt validating for a time, offering me a glimpse of how my behind-the-scenes research contributions could make a meaningful difference. However, even with this WHO work, I had become fairly disillusioned, questioning whether WHO was making a positive impact on health and wellbeing at all. "Where to from here?" I had often wondered.

When Covid-19 came along, the duality, freedom on one hand and isolation on the other, placed me in a fairly unique position. Whilst not having the backing of an esteemed organisation, I was unencumbered by the constraints of institutional or corporate allegiance. I was nobody's puppet, and no one could pull my strings. I could think and act with integrity. A wanderer in the world of science, charting my own course, I had no master.

However, the ivermectin mission required considerable voluntary effort, as my company, E-BMC Limited, could no longer sustain paying team members their usual wages for this work. While I directed some of my former colleagues to complete our remaining WHO and Cochrane contracts, others withdrew, unable to commit to my unconventional path challenging the official Covid-19 narrative.

It was clear that I would have to build a new team. As someone who tends to work alone, both by nature and practice, this became the greatest challenge of the next few years. For a brief period, it felt as though the pigeons outside my small corporate office, high up in the heart of Bath, with a view of the impressive Bath Town Hall, would be my only Covid-19 era companions. And, in truth, they made for excellent company!

MOVE 10: BIRD Delivers its Message to Health Authorities

After the extremely successful official BIRD meeting, I shifted my focus to the urgent task of contacting authorities to notify them of the BIRD recommendations. Together with my ivermectin-focused research assistant, Dr Claire Mock-Muñoz de Luna, during the final week of February 2021, we worked diligently to send evidence packs to all members of the WHO's Covid Team, led by Dr Maria van Kerkhove and Dr Janet Dias, as well as key individuals at health authorities and regulatory bodies in the USA, UK, South Africa, and Canada, among others.

A new Australian acquaintance, Prof. Emeritus Geoff Taylor, warned me not to get my hopes up though. He told me he had personally contacted a list of UK civil servants as well as some in the European Union during the preceding months with information about ivermectin. Prof. Taylor sent me this list!

1. Keir Starmer (4 October 2020) – the incumbent UK Prime Minister at the time of writing
2. Joe FitzPatrick, Scots Health Minister (25 September, 6 November, 2 December 2020)

3. Sir Patrick Vallance (20 October, 6 November, 1 December, 19 December 2020)
4. Sir Chris Whitty (28 and 29 December 2020)
5. Sir David Nabarro, WHO (15 October, 19 December 2020)
6. Vaughan Gething, Welsh Health Minister (16 October, 6 November 2020)
7. Edward Argar, Minister of State for Health (29 October, 19 December 2020)
8. Matt Hancock, Secretary of State for Health (2 January 2021)
9. Prof. Jonathan Van-Tam, JCVI Chair (12 October, 29 December)
10. Sir Simon Stevens, NHS (4 November, 30 December)
11. Royal College of Nursing (2 January 2021)
12. Andy Burnham, Mayor of Greater Manchester (19 October, 6 December 2020)
13. Royal British Nursing Association (10 October 2020)
14. Plus other assorted UK experts

The email from Taylor to me was emotional. He wrote:

"They wouldn't give a cheap safe drug to go in the middle of a dire situation. I am deeply concerned for you in Britain as a whole, as many of us share common ancestry, and for current friends and family there.

I also sent evidence to EU several contacts and received replies with EU health commissioner Stella Kyriakides and Olga Solomon finally telling me to write no more. There were also contacts with continental Health Ministers. Only the Bulgarians replied. Ivermectin is now available there, helped by the Huwepharma trial results.

I feel sad that I didn't succeed in being heard on the matter of ivermectin to prevent and treat Covid-19, in Britain especially. Normally I'd say 'they aren't going to listen to me', but the situation was so serious I thought it was worth a try."

I was thus braced by Taylor's experience and not expecting miracles from our BIRD communications. It was a significant move however, because we were drawing a line in the sand; we were saying "here is the evidence, and we're onto you".

Few recipients acknowledged the pack. Dr Peter Stein from the FDA did, however, as did Dr van Kerkhove, but only after being prompted by another member of the WHO team. We never received a response from anyone at the NIH, including Dr Clifford Lane, who appeared to have a long-standing professional relationship with Dr Fauci at the NIAID.

The response received from the UK's DHSC-led Covid-19 Antivirals and Therapeutics Taskforce epitomised the systemic resistance we faced in trying to bring truth to light. Their first reference was to the WHO's meta-analysis led by Dr Andrew Hill – how telling! His report, which formed the cornerstone of their stance, had not been peer-reviewed nor published in a journal and, as you know, was riddled with flaws yet they treated it as gospel. Their reliance on this controversial report showed the deep-rooted control mechanisms at play.

In addition to the compromised Hill review, the Therapeutics Taskforce also espoused the opinion of Merck on ivermectin's safety concerns, the very drug company profiting from alternative treatments! They added insult to injury in their position against the evidence, which they called our "view", by saying that C-TAP would be keeping everyone up to date on Covid-19 treatment. Remember Prof. Andrew Owen and his extensive Covid-19 conflicts of interest?

The Taskforce response would be mirrored, content verbatim, by other agencies and civil servants going forward. Annoyingly, correspondence sent to these bodies was fielded by a string of individuals without last names, and getting through to those whom we wished to engage and who were accountable for ignoring the evidence proved impossible.

MOVE 11: Engaging with the FDA

I knew our work on ivermectin and the BIRD recommendations would stir the pot, especially as public awareness around ivermectin began to grow. Those controlling the narrative could not afford to let our efforts gain too much traction, it threatened their entire strategy. Thus, early in March 2021 barely a week after our BIRD correspondence, it was no surprise that the FDA issued a warning against the use of ivermectin for Covid-19. Bar ivermectin being approved by the FDA, this felt like an excellent outcome! It demonstrated their fear – they were afraid of people power, and the power of ivermectin too.

In their statement, the agency announced that ivermectin intended for animals was being misused by people for Covid-19, leading to numerous reports of adverse reactions; they highlighted that even seizures and death were possible. The direness of this FDA warning, as well as the rate at which it was spread through mainstream press and social media, confirmed to me that ivermectin was not only a major threat to the EUA for Covid vaccines and novel drugs, but to the entire pandemic narrative itself.

Having received no further communication from FDA's Dr Stein, and in light of this new FDA media campaign against ivermectin, I sent an email on March 16th to Dr Janet Woodcock, the FDA's Acting Commissioner and a lead adviser to Operation Warp Speed (OWS). OWS was an interagency partnership between the Department of Health and Human Services (HHS) and the Department of Defence

(DOD) launched during the first Trump administration to **accelerate the development, manufacturing, and distribution of Covid-19 vaccines, therapeutics, and diagnostics**. OWS employed several strategies to accelerate vaccine development, including selecting multiple vaccine candidates, funding large-scale manufacturing, and combining or running clinical trial phases concurrently. As a result of these efforts, two novel gene-based vaccines (Moderna and Pfizer/BioNTech) received EUA from the FDA by January 2021.[1]

Thus, as the acting FDA Commissioner, Dr Woodcock played a significant role in these dangerous and unprecedented authorisations. Whilst the vaccines were ostensibly to prevent Covid-19 infection, Woodcock's particular OWS role was to accelerate the development and approval of new Covid-19 drug treatments. With regard to ivermectin then, in 2021, Woodcock seemed to be where the buck stopped.

This is what I wrote to Dr Woodcock on March 16th 2021:

Dear Janet Woodcock,

I am sharing with you the correspondence that I have had with Peter Stein and colleagues with regard to the use of ivermectin for the treatment and prevention of Covid. I am concerned that they have not yet seen the evidence that we sent to them on the 26th February, as the FDA's official position on ivermectin continues to be that there is no evidence to support its use and that ivermectin is intended for animals. The latter is particularly misleading and derogatory, given that ivermectin is widely used in humans around the world, including among the elderly in the US for the treatment of scabies. In addition, the FDA (and NIH) continues to refer to the in vitro Caly study to support the erroneous notion that ivermectin cannot be effective

1   Operation Warp Speed: Accelerated Covid-19 Vaccine Development Status and Efforts to Address Manufacturing Challenges. www.gao.gov/products/gao-21-319.

against covid at regular doses – there are at least 22 RCTs and 5 systematic reviews that show that ivermectin could have a significant impact on the pandemic and, in particular, reduce deaths.

I ask you to pay particular attention to the country example of India, which is four times more populous that the US, and where ivermectin is freely distributed in many states.

I attach the documents that I have shared to date with members of your organisation and trust that you will read them soon, so that we can agree to start saving lives with this cheap, safe and effective generic medicine. Honestly, what does the FDA have to lose?

Attached with this communication, I included the BIRD documents as well as a graph of alleged Covid-19 death rates in India and the USA for the preceding year. Daily Covid deaths in India were virtually zero in many states whereas the comparative death toll in the US was extraordinarily high. If you only watched CNN or the BBC, which would intermittently show people dropping like flies in foreign countries like India, you would never have known that one of the most technologically advanced countries in the world was experiencing among the highest death tolls from Covid.

You may have sensed a bit of tongue-in-cheek on my part by this email. The contrast between India's success and the ongoing struggles in the US made Operation Warp Speed's efforts to combat the 'deadly pandemic' seem absurd, and I was keen to convey this subtly. It felt like a scene from a British pantomime, where everyone is shouting about ivermectin and other effective treatment options, "It's over there!" but the man dressed up as a woman can't seem to find it.

Though "warp speed" is not a term by which I would frame her response to ivermectin evidence, Woodcock did respond pretty speedily to my email. Dispensing with the formalities of conventional email greetings, Woodcock wrote:

Thank you for writing. We are very aware of the wide use of ivermectin, including for scabies. The concern about animal use is that people are dosing themselves with doses intended for animals and getting serious toxicities. This is not good.

Ivermectin use for Covid-19 has been evaluated multiple times by experts in the US, not just at the FDA.

Janet Woodcock

This perfunctory reply from Woodcock was revealing. Here, she was actually acknowledging the widespread use of ivermectin in humans, including for scabies, before pivoting to highlight risks associated with overdosing on formulations intended for animals!

This focus on fringe cases of misuse was exactly the ruse the FDA had pulled in the media campaign against ivermectin to distract from the robust evidence BIRD had shared. Her assertion that "experts in the US" had repeatedly evaluated ivermectin reflected the approach of a bully, appealing to authority rather than inviting a genuine conversation about the data. Indeed, there were US experts in our BIRD team too.

The *I Ching* says of Woodcock's conduct, *Under certain conditions, intimidation without gentleness may achieve something momentarily but not for all time.*[1] In addition, *knowledge should be a refreshing and vitalising force. It becomes so only through stimulating intercourse with congenial friends with whom one holds discussion and practises. In this way learning becomes many sided and takes on a cheerful lightness, whereas there's always something ponderous and one sided about the learning of the self-taught.*[2]

By this brusque response Woodcock seemed intent on quelling

---

1   Hexagram 58, The Joyous, Lake. The Judgment. From I Ching, by Richard Wilhelm, 3rd Ed. p.224.

2   Hexagram 58, The Joyous, Lake, The Image. From I Ching, by Richard Wilhelm, 3rd Ed. p.224-5.

any opportunity for "stimulating intercourse" about ivermectin, at least not with me or BIRD. Yes, I'll admit, the language used by my ancient co-authors does make me chuckle sometimes!

My co-authors go on to observe, *True joy must spring from within. But if one is empty within and wholly given over to the world idle pleasures come streaming in from without. This is what many people welcome as diversion. Those who lack inner stability and therefore need amusement, will always find opportunity of indulgence. They attract external pleasures by the emptiness of their natures. Thus they lose themselves more and more, which of course has bad results.*[1]

Dr Woodcock was not just another bureaucrat during the Covid-19 chapter; she was integral to the deadly Covid-19 agenda, and her actions, as well as her inactions with respect to ivermectin, left an indelible mark on countless human lives. As Acting FDA Commissioner she wielded immense power. In my opinion, she used this power to facilitate and expedite dangerous drug products based on compromised processes and fraudulent data. It was her leadership that framed these efforts as rigorous and scientifically sound, emphasising safety, effectiveness, and manufacturing quality.

. Her sidelining of ivermectin was crucial to the vaccination agenda, but there was no way of doing this legitimately without being seen to act on the emerging evidence in some way. Thus, in what many saw as an attempt to stave off criticism, she would later add an ivermectin arm to the ACTIV trial, a token gesture to appear as though she and the FDA were willing to explore this avenue. Years later the trial would predictably find no role for ivermectin in the management of Covid-19.

Call me sexist, but I have always held women to higher standards of conduct than men. For example, I can tolerate a drunk man and even find him amusing for a period, but a drunk woman evokes

---

1   Hexagram 58, The Joyous, Lake, line 3. From I Ching, by Richard Wilhelm, 3rd Ed. p.225.

concern, disdain or disappointment in me. A woman behaving like a man feels disrespectful to our great Mother, Nature, who nourishes all people and all things, good and evil, and who has suffered a lot on our account.

In the professional sphere, time and again, I've witnessed women rise to positions of power and influence, only to behave in ways indistinguishable from men. In doing so, they discard the inherent intuition and ancient wisdom passed down through their maternal lineage. It's as if they lose themselves in a patriarchal system that diminishes the very qualities that would make their contribution significant. Women obstetricians were a case in point from my experience, more often reaching for their surgeon's knife to do unnecessary C-sections than empowering women through natural birth. Thus, professionally I too had to make difficult choices about how to navigate a patriarchal disease-based system that frames pregnancy as a medical condition in need of interventions.

By nature, women are engendered to nurture life, we don't take it away. In Woodcock's case, given her position and influence, she was not a passive participant, she was an active player of the Covid-19 game – a eugenics game, in essence. Why did she play it, I wonder? Perhaps it was easier to go along with the narrative, follow orders from those higher up, rather than risk rocking the boat with whomever or whatever is really in charge of the depopulation agenda. Or perhaps, like many individuals in powerful positions, Woodcock was driven by ambition and a desire for control.

In any event, Woodcock's actions were deeply troubling to me. When an authentic and compassionate woman's voice was most needed in a sea of fascist patriarchy, consider the potential for a woman in her position at that critical moment. Had she acted as a true advocate for public health, willing to consider all evidence on ivermectin and caution against using experimental Covid products, she could have made an extraordinarily good difference in the world.

My co-authors are more objective than me. They suggest that there is hope for Woodcock, as for us all, should she choose to heed some ancient wisdom. I have replaced *he* with *she* and *man* with *woman* for added clarity in this quote: *A vain nature invites diverting pleasures and must suffer accordingly. If a woman is unstable within, the pleasures of the world that she does not shun have so powerful an influence that she is swept along by them. She has given up direction of her own life and what becomes of her depends upon chance and external influences. Here it is no longer a question of danger, of good fortune or misfortune. Success may come, everything depends upon her seeking her happiness and that of others in one way only, that is, in perseverance of what is right. She must make herself strong by consciously casting out all that is inferior and degrading.*[1]

The *I Ching's* wisdom highlights a path of personal accountability and moral clarity, reminding us that true strength lies in resisting the pull of external pressures and aligning with what is just and right. The temptations of the world can be overwhelming, but they ultimately leave one adrift without purpose or integrity. The ancient text suggests that only through a conscious, deliberate choice to pursue what is noble and true can we reclaim our autonomy and determine our own fate. Success is not about fleeting power or external approval, but about finding inner strength and consistency in doing what is right.

MOVE 12: BIRD Informs the WHO's Covid-19 Team

BIRD certainly presented a challenge for the WHO. With professional appraisals of excellent and outstanding from the WHO in every work assessment domain, I was in good standing with my WHO colleagues in the Reproductive Health Research (RHR)

---

1   Hexagram 58, The Joyous, Lake, line 6. From I Ching, by Richard Wilhelm, 3rd Ed. p.226.

department that regularly hired me, and with whom I had worked for the better part of ten years. Our BIRD Evidence-to-Decision meeting had adhered to the guideline development process outlined in the WHO's Handbook on Guideline Development, which I had learnt and indeed helped refine over the years for the purpose of our specific RHR guideline work. The handbook provides step-by-step advice on the technical aspects of developing a WHO guideline and the methods used. As someone with extensive experience working in WHO Technical Teams, I, through BIRD, was in a unique position to tackle the official WHO misinformation on ivermectin. I knew their methods and WHO process to produce the evidence to support Covid-19 guidelines; I also knew that the WHO Covid Team was not following it!

BIRD communications alerting the WHO Covid-19 Team to the ivermectin evidence on the 23rd February 2021 had been addressed to Dr Maria van Kerkhove, and copied to the rest of the WHO Covid Team. Van Kerkhove played a central role during the so-called Covid-19 pandemic as the Technical Lead for the WHO's Covid-19 response. In this capacity, she was responsible for overseeing the evaluation of evidence and ensuring the integrity of the scientific guidance on prevention and management. She regularly communicated key findings and updates to the public and media, often serving as a spokesperson for the WHO's position on pandemic-related policies and treatments. Her role involved advising governments and health authorities globally and would evolve into also defending the organisation's stance against ivermectin.

Dr Janet Diaz, WHO's Emergency Programme Clinical Lead, also held significant responsibility for the WHO's clinical guidance on Covid-19. When I heard nothing further from Van Kerkhove, I reached out for support to one of my RHR colleagues, who kindly facilitated a direct introduction to Dr Janet Diaz. Perhaps we could get through to her? A limited correspondence followed, where I conveyed my disappointment over the failure of the WHO to recommend ivermectin promptly. I also highlighted the WHO's own guidance on the importance of rapidly sharing data during public health emergencies.

Diaz was courteous up to a point but made her position clear: The WHO Covid-19 Team had the ivermectin issue in hand, and we would have to wait for the outcome of their Covid-19 guideline development process. Notably within days of our BIRD correspondence, however, a new WHO "living systematic review" prepared by a team at McMaster University on ivermectin for Covid-19 prophylaxis (prevention) was posted to *medRxiv*, another preprint server.

Ivermectin's usefulness in Covid-19 symptom prevention was a bigger threat than its use as a Covid-19 treatment, as in prevention it was a direct threat to the novel Covid vaccine products, which were supposed to prevent infection and transmission (but did not). Unsurprisingly, this WHO-endorsed non-peer-reviewed review had significant methodological flaws. Acknowledging significant reductions in Covid-19 infection rates when ivermectin was used prophylactically, the authors undermined this favourable evidence in much the same way as was done in the Hill review pre-print.

I persisted with Dr Diaz, sending another email expressing my concerns about this development. Highlighting that the McMaster's review team had drawn different conclusions from the same collection of studies as used by BIRD, undermining the evidence. Supported by our statistician Bryant, I pointed out to Diaz the technical flaws in the grading of the evidence and the meta-analysis. In addition, I pointed out that Prof. David Tovey, Emeritus Editor-in-Chief of Cochrane, had personally noted these issues to me in correspondence too, suggesting there may be political motives behind the excessive downgrading of the evidence. My thoughts exactly.

I pointed out to Diaz that the WHO's reluctance to recommend this safe, affordable, and accessible treatment during a global crisis, raised serious concerns about WHO's objectivity. I signed off with a request that she urgently investigate these irregularities. On March 31st, two weeks later, the WHO published its treatment guideline called *Therapeutics and Covid-19*.

The gist of this 60-page WHO guideline document, which acknowledges that ivermectin "triggered" this version of the WHO guideline, was that "Ivermectin may increase the risk of serious adverse events (SAEs) leading to drug discontinuation [...] and may have little or no impact on time to clinical improvement". It further stated that "We currently lack persuasive evidence of a mechanism of action for ivermectin in Covid-19, and any observed clinical benefit would be unexplained". In addition "The panel believed that most well-informed patients would be reluctant to use a medication for which the evidence left high uncertainty regarding effects." The use of the term "well-informed" and the fact that a panel could decide what patients might think about ivermectin was, in itself, notably preposterous and an unconventional choice of language for a WHO guideline. I wonder what most well-informed people would say about the Covid-19 vaccines once they were, indeed, "well-informed".

The evidence presented by the WHO Covid-19 Team on ivermectin deeper within the document showed similar flaws as the other WHO-endorsed reviews, in particular with respect to "grading" the evidence to undermine it, and omission of studies. Based on what was known about the safety of ivermectin in WHO records alone, the emphasis on SAEs indicated the lengths the globalists were prepared to go to reinforce the official narrative. New, expensive therapeutics were on the way, like Molnupiravir and Paxlovid, and, like the Covid-19 vaccines, these would be needing rapid

EUAs too, so established safe, effective and low-cost medicines like ivermectin needed to be emphatically discredited.

With the fingerprints of globalist puppeteers all over it, I looked to see who had provided the technical support for the Covid-19 therapeutics guideline team. Not only did a team from McMaster University conduct the systematic review and meta-analysis, but influential individuals from McMaster such as Prof. Gordon Guyatt played key roles in the WHO's recommendations on ivermectin.[1] In, general, McMaster had conflicts of interest that needed examination when it came to Covid-19 therapeutics; the university was extensively involved in government funded vaccine research, with a particular focus on inhaled Covid-19 vaccines administered as aerosols. Such webs of intrigue, and the associated individuals, corporations, patents and funding, are beyond the scope of my intention with this book.

Specific to ivermectin though, McMaster University played a significant role in the subsequently announced TOGETHER trial, with Prof. Edward Mills serving as the principal investigator and other McMaster faculty members, including Prof. Guyatt, as co-investigators. The TOGETHER trial, centrally coordinated by Platform Life Sciences in Vancouver and conducted in Brazil, tested several repurposed drugs, including ivermectin. It received funding from the BMGF and the entity called Fastgrants. Thus, McMaster University's significant involvement in the TOGETHER trial, funded in part by the BMGF, raised serious concerns about impartiality in evaluating ivermectin for the WHO guideline. The authors of the TOGETHER Trial would later fail to address allegations of fraud raised by independent scientists about the conduct of this trial.

With regard to the WHO's "Global Norms" guidance, I

---

1   https://iris.who.int/bitstream/handle/10665/340374/WHO-2019-nCoV-therapeutics-2021.1-eng.pdf

referenced it in correspondence with Diaz too to support ivermectin's case. The original 2015 WHO meeting designed to set global norms for research in health emergencies, with its noble promises of ethical transparency and empowering local researchers, with hindsight, appeared to have been a carefully orchestrated effort to pave the way for experimental Covid-19 drugs and vaccines. Stakeholders included powerful journal editors (New England Journal of Medicine, British Medical Journal, and Nature), major private funders like the BMGF and Wellcome Trust, public health agencies, pharmaceutical giants like J&J and Sanofi, the US Department of Defence, and elite universities including Imperial College, Harvard, Oxford and McMaster. While the WHO's guidance had worked remarkably well to fast-track Covid-19 vaccines and would do so for other high-profit new drugs, its persistent disregard for ivermectin and other safe generics revealed glaring double standards. Thus, as mentioned, the guidance was unceremoniously removed from the WHO website and never referenced, to my knowledge, by the WHO during Covid-19 again.

What many people may not know is that the WHO's ACT-Accelerator, launched at the end of April 2020, claimed to unite governments, corporations, the same private foundations, and global health organisations in a coordinated effort to tackle Covid-19. With by no means humble ambitions, the ACT-Accelerator's initial funding request was a staggering US$31.3 billion to support the development of Covid-19 tests, treatments, vaccines, and "strengthen health systems" (with digital IDs and data harvesting) on a global scale.[1] It's Covid-19 slogan was "No-one is safe until everyone is safe".

From its outset, Covid-19 was a well-oiled machine engineered not just to respond to an immediate crisis, but to endure and transform the world as we knew it. Ivermectin, BIRD and I were inconvenient little nuisances in this regard.

---

1   https://www.who.int/initiatives/act-accelerator/about

After the publication of the WHO's Covid-19 therapeutics guideline, Van Kerkhove took to the airwaves to broadcast the position of the WHO, that the evidence was not sufficient and that ivermectin should only be used in clinical trials. Already the WHO's main pusher of the "safe and effective" vaccine narrative in the media, she became the WHO's leading spokesperson against "Covid-19 misinformation", especially about ivermectin.

I realised that I was not going to get any active engagement from Diaz or Van Kerkhove. Notably both women, why were they placed in these positions of WHO authority during the Covid-19 chapter? Were they really heartless individuals or simply pawns in a game they did not know they were playing? My co-authors' perspective suggests the latter. *However men may differ in disposition and in education, the foundations of human nature are the same in everyone. And every human being can draw in the course of his education from the inexhaustible wellspring of the divine in man's nature. But here likewise two dangers threaten: a man may fail in his education to penetrate to the real roots of humanity and remain fixed in convention – a partial education of this sort is as bad as none – or he may suddenly collapse and neglect his self-development.*[1]

With regard to Diaz, the *I Ching* commentary relates to a Hexagram called *Work on What Has Been Spoiled. Tolerating what has been spoiled by the father. In continuing one sees humiliation. This shows the situation of someone too weak to take measures against decay that has its roots in the past and is just beginning to manifest itself. It is allowed to run its course. If this continues, humiliation will result.*[2]

This suggest an authority figure had shaped Diaz's position, her WHO boss Tedros Adhanom Ghebreyesus perhaps, and she was not strong enough to resist its influence. Indeed, she might have

---

1   Hexagram 48, The Well, The Judgment. From I Ching, by Richard Wilhelm, 3rd Ed. p.186.
2   Hexagram 18, Work on what has been spoiled, line 4. From I Ching, by Richard Wilhelm, 3rd Ed. p.77.

experienced internal conflict, feeling caught in a system of compromise or passivity, but not having any agency to stand up to the forces of decay. This commentary obtained in hindsight helps me appreciate the complexity of the human condition and enables me to feel compassion now for these individuals, whose actions seem abhorrent to me. However, it was not always the case, as you will read below.

MOVE 13: Losing My Cow on Twitter

At the time, it was impossible to speak the truth about the vaccines anywhere, least of all on Twitter. The platform had become a minefield, where any wrong step could lead to your voice being erased. It claimed to be a space for free expression, but the reality was very different. Every post, every word, had to be carefully crafted to avoid censorship.

When I first started posting under my original research company E-BMC Limited's name, I kept things neutral – scientific articles on ivermectin with little commentary, just the basic information. But it did not take long before I realised my reach was being quietly restricted. Meanwhile, figures like Van Kerkhove and the Director General of the WHO, Dr Tedros Adhanom Ghebreyesus, were everywhere, spouting their killer lies with absolute freedom. They could say whatever their handlers wanted said about "the science", scripted according to a well-planned agenda, often with veiled threats about what would happen if people did not comply with masks, lockdown and injections, while I had to tiptoe just to post a scientific study.

Lies and more lies, it was maddening. My frustration grew by the day until, especially after the WHO had come out with their ivermectin guidelines, I couldn't resist the desire to say it how it was. I created a new Twitter account under a nickname, Tessarary. This one was not tied to my company, so I felt freer to say what I really thought. When Tedros, as he had become known, and Van Kerkhove posted yet another round of propaganda aimed at scaring people into getting the Covid shots, I replied to both of them with the same message using my new account: *"The new face of genocide."*

I meant it. The communications of Tedros and Van Kerkhove were facilitating the deaths of men, women and children around the world. I knew that it was risky and that my new account was likely to get deleted. But in that moment, I did not care. Someone had to say it. Someone had to call out their hypocrisy and the lies, even if their accounts were managed by others.

The fallout was immediate. Both the Tessarary and my E-BMC Limited company account were taken down within the hour. I had thought I was being savvy by using a separate account, but I hadn't realised that linking my phone number to both accounts would connect them. In my naivety, I had put everything at risk, and suffered the consequences.

The *I Ching* says of my conduct in this regard, *A wanderer should not demean himself or busy himself with inferior things he meets with along the way. The humbler and more defenceless his outward position, the more should he preserve his inner dignity. For a stranger is mistaken if he hopes to find a friendly reception through lending himself to jokes and buffoonery. The result will only be contempt and insulting treatment.*[1] The message is clear: shortcuts or compromises, made in the hope of quick wins or gaining favour, ultimately lead to contempt and greater harm. True strength lies in standing firm with honour and consistency, regardless of the external circumstances.

My company account had been steadily growing despite the censorship. When it was deleted, messages poured in – confusion, outrage. I couldn't bring myself to tell them that one angry tweet had brought the whole thing crashing down. So, I kept quiet about the

---

[1]   Hexagram 56, The Wanderer, line 1. From I Ching, by Richard Wilhelm, 3rd Ed. p.217.

reason for the deletion of my account and kept my guilt and my anger to myself. The *I Ching* line further stresses this point, *The birds nest burns up. The wanderer laughs at first, then must needs lament and weep. Through carelessness he loses his cow. Misfortune.*

The picture of a bird whose nest burns up indicates loss of one's resting place. The misfortune may overtake the bird if it is heedless and imprudent when building its nest. It is the same with a wanderer. If he lets himself go, laughing and jesting, and forgets that he is a wanderer, he will later have cause to weep and lament. For if through carelessness a man loses his cow – i.e. his modesty and adaptability – evil will result.[1]

Twitter seemed like a fitting platform for BIRD, despite the challenges of trolls and algorithms. Our BIRD bluebird symbolically mirrored Twitter's own, representing the contrast between truth and deception that both entities embodied on the platform. With support of a young volunteer, I focused on growing BIRD's presence on Twitter and building various group followings on Telegram, remaining careful not to mix my messages – one channel for ivermectin advocacy, others for the more challenging information related to the Covid vaccines, 5G and the other threats to humanity.

As for my personal and company Twitter accounts, I couldn't shake the feeling that I had inadvertently clipped my own wings. Moving forward, I knew I would need to be more cautious. However, when Twitter became a black X instead of a blue bird months later, it felt like a small victory for our bluebird of wholesomeness over evil. We had won the bird! Although Twitter's censorship and influence on the narrative remained, the X to me represented the unveiling of the media giant's colossal deception. It was after all, just another dead entity manipulating and harvesting humanity for its own gain.

Nevertheless, the injustice and horror of what was unfolding was at times too great to bear, and the powerlessness I felt led to many a

---

1   Hexagram 56, The Wanderer, line 6. From I Ching, by Richard Wilhelm, 3rd Ed. p.219.

sleepless night. One such night, borne out of a great frustration and need to stop the killing *somehow*, I tried another method to wake a few people up. At 4 o'clock in the morning I went for a brisk walk near my home in central Bath and, careful not to be seen wrote my first and only ever piece of graffiti on a prominent Bath stone wall. Armed with two tubes of lipstick, I wrote "Just say No!"

Perhaps one day someone will tell me that they saw it and it gave them courage. I hope so. I had intended to write a bit more – "Just say No to the jabs" perhaps – but the old, weathering stone gobbled up the lipstick in seconds and so I made do with the basic form of my message. Situated at a well-frequented crossing, where traffic usually stood for minutes on end, if it caught the eye of just one reflective driver over the years and helped them stand firm with their inner truth, it will have been worth it!

MOVE 14: Interview with Dr John Campbell

Securing an interview with John Campbell, a PhD nurse practitioner whose YouTube podcast practice was to examine studies and interpret them for the public, was a significant opportunity. His popularity had grown extensively during the Covid-19 chapter, reaching about 700,000 subscribers at the time of our interview in March 2021. Despite the disappointing responses from the authorities to the BIRD recommendations, access to his audience, comprised of both lay people and health practitioners, helped amplify our BIRD message and gave us much-needed exposure.

Circumstances often cause a man to seek a home in foreign parts. If he knows how to meet the situation and how to introduce himself in the right way, he may find a circle of friends and a sphere of activity even in a strange country.[1]

Campbell was impressed with my research work and WHO

---

1   Hexagram 56, The Wanderer, line 5. From I Ching, by Richard Wilhelm, 3rd Ed. p.219.

experience and began examining the evidence for himself, becoming a cautious ivermectin advocate thereafter. Shortly after our interview, he was invited to present the evidence on ivermectin to a group of investment managers; he reached out to me for more details. I too had been approached for such insights, and offered an eye-watering amount for the hour, which I declined. You might judge me careless to have done so, but I did not want to use my time advising moneylenders how to make more money; my time felt more valuable focused on helping everyday people.

The interview with Campbell was an important break, managing to escape YouTube censorship. It remained one of my most watched interviews at the time of writing. Campbell became a welcome support for the ivermectin corner and begun a slow journey of awakening to the Covid-19 corruption based on our sterling work.

MOVE 15. Interview with France-Soir

In mid-March I was also invited to an interview with Mr Xavier Azelbert, the director of France-Soir, which is an independent online News channel in France. This was a significant interview because it was the first time I spoke publicly about the shocking meeting I had with Dr Andrew Hill two months earlier. With respect to Hill and the corruption revealed, I had contemplated legal action and even made enquiries among human rights lawyers to see whether a case could be brought against the WHO. However, I was a "nobody" relative to the machine I was up against, as well as the huge sums of money required, therefore legal action was out of the question. So my options had either been to press on resolutely with BIRD, or to quit and move on. I had chosen the former.

In a resolute struggle of the good against evil, there are, however, definite rules that must not be disregarded, if it is to succeed. First, resolution must be based on a union of strength and friendliness. Second, a compromise with evil is not possible; evil must under all circumstances be openly discredited. Nor must our own passions and shortcomings be glossed over. Third, the struggle must not be carried on directly by force. [...]Finally, the best way to fight evil is to make energetic progress in the good.[1]

To be invited to a discussion with Azelbert, a mathematician and astute Covid commentator who had investigated the Covid hydroxychloroquine scandal thoroughly and formed the citizens advocacy group called Bon Sens (Good Sense), was a great honour. My French former sister-in-law informed me that he was well-respected in France and making great headway in standing up for people's rights. I found it both nerve-wracking and relieving to finally get what I knew about scientific corruption off my chest.

BREAK-THROUGH. One must resolutely make the matter known At the court of the king. It must be announced truthfully. Danger. It is necessary to notify one's own city. It does not further to resort to arms. It furthers one to undertake something.[2]

As with hydroxychloroquine, Azelbert would prove to be like a bloodhound at uncovering the deeper truth about Dr Hill's WHO ivermectin review. The *I Ching* notes in this regard, *When a man wishes to undertake an enterprise in extraordinary times, he must be extraordinarily cautious[...]This caution, though it may seem exaggerated, is not a mistake. Exceptional enterprises cannot succeed unless utmost caution is observed in their beginnings and in the laying of their foundations.*[3] Azelbert certainly was a cautious and thorough man. His rigour and clarity would stand BIRD in good stead.

After our interview that March, he set about commissioning an

---

1   Hexagram 43, Breakthrough, The Judgement. From I Ching, by Richard Wilhelm, 3rd Ed. p.167.

2   Hexagram 43, Breakthrough, The Judgement. From I Ching, by Richard Wilhelm, 3rd Ed. p.166.

3   Hexagram 28, Preponderance of the Great, line 1. From I Ching, by Richard Wilhelm, 3rd Ed. p.112.

independent forensic audit of Dr Hill's article. Once sure of the facts, he then instigated a complaint of scientific misconduct, requesting an investigation into Dr Hill's conduct from Liverpool University. More about this later. Overall, I am convinced that Azelbert's unwavering efforts and legal actions in France in respect to ivermectin were crucial to BIRD's solid foundation and our shared interest in protecting people around the world, not just in France, from their crazed governments. Meeting Azelbert was another breakthrough for BIRD!

Chapter 4

The Army

THE ARMY. The Army needs perseverance
And a strong man.
Good fortune without blame.[1]

The leader should be in the midst of his army, in touch with it,
sharing good and bad with the masses he leads. This alone makes
him equal to the heavy demands made upon him. He needs also
the recognition of the ruler. The decorations he receives are justified,
because there is no question of personal preferment here: the whole
army, whose centre he is, is honoured by his person.[2]

Since our BIRD efforts gave diverse and, perhaps, isolated individuals something tangible to get behind, it acted as a unifying force for those who had been seeking ways to push back against the Covid-19 narrative. Hence, the army metaphor suggested by my co-authors for this chapter feels appropriate. However, BIRD at this point was

---

1   Hexagram 7, The Army, The Judgement. From I Ching, by Richard Wilhelm, 3rd Ed. p.32.
2   Hexagram 7, The Army, line 2. From I Ching, by Richard Wilhelm, 3rd Ed. p.33.

simply a project, it would need anchoring, sustaining and reinforcing. There was much work to be done.

In the preceding chapters, my co-authors have highlighted my shortcomings as a leader, as well as the internal and external challenges I faced as an academic and professional outsider. Despite my achievements on record, I was in a lowly position in practice, with no influential associations. Like many ordinary human beings, I had a fairly low self-esteem too, and as previously mentioned, was afraid of public speaking. Overcoming these obstacles was crucial to getting BIRD's message out. The ivermectin battle was never going to be a quick one and so an army was needed.

About my personal situation, my co-authors observe, *It is the law of heaven to make fullness empty, and to make full what is modest [...] The destinies of men are subject to immutable laws that must fulfil themselves. But man has the power to shape his fate, according as his behaviour exposes him to the influence of benevolent and of destructive forces. When a man holds a high position and is nevertheless modest, he shines with the light of wisdom; if he is in a lowly position and is modest, he cannot be passed* by.[1] My co-authors highlight here that modesty, while often a hindrance to succeeding in this corporate world, could ultimately help me build the resilience needed to persevere, and to inspire a grassroots army of helpers.

Fortunately, people I had never met from all around the world had started to come to BIRD's aid. They flocked onto Twitter, Facebook, and other platforms where we had little presence or influence, defending BIRD, ivermectin, and me – both drawing and extinguishing fire on our behalf. One amazing individual called AJ, from the USA, set up a group on Telegram called the "BIRD Keyboard Warriors". I remain deeply indebted to the invaluable work of this feisty and dedicated group who swiftly countered the coordinated

---

1   Hexagram 15, Modesty, The Judgement. From I Ching, by Richard Wilhelm, 3rd Ed. p.63

attacks against BIRD and ivermectin. Not only were they a line of defence, but these online warriors also worked hard to spread our messages about ivermectin when many platforms were removing them.

Looking back, BIRD's Keyboard Warriors, comprising people from all walks of life, were the unseen force behind our campaign in 2021, pushing back against censorship and amplifying the truth when it was most needed. Another individual among our loyal and multi-talented BIRD volunteers was Linda Rae, who put heart and soul into helping disseminate BIRD's message. The passion and commitment of these individuals gave me hope; people all over the world were willing to step forward and fight for what was right. BIRD had a fighting chance! Without Linda, AJ and many others, BIRD's story might have had a very different ending.

MOVE 16. Finding BIRD Sustenance

The term David and Goliath has been used so often in the context of the globalist agenda that it's understandable if it's grown tiresome. But it was the reality of the situation. We had no money, no influence, and no power compared to the machinery of the global establishment. Yet, in building an army, securing provisions is crucial. Without provisions, no matter how strong the resolve or the will, the effort will falter, as many in the health freedom movement will attest. Even my personal pro bono work around ivermectin was not going to be sustainable in the medium term. My company, the Evidence-based Medicine Consultancy Ltd, had been covering the costs for additional technical and administrative support. However, the efforts required of me were so intense that, to continue, I had to outsource my existing contracts to colleagues. As ivermectin research pulled me and my company in a new direction, I declined new contracts with existing clients. Moreover, members of my existing remote-working team weren't excited about the new direction, especially with the risk of antagonising our biggest clients: the WHO and, indirectly, Cochrane. So, the only way forward was to find funding and a workforce that was willing and less costly. A crowdfunding appeal was suggested and implemented to cover our increasing financial needs, alongside volunteer efforts.

The fate of fire depends on wood; as long as there is wood below, the fire burns above.[1] At a time when wealth and status define so much of our world, few had any notion of the precarious position I found myself in on account of my new role. No longer receiving an income from traditional work – which I had outsourced to colleagues, and having little of material value to sell, I cashed in my modest pension as a first resort. Gratifyingly, our newly established GoFundMe campaign began raising a modest sum, comprised mainly of small donations from numerous grassroots supporters. It felt like a godsend not least because it indicated that our efforts were valued by those we wished to assist. However, GoFundMe had a nasty surprise in store for us five months later as they cancelled our fund-raising campaign without explanation or apology. We would never know for certain whether all donations made were received.

One is courageous and wishes to accomplish one's task, no matter what happens. This leads to danger. The water rises over one's head. This is misfortune. But one incurs no blame in giving up one's life that the good and the right may prevail. There are things that are more important than life.[2] My co-authors speak to the courage and determination behind continued efforts to push the BIRD initiative forward, despite lacking the resources required. Their commentary underscores the perilous path of self-sacrifice and commitment to a cause, even when the odds are stacked against you. It warns that the

---

1   Hexagram 50, The Cauldron, The Image. From I Ching, by Richard Wilhelm, 3rd Ed. p.194.
2   Hexagram 28, Preponderance of the Great, line 6. From I Ching, by Richard Wilhelm, 3rd Ed. p.114.

pursuit of something greater than oneself can lead to personal loss and hardship, but it also affirms that there is honour in giving everything for what is just and true. From my personal perspective, I was navigating purely by my instinct to do what was right, and having to trust that, in so doing, everything would be okay in the end.

Fortunately, while we had no intention of relying on large donors, mainly because such donations weren't forthcoming, one generous US businessman did offer us a much-needed gift of $50,000, with no strings attached. The businessman's act of generosity reflects a rare form of support that aligns with the principle of doing what is right without seeking reward, recognition, or control. This was a timely boost, but we knew we couldn't count on such funding to continue. In addition, my co-authors point out, *No blame. No praise. If in times of insecurity we give up alliance with those below us and keep up only the relationships we have with people of higher rank, an unstable situation is created.*[1]

The businessman would send a further donation later in the year. However, BIRD's lack of structure did not appeal to most wealthy donors. Since we weren't a charity, we couldn't offer tax advantages, and there was little to gain unless one could see, and valued the significance in, BIRD's potential to upset the globalist applecart – a vision that did not come with a traditional business plan, projections, or interest. It came with a lot of uncertainty. The reality was that vested interests were hard to find when it came to ivermectin. As a cheap, easily producible medicine, there were few opportunities for profit or control in supporting our cause. We had an army to feed and, whether the ivermectin warriors all knew it or not, we were fighting for the survival of mankind against those who had sold their souls for wealth and power. It would be the small individual contributions that would keep our fires burning in the long run.

---

1   Hexagram 28, Preponderance of the Great, line 5. From I Ching, by Richard Wilhelm, 3rd Ed.
     p.113-4.

Many remarked to me over the years that we should have reached out to American technology entrepreneur Steve Kirsch for funding. Kirsch had become, after all, well known for his generous wagers during the Covid era, offering anyone who could win a debate with him on Covid deaths statistics or, later, on the Covid vaccines a $1,000,000 dollar prize. Oddly enough, it was Kirsch who reached out to me very early in 2021 to convey his shock at the take-down of my YouTube video to PM Johnson. He offered to email YouTube's CEO to get it reinstated. It was reinstated for a time thereafter, not on my channel but on the FLCCC's one, demonstrating his considerable influence with those highly placed in the Big Tech arena.

We had numerous communications thereafter. He had set up a Covid-19 Early Treatment Fund (CETF) to fund research into re-purposing medicines for Covid-19. Kirsch was keen to share his research on fluvoxamine, a selective serotonin reuptake inhibitor or SSRI, with a scientist who would listen; he was convinced it worked. He showed me a slide presentation of the research on it, which I recall him saying had cost him in the region of $500,000 already.

Encouraged by his interest, I asked if he would consider funding a broader scope of work, including ivermectin, vaccines, as well as research into 5G wireless radiation on health. His main interest at the time, however, was in fluvoxamine. He said he would pay me to conduct a systematic review on fluvoxamine. It felt that implicit in his offer was the assumption that fluvoxamine worked. He had already looked at the evidence, conducted his own study, and now just needed someone with the right credentials to rubber stamp it.

Thus, I could not accept the commission; it was highly likely that our findings would not concur. There was very little evidence to include in a fluvoxamine systematic review, which would still take a significant amount of time to do properly. And there was no way I could divert our precious human resources to this task at that time, no matter how much money was involved. It would have been a massive distraction, and I was certain that fluvoxamine was not going to help anybody in the big scheme of things. There were already enough people around the world hooked on this unpleasant and addictive drug, and adding to that burden in the name of Covid-19 would have felt very irresponsible.

The *I Ching* describes the situation with Kirsch as *difficult at the beginning.*[1] He seemed taken in by the Covid-19 fearmongering propaganda and was searching for solutions to protect himself. From my perspective, the *I Ching* shrewdly observed, I had to *sort silk threads from a knotted tangle and binds them into skeins* to create order.[2] I had to make sense of the Covid therapeutics muddle to which Kirsch had just added fluvoxamine, and I had limited time in which to do so. My co-authors' advice speaks directly to the challenge of untangling a situation fraught with complexity and confusion. Clarity and patience were required to sift through the mess, separate the useful from the harmful, and craft a coherent approach in the midst of rapidly shifting dynamics. The task was not only one of sorting through external information but also of maintaining focus and integrity in a time of overwhelming pressures. I had to focus on that for which I had evidence – ivermectin.

Subsequently when I asked Kirsch if he would consider making a donation to our ivermectin advocacy work to help keep BIRD on the wing, he spun me a line I had never heard before, something to the effect of having only so many rabbits and needing to keep them breeding. So we never received a cent from him in the end.

In the context of the life and death battle with the globalist forces that was taking place, in which BIRD had recently gained us some ground, my ancient co-authors observed further about our

---

1   Hexagram 3, Difficulty in the Beginning, The Judgement. From I Ching, by Richard Wilhelm, 3rd Ed. p.16.

2   Hexagram 3, Difficulty in the Beginning, The Image. From I Ching, by Richard Wilhelm, 3rd Ed. p.17.

interactions: *The Illustrious Ancestor disciplines the Devil's Country. After three years he conquers it. Inferior people must not be employed.*[1] About the meaning of this, they elaborate, *The territory won at such a bitter cost must not be regarded as an alms house for people who in one way or another have made themselves impossible at home, but who are thought to be quite good enough for the colonies. Such a policy ruins at the outset any chance of success.*[2] They caution further that *the urge to expand, with its accompanying dangers, is part and parcel of every ambitious undertaking.*[3]

This commentary highlights that the battle for BIRD and the greater cause couldn't be sustained or supported by people who were driven by self-interest or whose actions betrayed a lack of moral clarity. It was not simply about funding; it was about the character of those who would align themselves with the mission. BIRD was not destined to rely on the fortunes of Kirsch or similar mega-rich elites, who, despite their influence, did not share the values needed for the cause. BIRD's success would come not through material support from the powerful, indeed this would be dangerous to our cause, but rather through the integrity of our grassroots supporters, who understood the greater stakes and were committed to honourable action.

Thus, in early 2021, it was Kirsch who received something of immense value from me: I gave him a pearl of wisdom. I warned him that the novel Covid-19 vaccines were dangerous and advised him and his family to stay well away from them.

MOVE 17. Creating BIRD's Nest: EbMCsquared CIC

As BIRD was an ivermectin-only initiative and covering the experimental vaccine issues would have alienated many of our following, the initiative needed to be nested in a broader health advocacy

---

1   Hexagram 63, After Completion, line 3. From I Ching, by Richard Wilhelm, 3rd Ed. p.246-7.

2   Hexagram 63, After Completion, line 3. From I Ching, by Richard Wilhelm, 3rd Ed. p.247.

3   Hexagram 63, After Completion, line 3. From I Ching, by Richard Wilhelm, 3rd Ed. p.247.

umbrella. Thus, we structured BIRD as a project within a broader organisation focused on advancing health for mankind. The natural name for this entity stemmed from my original Evidence-based Medicine Consultancy Limited company, E-BMC Limited. As the concept evolved on the fly, the name of the Community Interest Company (CIC) was obvious: EbMCsquared CIC. This name that drew directly from Einstein's equation, $E=MC^2$, and symbolised, to my mind, the energy and momentum we needed to drive this movement forward.

Einstein's theory of relativity profoundly resonates with the idea of change. It describes how the universe expands and accelerates, just like we needed peoples' awareness to expand and accelerate to beat this evil agenda. For me, the "E" represented the energy of transformation, "M" signified the mass awakening of humanity to truth, and "C^2", the speed of light squared, embodied the urgency and rapidity with which this awakening needed to occur.

EbMCsquared was to be the vehicle to challenge official health narratives, advocate for tools like ivermectin and other more natural health solutions, and ultimately put a spanner in the works for the globalists. It was ambitious, and at the time, I had no clear map of how it would be brought about. However, the universe was assisting, and the vision was clear: EbMCsquared would be the vehicle to spark a global awakening, turning individual energy into collective momentum for positive change.

Who could I call upon to get EbMCsquared's first project up and running with a visible presence? The situation with my estranged husband, Mark Lawrie, was complicated, but I knew I needed his help. Despite the history and emotional weight between us, as a jack of all trades in the film industry and still providing limited administrative support for E-BMC Ltd in my absence, he was already engaged in the ivermectin story, and his diverse skillset was perfect for our needs.

I approached him with sincerity and thankfully he agreed to help. *Great-hearted approach. Good fortune. No blame.* [1]

This line from the *I Ching* speaks to Mark's character. Despite everything that had transpired between us, he chose to set aside any personal grievances and extend his help when it was needed most. His kindness in this moment was an example of what I had always loved about him – a willingness to help others. And this would not only be good for us, but it would also benefit our family as a whole, expediting the healing of wounds caused by my sudden departure four years earlier.

We set about finding a web designer. A BIRD supporter who had been keeping me abreast of correspondence with authorities introduced me via email to Robert Trup, who had his own modest marketing company. Very soon, Mark and Rob worked very well together to get the nuts and bolts of EbMCsquared and its BIRD initiative in place as quickly as possible. Trup proved to be indispensable, not only for his gentleness and adaptability but also for his willingness to evolve with our needs. Initially, he had known nothing about ivermectin or BIRD and was aligned with the mainstream Covid-19 narrative when I'd approached him. Indeed, there was a possibility that he might even reject the work offered once he knew the task at hand.

Over time, it was gratifying to witness Trup's awareness grow through his involvement in our efforts, a satisfying demonstration of the power of the plain and simple truth. *Here [...] the nature of the dark force undergoes a change. It no longer opposes the strong principle by means of intrigues but submits to its guidance [...] Therefore all goes well.* [2] The uncomfortable information that would eventually be revealed to him through the course of his work with us, about the experimental Covid vaccines, may have caused him some inner

1   Hexagram 19, Approach, line 6. From I Ching, by Richard Wilhelm, 3rd Ed. p.81.
2   Hexagram 23, Splitting Apart, line 5. From I Ching, by Richard Wilhelm, 3rd Ed. p.96.

conflict, particularly as it contrasted with the prevailing views in his other environments. Yet, he took it in good stride, navigating the challenges provided by the new information with grace. It showed that when one is willing to face uncomfortable truths, no matter how discordant they may seem, the transformation is not only possible but deeply empowering.

MOVE 18: Building International Relationships

Following the BIRD Recommendation, small groups of ivermectin advocates, mostly doctors and other health professionals, began to form around the world. We had groups in Australia, Brazil, Canada, France, Grenada, Honduras, Iceland, India, Indonesia, Malaysia, Slovenia, South Africa, The Philippines, USA, and UK, as well as international networks like the World Doctors Alliance, the Alliance for Natural Health, and Doctors for Covid Ethics sign up. For groups based in countries such as Brazil, Malaysia, and the Philippines, where ivermectin was available over the pharmacy counter, the fuss about taking ivermectin for Covid-19 was incomprehensible as it was already a part of their basic health 'toolkit'. Ivermectin had been a useful drug in these countries for a range of infections for decades, and being cheap and accessible meant that their giving it a try for Covid-19 was only natural. By contrast, in countries like Canada, the UK and Australia, even mentioning ivermectin for Covid-19 risked persecution or prosecution, despite ivermectin being authorised for scabies and other skin conditions.

In general, what brought these groups to BIRD was the desire to team up with other ethical health professionals. In particular, doctors who were aware that something was very wrong in the official 'pandemic' approach, were very grateful that I had put my head above the parapet and assumed a counter-position to the Covid-19 narrative. Though eager to align themselves with BIRD, many preferred to keep a low profile so that they could continue to help people on the ground in their practices, hospitals and clinics. Being part of our international initiative lent them both credibility and the strength to continue their local efforts. It also fluffed up BIRD's feathers, amplifying our credibility.

At the beginning, our greatest BIRD ally was the Frontline Covid-19 Critical Care Alliance (FLCCC) in the USA. Dr Pierre Kory and Dr Paul Marik, two brilliant physicians, had become the voices of reason in a time of overwhelming uncertainty. They were grateful for the support we provided, and I felt an immense sense of love and respect for them as they stood firm in their convictions. As deeply embedded as they were within the medical system, there was an underlying charming naivety to their approach. They seemed to believe that, eventually, the weight of evidence would convince the authorities to change their stance. I knew, however, that it would not be that simple. I knew all too well that there were forces at play that would resist the truth, especially when it came to certain uncomfortable realities. Come hell or high water, the authorities had to get the novel, gene-based Covid-19 shots approved and into people.

Not only were these two FLCCC doctors facing conflict in the workplace with regard to their efforts to get proper help to patients diagnosed as having Covid 19, they were dealing with other struggles too. Their great and early article reviewing the literature on ivermectin, advocating for ivermectin as a treatment for Covid-19, had been rejected by *Frontiers of Pharmacology*, even after it had gone through peer review and proof reading, moments before it was set to be published. A resubmission to the *American Journal of Therapeutics* saw their article published at last, but not without them realising that they were trapped in a system that was designed to stifle honest scientific and medical debate. Thus, they welcomed the reinforcements and international collaboration represented by BIRD from across the

Atlantic ocean. My professional background impressed them, but it was clearly not a guarantee of success, especially after Cochrane's rejection of our submission. Together, we all waited in apprehension to see what *Lancet Respiratory Medicine* editors would decide about our review team's paper.

The *I Ching* says about Kory, *Treasure of the house. Great good fortune.*[1] It doesn't surprise me that the ancients have such high praise for him. This hexagram is all about the family, and it definitely felt like we were building one, with Kory as a central member. He was solid and upright. His integrity, openness, and friendliness would be the cornerstone on which the wellbeing of the family depended. *Wellbeing prevails when expenditures and incomes are soundly balanced. This leads to great good fortune. In the sphere of public life, this line refers to the faithful steward whose measures further the general welfare.*[2] I believe this described Pierre's character and sentiment well – he was in it because he cared about humanity. Once he knew the truth, he could do no other but to stand up for the good of all.

Between us, the vaccines became a delicate subject though. Dr Marik, especially, made it clear that he was a strong supporter of the vaccines in those days. Marik's opinion would change later when the evidence stacked up against them, but at this stage he did not want to say anything that might upset the authorities or risk being labelled as "anti-vax." I understood his position. But despite our differing perspectives on vaccines at that time, our bond was crucial. We needed one another, and I was not sure who needed whom the most. It was a relationship built on mutual respect, but I had to be careful not to openly voice my concerns about the shots. *Conflict develops when one feels himself to be in the right and runs into opposition. If a man is entangled in conflict, his only salvation lies in being so clear headed*

---

1   Hexagram 37, The Family, line 4. From I Ching, by Richard Wilhelm, 3rd Ed. p.146.
2   Hexagram 37, The Family, line 4. From I Ching, by Richard Wilhelm, 3rd Ed. p.146.

and inwardly strong that he is always ready to come to terms by meeting the opponent halfway. [1] In many ways, we were both walking a fine line, but his position in the US was more precarious than mine. I was happy to meet him halfway.

Originally from South Africa, a brilliant academic, dedicated physician and former Professor of Medicine, Dr Marik had had to work harder than most to maintain his reputation in the US health-care system. Already severely criticised for his advocacy of vitamin C in the treatment of sepsis in ICU settings, he knew the price for taking a stand against the pharmaceutical industrial complex. Prone to standing up for his patients, good medicine and his Hippocratic Oath, his personal and professional challenges had only intensified with his stance on ivermectin. This understandably made him very cautious in his approach, especially with regard to the Covid-19 vaccines. Opposing these in 2021 might have meant the final blow to his professional standing.

However, in the early months, Dr Marik still had faith in the medical system and, hence, the Covid-19 vaccines. Just like most others, he could not believe we were living in a world where so-called health authorities would intentionally harm us. *There is a temptation to fall in with the evil element offering itself – a very dangerous situation. Fortunately circumstances prevent this; one would like to do it, but cannot. This leads to painful indecision in behaviour. But if we gain clear insight into the danger of this situation, we should at least avoid more serious mistakes.* [2] Having taken a Covid-19 vaccine himself, Dr Marik would subsequently become an important and credible advocate against these harmful shots.

Dr Marik's journey mirrors the struggle many faced, caught between trust in long-established systems and the unsettling reality

---

1   Hexagram 6, Conflict, The Judgement. From I Ching, by Richard Wilhelm, 3rd Ed. p.28-9.
2   Hexagram 44, Coming to Meet, line 3. From I Ching, by Richard Wilhelm, 3rd Ed. p.172.

of what those systems were capable of. The key, as my co-authors suggest, is not to act impulsively or succumb to the temptations presented by external pressures, but to reflect, gain clarity, and stand firm when faced with the truth, no matter how difficult it may be. Fortunately, as time passed and the true dangers of the vaccines was revealed, we would all be on the same page. In fact, in the months and years that followed, I was amazed by both Kory and Marik's adaptability, growth and authenticity, as they navigated the emerging revelations about the shots, the WHO, and the bigger globalist agenda, with courage and clarity. Few seemed capable of this. *By cultivating in himself an attitude of compliance and voluntary dependence, man acquires clarity without sharpness and finds his place in the world.*[1] This process, though challenging, revealed the power of humility and adaptability, qualities that allowed them to not only survive the storm but to emerge with a deeper understanding of themselves and the world around them. True strength comes not from resisting change, but from embracing it with grace and integrity, always seeking what is right, no matter the cost.

As highlighted, the bulk of the real-world experience of using ivermectin came from the East, Africa and South America, where it has been widely used for decades as both prophylaxis and treatment of various parasitic diseases. In addition, it had been deployed against some viral diseases such as Dengue and Zika too in regional health emergencies. When health authorities started restricting use of ivermectin, South African and Malaysian groups were among the first to reach out to ask for support in their legal actions against their governments to demand access to ivermectin for Covid-19 prevention and treatment. I was invited to speak at online meetings in South Africa, Malaysia and The Philippines at this time, to share the BIRD evidence at the requests of country doctors, scientists and lawyers, in which there were

---

1   Hexagram 30, The Clinging, The Judgement. From I Ching, by Richard Wilhelm, 3rd Ed. p.119.

occasionally obstinate, defensive, and/or antagonistic medical, CDC and government representatives present. I also had several interviews with journalists in these countries who were trying to bring an enlightened perspective to the rigged Covid game.

Malaysia's Captain Dr Ang Wong Peng was an extraordinary advocate for ivermectin, a dedicated naturopathic healer, and a passionate individual. I was fortunate to meet him during the many discussions with Malaysian doctors and lawyers early in 2021. I learned early on that he was no stranger to strategy. Having led armies into battle, I heard that he had narrowly escaped death on several occasions in the line of duty. Needless to say, when he appeared at online meetings in decorated military regalia, he made quite an impression!

Cpt Dr Peng's efforts to help Malaysians in the face of overwhelming opposition and draconian Covid-19 restrictions were exemplary. My ancient co-authors describe Cpt Dr Peng *as one occupying a high position and striving to let his light shine forth. To do this he needs helpers, because he cannot attain his lofty aim alone. With the greed of a hungry tiger he is on the lookout for the right people. Since he's not working for himself but for the good of all, there's no wrong in such zeal.*[1]

My experience of Cpt Dr Peng was that of a hungry tiger indeed, eager to elicit our help for his efforts in Malaysia, as well as to support us. I took to him immediately and valued his enthusiasm, directness and strategy, which would be unwavering. His approach, though driven and relentless, was rooted in a deep sense of purpose and commitment to a cause much larger than himself. His determination to rally others, even in the face of tremendous adversity, was a clear reflection of his resolve and belief in the greater good, a reminder that great leaders often forge their path through persistence and clear vision.

---

[1]   Hexagram 27, The Corners of the Mouth, line 4. From I Ching, by Richard Wilhelm, 3rd Ed. p.110.

As much as Peng's warrior attributes were bold, Dr Lucy Kerr 's were gentle, though both were equally strong characters. A persevering warrior of note, Dr Kerr was the leader of the Medicos Pela Vida (Doctors for Life) group in Brazil. Ivermectin was available over the counter in her country, but Kerr especially wanted to share her expertise, as well as her wisdom. Her aim was clearly to enlighten Western and other countries about the benefits of using ivermectin, with which she had extensive experience using for various diseases, so that their populations could benefit too.

Kerr provided BIRD not only her own medical protocol on how to treat and prevent Covid symptoms with ivermectin in combination with other supplements, but she would also in due course publish the largest ivermectin population-based study proving beyond a shadow of a doubt that ivermectin, when used regularly as prophylaxis, prevented Covid-19 infections, hospitalisation and deaths, in sharp contrast to Big Pharma's experimental jabs. Kerr was a wellspring of knowledge and, my ancient co-authors highlight, her wisdom was available for everyone. *The well is there for all. No one is forbidden to take water from it. No matter how many come, all find what they need, for the well is dependable. It has a spring and never runs dry. Therefore it is a great blessing to the whole land. The same is true of the really great man, whose inner wealth is inexhaustible; the more that people draw from him, the greater his wealth becomes.*[1]

Kerr's generosity of spirit and her unwavering commitment to sharing her insights exemplified the true nature of selfless leadership. Her contributions, both in knowledge and action, did not diminish with use; rather, they grew, benefiting countless others and amplifying the impact of her work. Just as a well that never runs dry nourishes an entire land, so too does a great individual's wisdom flow endlessly, enriching all who come in search of it.

---

1   Hexagram 48, The Well, line 6. From I Ching, by Richard Wilhelm, 3rd Ed. p.188.

These are but a few of the many incredible new international connections I made and valued during those first few months, reminding me that irrespective of language, creed or culture, we are all the same when it really matters. In the face of adversity, otherwise ordinary human beings come together, transcending their differences, united by a shared sense of purpose and the belief that collective action can bring about meaningful change. It was a powerful reminder that in times of crisis, humanity's capacity for collaboration and mutual support is boundless.

MOVE 19. Gathering Birds of a Feather Together

Human life on earth is conditioned and unfree, and when man recognises this limitation and makes himself dependent upon the harmonious and beneficent forces of the cosmos, he achieves success.[1] As the *I Ching* suggests, individually, we are often powerless in the face of larger forces. Recognising this limitation is what made trust and collaboration all the more vital. By gathering together and trusting oneself, one another, and in a greater power, our individual efforts were no longer isolated; by combining our strengths, a capable international network began to emerge to lead our health freedom movement forward.

Dr Jennifer Hibberd, a Dental Surgeon from Canada who was working with the newly established Canadian Covid Care Alliance, was among the first to respond to the ivermectin information. A passionate, and well-connected individual, Jennifer maintained her busy practice and lecturing schedule, whilst also hosting an alternative health podcast that accrued a keen audience during the Covid-19 chapter. Dr Hibberd had been drawn to my ivermectin work early on, perhaps by the Boris video or the original BIRD press release, and I was grateful to be invited to an interview on her podcast. Jennifer

---

1   Hexagram 30, The Clinging, The Judgement. From I Ching, by Richard Wilhelm, 3rd Ed. p.119.

had interviewed several international doctors with 'alternative' views on how to treat Covid symptoms and was facing censorship even before our interview was deleted censoriously from her channel months later. Working with the Canadian Covid Care Alliance, which partnered with BIRD thereafter, a natural camaraderie developed between us based on a common desire to get truthful information out.

Great possession consists not only in a quantity of goods at one's disposal, but, first and foremost, in their mobility and utility, for then they can be used in undertakings, and we remain free of embarrassment and mistakes. The big wagon, which will carry a heavy load and in which one can journey far, means that there are at hand able helpers who give their support and are equal to their task. One can load great responsibility upon such persons, and this is necessary in important undertakings.[1] As my *I Ching* co-authors note, Jennifer was a very capable individual, someone who did not shy away from *great responsibility*, and I very much valued her help, our hilarious brain-storming sessions, and her friendship. In many ways, Jennifer embodied the essence of what my co-authors describe: a person who could bear significant responsibility without hesitation and rise to the challenge when the stakes were high. Her willingness to support BIRD in such a pivotal moment, combining her own expertise with the collective vision, made her an invaluable ally in our shared mission.

Similarly, Shabnam Palesa Mohamed, a South African activist lawyer and founder of Transformative Health Justice, quickly grasped the issues surrounding the suppression of ivermectin and tenaciously searched for opportunities to raise awareness as well as bring legal actions in South Africa. Shabnam had very creative ideas about how to engage the public too. Through her close association with South

---

[1]   Hexagram 14, Possession in Great Measure, line 2. From I Ching, by Richard Wilhelm, 3rd Ed. p.60-1.

African cartoonist Nanda Soobbens, Shabnam produced a short, animated video titled *Set Ivy Free* about ivermectin. The concept was simple but powerful: a bird drops a book of evidence onto a virus, unleashing many more birds that then fly around spreading the message. Soobbens' execution was really charming and effectively conveyed the power of our cause.

Shabnam had her sights set on exposing the corruption within the World Health Organization (WHO), for which I obviously had useful insights and experience. She was no stranger to corruption and injustice having experienced this professionally and personally, not least at the hands of the South African police during apartheid. As a South African by birth, I also had lived perspectives pre- and post-apartheid and thus there was a natural sisterhood between us. Our shared experiences of facing systems built on injustice and oppression forged an unspoken bond that made our partnership stronger. In many ways, Shabnam's determination and courage to confront powerful institutions reminded me of the resilience that people develop when they have no other choice but to stand up for what is right. Her approach, both strategic and creative, aligned with my essential drive to challenge the status quo and turn the tables on those seeking to exploit mankind.

Following the success of the *Set Ivy Free* animation, Shabnam suggested we work together on a longer animation script to highlight the WHO's questionable Covid-19 policies. Though this particular project did not come to fruition, it was during this creative collaboration that we discussed forming a new world health organisation – a people's organisation that would challenge the WHO's regime and focus on providing real help to people, rather than merely benefiting its funders. It was Shabnam's idea. However, while creating a new health organisation sounded noble, it felt too daunting an aspiration and, if anything, a pipe dream, much easier said than done, and I did not want to be involved. I had no interest in being part of another bureaucratic organisation. Still, the seed of Shabnam's ideal remained, and in the back of my mind, I couldn't completely shake the notion of a better, more ethical approach to "global health". Though I was hesitant to take on something so monumental, the idea of it lingered and was regularly watered by my new friend and warrior, Shabnam!

Shabnam was acutely aware of the harms wreaked by the WHO, in collaboration with Big Pharma, Bill Gates and others, in African countries like Kenya. *A decrease in the prosperity of the people in favour of the government is an out-and-out decrease.*[1] She was righteously angry and with this anger came a powerful presence. Her determination to expose and fight back against these entities became a driving force for her, propelling her to speak out, and her courage inspired those around her to take action as well. *Therefore decrease is necessary; anger must be decreased by keeping still, the instincts must be curbed by restriction. By this decrease of the lower powers of the psyche, the higher aspects of the soul are enriched.*[2] Shabnam's deep spirituality enabled her to transform her anger, as well as her hurt, into positive actions. Rather than allowing her emotions to cloud her judgement, Shabnam channelled her energy into constructive avenues, using her inner calm to guide her through the turbulence. This balance between passion and control allowed her to navigate the difficult terrain of activism with purpose and clarity, ensuring that her efforts remained focused and impactful, rather than becoming mired in frustration or despair.

Shabnam's perspective gave me cause for consideration. She had high hopes of me and what we could achieve together and I was not ready for them. My co-authors say of this, *To make a fool develop, it furthers one to apply discipline. The fetters should be removed. To go on in this way brings humiliation. Law is the beginning of education.*[3] In case you are wondering, I am the fool referred to here. Focused on my

---

1   Hexagram 41, Decrease. From I Ching, by Richard Wilhelm, 3rd Ed. p.158.
2   Hexagram 41, Decrease, The Image. From I Ching, by Richard Wilhelm, 3rd Ed. p.159.
3   Hexagram 4, Youthful Folly, line 1. From I Ching, by Richard Wilhelm, 3rd Ed. p.22.

own plans, I wanted to get the word on ivermectin out, oppose the so-called vaccines, and then move on to the issues of 5G and wireless technology. What "moving on" looked like, I was not entirely sure, but I knew that setting up a massive international health organisation was not something I would be taking on. Apart from sounding extremely ambitious, it would be all-consuming. What's more, I did not like institutions and big organisations, I had seen their propensity for corruption first hand, and I certainly would not be persuaded to set up any more of them! Shabnam's perspective demanded discipline and a burdensome, long-term plan.

Dr Edmund Fordham, also became a solid member of our BIRD team, proving to be an invaluable asset to our efforts to fight back on the science. His unwavering commitment to truth and justice set him apart from many scientists I have met over the years. In addition, his very comprehensive knowledge of British politics, of which I was blissfully naïve, would stand us in good stead in the long run. You may recall that I asked Fordham to be the consumer representative on the Cochrane Review after the successful outcome of the BIRD meetings. In particular, I asked him to write the sections in our paper on the mechanisms of action of ivermectin, a task he immediately took on during a family trip to Kenya.

When you have a critical task that needs to be done, the common adage is to give it to the busiest person, because they know how to prioritise and deliver. This was Fordham in a nutshell. *The king uses him to march forth and chastise,*[1] my ancient co-authors observe. *It is not the purpose of chastisement to impose punishment blindly but to create discipline. Evil must be cured at its roots.*[2] Fordham's unrelenting determination to ensure every fact was checked, every piece of information cross-referenced, made him indispensable. In Kenya, diligently working

---

1   Hexagram 30, The Clinging, line 6. From I Ching, by Richard Wilhelm, 3rd Ed. p.121.
2   Hexagram 30, The Clinging, line 6. From I Ching, by Richard Wilhelm, 3rd Ed. p.121.

on his allotted task, Fordham was notably gutted but thankfully not deterred when we received the Cochrane editors' rejection.

Much later, Fordham would tell me that he had shown my original rapid review to the British-educated Chief Medical Officer (CMO) of Kenya's large Kitui County. The CMO, after reading the content, looked him in the eye and said, "If you go on with this, your life will be in danger." Despite receiving this ominous warning, he still committed wholeheartedly to working with us. He had to hurry back home soon after this chat as the UK government began implementing quarantine hotels to ramp up pandemic panic for travellers. Thus, to my mind Edmund also had the key character pre-requisite for the nature of BIRD's efforts – courage.

Another invaluable team member was Dr Andy Bryant, the statistician from Newcastle University and first author on our ivermectin review, whose niche expertise really helped focus the review team. I already knew Bryant to be a man of principle through occasional collaborations on Cochrane reviews for the Cochrane Gynaecological, Neuro-oncology and Orphan Cancer Review Group. Notably, he always approached the science from a position of neutrality. It was a boon to have him as co-author on the ivermectin review, which he oversaw with remarkable precision and commitment.

With many professional options had he sought them, Bryant had always struck me as someone who did not really belong in institutionalised academia. Whilst he did not voice any disillusionment, it always seemed to me that he found his normative work a tad unstimulating. Which is why he played golf – his true passion! Having worked with him over several years, I'd often had a sense that he was waiting for his life to get more interesting, and with BIRD it unwittingly and most certainly had!

However about Bryant's position at the time, my co-authors observe, *The power of the inferior people is growing. The danger draws*

close to one's person; already there are clear indications, and rest is dis-
turbed. Moreover, in this dangerous situation one is as yet without help
or friendly advances from above or below. Extreme caution is necessary
in this isolation. One must adjust to the time and promptly avoid the
danger. Stubborn perseverance in maintaining one's standpoint would
lead to downfall.[1]

Bryant certainly faced some difficulties at work on account of his association with BIRD and the ivermectin review, as well as his refusal to take a Covid vaccine. Despite this, his sense of responsibility to this novel cause outside of his university scope of work kept him resolute.

I was pleased to hear that he did not take the Covid shots, as people working in the hallowed halls of science and academia were under extreme pressure to do so at the time. Ironically, it was not that he had looked at the evidence that had saved him from this partic-ular evil. Rather, it was that health was not exactly high on his list of priorities, having a particular disdain for fresh fruit, vegetables and doctors, I recall! This combined with a cautious scepticism, coupled with an inculcated inclination to follow the science, meant that by the time we had had the conversation, and I had shared what I knew, he had thankfully not been jabbed. Thereafter, he kept his opinion on the vaccines to himself, though occasionally had to defend his posi-tion among his peers.

When it came to our ivermectin review too, Bryant had no dif-ficulty holding his ground with affable demeanour and equipoise, always letting the statistics and the science speak for themselves. This is one of the qualities I respected most about him and what rein-forced BIRD's integrity immensely. I have often felt that he must be one of the few remaining *superior men* in academia, and my ancient co-authors agree that he is indeed a rare bird.

It was a great honour too that Dr Tina Peers joined BIRD and,

---

1   Hexagram 23, Splitting Apart, line 2. From I Ching, by Richard Wilhelm, 3rd Ed. p.95.

despite her busy clinical practice, agreed to be part of the Steering Group for our February 20th BIRD recommendation meeting. Dr Peers had a clarity of mind that shone brightly along with her beautiful smile. No pushover, Peers very thoughtfully weighed the evidence presented on ivermectin early in 2021, and once she had deduced that there was a high chance it would help her patients, and then found that it worked, she became a powerful advocate for its cause. About Dr Peers, my coauthors agree, that her approach was cautious and considered. *When talk of change has come to one's ears three times, and has been pondered well, he may believe and acquiesce in it. Then he will meet with belief and will accomplish something.*[1] Dr Peers' integrity, wisdom and eloquence on ivermectin matters would become invaluable to our shared mission to help at this time of crisis.

These are but a few of the individuals whose collaborative efforts were essential to the development of what would ultimately become a powerful health and sovereignty movement. Each of us brought something unique to the table, yet it was the collaboration, our ability to work in concert, despite our varied backgrounds, that gave us the momentum to challenge the overwhelming tide of corruption. Just as birds of a feather flock together for mutual support, so too did our alliance rooted through BIRD and EbMCsquared strengthen with every new voice, every new contribution. Our shared purpose created a collective voice that could not be easily dismissed. Courage, open-mindedness, and the desire to find the truth were the common factors.

MOVE 20. The Lancet Respiratory Medicine Submission Outcome

By the end of February, we received some rather good news from *The Lancet Respiratory Medicine*, which we approached with cautious optimism. Four appointed peer reviewers had returned their

---

[1]   Hexagram 49, Revolution, line 3. From I Ching, by Richard Wilhelm, 3rd Ed. p.191.

feedback, requesting a few revisions and corrections, nothing that we felt would be difficult to address. My *I Ching* co-authors highlight here that: *The conditions are difficult. The task is great and full of responsibility. It is nothing less than that of leading the world out of confusion back to order. But it is a task that promises success, because there is a goal that can unite the forces now tending in different directions. At first we must move warily, however, like an old fox walking over ice.*[1]

Confident that we could make the necessary adjustments with relative ease, and approaching it thoroughly and meticulously so that there could be no reason for rejection, Bryant sent the revised manuscript back to the editors within a week.

However, to our surprise, we received the following email back stating that, despite the fact that the review had passed full peer review and upon re-review all four reviewers were satisfied with the revisions, the editorial team had decided not to publish the paper! After all the work we had put in, this was a bitter pill to swallow. The part that was particularly galling was the line in the rejection letter that read, "We don't doubt that this is an important paper."

Dear Mr Bryant,

We have now received all of the peer reviews reports for your manuscript. Unfortunately, after some lengthy discussions with the editorial team, we do not feel that we can pursue the paper at *The Lancet Respiratory Medicine*. It was felt that there is just not enough evidence at the moment on ivermectin to be confident in a study such as this at this time, and we encouraged waiting until several more studies are published to help improve confidence in the paper.

We don't doubt that this is an important paper, and would be

---

1   Hexagram 64, Before Completion, The Judgement. From I Ching, by Richard Wilhelm, 3rd Ed. p.249.

widely picked up, and as such, we want to make sure that it includes as high quality evidence as possible to ensure we spread a message that is strongly supported by the evidence.

Therefore, on this occasion we have decided not to publish your manuscript, but would perhaps consider an updated paper that includes more published evidence later down the line. The re-review comments we received from the reviews are presented below:

Reviewer 1: authors have responded to my comments.

Reviewer 2: the authors have replied to my comments from my review period

Reviewer 3 : thanks for addressing most of the issues. Now it looks better.

Reviewer 4: the authors have addressed my comments satisfactorily.

I can't say I was really surprised. I had been more surprised that we had been invited to revise the paper in the first place. Why lead us a merry dance when they were going to reject it irrespective of the outcome of the peer review? Fordham had never been particularly optimistic about our Lancet submission after their publication of the fraudulent study that discredited hydroxychloroquine, but he did not stop us from going ahead anyway. However, the immortal words "we don't doubt this is an important paper" would have a special place in all of our memories.

My co-authors observe of our continuingly naïve approach in pursuit of publication in a high-impact journal: *If we wish to achieve an effect, we must first investigate the nature of the forces in question and ascertain their proper place. If we can bring these forces to bear in the right place, they will have the desired effect, and completion will be achieved. But in order to handle external forces properly, we must above all arrive at the correct standpoint ourselves, for only from this vantage can we work correctly.* [1]

Finally, we had arrived at the correct standpoint; if *The Lancet*, and Cochrane were no longer trustworthy options, all the 'high-impact' journals were likely corrupted too. The *British Medical Journal* (*BMJ*), *New England Journal of Medicine, JAMA, PLOS* and others, with their links to the drug industry and/or the WHO would be a no-go. We clarified our purpose and adapted our expectations and egos accordingly. The main task was to get the review published.

Bryant took the lead again and redrafted the paper once more for submission to yet another journal. *Thus the superior man is careful in the differentiation of things, so that each finds its place.* [2] Based on the success of the FLCCC's successful submission to the *American Journal of Therapeutics*, we decided to submit our work there as well, with fingers and toes crossed.

Move 21. *Trialsite News* Gives Bird Some Air

TrialSite News had been one of the very few credible sources providing scientific perspectives on the ongoing 'pandemic', often taking significant risks in sharing them. There was always the possibility that YouTube's spurious algorithms would mark episodes for deletion. Daniel O'Connor, *TrialSite News*' founder, was a welcome support to our efforts to raise awareness about ivermectin and his platform's interest in alternative approaches to Covid-19 prevention and treatment boosted BIRD's following. *Fundamental sincerity is the only proper basis for forming relationships.* [3] O'Connor was very aware of the hostile landscape surrounding re-purposed Covid treatments, and ivermectin in particular, so his approach to me was cautious but sincere; he was clearly very much interested in sharing good science.

---

1   Hexagram 64, Before Completion, The Image. From I Ching, by Richard Wilhelm, 3rd Ed.
     p.249-50.
2   Hexagram 64, Before Completion, The Image. From I Ching, by Richard Wilhelm, 3rd Ed.
     p.249.
3   Hexagram 8, Holding Together, line 1. From I Ching, by Richard Wilhelm, 3rd Ed. p.37.

My co-authors comment, *Here the relations with a man who is the centre of union is well established. Then we may, and indeed we should, show our attachment openly. But we must remain constant and not allow ourselves to be led astray.*[1] The *I Ching* speaks about O'Connor's approach. Putting his support behind our efforts to raise awareness of ivermectin for Covid-19, and even participating as a host in our first ivermectin conference in April 2021, he remained cautious in relation to my opinion of Covid-19 vaccines. As the "anti-vax" narrative and YouTube censorship increased, he and *TrialSite News* were reluctant to go in the direction I was headed – the dangerous reef of the experimental Covid vaccines, where many a sound reputation would soon be wrecked. Nevertheless, it was our good fortune to have our efforts highlighted on *TrialSite News* in those early days and I remain grateful to O'Connor for the lift he gave us during a time when BIRD desperately needed to garner the public's attention.

MOVE 22. Finding Reinforcements

Establishing a counter-narrative was filled with challenges. One of these was finding professionals not afraid to be associated with me publicly. A game of fear was being played by the globalists. With many of BIRD's members unaware of the scope of the battle being raged, combined with the widespread fear of speaking out, this meant few were prepared to be seen to counter the official draconian agenda in the public domain. Given my WHO background, and established academic credibility, combined with the fact that I had dropped my career and all other commitments for this battle, it was natural that I assume a front facing role.

Thus, initially I was the sole director of EbMCsquared CIC. This was a risky position and not accompanied by accolades. It took a few months before I found others willing to assume a named role on the

---

1   Hexagram 8, Holding Together, line 4. From I Ching, by Richard Wilhelm, 3rd Ed. p.38.

company website. As mentioned, with many scientists and doctors still afraid to stand up, the selection was scanty. I reached out to Dr Mike Yeadon, who was already a public figure in the "resistance", Mr Hedley Rees and Prof. Dana Flavin, whom I barely knew to ask if they would be prepared to hold a position with EbMCsquared. As a respected cancer clinician in private practice, Flavin was thankfully unafraid to be associated with us publicly. EbMCsquared's mission "to advance health for mankind" through repurposed and natural medicines aligned very much with her clinical perspective. I was introduced to Dr Flavin by Rees, a freelance pharmaceutical regulatory consultant whom we hired to assist with the application to get ivermectin approved for use in the UK. He too was happy to come on board for the period that we could afford his consultancy fees. Later, Dr Katherine MacGilchrist, an experienced systematic reviewer, would later add to these reinforcements.

These individuals took a backseat with regard to our health advocacy activities. Nevertheless, their support in 2021 was helpful. In particular, Dr Yeadon's public contributions in defence of ivermectin for Covid-19 were significant. In May 2021, in an excellent article entitled *Why are we being lied to about Covid? There's no good reason*, published in *The Conservative Woman*, Yeadon wrote:

"Please allow me to illustrate with an example close to my heart why it is high time for us to change our response. Ivermectin is one of the WHO's 'essential drugs' which all countries should have access to. It's very cheap as its patent has long expired; it's one of the most-used drugs in world history; it's extraordinarily safe; it is often life-saving against parasitic infections. It is also one of the best-established pharmaceutical treatments for Covid-19, showing benefit in every stage of the disease, in multiple independent clinical trials of varying quality. On January 3, 2021, Dr Tess Lawrie attempted to alert the Prime

Minister to the potential of ivermectin. Her video here was pulled from YouTube within hours of posting, though it survives on Vimeo. The paper by the FLCCC group of US intensivists (whose survival rates for severe Covid-19 are best in class) that was the inspiration for Dr Lawrie's work was accepted after extensive open peer review (including two career employees of the FDA) and 'provisionally accepted' by the 'open science' journal Frontiers in Pharmacology. The screenshot of the abstract tweeted by Clare Craig shown here attracted more than 100,000 views. Then, mysteriously, it was rejected and pulled by the Frontiers editor in chief. It is still here in cached form though the Ministry of Truth has been at work and placed it in a memory hole, so no trace survives on Frontiers' own website.

Intended for a Special Issue on 'repurposed drugs' for Covid-19, various guest editors were so incensed at this behaviour that they resigned in protest. You can read their letter here. They concluded that 'these unfortunate events constitute gross editorial misconduct by Frontiers.' Fortunately this major paper is now published by the American Journal of Therapeutics and can be read in its final form here.

This nevertheless successfully delayed by nearly six months its circulation to leading public health bodies starting mid-November. A copy was sent to Sir Jeremy Farrar (boss of the Wellcome Trust and member of Sage) who passed it on to Professor Peter Horby (also on Sage), amongst others, on November 18, 2020. So the efficacy of ivermectin must be well known to the Government's advisers, but they have done nothing about it. Likewise, the formal and rigorous meta-analysis performed by Dr Tess Lawrie's team at the Evidence-Based Medicine Consultancy Ltd has been communicated to Matt Hancock, but without reply. I am telling you about this, because all that governments, their scientific advisers, big pharma (here's Merck, who originally developed & marketed it) and regulatory agencies will tell you is that ivermectin doesn't work in

Covid-19. They are lying. I am inviting any of them to sue me, but they won't, for I would win easily. If ivermectin was more widely used, there'd be no need for vaccines."[1]

As an ex-Pfizer executive, as well as having scrutinised the BIRD evidence on ivermectin for Covid-19, Mike's bold opinion held significant weight with the public. Pointing out that UK government's SAGE advisers knew in 2020 about ivermectin was news to my ears. In addition, his inclusion of "If ivermectin was more widely used, there'd be no need for vaccines" was a validation of our efforts.

Prof. Horby was a controversial member of SAGE not least because of his role as co-investigator in the RECOVERY Trial. The RECOVERY Trial evaluated another cheap generic drug, hydroxychloroquine (HCQ) and, for reasons that were never explained, very high doses of HCQ were used, more than double the usual dosage and duration. In addition, the trial did not focus on early treatment of symptoms but rather recruited hospitalised patients. Needless to say there were safety issues; 25% of people in the HCQ arm died and the trial had to be halted prematurely. The result achieved by the trial was that anyone suggesting that HCQ at normal doses was effective for early Covid treatment was ridiculed.

About Horby's role in the RECOVERY Trial, my co-authors suggest that the decision to use exceptionally high doses of HCQ might have been driven by a desire to obtain clear (negative) results quickly – *Here the ritual is only superficially fulfilled.*[2] Expediency was the name of the game, in other words. In addition, their comments suggest Horby could have been influenced by external pressures – funding bodies, associates, government, or other influences to rig the game against HCQ and the unfortunate trial participants.

---

1   https://www.conservativewoman.co.uk/why-are-we-being-lied-to-about-covid-theres-no-good-reason/

2   Hexagram 54, The Marrying Maiden, line 6. From I Ching, by Richard Wilhelm, 3rd Ed. p.212.

Certain relationships require tactful reserve. *A girl who is taken into the family, but not as the chief wife, must behave with special caution and reserve. She must not supplant the mistress of the house, for that would mean disorder and lead to untenable relationships.*[1]

With regard to my pragmatic approach to EbMCsquared's temporary front-facing team, my co-authors warn, *Perchance the army carries corpses in the wagon. Misfortune.*[2] My approach could potentially have led *to defeat because someone other than the chosen leader* could *interfere[s] with the command.*[3] I did not know any of these individuals well and having people whom I did not know *ride in the wagon* was definitely a risk. The danger of external influences, even well-intentioned ones, was that they could dilute the focus and unity needed for success. In the chaos of navigating a complex and evolving battle, it was all too easy for conflicting priorities and loyalties to undermine the collective effort, leaving the mission vulnerable to failure.

On the other hand, these individuals provided invaluable reinforcement, albeit for a short period only, at a time when our fledgling company needed a robust countenance. Not only did Mike Yeadon share my concerns about the dangers of the experimental Covid-19 shots, but as one of the few prominent voices in the pharmaceutical industry speaking out, his vocal opposition to what was going on carried significant weight. As it had been politely suggested by several BIRD colleagues that I focus on ivermectin and mute my stance on the injections to avoid alienating potential allies, especially doctors starting to question the official Covid position, I was especially grateful for Mike's relative freedom to do so. My approach to the experimental vaccine issues had to be more indirect in the early months of 2021. The need to keep BIRD separate from vaccine issues was great.

---

1   Hexagram 54, The Marrying Maiden, The Judgement. From I Ching, by Richard Wilhelm, 3rd Ed. p.209.

2   Hexagram 7, The Army, line 3. From I Ching, by Richard Wilhelm, 3rd Ed. p.34.

3   Hexagram 7, The Army, line 3. From I Ching, by Richard Wilhelm, 3rd Ed. p.34.

Chapter 5

Obstruction

Water on the mountain:
The image of OBSTRUCTION.
Thus the superior man turns his attention to himself
And moulds his character.[1]

The hexagram pictures a dangerous abyss lying before us and steep, inaccessible mountain rising behind us. We are surrounded by obstacles; at the same time, since the mountain has the attribute of keeping still there is implicit a hint as to how we can extricate ourselves.[2]

Despite being careful to play the science game, the globalist artificial intelligence (AI) beast, with its social media algorithms, was certainly awakening to BIRD's song. Though at first appearing to simply watch out the corner of the eye, it was readying its minions and soon thousands of 'fact checkers', hired hands and algorithmic censors were ready to be deployed whenever we moved.

---

1   Hexagram 39, Obstruction. The Image. From I Ching, by Richard Wilhelm, 3rd Ed. p.152.
2   Hexagram 39, Obstruction. The Image. From I Ching, by Richard Wilhelm, 3rd Ed. p.152.

Though I would have liked to do so, it was clear that I could not come out with guns blazing about the dangerous genetic injections being deployed in the name of vaccines. If I were to be labelled "anti-vax" at this delicate stage of BIRD's efforts, which relied to a large extent on my professional credibility, it would have been a home goal. Already there was significant energy being spent to undermine us; however, with my personal credibility endorsed by my excellent WHO standing and appraisals, as well as by objective academic metrics, the most the enemy could do at this stage was ignore us, send in the trolls on social media, or cancel our videos and articles. Having learnt my lesson on Twitter with my ill-informed "new face of genocide" tweets, I kept fairly still on social media platforms. Meanwhile, BIRD's followers on Twitter and Telegram continued to grow despite the trolls.

Dr Andrew Hill quietly faded into the background during this period, deleting his previously optimistic tweets and retreating from social media. The next time I would see his name on a scientific article (other than one undermining ivermectin), would be as a co-author on a paper promoting worldwide access to Pfizer's Paxlovid. Paxlovid was experimental, prohibitively expensive, and a direct competitor to the low-cost ivermectin. The Paxlovid study was funded by the International Treatment Preparedness Coalition (ITPC)/Make Medicines Affordable Campaign (MMAC). As one might have expected, ITPC and MMAC received funding directly and indirectly from Unitaid, the BMGF, and USAID.

Apparently the BMGF, a founding partner of the Global Alliance for Vaccines and Immunisation (GAVI), also called The Vaccine Alliance, even took out Google ads telling people not to use ivermectin. In terms of obstacles, therefore, I would note to myself that we had climbed the Hill but would have to get over the Gates sooner or later! How could one help people impressed by material wealth to connect the dots about Bill Gates – a man who had sold the image of a self-less philanthropist, all while being deeply entrenched in anti-human agendas that served his financial and ideological interests?

Going leads to obstructions, coming leads to union. This too describes a situation that cannot be managed single handed. In such a case the direct way is not the shortest. If a person were to forge ahead on his own strength and without the necessary preparations, he would not find the support he needs and would realise too late that he had been mistaken in his calculations, in as much as the conditions on which he hoped he could rely would prove to be inadequate. In this case it is better, therefore, to hold back for the time being and to gather trustworthy companions who can be counted upon for help in overcoming the obstructions.[1]

MOVE 23. Submission to Parliament Thwarted

In addition to putting together an application to the MHRA for ivermectin approval, and supporting various legal initiatives in distant countries, I was urged by a supporter to make a formal submission to the British Parliament. They were full of hope that upon receiving our evidence, British parliamentarians would finally correct their mistakes and allow doctors to treat their patients with ivermectin. I knew in my heart that it would come to nothing, but I went along with it. Such steps served other purposes too. At the very least, it would help build the body of evidence we would need for accountability, to show how badly the game had been rigged – and who in government were playing for the opposition.

My submission was courteously forwarded by Member of Parliament Mrs Andrea Jenkyns to the Right Honourable Mr Jeremy Hunt on March 24th. In 2021, Hunt was not in a cabinet position but, rather, held an influential role as the Chairman of the Health and Social Care Select Committee, where he could provide alternative

---

[1]   Hexagram 39, Obstruction, line 4. From I Ching, by Richard Wilhelm, 3rd Ed. p.153.

opinions on healthcare management, including for the Covid-19 "pandemic". Mrs Jenkyns wrote on my behalf to Mr Hunt:

> Good morning,
>
> I hope you are well.
>
> I am writing following an e-mail that I have received from Dr Theresa Lawrie who has contacted me with regard to the use of Ivermectin for the prevention and treatment of COVID-19.
>
> Please find attached the documentation that she has sent to me which includes a letter directly from her.
>
> They are looking for a meeting with you, in your role as the Chair of the Health and Social Care committee, as they are keen to discuss their issues with you further. Her e-mail address can be found here: [...]
>
> Kind regards,
>
> Andrea Jenkyns MP

I included with the cover letter our expert systematic review on ivermectin, and the British Ivermectin Recommendation Development (BIRD) documents detailing the BIRD methods, findings and Covid-19 recommendations (Exhibit 12).[1] The cover letter of approximately seven pages explained my experience, involvement in the ivermectin story, issues with the controversial Dr Hill pre-print, and the extraordinary departure of the World Health Organization from an evidence-based approach concerning ivermectin. I also discussed the basis of UK guidance on Covid-19 evidence, which was pragmatic in the sense that it was less stringent than usual due to the emergency context. Despite this relaxation of the UK's rules, I explained that our systematic review was even more comprehensively prepared than the National Institute for Health and Care Excellence

---

1   Exhibit 12. Submission to British Parliament, 24th March 2021.

(NICE) guidance for evidence in emergencies required.

In addition, I presented WHO pharmacovigilance data in the form of a table including Deaths and Adverse Drug Reaction (ADR) data on ivermectin, aspirin, remdesivir, tocilizumab, and the Covid-19 vaccines. At the time of extracting and reviewing these data, it was clear that the average annual deaths attributed to ivermectin numbered less than one and that the number of ADR reports linked to ivermectin was extraordinarily low. These data looked stark compared with 9,612 deaths reported within just three months of the Covid-19 vaccine roll-out. In the same 3-month period of the roll-out, there were also 309,403 ADR reports linked to the Covid-19 vaccines, which Hunt could not have missed, as they were highlighted in red ink.

I also included data on the tetanus vaccine, for which ADR reports had been documented since 1968 by the WHO. The pharmacovigilance data showed that it too was associated with fewer than one death per year and had accumulated 14,725 ADR reports in total. While I did not explicitly mention the Covid-19 vaccine or its shocking ADR data in the body of the letter, I noted that ivermectin had been shown over a long period of time to be very, very safe in comparison with most drugs. Even Prof. Chris Whitty, the UK's Chief Medical Officer during the Covid Chapter, had claimed ten years earlier in a scientific paper that "(Ivermectin) has proven to be safe. Doses up to 10 times the approved limit are well tolerated by healthy volunteers".[1] When so much intentional doubt had been created about ivermectin's safety, isn't it crazy that the UK's Chief Medical Officer knew all along that it was safe?

One can never presume anything about anyone, and having prepared the submission, and pointed out to Hunt that, despite our efforts, we had yet to receive a considered response from any UK

1   Chaccour, Lines and Whitty. Effect of Ivermectin on Anopheles gambiae Mosquitoes Fed on Humans: The Potential of Oral Insecticides in Malaria Control (2010). doi. org/10.1086/653208

health authorities, including the MHRA, the Therapeutics Task Force, Public Health England, NICE, SAGE, and others, I had high hopes that, despite my earlier misgivings, he would recognise the urgency of the situation and respond appropriately.

To the contrary, it took Hunt five weeks to send his brief response, which arrived by email on May 7th, 2021. Shirking any accountability, as would become the trademark of all those in positions of real authority during the Covid-19 scam, it was predictably negative.

Dear Dr Lawrie

Thank you for your letter regarding the use of Ivermectin for the prevention and treatment of Covid-19.

The role of the Health and Social Care Committee, of which I am Chair, is to scrutinise the policy, administration and expenditure of the Department of Health and Social Care and its arms' length bodies.

While I am grateful for the information you have provided, the role of the Committee is not to advocate for specific therapies so I regret that I will not be able to meet with you on this occasion.

Best wishes

Jeremy Hunt

Rt Hon Jeremy Hunt MP

Where there is hoar frost underfoot, solid ice is not far off.[1] Frankly, I have never trusted politicians but, about this interaction with Hunt, the *I Ching* notes that this was the first tangible sign to me of systemic corruption in the ruling British Government. *Just as the light giving power represents life, so the dark power, the shadowy represents death. When the first hoar frost comes in the autumn, the power of darkness and*

---

1   Hexagram 2, The Receptive, line 1. From I Ching, by Richard Wilhelm, 3rd Ed. p.13.

cold is just at its beginning.[1] It signalled the initial stages of the power of darkness and cold, an omen that decay had begun. *After these first warnings, signs of death will gradually multiply, until, in obedience with immutable laws, stark winter with its ice is here.*[2] The appearance of this first hoar frost from Hunt was a reminder that after such early, seemingly insignificant signs, the force of destruction will only grow stronger until it culminates in the harshness of winter, symbolising final dissolution. In the context of Hunt's response to me, this metaphor becomes strikingly clear. Hunt's failure to act on crucial evidence, and his refusal to respond with integrity and honesty, was a significant sign of systemic decay. His actions, or lack thereof, were a clear indication that corruption had taken root at the highest levels of government. This failure to act on the mounting evidence would have dire consequences, not only for the health and wellbeing of the British people, who would literally die in droves from the experimental jabs, but for the British government itself, which would eventually collapse under the weight of its own indifference and deceit. As the *I Ching* suggests, these signs of decay were not to be ignored, and I did not ignore them.

In the interim, we had sent our ivermectin evidence pack to PM Boris Johnson, delivered on 21st April 2021 to 10 Downing Street, with a covering letter outlining the difficulties we were having engaging the responsible authorities on the matter, asking for his intervention. (Exhibit 13.)[3] Again, we heard nothing back from the PM.

I took note, recognising that, at this point, we had moved beyond the realm of conspiracy theory, where no evidence of systemic indifference or active intent could be proven. It was now a reality, an undeniable truth that the system itself had failed. Worse, individuals in government had colluded.

---

1   Hexagram 2, The Receptive, line 1. From I Ching, by Richard Wilhelm, 3rd Ed. p.13.
2   Hexagram 2, The Receptive, line 1. From I Ching, by Richard Wilhelm, 3rd Ed. p.13.
3   Exhibit 13. Letter to PM Boris Johnson (19 April 2021).

MOVE 24. A Revealing Freedom of Information Request

Shortly after the parliamentary disappointment I submitted a Freedom of Information (FOI) request to the DHSC. Of the many FOI requests done over the Covid-19 years, this is one that I found particularly revealing in its frankness.

Freedom of Information Request Reference FOI-1321606

Dear Mrs Lawrie

Thank you for your request dated 8 April, in which you asked the Department of Health and Social Care (DHSC):

"I notice that there are no medical doctors or health professionals/researchers among the team of directors that heads up the Therapeutics Taskforce. Could you at least tell me how many of the 44 members of the taskforce are 1) medical doctors, and 2) medical researchers?"

Your request has been handled under the Freedom of Information Act (FOIA).

DHSC holds information relevant to your request. The Therapeutics Taskforce is a director-led team of civil servants employed by or seconded to DHSC; **none are currently medical doctors or medical researchers.** The Taskforce works closely with medical and scientific experts in the UK COVID-19 Therapeutics Advisory Panel (UK C-TAP) and RAPID C-19, a multi-agency initiative including NIHR, NICE, MHRA, NHSE-I and representatives from the Devolved Administrations.

The programme is overseen by Deputy Chief Medical Officer Jonathan Van-Tam.

Etc.

There it was, in black and white. There was no one with any medical or scientific expertise in charge, just a bunch of order followers who lacked the knowledge to make informed decisions, and no one with authority to take the blame when things inevitably went wrong. The revelation was an eye-opening look at how public health decisions during Covid were being guided not by science and expertise, but by bureaucratic cogs and political calculation. This FOI provides a critical piece of the puzzle that explains the true nature of the official 'pandemic' response. No one would claim to be at the wheel of the Covid-19 bus, because no one could.

MOVE 25. Documenting Covid-19 Vaccine Harms

For the first few months of 2021, whilst overtly engaged in ivermectin advocacy and science, behind the scenes I was working on how to present the dangers of the experimental Covid-19 vaccines within an evidence-based framework. We had a teeny team, yet it was imperative to me that we began addressing this. However, most of my new BIRD acquaintances – individuals and groups – were either unaware of the potential dangers at this stage or, if they were, hesitant to raise them publicly. The risk of being labelled "anti-vax" was very real and a deterrent for many. This fear was not unfounded, given the Trusted News Initiative's reputation for branding anyone who questioned the official narrative as dangerous or untrustworthy.

In addition, there were many obstacles to highlighting the problems with the Covid-19 shots from a scientific perspective: the main problem with the literature on gene-based vaccines was that there simply was not enough of it to show that these genetic products might ever be a good idea, let alone to conduct a systematic review on them! The drug company studies generally hadn't been published, with sequential clinical trial phases expanded into the next phase without reaching their outcomes so there was almost no publicly available scientific evidence to analyse despite the widespread roll-out. Data from Pfizer, Moderna, and the other vaccine producers were going straight to regulatory bodies, ostensibly to inform rapid decision-making, which meant that they bypassed critical analysis by independent scientists.

Whilst authorities were quick to hail the vaccines a miraculous feat of modern science in their effectiveness in preventing transmission of the virus (for which they had *no evidence*), they were as quick to dismiss concerns raised about safety because there was *no evidence* to show that they were *not* safe. Thus, all we had to go on was the massive gap in the literature, the theoretical probabilities of harms likely with these novel gene-based products, and the reports of harms recorded on pharmacovigilance databases (which monitor drug side effects and adverse reactions for safety purposes). Meanwhile, most people convinced to take the jabs did not even realise that these products were still in clinical trials, or that they were gene-based products that could change their biology.

Though not familiar with specific country pharmacovigilance databases, I was talking with individual scientists who were analysing the Vaccine Adverse Events Reporting System (VAERS) database in the US and drawing some pretty concerning correlations between the Covid-19 vaccine rollout and clotting diseases, such as stroke. However, what I *was* familiar with was the WHO's pharmacovigilance database, Vigibase, a WHO collaboration with the University of Uppsala in Sweden. This database had been collecting drug harms data for decades, from all around the world, and already in early 2021, the reports on the Covid-19 vaccines were mounting up.

In fact, it was the WHO's Vigibase data on ivermectin that had supported its use for scabies and led to its inclusion on the WHO's list of essential medicines. This inclusion was a direct result of ivermectin's impeccable safety record over many years. It was precisely because it was so safe that it had been recommended for mass administration for river blindness and, by Prof. Whitty et al, potentially malaria. A Nobel prize awarded to its discoverers Prof. Satoshi Ōmura and Dr William

Campbell in 2015 defined it notably as a medicine of immeasurable benefit to mankind. The Uppsala Vigibase team updated their international safety data weekly, and so I asked one of our young volunteers to start recording the data every week. Specifically, I asked her to record data on the Covid-19 vaccines, remdesivir (Dr Anthony Fauci's favourite drug for Covid-19 treatment) and ivermectin.

The first data we have on record were from February 16th, 2021. At this date, Vigibase already showed 84,489 ADRs and 922 deaths linked to the Covid-19 vaccines – undeniably unprecedented. What stood out immediately when plotting the data was how the Covid-19 vaccine numbers just skyrocketed week on week, while ivermectin remained virtually flatlined despite its widespread use. In over just one month to March 16th, 2021, the ADR reports for the vaccines doubled to 243,000, with 2,000 deaths. I was watching these figures unfold, desperate to communicate what I could see happening, all the while the government propaganda kept blazing "safe and effective" across all screens. Thus, one of the methods I subtly employed in our BIRD work was to include the Vigibase data for ivermectin, remdesivir and the Covid-19 vaccines in all presentations, interviews, reports and discussions on ivermectin.

I added the Covid-19 vaccine data from the Yellow Card Scheme to my watch list too. It seemed few doctors in the UK were aware of the Yellow Card Scheme for reporting adverse reactions to drugs in general, let alone that Covid-19 vaccine harms could be reported. It's as if critical thinking had been switched off in their brains and they just assumed the vaccine was "safe and effective" because they were told it was so. Nevertheless, in combination with non-medical individuals self-reporting, significant data were accruing to the Yellow Card Scheme too. These data were particularly difficult for us to work with because they were presented in a fixed Portable Document Format (PDF) instead of spreadsheets – a separate one for each Covid vaccine type. The intention by doing this was obviously to make it extremely labour-intensive for independent scientists to abstract and analyse. One had no sooner abstracted data, than the update would be published with new data. It was near impossible to compare one week with another, until I discovered the UK Column's initiative. The UK Column, an independent media group was diligently copying and updating these data onto their website each week, which was tremendously helpful. Another small group, called the UK Freedom Project, whose active members mainly comprised a couple of determined women with data capturing and Excel skills, kindly updated spreadsheets for me and assisted in supporting a number of my analytical requests. What was notable with the UK data was how the data changed. Deaths in different categories could go up or down, for example. There was definite fiddling going on, but no amount of fiddling the books could alter the fact that the deaths and disease post-vaccination were horrendously high.

I would like to point out how this crucial documentation process was a collective effort by strangers around the world, all coming together for the good of all. It might have appeared to be my work in the end, but in reality, it was only through the support and dedication of countless individuals, most of whom I had never met, that we were able to gather this essential evidence to ensure that justice could eventually be done. My wise co-authors remind me that as a *wanderer,* it was important to be *modest and reserved.*[1] If *he does not lose touch with his inner being, hence he finds a resting place. In the outside world he does not lose the liking of other people, hence all persons further him, so that he can acquire property.*[2] This resonates because, despite the tumultuous and often isolating nature of this journey, I trusted that by holding firm with integrity, I would attract the right kind

---

1   Hexagram 56, The Wanderer, line 2. From I Ching, by Richard Wilhelm, 3rd Ed. p.218.
2   Hexagram 56, The Wanderer, line 2. From I Ching, by Richard Wilhelm, 3rd Ed. p.218.

of people to help push the mission forward. *Moreover, he wins the allegiance of a faithful and trustworthy servant – a thing of inestimable value to a wanderer.*[1]

At this stage I must make a request to the reader: if certain words, such as *servant, superior man, inferior man, ruler,* and *lowly* are uncomfortable, please explore the meaning and make allowances for the old-world language used by my co-authors. They speak in ancient tongue and metaphor that in a hypersensitive and polarised society such as ours can easily lead to offence being taken on reflex. What they mean by a *faithful and trustworthy servant* in this context are the volunteers, scientists, mothers and fathers who stepped up to help without need of recognition or compensation. The value of their many and varied contributions and support cannot be overstated. My co-authors have taken the opportunity to highlight here that when we align ourselves with truth and humility, the universe itself conspires to help us, and those who believe in the cause will step forward, often from the most unexpected places.

MOVE 26. Holding the First Ever Covid-19 Conference

On the 24th and 25th of April 2021, amidst an atmosphere thick with fear and uncertainty, BIRD held the first ever Conference on Covid 19 prevention and treatment. In the UK, the government had put Step 2 of its arbitrary Four-Step Plan into action, restricting indoor gatherings, prohibiting travel, and limiting public events. There was no mixing indoors with anyone outside your household or "support bubble". Funerals could have up to 30 attendees and weddings up to 15 attendees. Travel abroad remained prohibited, except for a small number of permitted reasons, and people were advised to work from home. It was imperative that we find a way around these government obstacles to open discussion and communication

---

1   Hexagram 56, The Wanderer, line 2. From I Ching, by Richard Wilhelm, 3rd Ed. p.218.

about Covid issues. What better way to do so than to hold the first ever medical conference on Covid-19? It would have to be online, of course.

In the midst of the greatest obstructions, Friends come. Here we see a man who is called to help in an emergency. He should not seek to evade the obstructions, no matter how dangerously they pile up before him. But because he is really called to the task, the power of his spirit is strong enough to attract helpers whom he can effectively organise, so that through the well-directed cooperation of all participants the obstruction is overcome.[1]

Like all our activities, we pulled the conference together in a very short time and with limited means, yet managed to arrange a great panel of international speakers. And the focus? Ivermectin – we called it the International Ivermectin for Covid Conference (IICC)! The conference was not just about ivermectin though. It was about pushing back against the official Covid-19 narrative and offering people an alternative approach. It was a major milestone. For the first time, medical professionals were speaking openly about how we could actually treat and prevent Covid-19, without waiting for permission to do so, or for validation from the establishment. YouTube Medical educator Dr Mobeen Syed chaired the proceedings, and the superb presentations from doctors and scientists, with panel discussions, felt like the first rains after a buildup of clouds – such a relief for all. As we spoke out together, sharing knowledge, discussing the latest studies and real-world data, and offering solutions, it was obvious that the Covid narrative would not have been able to take hold had people had access to our information and expertise. A particularly excellent presentation was given by Prof. Matjaž Zwitter from Slovenia on the ethics of withholding effective, low-cost medicines in favour of expensive novel vaccines. It should still be available for viewing and downloading at www.bird-group.org.

---

1   Hexagram 39, Obstruction, line 5. From I Ching, by Richard Wilhelm, 3rd Ed. p.153.

This is the press release that followed the conference. Perhaps you would have wanted to attend this conference if you had known about it.

Press release
From the British Ivermectin Recommendation Development Group
29 April 2021

The long established and safe drug ivermectin – costing just pennies – is beating Covid worldwide, and health regulators should authorise it for use as soon as possible to save lives. This was the message broadcast loud and clear to over 500 medical professionals attending an international medical conference focused on this pressing issue.

United by their passion to save lives, the International Ivermectin for Covid Conference held last weekend, featured talks and discussions from 12 world-class medical researchers, frontline medics and data analysts. The event, hastily assembled in just 10 days by a network of dedicated medical professionals known as the British Ivermectin Recommendation Development (BIRD) group, was unwavering in its mission; to share the most up-to-date evidence on ivermectin for prevention and treatment of Covid-19, and to overcome regulatory obstacles that currently prevent GPs from prescribing it to save and improve lives.

Internet medical sensation and chair of the conference, Dr Mobeen Syed – or 'Dr Been' to his 280,000+ followers – quickly established in precise scientific detail exactly how ivermectin works to block the Covid-19 virus from reproducing and causing inflammation. Notably, for forty years, ivermectin has been prescribed in the UK and worldwide as an anti-parasitic drug. Billions of doses have been administered, leading to the near eradication of the debilitating River Blindness disease in most of Africa, with very few adverse events recorded.

For its immeasurable contribution to the health of humanity its inventors won a Nobel Prize in 2015. Now it is a generic drug, the tablets cost just a few pence, doesn't need refrigeration, and can be taken at home, making deployment much simpler and with a broader reach than novel treatments and vaccines.

The scientific basis for ivermectin's mechanisms against Covid-19 outlined by Dr Been is unequivocally borne out by the data according to Dr Tess Lawrie, founder of the BIRD group. "The most up-to-date trial data shows that primary and secondary outcomes significantly favour ivermectin for the treatment and prevention of Covid-19." Viewing ivermectin's effectiveness and long-term safety record stretching back 40 years, she is baffled by the slow progress in gaining approval. "We are seeking health equity for people in all countries through the immediate approval of this safe means of preventing and treating of Covid symptoms," Dr Lawrie added.

Dr Lawrie expressed the frustration of many; that while governments have fast tracked the approval of a variety of novel treatments and backed their development with massive injections of public funding, the evidence base and long-term safety track record is much smaller compared to that of ivermectin. Since the rise of the virus, practitioners and researchers around the world seeking early treatment options for Covid have been astounded to discover that this unassuming tablet is delivering outstanding results in helping to fight the pandemic.

The pressing topic of Long Covid and ivermectin was also discussed during the conference. Prof. Hector Carvallo from Argentina, and Dr Tina Peers from the UK delivered compelling real-world evidence to show that ivermectin may reduce the risk of hospitalisation and intubation, and clear up long-term symptoms associated with Long Covid. Prof. Carvallo's data showed resolution of all Long Covid symptoms in 100% of patients treated with ivermectin, after an average of 36 days. Speaker after speaker delivered compelling evidence for using ivermectin and their despair with regulators stalling on this issue.

"It's a NO BRAINER to prescribe ivermectin for Covid!" declared Dr Manjul Medhi, a front-line NHS doctor and expert in quantitative and qualitative research, after studying real-world data, RCT data, mass epidemiological data and the experiences of physicians and patients using ivermectin.

"The earlier ivermectin is administered, the better the results," concluded Prof. Eli Schwartz having conducted a randomised, double-blinded trial in Israel, that looked into the viral shedding among patients with mild-to moderate Covid-19, in non-hospitalised community-based settings.

In places like Mexico City that are widely deploying ivermectin: "There is only one explanation for the sharp drop in new cases and fatalities – ivermectin," declared Juan Chamie a data analyst who forensically dissected the evidence across both outpatient and hospital settings. Andrew Bryant a statistician at the University of Newcastle, backed Chamie's findings, and asked with so much positive data "why delay implementation of ivermectin for Covid-19 now?"

The reluctance by authorities to accept the evidence is viewed as incomprehensible by many in the medical community– and it was a consistent theme throughout the two days. The frustration is leading many in the medical community to fear that the emphasis on the financial gain of novel and expensive treatments may be blocking the approval of ivermectin.

In a moving final address, Dr Tess Lawrie made an impassioned appeal to clinicians and regulators, asking them to evaluate the huge body of evidence on ivermectin for Covid-19. She urged regulators to support medical doctors to practice medicine according to their obligations as outlined in the Hippocratic Oath. Lives are at stake.

Despite the significance and the success of this event, attended by around 500 people, it was ignored by the mainstream. Undeniably, however, it was a defining moment in the health sovereignty movement. It proved that people could come together, develop their own solutions, and stand up to the forces that were trying to control the global response. The courage of BIRD members and the medical professionals who participated in International Ivermectin for Covid Conference should not be underestimated. Very few professionals were speaking out at this time. Many, like Dr Mobeen Syed, with an income dependent on his You Tube channel, had a lot to lose.

About the cautious enthusiasm, courage and steady support of Dr Been and others like him, my co-authors note, *Before completion, at the dawning of a new time, friends foregather in an atmosphere of mutual trust, and the time of waiting is passed in conviviality. Since the new era is hard on the threshold, there is no blame in this. But one must be careful to keep within proper bounds. If in his exuberance a man gets drunk, he forfeits the favourableness of the situation through his intemperance.*[1]

The conference was not just about ivermectin, however. Whether the speakers and attendees were aware of it or not, we were also standing up for the right of people to choose, to make informed decisions about their own health without being dictated to by politicians. By standing up together to discuss the science, in friendliness, we gave others the courage to do the same. In this way, we shared a silent promise to help our fellow man.

MOVE 27. BIRD's Helpers Are Obstructed

Since the release of the BIRD recommendation in February 2021, followed by the multiple documents, press releases, interviews and other methods we had used to get BIRD's message across to the public, a fleet of motivated individuals had set forth to help us disseminate the

---

1   Hexagram 64, Before Completion, line 6. From I Ching, by Richard Wilhelm, 3rd Ed. p.252.

good news. Thus, thousands of emails and letters winged their way to political representatives and other leaders, often with me cc'd.

An example of such a communication is this one from Dr Graham Taylor to his UK Member of Parliament Mr Oliver Dowden, sent the week before the International Ivermectin for Covid Conference.

Sent: 20th April, 2021
  Subject: First International British Ivermectin Recommendation Development (BIRD) group conference.

Dear Mr Dowden,

I write to you because you are my local MP, a government minister, and because I am a physician observer of the devastation the Covid pandemic has caused over the last 15 months.

For many months now we have been ignoring the availability of a cheap, safe, highly effective, easily-producible and readily available medicine for both the prophylaxis and treatment of Covid19, the latter seemingly at all stages of the illness.

An illness which could, and should, have been managed in primary care has instead been one in which people with early symptoms have been told to isolate, take paracetamol, and to call 111 if they can't breathe, or are turning blue, by which time a sizeable minority will inevitably progress to a devastating whole body disease, and for many, death.

This is an appalling dereliction of duty as far as I am concerned, and has resulted in doctors and other healthcare workers having to discard their obligations to the Hippocratic Oath, which in essence mandates that we first do no harm, but that we also don't withhold effective medicines from patients. Faced with a disease projected to potentially kill hundreds of thousands of vulnerable people in the UK, I believe our willingness to sideline Ivermectin has been unforgiveable, particularly in recent months during which evidence of effectiveness and safety has been accumulating rapidly, and in which world renowned, widely published, physicians and associated researchers in pulmonary and critical care have been using it successfully with significant benefit for their patients. They have saved countless lives which would otherwise have been lost.

The BIRD group is holding its first hastily arranged conference this weekend. PLEASE attend. PLEASE distribute the attached flyer to friends, acquaintances and colleagues.

I implore you to take this seriously. It isn't PR speak to state categorically that lives are at stake.

And please lobby to have Ivermectin's status as a treatment option prescribable by GPs at the earliest suggestion of Covid symptoms with a positive test. This is utterly vital.

GPs must be allowed to help in primary care, rather than be witness to their patients dying, and must be allowed to fulfil the Hippocratic Oath to which they have sworn allegiance.

Thank you.

Graham.

Graham Taylor BSc MBBS MRCGP MBA
Independent Consulting Pharmaceutical Physician

In my opinion, Dr Taylor's sincerity and quiet authority comes across clearly in this letter. His medical expertise, concern, dedication and decency should have caused his local political representative to sit up and take notice. However, this was Dowden's response six days later.

Sent: Monday, April 26th 2021, 09:34
Subject: RE: First International British Ivermectin Recommendation Development (BIRD) group conference.

Dear Graham,

Thank you very much for your email.

I am very grateful for your email and I am pleased that you have brought your interest in Ivermectin and the potential benefits it could bring as a treatment for Covid-19 to my attention.

As I understand it, currently Ivermectin for oral use is not a licensed human medicine in the UK. For Ivermectin to be granted a marketing authorisation in the UK, an application must be submitted to the Medicines and Healthcare products Regulatory Agency (MHRA) for review. I am reassured that the MHRA has processes in place to expedite individual applications, and assess this for quality, efficacy and safety.

The MHRA is aware that Ivermectin, administered orally, is being studied for safety and efficacy in numerous clinical trials worldwide and is used in some countries in the treatment of COVID-19. While some studies have reported findings, and some are inconclusive, I do know that other large studies are still on-going.

I can absolutely assure you that the Government's Therapeutics Taskforce will continue to monitor these ongoing trials to assess the evidence available on whether Ivermectin is an effective treatment for Covid-19.

I also know that researchers across the country are working on a range of possible treatments for Covid-19 and have already been able to identify a whole series of drugs which are effective in treating Covid-19. The search for new treatments for Covid-19 is ongoing and I will of course continue to follow these closely.

Thank you again for your email and for raising this with me.

Yours sincerely,

Oliver

The Rt Hon Oliver Dowden CBE MP Member of Parliament for Hertsmere

This letter is typical of many that were received by concerned health professionals and others, who attempted to educate their MPs – those who undertook to represent and serve their constituencies. Sections of such letters were repeated verbatim, whether in England, Scotland, or Wales, as political puppets around the country danced to the tunes, and whistled the deceptions, of their masters.

Wikipedia lists Dowden as Right Honourable Sir Oliver Dowden. After apparently studying law at Cambridge, he became a Conservative politician in 2004, interrupted only by a two-year stint in a PR company, working as a special adviser and David Cameron's deputy chief of staff. For this service, he was awarded the title Commander of the Order of the British Empire (CBE) in 2015. He was also elected as MP for Hertsmere in 2015 and knighted in July 2024, at the age of 46, to become a "Sir."

This *indicates a rather vertical ascent – direct rise from obscurity and lowliness to power and influence.*[1]

A vertical ascent to power, as we know, often comes with a price – allegiance.

In such times, the mind of an able man is set upon going out into life and accomplishing something.[2]

Dowden's ties to the World Economic Forum (WEF) serve as proof of such allegiance and ambition. His participation in WEF events, particularly in Davos, where global leaders, policymakers, and business executives convene to discuss economic and social issues, speaks to a clear prioritisation of international networks, over his constituency's concerns. Dowden's rise to power, facilitated by such networks makes me wonder how much of his dismissal of Dr Taylor's concerns was guided by the needs of his Hertsmere constituents versus the agendas pushed by these globalist circles?

---

1   Hexagram 46, Pushing Upward. From I Ching, by Richard Wilhelm, 3rd Ed. p.178.
2   Hexagram 11, Peace, line 1. From I Ching, by Richard Wilhelm, 3rd Ed. p.49-50.

True fellowship among men must be based upon a concern that is universal. It is not the private interests of the individual that creates lasting fellowship among men, but rather the goals of humanity.[1]

Dr Taylor, on the other hand, was an ethical doctor and moral man acting out of concern for his fellow human beings. The *I Ching* comments that *If one is in the difficult and responsible position of counsellor to a powerful man, one should restrain him in such a way that right may prevail. Therein lies a danger so great that the threat of actual bloodshed may arise. Nonetheless, the power of disinterested truth is greater than all these obstacles. It carries such weight that the end is achieved, and all danger of bloodshed and fear vanish.*[2]

A member of the Faculty of Pharmaceutical Medicine, a UK-based professional membership organisation that comprises physicians with a professional interest in pharmaceutical medicine, Dr Taylor's expertise and interest lay in the science of discovering, developing and testing new drugs, their regulation, and safety monitoring. He was perfectly qualified to be *counsellor* to Dowden, the *powerful man* in this context. Obstructed in his authoritative capacity, Dr Taylor gave up on Dowden. *A reasonable and resolute man will not expose himself to a personal rebuff, but will retreat with others of like mind. This brings good fortune, because he does not needlessly jeopardise himself.*[3]

Dr Taylor continued to send emails to other public officials and organisations. Testimony to his strong character, he resigned from the Faculty of Pharmaceutical Medicine when it failed to respond to his requests to investigate and intervene on the ivermectin issue, demonstrating a stark contrast with Dowden's character and set of priorities.

Ambitious career politicians such as Dowden, whose failure

---

1   Hexagram 13, Fellowship with Men, The Judgement. From I Ching, by Richard Wilhelm, 3rd Ed. p.56.

2   Hexagram 9, The Taming Power of the Small, line 4. From I Ching, by Richard Wilhelm, 3rd Ed. p.42.

3   Hexagram 9, The Taming Power of the Small, line 2. From I Ching, by Richard Wilhelm, 3rd Ed. p.42.

to serve his constituency's interests was a betrayal typical of most MPs, had their true colours revealed during the Covid experiment – with ivermectin serving as a meaningful litmus test. The efforts of the many individuals like Dr Taylor, although thwarted, effectively showed to everyone a political system so deeply corrupt that it was entirely obsolete. Like the deathwatch beetles that infest the structural timber of old buildings, the entire Houses of Parliament would soon come crashing down, not from outside forces, but from the rot of their own making. As the *I Ching* reiterates, *the power of disinterested truth is greater than all these obstacles.*[1]

MOVE 28. My International Ivermectin for Covid Conference Closing Speech

I have included my closing conference speech as a separate 'move' because it was distinct from the IICC event itself in that it acted as a catalyst for what was to come. The speech below was, upon request, subsequently translated into many languages and shared worldwide on social media.

> I would like to thank all the esteemed speakers of today and yesterday – your valuable research, clinical experience and expert opinion have provided the key that we needed to turn this pandemic around.
>
> To our amazing Chair, Dr Been, I am so grateful that we have had your wisdom, humour and generosity of spirit to guide our discussions this weekend. From the bottom of my heart, thank you Dr Been. Thanks also to our technical team, Rob, Mark and Ronan, who have kept things running smoothly.
>
> To the wonderful participants from every continent and many

---

1   Hexagram 9, The Taming Power of the Small, line 4. From I Ching, by Richard Wilhelm, 3rd Ed. p.42.

countries, thank you for your engagement throughout this two-day conference, and the stimulating discussions.

Before you go, I would like to share with you a few reflections on ivermectin and my opinion on the state of affairs with regard to Evidence-Based Medicine.

As a scientist tasked with providing evidence along Evidence-Based Medicine principles, I have become aware that the hierarchi -cal approach to evidence synthesis, where systematic reviews sit at the top of the evidence pyramid and expert opinion and consensus at the bottom, is no longer appropriate. This is partly because the latter has become degraded by the increasing requirements of randomised controlled trials – the so-called gold standard of clinical studies. Large, randomised trials have become hugely resource intensive – 70-page trial protocols and grant applications require months of time and expertise to jump through all the hoops required for processing and authorisation.

These requirements play into the hands of Big Pharma, who are the only ones who can afford such trials, which cost millions of dollars. This is why large randomised clinical trials of generic medicines like ivermectin, which deserves to be evaluated for a number of viral conditions, are rare – if there is no money to be made, there are few trials. In my experience of evaluating trials of novel anti-cancer agents guaranteed to reap its developer billions, it is common that early trial findings showing benefit leading to the drugs' approval are contradicted by later evidence showing no benefit.

This is why I caution against the unquestioning acceptance of data provided by the developers of novel treatments and strongly suggest these their data are independently evaluated. Not by academics and institutions receiving unlimited research grants and funding from this industry either, but by independent objective scientists with no conflicts of interest. It is time we recognise and scrutinise the involvement of industry in institutions once known for their scientific integrity and all the so-called public private partnerships and charitable foundations that have facilitated the corruption of science. They who design the trial and control the data, also control the outcome. And this needs to stop. Data from on-going and future trials of novel treatments needs to be independently controlled and analysed.

With regard to the evidence pyramid, there needs to be a new approach. An integrated evidence approach instead of a tiered, hierarchical approach. I suggest that instead of a pyramid a doughnut shape would be more appropriate – with the centre hole representing the integrated evidence from different sources. Systematic review and meta-analysis of randomised trials would then represent one of several types of evidence, including observational studies, real world data and doctors' expert opinion to inform clinical practice decision-making in a more holistic way. All these data are vital and should be part of the decision-making process. Cherry picking large, randomised trials funded by private industry should not be the only tool used to make decisions. And then one could see, for ivermectin, which has evidence from all of these sources, there would be a pile of evidence in the middle of this doughnut – a veritable pyramid.

However, the story of ivermectin shows that we as the public have misplaced our trust in the authorities and have underestimated the extent to which money and power corrupts. The story of ivermectin and covid has highlighted that we are at a remarkable juncture in medical history – where rigorous scientific evidence, our training and experience, the tools that we use to heal, and our connection with our patients, are being systematically undermined by relentless disinformation stemming from corporate greed.

Had ivermectin been employed in 2020, when medical colleagues around the world first alerted the authorities to its efficacy, millions of lives could have been saved and the pandemic, with all of the associated suffering and loss, brought to a rapid and timely end. Since then, hundreds of millions of people have been involved in the largest medical experiment in human history – mass vaccination with an unproven novel therapy.

With politicians and other non-medical individuals dictating to us what we are allowed to prescribe to the ill, we, as doctors, have been put in a position such that our ability to uphold our Hippocratic Oath is under attack. At this fateful juncture, we must therefore choose: will we continue to be held ransom by corrupt organisations, health authorities, Big Pharma and billionaire sociopaths? Or will we do our moral and professional duty to do no harm and always do our best for those in our care? The latter includes urgently reaching out to colleagues around the world to discuss which of our tried and trusted safe older medicines can be used against covid, holding medical forums free of conflicts of interest like this one, and banding together as health professionals to stand up to the medical tyranny that has been imposed on us and the public over the past year.

To this end, I suggest we form a new world health organisation, a health organisation that represents the interests and wellbeing of the people, not big corporations and billionaires. An organisation focused on optimising human health and potential, not contraception and population control. A people-centred health organisation.

Never before has our role as doctors been more important – never before have we been complicit in potentially causing so much harm. I ask all doctors here today to look into their hearts and remember their Oath so that we can move forward united in the protection of those we serve and with great courage. Thank you.

As you may have gathered from the speech, the second day of the conference had been deeply emotional for me. The weight of the harms deliberately caused by an anti-human agenda, executed by millions of ignorant people, had truly hit home. On top of this, I could sense the return of despondency among attendees begin to seep in as the conference drew to a close. When I had written the speech I had felt it lacked a punchline, a solution that could inspire hope and rally people around a cause. Thus, speaking with Shabnam the night before, I had modified my speech and added the bit about forming a new world health organisation. Bolstered by two days of ethical, intelligent company, combined with the need to address the question "what's next?", it felt important to give attendees hope, even if it sounded a bit unrealistic. Still, it was a bold move, a step over the 'Gates', so to speak. Setting my reservations aside I took the leap.¹ I hoped others could set up such an organisation. Even as I spoke the words, I doubted I would be involved.

A wanderer by nature, as the *I Ching* has revealed about me, I hadn't really wanted to be public facing or involved in large organisational activities for the long haul. My intention had been to highlight what needed sorting out regarding Covid-19, and then disappear into the background once more to help figure out how to stop the escalating 5G and artificial radiofrequency technology, which I believed to be the greatest threat to mankind. I did not want further distractions. My co-authors remind me of this fact. *This refers to a man who has already left the world and its tumult behind him. When the time of obstructions arrives, it might seem that the simplest thing for him to do would be to turn his back upon the world and take refuge in the beyond. But this road is barred to him. He must not seek his own salvation and abandon the world to its adversity. Duty calls him back once more into the turmoil of life. Precisely because of his experience and inner freedom, he is able to create something both great and complete that brings good fortune. And it is favourable to see the great man in alliance with whom one can achieve the work of rescue.*¹

---

1   Hexagram 39, Obstruction, line 6. From I Ching, by Richard Wilhelm, 3rd Ed. p.154.

I feel the *great man* to whom they refer is not just an individual, but the many great people I would need to work alongside, both within my existing circle and new allies, for the massive undertaking of creating a peoples' health organisation to replace the WHO. The *I Ching's* reference to *alliance* indicates the power of collective action, suggesting that my work could only truly progress and succeed if I was united with others who had the same purpose and dedication. Very true. The *I Ching* highlights that I needed to seek out those people and work together with them.

On a personal and physical level, the speech had a rather peculiar consequence. Unable to hold my tears back during its delivery, I admonished myself afterwards for this outward show of vulnerability. I wished I hadn't cried and vowed to be stronger. From that point on, I became unable to cry. Instead, when I felt emotional, my nose became itchy and I sneezed! This anomaly is still largely present at the time of writing.

MOVE 29. Censored by Vimeo, YouTube, LinkedIn & Twitter

Thinking back, I am reminded how this period was marked by taking two steps forward and one-and-a-half steps backward. The success of the IICC, BIRD's expansion, and a flurry of interest on social media, led to a series of cancellations which could not help but make one feel a little despondent. The sense that there was nowhere left to manoeuvre, with the feeling of being surrounded by pawns, was overwhelming.

My company's YouTube account had previously been trimmed of a few posts. On this next occasion though, a particular two-minute video that we had put effort into translating into numerous languages, aimed at doctors explaining the suppression of ivermectin and urging them to uphold their Hippocratic Oaths, was targeted.

The translated versions went down too.

YouTube's email notified me about their Covid-19 medical misinformation policy: "Safety of our creators, viewers, and partners is our highest priority" they stated, elaborating that YouTube does not allow content contradicting local health authorities or the World Health Organization (WHO) on matters like Covid-19 treatment, prevention, diagnosis, transmission, and social distancing. They specifically flagged content recommending ivermectin or hydroxychloroquine for treating or preventing Covid-19, as misinformation. (Exhibit 14.)[1]

LinkedIn's censorship was triggered by my sharing of a scientific article by Massachusetts Institute of Technology (MIT)'s Dr Stephanie Seneff and Greg Nigh, entitled "Worse than the disease? Reviewing some possible unintended consequences of the mRNA vaccines." (Exhibit 15.)[2] This well-researched scientific paper, which had taken its esteemed authors six months to write, discussed the potential for mRNA technology to integrate into human DNA, a concern that has since been supported by hard evidence. The article's authors sensibly recommended increased surveillance to properly assess the risks and benefits of these new genetic vaccines – what a crime. LinkedIn removed the post, referring me to their "professional community guidelines".

As for Vimeo, while YouTube simply removed videos and issued warnings, and LinkedIn educated me on their policies, Vimeo took a more drastic step, terminating my entire account for allegedly violating their terms of service. With no room given for negotiation, Vimeo also cited misinformation regarding vaccine safety and claimed my content could mislead people into taking dangerous or unproven treatments, or refraining from necessary precautions

---

1   Exhibit 14. YouTube's Misinformation Notice (14 May 2021).
2   Exhibit 15. Seneff & Nigh. Worse than the disease? Reviewing some possible unintended
      consequences of the mRNA vaccines (2021).

(Exhibit 16).[1] Once more, the irony was breath-taking. They were kind enough to wish us luck in finding a platform better suited to our needs.

As for LinkedIn, while I should not have been surprised, I had pushed the envelope to see what it would take and, clearly, it did not take much. I learned that Mr Bill Gates, who owns far too much, owned LinkedIn too (through Microsoft), hardly a surprise given the platform's obvious ties to global interests. LinkedIn was another beastly lair, as were YouTube and Facebook – which I never bothered with as ivermectin was a clear trigger word for cancellation – and Twitter. The connections between these platforms and powerful global entities had become glaringly evident, and their censorship practices were increasingly designed to silence dissenting voices.

Like Gates and his 'philanthropic' foundation, Google's parent company, Alphabet, was deeply intertwined with the vaccine industry, through various subsidiaries and investments. Verily, Alphabet's health and life sciences division, had partnerships with major pharmaceutical companies like Pfizer, Novartis, and Sanofi. In addition, the Google search engine reports upon enquiry that Google collaborated extensively with the Defence Advanced Research Projects Agency (DARPA), a government agency responsible for advanced defence research, notably in AI systems, self-driving cars and advanced chip designs. DARPA funded and influenced Google's development of these key technologies. Illustrating this deep entanglement were the career histories of individuals like Regina Dugan, the former director of DARPA. After leading DARPA, a Google search reveals she became head of Google's Advanced Technology and Projects (ATAP) group, overseeing the development of mobile technologies, some of which remain shrouded in secrecy. During her time at Google, Dugan's group continued to collaborate with DARPA on a range of projects.

---

1   Exhibit 16. Vimeo's account termination notice (13 May 2021).

Dugan later moved to Facebook, where she apparently led the secretive Building 8 lab for Zuckerberg, focused on innovations like brain-computer interfaces and augmented reality.

With all of these cancellations, our presence on Twitter was increasingly important and we had to tread delicately not to trigger the algorithms. On occasion, our supporters would suggest we appealed to Elon Musk, a technology tycoon with a huge Twitter following, who occasionally championed the case of those with lesser influence. To this end we were unsuccessful. When Twitter was bought by Musk a while later, he would change its name to X, a symbol evoking notions of death to truth, rather than freedom. Asked to comment on my somewhat cynical perspective of Musk's Twitter acquisition and nomenclature, my co-authors made several observations. *If help comes to a man from on high, this increased strength must be used to achieve something great for which he might otherwise never have found energy, or readiness to take responsibility. Great good fortune is produced by selflessness, and in bringing about great good fortune, he remains free of reproach.*[1]

Suggestive to me that Musk's own *great good fortune* was pre-destined by *help* from *on high*, his position as owner of X presented a curious balancing act between alleging publicly to stand for the liberation of speech, yet contributing in deed to the same system that silenced the truth and had enslaved the world's people. I was not convinced that Musk had what it takes in terms of *selflessness* to be bringing about *great good fortune* for the rest of us. X seemed more like the same old tyranny with a fresh coat of paint.

But about Musk's potential, my co-authors further pointed out, *It is important that there should be men who mediate between leaders and followers. These should be disinterested people, especially in times of increase, since the benefit is to spread from leader to the people. Nothing of this benefit should be held back in a selfish way; it should really reach*

---

1   Hexagram 42, Increase, line 1. From I Ching, by Richard Wilhelm, 3rd Ed. p.163.

those for whom it is intended. This sort of intermediary, who also exercises a good influence on the leader, is especially important in times when it is a matter of great undertakings, decisive for the future and requiring the inner assent of all concerned.[1] This response contextualises Musk's later role with regard to Mr Donald Trump perhaps. As mediator between the newly elected leader and the American people, who were extremely divided between Republican and Democratic political camps, a correct attitude was crucial. With immense financial power and influence in hand, my co-authors caution that those in such positions, as Musk, must be selfless, ensuring that their actions benefit the higher good rather than advancing their own interests.

Were Musk to sever his ties with the dark forces, such a sacrifice would fill people *with a sense of joy and gratitude* and would lead to a *flowering of the commonwealth. The meaning here is that through renunciation those in high place should bring increase to those below. By neglecting this duty and helping no one, they in turn lose the furthering influence of others and soon find themselves alone.*[2] This is particularly relevant when considering Elon Musk's connections to DARPA, with which several of Musk's companies, particularly SpaceX and Neuralink, were heavily involved. SpaceX's collaboration with DARPA began with the Falcon HTV-2 program, while Neuralink's brain-computer interface projects aligned closely with DARPA's own interests in transhumanism and mind control. These partnerships provided Musk's companies with massive funding and government support, cementing his ties to the military-industrial complex.

The *I Ching's* wisdom suggests that for those in high positions, like Musk, true accomplishment comes not from accumulating more power or resources, but from renouncing the self-serving dynamics of the corrupt, elitist system. If Musk were to distance himself from

---

1   Hexagram 42, Increase, line 4. From I Ching, by Richard Wilhelm, 3rd Ed. p.164.
2   Hexagram 42, Increase, line 6. From I Ching, by Richard Wilhelm, 3rd Ed. p.165.

these entanglements, he would inspire widespread admiration and trust; people would rally behind him, and this could lead to a flourishing of society, benefiting all people. However, by remaining closely aligned with DARPA and the military, Musk risks failing in his duty and, instead of serving, harming all creatures, the heaven, and the earth. His continued involvement with these evil agencies could isolate him from the people who once saw him as a champion of innovation and free speech, though I could find no evidence of the latter apart from empty promises. Any attitude misaligned with the true needs of the time invites misfortune, my co-authors warn. Only by stepping away from his entanglements with DARPA and the deep state could Musk realise his full potential. Instead, he seems intent on leveraging his new extension of power to further entangle himself. Not content with being the most powerful man in the private domain, he appears set on being the most powerful man in the public domain as well. *An attitude not permanently in harmony with the demands of the time will necessarily bring misfortune with it.*[1]

Becoming aware of this web of interconnections between Tech Giants, DARPA, and Big Pharma – the military industrial complex – helped me grasp the full extent of what we were up against. Recognising the grotesque countenance of humanity's true enemy for what it was, far from a deterrent, made me even more resolute. This anti-human collective of dark forces could never succeed. As my wise co-authors conclude, *Only collective moral force can unite the world.*[2]

---

1   Hexagram 42, Increase, line 6. From I Ching, by Richard Wilhelm, 3rd Ed. p.165.
2   Hexagram 45, Gathering Together, The Judgement. From I Ching, by Richard Wilhelm, 3rd Ed. p.174-5.

Chapter 6

Deliverance

DELIVERANCE. The southwest furthers.
If there is no longer anything where one has to go, return brings good
fortune.
If there is still something where one has to go,
Hastening brings good fortune.[1]

This refers to a time when tensions and complications begin to be
eased. At such times we ought to make our way back to ordinary
conditions as soon as possible; This is the meaning of the "southwest".
These periods of sudden change have great importance. Just as rain
relieves atmospheric tension, making all the buds burst open, so a
time of deliverance from burdensome pressure has a liberating and
stimulating effect on life. One thing is important, however: in such
times we must not overdo our triumph. The point is not to push on
farther than is necessary. Returning to the regular order of life as

---

1   Hexagram 40, Deliverance, The Judgement. From I Ching, by Richard Wilhelm, 3rd Ed. p.154-
     5.

soon as deliverance is achieved brings good fortune. If there are any
residual matters that ought to be attended to, it should be done as
quickly as possible, so that a clean sweep is made and no retarda-
tions occur.[1]

June 2021 provided us with the opportunity for completion on two
important matters. First, together with hardworking members of the
UK Freedom Project, we finally managed to get on top of the weekly
vaccine harms data reported to the Yellow Card Scheme, publishing an
urgent preliminary report that clearly described the nature of reported
harms linked to the Covid-19 vaccines in the United Kingdom. The
urgency behind this tremendous effort was driven by the government's
upcoming Joint Committee on Vaccination and Immunisation
(JCVI) meeting scheduled for June 10th, where the issue of Covid-19
vaccinations for children was to be discussed. The JCVI alleged to be
an expert scientific advisory committee that advised the UK government on "vaccination and immunisation matters".

Second, the obstructions facing BIRD and EbMCsquared began
to ease. The submission process with the American Journal of Therapeutics had gone smoothly, and the revisions to our manuscript had
been accepted. As we excitedly signed off the proofs, editor Dr Peter
Manu notified Dr Andy Bryant that our systematic review would be
published soon. While we tried not to get our hopes up, knowing
how easily things could go wrong, like what had happened to Dr
Pierre Kory's team, we allowed ourselves a cautious optimism.

Fingers crossed; it was going to be a busy month at EbMCsquared.
In all likelihood, we would have these two critical documents to disseminate, which would provide people with the tangible evidence
they needed to lobby their representatives, as well as to make their

---

1   Hexagram 40, Deliverance, The Judgement. From I Ching, by Richard Wilhelm, 3rd Ed. p.154-
     5.

own informed health decisions. Our greatest task now would be how to get this information to them.

MOVE 30. URGENT: Independent Analysis of Yellow Card Scheme Vaccine Data

For the Yellow Card Scheme report, I had been impatiently biding my time, waiting for the right moment to present the evidence we had been gathering. It had been a delicate balancing act. I did not want to alienate those within the BIRD group or our wider support base who were still holding on to the narrative of vaccine safety despite the mounting evidence and testimonials that suggested otherwise. Many people, including some of our closest allies, were so afraid of challenging the mainstream narrative, even though they knew it was not quite right. Thus, we kept the report separate from BIRD's activities, preparing it under the joint banner of Evidence-based Medicine Consultancy Limited and EbMCsquared CIC. Whilst the hastily written report was authored by me, it was the result of a friendly collaboration between veritable strangers – folk at the UK Freedom Project and me. Entitled 'Urgent preliminary report of Yellow Card data up to 26th May 2021', it was satisfying to dispatch this correspondence to the MHRA's leader Dr June Raine (Exhibit 17).[1] With the timing and content intended to block the authorisation of the Covid-19 vaccines for children under consideration by the JCVI panel on June 10th 2021, our report dated June 9th just made it! Of course, in addition to Raine, we sent it to Van-Tam and other members of the JCVI too.

The prevailing situation was succinctly captured by Dr K. Polyakova in her 'Rapid Response' discourse on "Do doctors have to have the Covid-19 vaccine?" published on the *BMJ*'s website in April 2021. In her letter, Dr Polyakova voiced grave concerns about the

---

1   Exhibit 17. Urgent preliminary report of Yellow Card data up to 26th May 2021.

Covid-19 vaccines, particularly with respect to the NHS worker population. She spoke of the unprecedented sickness and the strain that the UK's mandatory vaccination program was placing on both staff and healthcare provision. Her words were a voice of reason in the NHS madness: the vaccines, still under emergency licensing with limited safety data, were causing harm, and the risks far outweighed the unsubstantiated benefits. Dr Polyakova's letter was a rare insider's perspective. Here it is:

Do doctors have to have the Covid-19 vaccine?

Dear Editor,

I have had more vaccines in my life than most people and come from a place of significant personal and professional experience in relation to this pandemic, having managed a service during the first 2 waves and all the contingencies that go with that.

Nevertheless, what I am currently struggling with is the failure to report the reality of the morbidity caused by our current vaccination program within the health service and staff population. The levels of sickness after vaccination is unprecedented and staff are getting very sick and some with neurological symptoms which is having a huge impact on the health service function. Even the young and healthy are off for days, some for weeks, and some requiring medical treatment. Whole teams are being taken out as they went to get vaccinated together.

Mandatory vaccination in this instance is stupid, unethical and irresponsible when it comes to protecting our staff and public health. We are in the voluntary phase of vaccination, and encouraging staff to take an unlicensed product that is impacting on their immediate health, and I have direct experience of staff contracting Covid AFTER vaccination and probably transmitting it. In fact, it is clearly stated that these vaccine products do not offer immunity or stop transmission. In which case why are we doing it? There is no longitudinal safety data (a couple of months of trial data at best) available and these products are only under emergency licensing. What is to say that there are no longitudinal adverse effects that we may face that may put the entire health sector at risk?

Flu is a massive annual killer, it inundates the health system, it kills young people, the old the comorbid, and yet people can choose whether or not they have that vaccine (which had been around for a long time). And you can list a whole number of other examples of vaccines that are not mandatory and yet they protect against diseases of higher consequence.

Coercion and mandating medical treatments on our staff, of members of the public especially when treatments are still in the experimental phase, are firmly in the realms of a totalitarian Nazi dystopia and fall far outside of our ethical values as the guardians of health.

I and my entire family have had Covid. This as well as most of my friends, relatives and colleagues. I have recently lost a relatively young family member with comorbidities to heart failure, resulting from the pneumonia caused by Covid. Despite this, I would never debase myself and agree, that we should abandon our liberal principles and the international stance on bodily sovereignty, free informed choice and human rights and support unprecedented coercion of professionals, patients and people to have experimental treatments with limited safety data. This and the policies that go with this are more of a danger to our society than anything else we have faced over the last year.

What has happened to "my body my choice?" What has happened to scientific and open debate? If I don't prescribe an antibiotic to a patient who doesn't need it as they are healthy, am I anti-antibiotics?

Or an antibiotic-denier? Is it not time that people truly thought
about what is happening to us and where all of this is taking us?[1]

I was very grateful to read this letter as the silence among doctors
and nurses up to this point about what they must be witnessing in
the hospitals was deafening. The Medicines and Healthcare products
Regulatory Agency (MHRA)'s Yellow Card Scheme was meant to
monitor vaccine safety but instead it had facilitated the roll-out of
a variety of experimental Covid products known as 'Covid-19 vaccines'. MHRA's Dr Raine, the horse's mouth, openly acknowledged
the conversion of the UK's 'regulatory' body from drug "Watchdog
to Enabler". She gave a presentation about it in Oxford University in
March 2022, so it was no secret.[2,3]

Given the urgency, as well as the complexity in accessing, capturing
and analysing the MHRA data, our report was focused on pragmatism,
not perfection. The problem we had faced, specific to the Yellow Card
Scheme database, was that the data were reported as 70-page PDF documents for each vaccine brand, e.g. Pfizer, Moderna, AstraZeneca, and
these documents comprised long lists of diverse adverse drug reactions
categorised by organ system, e.g. blood, cardiac, gastrointestinal, with
random nomenclature for diseases that made it feel less like an official
repository and more like a school project.

The brief report to Raine was a formal demand for transparency
and accountability. It was quite a race to get this done. With MHRA
numbers changing weekly, we had less than a week to collect the data
and prepare the document. Through our novel approach of classi-
fying the adverse reactions according to how a patient might present,

---

1   https://www.bmj.com/content/372/bmj.n810/rr-14 Dr Polykova's letter was removed by the
     BMJ allegedly for spreading misinformation.
2   www.conservativewoman.co.uk/the-mhra-the-watchdog-covering-up-the-truth-about-vaccine-
     deaths-and-injuries/
3   From Watchdog to Enabler - Regulation in Covid and after. Dr June Raine. Oxford University
     Medic's Day, 5th March 2022. https://www.youtube.com/watch?v=xUQfzTqPUm4

we hoped to translate the numbers into an accessible albeit limited clinical perspective. In this way, even if the MHRA did not share the findings, the information might still make sense to medical doctors who came across it. NHS doctors at the time were being mainlined with MHRA propaganda via 'no-reply' official channels, which kept them in the dark about vaccine harms, assuming that everything was 'business as usual.' In addition, it's widely known that many doctors were hugely incentivised to give vaccines. We would subsequently send the report out to practices countrywide in the hope that it would break through the veil of ignorance and get doctors rejecting their official drip feeds.

In May 2006, there was a campaign to raise awareness of pharmaceutical drug side effects in the UK. At the time, Raine was quoted in *The Guardian* as saying about the Yellow Card Scheme: "There is no need to prove that the medicine caused the adverse reaction, just the suspicion is good enough."[1] *The Guardian* article goes on to highlight that, for this awareness-raising campaign, posters had been provided by the MHRA and British Medical Association for doctors to hang in their surgeries to encourage patients to report any drug side effects too. None of this had been said or done during the so-called Covid-19 pandemic, where millions were being coaxed into taking experimental vaccines, ostensibly for the safety of Granny!

Thus the Urgent Yellow Card Report to Raine began with a reminder that the MHRA's Yellow Card system is designed to act as an early warning mechanism, identifying potential drug safety concerns. At the risk of seeming patronising, I felt it my duty to remind Raine of the MHRA's key and objective role. I also noted that the MHRA itself acknowledges that some safety issues may not become apparent until a large number of people are exposed to the drug.

---

1   The Guardian. Doctors urged to be more vigilant over drug side effects. Sarah Boseley, 12th May, 2006.

But there were so many data now in hand! Since the roll-out of the Covid-19 vaccines in the UK on 8th December 2020, more than 39 million people in the UK had received their first dose and 24 million had received both doses. Thus, since a very large number of people had been exposed to the vaccines, it was appropriate that the MHRA analyse their safety data. Indeed, it was imperative.

I drew Raine's attention to the concerning number of deaths and ADRs linked to the Covid vaccines on the MHRA's own database, indicating that within the first five-month period of roll-out, there had been 256,224 individual UK reports of harms linked to the injections, including 1,253 UK deaths and 888,196 ADRs. At the same time, the WHO's database had about one million ADRs linked to the Covid-19 vaccines and thousands of deaths. Whilst the UK's Yellow Card Scheme did not provide nor report demographic data, the WHO's data indicated most of these data were people between 18 to 60 years of age. It's important to bear in mind that most people receiving the shots were not ill to begin with, and, as nobody was told about potential harms or encouraged to report them, these data were grossly under-reported.

The contents of the injections did not remain in the arm muscle but were widely disseminated around the body. Citing research by Seneff and Nigh, I highlighted that scientists had, in fact, warned of potential short and long-term health risks with this new-style of vaccine, including multisystem inflammatory diseases, autoimmune reactions, allergic responses, activation of latent viral infections like Epstein-Barr and Herpes, neurodegeneration (e.g. dementia and Parkinson's), and the potential for the foreign gene material to integrate into human DNA. The diseases and ADRs reported to the MHRA aligned with these concerns.

I explained our methods, how we had grouped the Yellow Card ADRs into six key categories, that of bleeding, clotting and ischaemic disorders, immune system disorders, pain disorders, neurological disorders, disorders of sight, hearing, speech or smell, and pregnancy disorders. In a nutshell, I told Raine that these early Yellow Card Scheme data already indicated unprecedented levels of death, pain and suffering among the British people. Here is a summary of key findings of MHRA data up to May 26th 2021:

A. Bleeding, Clotting, and Ischaemic ADRs

A total of 13,766 reports related to bleeding, clotting, and ischaemia were identified, with 856 of these being fatal. Thromboembolic events were reported in a wide range of veins and organs, including the brain, heart, lungs, and kidneys, with serious consequences. Notably, there were 24 fatalities related to cerebral venous sinus thrombosis, the latter being one of the few ADRs raised by the MHRA as a potential concern.

B. Immune System ADRs

54,870 entries were linked to immune system reactions, including infections, inflammation, and autoimmune responses, with 171 associated fatalities. There was a notable number of cases involving the reactivation of latent viruses, such as shingles, and immune-mediated conditions like Guillain-Barré syndrome, even a case of rabies! Allergic reactions also contributed to significant numbers of ADRs.

C. Pain ADRs

Pain-related entries accounted for 18% of total reports, with common complaints including joint and muscle pain, as well as headaches. A rare genetic condition, Paroxysmal Extreme Pain Disorder (PEPD), was reported in 11 cases, and headaches were associated with four fatalities.

D. Neurological ADRs

Approximately 21% of entries were neurological, including seizures, paralysis, and neurodegenerative disorders like dementia. Serious conditions like encephalopathy and Parkinson's were reported, with 127 out of 180 fatalities mainly resulting from haemorrhages (latter are counted in A).

E. Loss of Sight, Hearing, Speech, or Smell

There were 4,771 entries of visual impairment, including blindness, and 704 reports of hearing impairment. Taste and smell issues were also widely reported.

F. Pregnancy ADRs

Pregnancy-related entries included 307 reports, with one maternal death, 12 stillbirths, and 150 spontaneous abortions. We would have preferred to expand this category to all reproductive harms including fertility and cancers, but we ran out of time. However, there were many reports of vaginal bleeding, including amongst women long past having periods, and at least 50 breast cancers on the data base at this time.

Calling for an immediate cessation of the vaccination programme, I told Dr Raine in conclusion:

"The MHRA now has more than enough evidence on the Yellow Card system to declare the Covid-19 vaccines unsafe for use in humans. Preparation should be made to scale up humanitarian efforts to assist those harmed by the Covid-19 vaccines and to anticipate and ameliorate medium to longer-term effects. As the mechanism for harms from the vaccines appears to be similar to Covid-19 itself, this includes engaging with numerous international doctors and scientists with expertise in successfully treating Covid-19."

In her response, which we received around six weeks later, Dr Raine reiterated the official position: which was "as with any vaccine, the Covid-19 vaccines will cause side effects in some people. The total number and the nature of yellow card reports so far is not unusual for a new vaccine for which members of the public are encouraged to report any suspected adverse reaction" (Exhibit 18).[1] This was a blatant lie, as the public were not encouraged at all to report ADRs, neither were doctors. However, there was a rather telling moment in Dr Raine's response. She stated that "the nature of Yellow Card reports means that reported events are not always proven side effects," suggesting that *some events may have happened coincidentally, regardless of vaccination.*" Her phrasing actually implies that many of the reported events were indeed caused by the vaccine, though she did not clarify how many. The obvious question was then: How many of the 256,224 reports were actually due to the vaccine, and how many were coincidental? Was it 10%, 20%, or perhaps even 90% of those reports? The truth seemed to be that she and the MHRA either did not know or did not care enough to investigate further. What was clear by Raine's dismissive transmission though was that evil was deeply entrenched in the MHRA leadership.

About such individuals, like Raine, my ancient co-authors observe, *The hawk on a high wall is the symbol of a powerful inferior in a high position who is hindering the deliverance. He withstands the force of inner influences, because he is hardened in his wickedness. He must be forcibly removed, and this requires appropriate means.*[2] Our consistent efforts to highlight the serious failings of the MHRA, and specifically Dr Raine's hand in defence of the dangerous injections

---

1   Exhibit 18. Dr June Raine's response, 18th July 2021.
2   Hexagram 40, Deliverance, line 6. From I Ching, by Richard Wilhelm, 3rd Ed. p.157.

unleashed on the British public would continue and, perhaps, may have contributed to her stepping down in due course. However, this is how the game was played – the controllers reset the board from time to time so that key individuals could not be held to account.

However, the short-term outcome of our urgent report was successful, at least; the JCVI panel voted against rolling out shots to UK's children at that June 10th meeting. We had helped to kick the ball down the road for the children at least! Whilst we could not be 100% certain of this, as it is not mentioned in the JCVI meeting minutes, it felt true.

It was satisfying knowing that we had put our cards on the table and delivered a modest yet significant victory. It demonstrated how, when a bunch of strangers create together for a common goal, we can make a difference. Of course, there would be other meetings soon with different attendees that would override this June 2021 decision, but Raine and her cronies could not intimidate us, we had made it clear that we meant business. What was once the public watchdog acting with impunity now knew that it was being watched – by the birds no less! The days that such influential order-followers could do the Devil's work were numbered. After all, birds are everywhere.

Times of deliverance demand inner resolve. Inferior people cannot be driven off by prohibitions or any external means. If one desires to be rid of them, he must first break completely with them in his own mind; they will see for themselves that he is in earnest and will withdraw.[1]

With reinforcements arriving in the form of the meticulous UK researcher, Dr Katherine McGilchrist, we would submit another report to Raine in August 2021 to keep her and the MHRA on their toes. For the moment though, we quietly appreciated our short-term win. *In keeping with the situation, few words are needed. The hindrances past, deliverance has come. One recuperates in peace and keeps still. This*

---

1   Hexagram 40, Deliverance, line 5. From I Ching, by Richard Wilhelm, 3rd Ed. p.157.

is the right thing to do in times when difficulties have been overcome.[1]

MOVE 31. Our Gold Standard Ivermectin Review Is Published at Last!

Our concerns about being rejected for the third time turned out to be unwarranted. This time there was no need to worry, the article entitled "Ivermectin for Prevention and Treatment of Covid-19 Infection: A Systematic Review, Meta-analysis, and Trial Sequential Analysis to Inform Clinical Guidelines", was published as promised by American Journal of Therapeutics for all to read on June 21st, 2021. (Exhibit 19.)[2] The addition of the trial sequential analysis, statistically demonstrating the point at which accumulated trial data reached a threshold of significance, thereby confirming that further clinical trials of ivermectin for Covid-19 were superfluous, was a streak of genius from Bryant, making the full package a veritable magnum opus.

To say it had been a gruelling marathon to get to this endpoint was an understatement. But we made it, with two certain victories in a single month, what a gift! The journal costs, and indeed our team's wages, were covered by members of the public through donations to our GoFundMe campaign. I am quite certain we would not have got this far without this broad-based and modest financial support. An army, even one comprised of birds, must be able to feed their families. With our scientific review conducted to the highest standards and published, BIRD had something powerful in hand to further the work of rescue. Hooray!

About this, my co-authors note that the situation was that *heaven and earth are out of communion and all things are benumbed. What is above has no relation to what is below and on earth confusion and*

---

1   Hexagram 40, Deliverance, line 1. From I Ching, by Richard Wilhelm, 3rd Ed. p.155.

2   Exhibit 19. Bryant et al, Ivermectin for Prevention and Treatment of Covid-19 Infection: A Systematic Review, Meta-analysis, and Trial Sequential Analysis to Inform Clinical Guidelines (2021).

disorder prevail.[1] In this context, nothing less than sublime success had been achieved. *Here the effects of the light-giving power begin to manifest themselves.*[2] Finally, with this excellent publication, there existed the possibility of exerting real influence, particularly among those who might only believe what they can read in a scientific journal, or newspaper – would mainstream reporters now write about this?

The influence being sought was not a matter of ambition or glory but that of rescue. Thus, despite the victory, *All day long the superior man is creatively active. At nightfall his mind is still beset with cares. Danger. No blame.*[3] *[...]* The *I Ching* observes and cautions, *He who remains in touch with the time that is dawning, and with its demands, is prudent enough to avoid pitfalls, and remains blameless.*[4] This milestone would only intensify our work.

MOVE 32. Sea Turtles Are NICE But Don't Do Much for Covid-19

Keyboard warriors, men and women around the world, as well as our BIRD administrative crew, Linda and Claire, set about sharing the news of our finally published ivermectin review. Linda took charge of emailing country health departments with the document, while Claire focused on urgent follow-up communications with UK authorities. Claire's primary correspondence was with the MHRA, marked as an urgent matter. The message was clear and simple:

"Further to our previous correspondence, please note that the evidence on ivermectin has recently been significantly bolstered by the publication of a gold-standard review, which analysed 24 randomised trials conducted across 15 countries involving more than

1   Hexagram 12, Standstill, The Judgement. From I Ching, by Richard Wilhelm, 3rd Ed. p.52-3.
2   Hexagram 1, The Creative, line 2. From I Ching, by Richard Wilhelm, 3rd Ed. p.8.
3   Hexagram 1, The Creative, line 3. From I Ching, by Richard Wilhelm, 3rd Ed. p.8-9.
4   Hexagram 1, The Creative, line 3. From I Ching, by Richard Wilhelm, 3rd Ed. p.8-9.

3,400 participants. The results demonstrated that ivermectin administration led to a reduction in infections and a dramatic decrease in deaths. This review was published in the American Journal of Therapeutics, with the highest statistical standards applied by world-leading researchers. Dr Tess Lawrie would be happy to discuss the evidence with clinical experts at their convenience."

The response was as predictable as it was frustrating:

"Please note that the WHO has recently issued a guidance note advising that ivermectin should only be used to treat Covid-19 within clinical trials. There is an ongoing clinical trial in the UK evaluating ivermectin for Covid-19, and once adequate, robust evidence of its efficacy and safety is available, it could be authorised. Additionally, the FDA has recently advised that it has not reviewed data supporting the use of ivermectin for Covid-19 treatment or prevention. Taking a drug for an unapproved use can be very dangerous. If you wish to obtain scientific advice on any data you have available, please refer to our website for details."

The absurdity of the situation cannot be overstated. The media was screaming panic, everything seemed so dire, people were dying, only the vaccine could save us, yet we were being referred to the MHRA's website for useless details. Signed by Ella at the MHRA customer service centre, this was not just a faceless reply from a nameless bureaucrat – it was a symbol of the systemic denial we had come to expect. Ella, no doubt, was dispatching hundreds of similar emails a day.

If one devotes himself wholeheartedly to the task of deliverance, he develops so much inner strength from his rectitude that it acts as a weapon against all that is false and low.[1]

---

1   Hexagram 40, Deliverance, line 2. From I Ching, by Richard Wilhelm, 3rd Ed. p.155-6.

Undeterred, Claire followed up extensively with several key figures at the National Institute for Health and Care Excellence (NICE). NICE, as the body responsible for assessing the evidence on Covid-19 therapeutics and issuing treatment guidelines for the NHS, had a clear duty to respond to our concerns. However, despite our professional inquiries with NICE, which began in March and April 2021, its leadership never once engaged with us in meaningful communications. NICE's Program Director, Dr Fiona Glen – a zoologist with a PhD in sea turtles – was, according to correspondence received from Carla Deakin, responsible for NICE's Covid-19 Guidelines.

Originally a biomedical scientist, Deakin, Program Director for Commercial & Managed Access at NICE, acknowledged receipt of our paper and indicated that Glen's team would review the evidence. She also mentioned that Glen was available to discuss the guidelines procedures if needed. We have no idea whether our evidence was ever formally reviewed by NICE. We heard nothing from Glen and at no point did any of the other named NICE civil servants with whom we communicated engage in the substance of the evidence, nor did anyone explain why ivermectin, despite being backed by robust data, was being overlooked as a potential prevention and treatment option.

One thing that Covid-19 revealed was how even well-intentioned, NICE people can inadvertently facilitate terrible things. Dr Glen, clearly a nature lover, though not a medical doctor bound by a Hippocratic Oath to care for patients, perhaps epitomised the many individuals in positions of influence within various government organisations who were simply taken in by the official Covid-19 narrative. These individuals followed orders from unspecified authority figures, acting in good faith but without the skills or insights needed to navigate the Covid-19 minefield. Their lack of experience, medical knowledge, responsibility of care, and critical analysis made them susceptible to being swept along by the tide of government directives.

The NICE website shared that Glen had an interest in equality and human rights, which makes it all the more perplexing that she seemed to turn a blind eye to the obvious injustice at hand; a safe, well-established medicine was being withheld from the British public, while experimental and potentially dangerous drugs were pushed forward. From the details on the NICE website, Fiona Glen appeared to be someone who would have deeply cared about this. NICE was a far cry from working outdoors with sea turtles, which must have been a far simpler and more fulfilling endeavour in comparison.

A lack of discernment to understand the far-reaching consequences of actions and inactions afflicted many in the civil service during Covid-19. If *the beginning is not right, there is no hope of a right ending. If we have missed the right moment for union and go on hesitating to give complete and full devotion, we shall regret the error when it is too late.*[1]

Many of the individuals working at NICE, Glen included, likely had misgivings. Following our correspondence about ivermectin, they were given the opportunity to do the right thing, to prioritise the health and wellbeing of men, women and children. Yet they chose to remain passive, and thereby complicit, not only in the withholding of a life-saving treatment, but in the facilitation of dangerous injections and other novel new drugs. In time, some would likely come to regret their inaction, as the consequences of their decisions became painfully clear. To reassure such people, I would like to add that it is seldom too late to take actions to rectify one's mistakes.

Lastly, the Therapeutics Taskforce (TTF) response was unrepentantly ignorant and coordinated. Upon receiving the latest expert ivermectin evidence from Claire, they dismissed it out of hand, referring us to the WHO's out-of-date recommendation from March 2021 and, not least, to the PRINCIPLE Trial, which had announced afresh, on the 23rd June 2021, that it would add ivermectin to its study interventions.

---

1   Hexagram 8, Holding Together, line 6. From I Ching, by Richard Wilhelm, 3rd Ed. p.39.

The Therapeutics Taskforce is monitoring the data from trials of ivermectin as a treatment for COVID-19. As you mention, on 23 June, the PRINCIPLE trial announced that ivermectin has been added to its platform investigating potential COVID-19 treatments for use in community settings. PRINCIPLE is one of UK Government's national priority platform trials of COVID-19 treatments, and the world's largest currently taking place in community settings looking for treatments at home. We will continue to closely monitor the data that emerges from PRINCIPLE, as well as from further emerging clinical trials worldwide to expand our evidence base on the efficacy of ivermectin in treating COVID-19.

You can find out more about PRINCIPLE's announcement here: Ivermectin to be investigated as a possible treatment for COVID-19 in Oxford's PRINCIPLE trial | University of Oxford

You may have seen that the WHO issued a statement on 31 March 2021 advising that an independent WHO guideline development group has reviewed the current evidence on the use of ivermectin for treating COVID-19 and found that is "inconclusive". The WHO recommendation at this stage is that ivermectin should only be used within clinical trials until more data is available.

With no human name attached to the missive, the email was signed, the 'Therapeutics Taskforce Secretariat'.

Nevertheless, a significant event took place on June 26, 2021, when the UK's Health Secretary, MP Mr Matthew Hancock, a key UK puppet of the globalist agenda, resigned just days after the publication of our review. Clearly contrived, attempts were made to portray his departure as graceful when he admitted to breaching social distancing guidelines by kissing and embracing his aide in his office, which was conveniently captured on CCTV and published by *The Sun* newspaper.

Whilst our efforts to expose the corrupt Covid policies no doubt contributed to his sudden departure, I felt more irritated by his resignation than thankful. His resignation meant little; he would simply be replaced by someone of the same calibre. Such salacious news, combined with regret over his improper conduct, was eagerly consumed by the British public and soon found him a new role on *I'm a Celebrity, Get Me Out of Here*, highlighting the public's obliviousness to the immense harm Hancock had been instrumental in unleashing on British families. As the *I Ching* observes about the public's response: *No matter how lowly he may be, provided he is ready to purify himself, he is accepted.*[1]

The contempt such figures appeared to have for the public was staggering, and real accountability seemed unlikely. On popular television, Hancock attained *a station in which he* could *prove himself fruitful in accomplishment, and as a result, he* gained *recognition,*[2] celebrity status, no less! To do this, however, he needed to show *constant self-abnegation*, and *having achieved this attitude*[3] on the show with a confession and some crocodile tears, he found public support instead of retribution. Hancock's resignation and newfound adoration by the British public demonstrated how the cycle of appointments and resignations would continue, ensuring that no one would be held accountable for the disastrous Covid policies that had unfolded.

MOVE 33. PRINCIPLE Adds Ivermectin (Again)

If you experienced any déjà vu in reading the TTF correspondence above, you're not alone. Just two days after our landmark publication in the *American Journal of Therapeutics*, we learned that the Oxford-led PRINCIPLE Trial had announced the addition of an ivermectin arm – again. This move was clearly another direct response

---

1   Hexagram 50, The Cauldron, line 1. From I Ching, by Richard Wilhelm, 3rd Ed. p.194-5.
2   Hexagram 50, The Cauldron, line 5. From I Ching, by Richard Wilhelm, 3rd Ed. p.196.
3   Hexagram 50, The Cauldron, line 5. From I Ching, by Richard Wilhelm, 3rd Ed. p.196.

to our work, as if they had forgotten they had already announced an ivermectin arm back in January 2021, right after our very first BIRD meeting. It was like the announcement, made so casually on their website, was a fresh revelation.

In the press release, Prof. Chris Butler ironically stated that ivermectin was "a well-known medicine with a good safety profile," yet he claimed that the PRINCIPLE Trial would "generate robust evidence to determine whether there were benefits or harms associated with its use."[1] Essentially, they set out to determine whether a drug, which they knew to be safe, was indeed safe. This was a classic case of doubling down on a narrative that could not afford to acknowledge the growing body of evidence supporting ivermectin's effectiveness.

The flawed protocol itself had not changed materially since the previous February announcement, further undermining any notion of true scientific curiosity or intent. There was no effort to reflect on the accumulated body of evidence or distinguish participants by vaccination status. In addition, enrolment could extend up to 14 days of symptom onset, which was far too late for an anti-viral to have any benefit at all. Upon our request, they refused to disclose their plan for analysis.

Oxford University, which had already demonstrated its willingness to muddy the waters around effective and safe repurposed medicines in favour of promoting the Covid-19 vaccines, had a track record of questionable Covid-19 treatment protocols. This was particularly evident with the RECOVERY Trial, discussed in relation to Prof. Horby's conduct in Chapter 4. Among other re-purposed drugs, the RECOVERY Trial investigated HCQ and, despite a growing body of evidence from clinicians that this well-established medicine was effective in treating Covid-19, was abruptly halted because patients were dying from HCQ overdosing. *The Real Anthony Fauci* is the

---

1   https://www.clinicaltrialsarena.com/news/ivermectin-principle-trial-covid/?cf-view

best book for delving into the details about how HCQ was buried. Meanwhile, Oxford's poker-faced RECOVERY Trial investigators declared that HCQ did not work.

First HCQ, then ivermectin. The entire process felt like a coordinated attempt to suppress safe, effective therapies, regardless of the mounting evidence, in keeping with their paymasters' designs. Oxford University's dubious role in these trials should have raised critical questions, especially when considering the substantial financial ties between the university, the BMGF, and AstraZeneca, all of whom had vested interests in the novel Covid-19 vaccines continuing to be widely deployed.

MOVE 34. How and Whom to Broadcast the News?

We sent our Urgent Yellow Card Report to over 100 journalists across multiple countries, both mainstream and independent. While it was picked up by several independent outlets eager for solid scientific evidence that exposed the truth, we were also fortunate to secure an unsolicited interview with mainstream host Mr Mark Dolan on TalkRadio at NEWS UK Studios. The timing was purely coincidental, TalkRadio had no prior knowledge of our new pharmacovigilance report. They needed a scientist who could speak about the vaccines and, with none of the usual establishment voices available, I received a hastily forwarded email from a Health Advisory & Recovery Team (HART) colleague asking if I could take the slot. I was both delighted and excited.

It was a rare opportunity to reach a broader audience, especially since we had been largely ignored by the mainstream media until then. While TalkRadio was marketed as an alternative to the BBC, it was far from independent, pushing the government narrative about the vaccines. They were seeking a doctor to calm fears about "vaccine hesitancy", a term coined by the needle pushers to stigmatise people with common sense, so the TalkRadio team was certainly in for a surprise getting me for the gig! The interview, which took place on July 14, 2021, was brief, but I felt I made my point clearly, to the viewers at least.

Despite my natural anxiety about interviews, which still stressed me out despite my increasing media experience, I found myself enjoying this one. I felt so grateful to share our information with a wider audience than we'd previously been afforded. I explained our report findings, highlighting that people did not need to take the experimental vaccines because there were alternatives, such as ivermectin. Enduring a pointed question from Mark Dolan about my personal Covid-19 vaccination status, I highlighted the thalidomide tragedy of the 1960s, stressing the importance of paying attention to early warning signals, such as the Yellow Card Scheme data that I had described, and that of applying the precautionary principle.

As if instructed via his earpiece to salvage the situation, Dolan asked, "But surely, Dr Lawrie, given that the vaccine has been distributed around the world in different forms and formulas, it's not comparable to that particular tragedy you mentioned – thalidomide?" I assured him that, in fact, that was the road we were headed down. Nevertheless, at the end of the interview, Dolan overrode my expertise and the data I'd shared live on air, falsely reassuring his audience with "I've got to say, I've had the vaccine, both jabs, and I am confident it's safe."

I am grateful to those who archived this interview, as historic recordings like these, in an age of extreme censorship, have become increasingly difficult to find. On a BitChute channel, I saw the video posted with the description: "Aunty Tess dropping some KNOWL-EDGE on the unwitting vaccine salesmuggle", an amusing yet fitting description of the moment. It was strange, too. Dolan had the opportunity to learn from me, to protect himself from potential harms, yet he chose to dismiss my expertise and what I had shared to help his audience make informed health choices. As a result, he and others like him unwittingly used their influence to undermine me and other independent experts, aligning with the interests of drug companies, billionaire elites, and governments. The role of media personalities in propagating tyranny cannot be understated.

About this particular situation, my ancient co-authors remind us that *If we wish to know whether anyone is superior or not, we need only observe what part of his being he regards as especially important. The body has superior and inferior, important and unimportant parts. We must not injure important parts for the sake of the unimportant, nor must we injure the superior parts for the sake of the inferior. He who cultivates the inferior parts of his nature* – those governed by base instincts or shallow desires – *is an inferior man. He who cultivates the superior parts of his nature* – those rooted in intellect, wisdom, and compassion – *is a superior man.*[1] The *I Ching*'s shared wisdom here is essentially about nourishment, *what a man seeks to fill his own mouth with,* what *part of his being* he values most. Is it the higher faculties, like the critical thinking mind, the capacity for discernment, and the empathy that resides in the heart? Or does one, perhaps unwittingly, place more value on the lower faculties: the sex organs, the mouth (for words and food), and the physical aspects of the skin that represent our immediate, sensory pleasures?

In truth, a willingness to confront and engage with difficult, uncomfortable ideas, those that may challenge deeply held beliefs or require courage to face, reveals much about the higher faculties at play. Valuing the truth, even when it is hard or scary, is what determines the measure of our own integrity and wisdom.

Finally about the TalkRadio interview with Dolan, my co-authors

---

[1] Hexagram 27, The Corners of the Mouth, The Judgement. Excerpt from the Book of Mencius, bk, VI, sec. A, 14. [Mencius lived from 389 to 305 B.C.]. From I Ching, by Richard Wilhelm, 3rd Ed. p.108.

observe that *As a result of misunderstandings, it has become impossible for people who by nature belong together to meet in the correct way. This being so, an accidental meeting under informal circumstances may serve the purpose, provided there is an inner affinity between them.*[1] It is possible that our chance encounter may have had an impact on Mark Dolan after all.

Similar to Dolan, when I enquired about Russell Brand, a British podcaster on YouTube who was widely seen to be exposing various truths, my co-authors observed the following: *Pay heed to the providing of nourishment And to what a man seeks To fill his own mouth with.*[2] *In bestowing care and nourishment, it is important that the right people should be taken care of and that we should attend to our own nourishment in the right way. If we wish to know what anyone is like, we have only to observe on whom he bestows his care and what side of his own nature he cultivates and nourishes.*[3]

Previously a stand-up comedian, Brand's YouTube show had garnered millions of followers, more than 6 million the last time I looked, whom he affectionately referred to as his "awakening wonders." It was obvious that if we had been invited onto his show, it would have catapulted BIRD into the awareness of millions of people in 2021, a visibility we desperately needed. We weren't the only ones who believed this. People frequently told me, "Dr Lawrie, you must get on Russell Brand's show. He's got millions of viewers, and I'm sure he'd love to have you on."

However, it was not for lack of trying. Linda Rae, my BIRD team mate and a dedicated health professional passionate about raising awareness of ivermectin's potential, was a follower of Brand's show. She tried to reach him one way or another, hopeful for a response. It

---

1   Hexagram 38, Opposition, line 2. From I Ching, by Richard Wilhelm, 3rd Ed. p.149.

2   Hexagram 27, The Corners of the Mouth, The Judgement. From I Ching, by Richard Wilhelm, 3rd Ed. p.107-8.

3   Hexagram 27, The Corners of the Mouth, The Judgement. From I Ching, by Richard Wilhelm, 3rd Ed. p.107-8.

was Linda who, working with BIRD, sent out our Joint Statements with the FLCCC to health ministers and heads of state around the world in July and August of 2021, advising them on how to treat Covid-19. (Exhibit 20.)[1]

Over the years of the Covid crisis, I would hear about Brand interviewing many others on topics related to ivermectin, including John Campbell, whom I had personally initiated on the subject, as well as discussions surrounding the WHO, vaccine harms, and other issues that BIRD and EbMCsquared had been pioneering. Yet despite our efforts, none of the attention seemed to acknowledge the foundational work we were doing. It left us feeling somewhat ignored, if not bemused, to see these important subjects discussed with Brand by others without any reference to our contributions. Was he avoiding us and, if so, why?

My co-authors' expanded commentary on Russell Brand, about how we nourish ourselves and where we direct our attention, starts with an observation, or scolding even, that *You let your magic tortoise go.*[2] This depicts *a man fitted by nature and position to live freely and independently,* [yet who] *renounces this self-reliance and instead looks with envy and discontent at others who appear to be in better circumstances.*[3]

Further reflections are offered. *Normally a person either provides his own means of nourishment or is supported in a proper way by those whose duty and privilege it is to provide for him. If owing to weakness of character, a man cannot support himself, a feeling of uneasiness comes over; this is because in shirking the proper way of obtaining a living, he accepts support as a favour from those in higher place. This is unworthy, for he is deviating from his true nature. Kept up indefinitely, this course*

---

1   Exhibit 20. Example of the Joint Country Statement on Ivermectin.

2   Hexagram 27, The Corners of the Mouth, Line 1. From I Ching, by Richard Wilhelm, 3rd Ed. p.108.

3   Hexagram 27, The Corners of the Mouth, Line 1. From I Ching, by Richard Wilhelm, 3rd Ed. p.108.

leads to misfortune.[1] When someone lacks the strength of character to stand on their own and instead seeks support or validation from those in positions of power, they deviate from their true nature. A reliance on external favours, especially when it comes at the cost of self-reliance and truth, ultimately leads to unease and misfortune according to my co-authors. Brand's failure to acknowledge the foundational work of groups like ours could be perceived as a sign of weakness or a deviation from a path that truly serves the higher good.

He who seeks nourishment that does not nourish reels from desire to gratification and in gratification craves desire. Mad pursuit of pleasure for the satisfaction of the senses never brings one to the goal. One should never follow this path, for nothing good can come of it.[2] This passage suggests that someone in a prominent position, like Brand, would be better off using their influence for the collective good rather than seeking validation, popularity, or praise for selfish reasons. It underscores the importance of aligning one's actions with a higher purpose, working not just for personal benefit but for the wellbeing of others with a sense of duty.

With his high profile and large platform, Brand had the potential to be of great service to mankind. This potential is ever present – *if one is occupying a high position and striving to let his light shine forth. [...] Since he is not working for himself but for the good of all, there is no wrong in such zeal.*[3] Thus, again, my co-authors emphasise that there is no blame in following a noble path that brings benefit to others.

However, individuals with celebrity status, like Brand, may be well aware of their limitations. *A man may be conscious of a deficiency in himself. He should be undertaking the nourishment of people, but*

1　Hexagram 27, The Corners of the Mouth, line 2. From I Ching, by Richard Wilhelm, 3rd Ed. p.109.

2　Hexagram 27, The Corners of the Mouth, line 3. From I Ching, by Richard Wilhelm, 3rd Ed. p.109-110.

3　Hexagram 27, The Corners of the Mouth, line 4. From I Ching, by Richard Wilhelm, 3rd Ed. p.110.

he has not the strength to do it. Thus he must turn from his accustomed path and beg counsel and help from a man who is spiritually his superior but undistinguished outwardly. If he manifests this attitude of mind perseveringly, success and good fortune are his. But he must remain aware of his dependence. He must not put his own person forward nor attempt great labours, such as crossing the great waters.[1] In the context of someone in a position of influence, such as Brand, this commentary suggests that if one was unable to carry out the nourishment or guidance he was meant to offer, whether due to a lack of understanding, strength, or spiritual clarity, he should seek assistance from someone who has the knowledge necessary, even if that person is not outwardly distinguished or well-known. The lesson here is that humility and recognition of one's own weaknesses are essential. It's not wrong to seek counsel from someone who might be less visible in the public eye but more spiritually or intellectually aligned with the higher goals of truth and service. By doing this, Russell Brand, and others like him, would be on the path to success and good fortune, especially in terms of spiritual growth and self-fulfilment.

Finally, my co-authors suggest an ideal worth striving for is to be *a sage of the highest order, from whom emanates all influences that provide nourishment for others. Such a position brings with it heavy responsibility. [...] These undertakings bring general happiness for him and for all others.*[2] By serving others selflessly and fulfilling a higher calling, one not only contributes to the general good but also experiences personal fulfilment. Thus, one's own happiness becomes inseparable from the happiness of those one serves.

Phew. My co-authors certainly offered a lot to think about when it comes to influencers like Brand who like to lead!

---

1   Hexagram 27, The Corners of the Mouth, line 5. From I Ching, by Richard Wilhelm, 3rd Ed. p.110.

2   Hexagram 27, The Corners of the Mouth, line 6. From I Ching, by Richard Wilhelm, 3rd Ed. p.110-11.

Meanwhile, Dr Bret Weinstein with his *Dark Horse* podcast stepped forward with an invitation from across the Atlantic to speak about our ivermectin review in early August 2021. Cautious and intellectually curious by nature, he and his wife Heather, both evolutionary biologists, had chosen not to take the Covid-19 vaccines. No stranger to going against the herd, in 2017 they had found themselves mired in controversy when they had objected to an official event that in effect formalised racial segregation at Evergreen State College. In the business of closely examining scientific evidence on their podcast, in the case of the experimental Covid-19 vaccines, they found there was not much and, as such, remained sceptical. On the other hand, there was a mountain of evidence on ivermectin, which they duly noted, and it is with much gratitude that BIRD's efforts were highlighted to their growing and questioning audience. At this time, one could not mention the word 'ivermectin' on YouTube, so their engagement in this no-go topic was brave indeed.

My co-authors note that the situation in 2021 required people to persevere in search of the truth, much like the heavenly bodies that maintain their steady orbits. *So, likewise the dedicated man embodies an enduring meaning in his way and life.[1] The laws governing nature endure. Whilst the actions of the wind and thunder are not fixed, the laws governing their movements are. In the same way the independence of the superior man is not based on rigidity and immobility of character. He always keeps abreast of the time and changes with it. What endures is the unswerving directive, the inner law of his being, which determines all his actions.[2]* This approach accurately summed up Weinstein, who was anchored by his integrity. His unwavering principles allowed him to navigate diverse situations, adapting his approach while remaining steadfast to the core values that guided him.

---

1   Hexagram 32, Duration, The Judgement. From I Ching, by Richard Wilhelm, 3rd Ed. p.126-7.

2   Hexagram 32, Duration, The Image. From I Ching, by Richard Wilhelm, 3rd Ed. p.127.

As a regular viewer of the *Dark Horse* podcast, I felt that I could have helped Bret reach his conclusions quicker as, in 2021, he seemed innocent to the bigger globalist agenda. My co-authors agree that *There might be an opportunity of surreptitiously easing the way, [...] but a self-contained man scorns help gained in a dubious fashion. He thinks it more graceful to go on foot than to drive in a carriage under false pretences.*[1] In the end, Bret and Heather reached the same destination as me and many others. I developed a great respect for this erudite couple, who were committed to their slow and sound approach.

Over time, clearly affected by the downfall of academia, a foundation stone of their worldview, they began to appreciate us as potential allies. My co-authors highlight that *at first it may be disappointing to renounce comforts that might have been obtained, yet one finds peace of mind in a true relationship with the friend who courts him.*[2] Thus we are reminded that, during the Covid chapter, people often had to choose between historic allegiances and genuine relationships that offered authentic support.

Covid content that filled me with dismay whenever I tuned in, was that produced by Dr John Campbell, the increasingly more popular YouTube nurse educator, especially with regard to the Covid-19 vaccines. The interview I had with Campbell on the ivermectin evidence had been such a great boost months earlier. Clearly, he had taken a risk by giving it a platform. Of course, I understood the challenges he faced, particularly with the draconian censorship and controlled narrative surrounding the vaccines, and I could appreciate why he might hesitate to highlight their associated risks. However, what I couldn't understand was why he was effectively promoting and endorsing them, despite the evidence and concerns I had shared with him, including our MHRA Yellow Card Report.

---

1   Hexagram 22, Grace, line 1. From I Ching, by Richard Wilhelm, 3rd Ed. p.91-2.
2   Hexagram 22, Grace, line 4. From I Ching, by Richard Wilhelm, 3rd Ed. p.92.

On one particular occasion, I directly asked Campbell where he had sourced his information that vaccines resulted in less severe symptoms if one contracted a Covid infection. This was a highly dubious claim, unsupported by independent scientific data. His response was disappointing: he was relying on various government claims and a certain Dr Tim Spector. A prominent TV Covid-19 expert, Spector was also founder of the ZOE Covid Symptom Study app, and widely seen as a spokesperson for the government-promulgated narrative. Spector's hasty dismissal of ivermectin and his unwavering promotion of the experimental Covid-19 vaccines raised significant concerns about his objectivity.

I discovered that, in August 2020, the UK's Department of Health and Social Care (DHSC), chaired by Mr Jeremy Hunt, awarded a £2 million grant for the app to Spector, who was also a Professor of Genetic Epidemiology at King's College London. Additional funding was provided in June 2021, the same time as our report to the MHRA. Thus, his profiting from government-funded pandemic projects cast serious doubt on Spector's ability to be impartial, and I was surprised that Campbell did not see Spector's potential conflict of interest.

As such, the influence of individuals like Campbell and Spector, who effectively endorsed the Covid-19 vaccines, led to a significant standstill in our efforts to raise public awareness and protect the public from the Covid-19 vaccines. As much as I valued Campbell's support on ivermectin, not only was it tremendously frustrating to hear non-science promulgated by such an influential educator on health, but it was also traumatic, akin to the powerlessness of watching a train crash every time he went on air to speak about the vaccines. I could not reconcile his endorsement of the vaccines with his reassurances to me that he appreciated my time and expertise whenever he reached out about ivermectin matters.

My co-authors illuminate that *Inferior people are ready to flatter their superiors in a servile way. They would also endure the superior man if he would put an end to their confusion. This is fortunate for them. But the great man calmly bears the consequences of the standstill. He does not mingle with the crowd of the inferior; that is not his place. By his willingness to suffer personally he ensures the success of his fundamental principles.*[1]

About the prevailing situation my co-authors observe *Within are the inferior, and without are superior. The way of inferior people is in ascent; The way of superior people is on the decline.*[2] Was Campbell, like others, receiving commissions to prevent "vaccine hesitancy", I wondered? Was he seduced by his rapidly growing online influence as a credible spokesperson on Covid-19 that he followed the government narrative, instead of asking for the evidence of safety and efficacy? Or perhaps cognitive dissonance took hold of him, as it did with so many people and it was this that prevented him from recognising the dangers of the experimental genetic injections? It is indeed challenging to reconcile the rollout of potentially dangerous vaccines with the belief in a fundamentally benign government.

Whatever the case, my co-authors don't doubt that he furthered the confusion and disorder of the time. *When owing to the influence of inferior men, mutual mistrust prevails in public life, fruitful activity is rendered impossible because the fundamentals are wrong.*[3]

Positioned as a trustworthy voice on Covid-19 matters, Campbell accumulated a substantial YouTube following. As Confucius warns, *Dangers arise when a man feels secure in his position. Destruction threatens when a man seeks to preserve his worldly estate.*[4] With influential and seemingly authentic individuals like Campbell among

1   Hexagram 12, Standstill, line 2. From I Ching, by Richard Wilhelm, 3rd Ed. p.54.
2   Hexagram 12, Standstill, The Judgement. From I Ching, by Richard Wilhelm, 3rd Ed. p.52-3.
3   Hexagram 12, Standstill, The Image. From I Ching, by Richard Wilhelm, 3rd Ed. p.53.
4   Hexagram 12, Standstill, line 5. From I Ching, by Richard Wilhelm, 3rd Ed. p.55.

the foremost authorities from whom many sought clarification and reassurance in an incredibly confusing Covid landscape, it became impossible for us to break through to the mass public. People, many health professionals included, hung on Campbell's every reassuring word and shared his videos widely.

Whilst years later Campbell would apologise for misinforming the public about the safety of the Covid-19 vaccines, for millions the damage was done. His delay in acknowledging the consequences of his public endorsements left many feeling betrayed. However, my co-authors explain that even in such situations, there is a turning point. *Inferior people who have risen to power illegitimately do not feel equal to the responsibility they have taken upon themselves. In their hearts they begin to feel ashamed, although at first they do not show it outwardly. This marks a turn for the better.[1]* Thus, it is in Campbell's reflection and apology that growth and redemption could begin, leading to more responsible actions in the future, one hopes.

On the matter of deliverance and of fair-weather friends, my co-authors' urge, *When the time of deliverance draws near, with its call to deeds, a man must free himself from such chance acquaintances with whom he has no inner connection. For otherwise the friends who share his views, on whom he could really rely and together with whom he could accomplish something, mistrust him and stay away.[2]* This insight served as a poignant reminder that in times of significant action or change, it is essential to distance oneself from those whose loyalties are superficial or contingent on convenience. Genuine allies, those with shared values and principles, will recognise the integrity of one's actions and remain steadfast. However, those who have only been companions in more comfortable times may falter when the situation becomes more challenging, revealing the importance of cultivating

---

1   Hexagram 12, Standstill, line 3. From I Ching, by Richard Wilhelm, 3rd Ed. p.54.
2   Hexagram 40, Deliverance, line 4. From I Ching, by Richard Wilhelm, 3rd Ed. p.156-7.

authentic, meaningful relationships based on mutual respect and purpose for times such as these.

THE IMAGE
Thunder and rain set in:
The image of deliverance.
That's the superior man pardons mistakes
And forgives misdeeds.

A thunderstorm has the effect of clearing the air; the superior man produces a similar effect when dealing with the mistakes and sins of men that induce a condition of tension. Through clarity he brings deliverance. However, when failings come to light, he does not dwell on them; he simply passes over mistakes, the unintentional transgressions, just as thunder dies away. He forgives misdeeds, the intentional transgressions, just as water washes everything clean.[1]

These last words from my wise co-authors about deliverance are firm and reassuring. If we are to strive to be *superior* men, we should not dwell on mistakes of others but, rather, help to clear the air, offering clarity on the situation and renewal. Like a thunderstorm clearing the skies, we should help dissolve tension to allow everyone to move forward. We should forgive misdeeds, not to excuse them, but instead to create space for growth and healing, freeing our own hearts from despair and judgement, and individuals from the weight of their past actions.

---

[1] Hexagram 40, Deliverance, The Image. From I Ching, by Richard Wilhelm, 3rd Ed. p.155.

Chapter 7

Peace

PEACE. The small departs,
The great approaches.
Good fortune. Success.[1]

Here the small, weak, and evil elements are about to take their
departure, while the great, strong, and good elements are moving
up. This brings good fortune and success.[2]

As my co-authors suggest, in times of change, the forces of good
rise and the forces of evil fade. After our dual publications in June,
we began to feel the shift in our favour. The attention we drew
from our critics following the delivery of two significant pieces of
work, one on ivermectin and the other on the Covid-19 vaccine
harms, was clear proof that we were making an impact. One could
almost feel the hired hands scrambling to regroup and re-strategize
in response to the nuisance posed by BIRD, Dr Tess Lawrie – a

---

1   Hexagram 11, Peace, The Judgement. From I Ching, by Richard Wilhelm, 3rd Ed. p.48.
2   Hexagram 11, Peace, The Judgement. From I Ching, by Richard Wilhelm, 3rd Ed. p.48.

WHO consultant of good standing but a nobody in essence – and EbMCsquared, our vehicle for great change.

Thus, we benefited from a brief period of reprieve, during which we attracted the interest of some prominent activists both abroad and at home. One of these individuals was Mr Robert F. Kennedy Jr of the Children's Health Defense organisation, whose high-profile advocacy for public health and children's rights brought a significant boost to our cause. The other was retired Metropolitan police officer Mr Mark Sexton, whose commitment to exposing the truth about Covid-19 and its related policies spearheaded various initiatives in the UK targeting the law enforcement community. Together, their support lent us credibility and helped us retain equilibrium against the mounting opposition.

With the ivermectin review publication in hand, we ramped up our efforts to get ivermectin approved in the UK – we now had a tangible product that could substantiate our cause. Regulatory consultant Mr Hedley Rees took charge of negotiating with a Bulgarian ivermectin producer, Huwepharma, a company primarily focused on veterinary applications, but which had also conducted a promising study on ivermectin's efficacy against Covid-19 symptoms. While these talks were a critical part of our strategy and the effort costly, they would eventually break down, leaving us with little to show for these efforts in the long run.

Anticipating the spurious attacks that followed from pharma-funded academics, the brilliant Drs Fordham and Bryant got to work preparing the rebuttals, firing them off at an awe-inspiring rate. It was particularly gratifying however, to see our ivermectin initiative grow stronger as legal challenges were initiated and supported around the world by our efforts.

Nevertheless, following the publication of our robust scientific ivermectin article, and letting the UK's MHRA know that the experimental vaccines were not fit for human use, there was a brief period where we felt like we were in the eye of the storm, untouchable, shielded from the fierce winds of opposition. During this time, it seemed as if our position had been solidified, and we were given a window of relative peace with effective tools to continue advocating for our cause. In addition, we were able to make meaningful contributions to, and amplify, the efforts of others raising awareness of Covid-19 crimes and its culprits.

MOVE 35. The Metropolitan Police Are Informed

Have you ever wondered why police officers were so silent during the Covid-19 crisis? Why did they fail to defend individuals against what many saw as tyrannical mandates and policies? This question troubled me deeply, particularly as I observed the widespread compliance of law enforcement with government directives that seemed to violate fundamental rights and freedoms. Amidst this silence, however, there was one notable exception: Mr Mark Sexton, a retired police officer who courageously spoke out against the corrupt policies surrounding Covid-19 in the UK. For several months, I had been following his efforts, and I was heartened to learn that he had decided to take further action by laying a formal complaint against British parliamentarians with the Metropolitan Police.

Sexton's decision to challenge the politicians represented a rare act of courage from within this profession, like the doctors I suppose, that had, largely, complied with unlawful directives. When Sexton asked for an expert testimony I felt compelled to support him. In response, I prepared an email to Superintendent Pete Hill, with a CC to his police colleague Debbie Tedds. This email was a formal submission, providing evidence to support the complaint. I included five key documents that I believed would make a compelling introduction:

1. **The BIRD proceedings document** with ivermectin recommendations, highlighting its efficacy and safety for Covid-19 treatment.

2. **The MHRA report**, detailing the high numbers of vaccine injury cases reported to the UK's yellow Card scheme.

3. **The Bryant-Lawrie et al ivermectin review**, which provided a high-quality peer-reviewed analysis of ivermectin's benefit for Covid-19 symptoms.

4. **The submission to Parliament**, which laid out the urgent need for transparency and accountability with regard to ivermectin and the Covid-19 shots.

5. **The expert paper by Seneff and Nigh**, which detailed the risks associated with mRNA vaccine biotechnology, further illustrating the dangers posed by the government-endorsed vaccine rollouts.

I crafted this submission not only as a support for Sexton's efforts but as a call to action for the police to consider their duty to the public, rather than unquestioning compliance with government directives. The hope was that, with evidence in hand, the Superintendent and others in his team might reconsider their stance and begin to act in the public's best interests, as law enforcement is meant to do in times of moral and social crisis.

From: Dr Tess Lawrie
Subject: In support of Mark Sexton's allegations of Misconduct and Misfeasance
Date: 24 June 2021 at 10:57:21 BST
To: Superintendent Pete Hill
Cc: Debbie Tedds

Dear Detective Superintendent Hill,

My name is Dr Tess Lawrie and I am a medical doctor and research consultant based in Bath, UK. My professional qualifications are MBBCh, PhD. As the Director of the Evidence-based Medicine Consultancy (E-BMC) Limited and EbMCsquared, a Community interest research Company, I am committed to improving the quality of health and health care through rigorous independent research. The World Health Organization has been one of E-BMC Limited's clients since 2012. Because we have no conflicts of interest, our work is highly valued. In addition, my personal ResearchGate score is among the top 5% of ResearchGate scientists and my work is highly cited.

I am making contact with you with regards to the criminal complaint of Misconduct and Misfeasance in public office made against Members of Parliament by Mr. Mark Sexton. I would like to make you aware of the following as I believe this supports Mr. Sexton's assertions and validates a number of the allegations he is making.

On January 4th, 2021, I sent an urgent communication to the UK government (Mr Matt Hancock, and others) regarding an old generic medicine called ivermectin. After reviewing the evidence on ivermectin for Covid-19, I concluded in the report that deploying ivermectin against Covid-19 would have a dramatic effect on the pandemic as the evidence showed that it was effective and safe in treating and preventing Covid-19. Currently, there is no effective anti-viral treatment approved by the government for Covid-19, and a special task force has been put together to find early treatments. This is ridiculous, as a safe early treatment already exists, and the government has been informed of this. As mentioned, ivermectin is a generic medicine, it costs pennies to make and many pharmaceutical companies can make it. It's on the

World Health Organization's list of essential medicines because it's been such a useful medicine over the decades and its developers won a Nobel Prize for it in 2015. There is therefore little profit to be made from this medicine unlike the novel therapies in which the government has invested. Remdesivir, made by Gilead, costs around £3,000, and is approved for use in the UK with very little evidence that it works and serious safety concerns. ivermectin costs around 50p.

The evidence that I have supplied to the government and their Agencies over the past 6 months has been consistently ignored. This has been surprising to me as I expected that they would have been very interested in this safe and effective low cost medicine. I have since become aware that key figures in government had already been informed about ivermectin's promise last year. In addition, Prof. Chris Whitty has extensively studied ivermectin in his career and even wrote a paper in 2010 highlighting how safe this low-cost medicine is for widespread use in malaria areas. When thousands of people were dying every day, they couldn't give this safe cheap old medicine a go in the interest of saving lives. As it is most widely used as a de-worming medicine, the worst that would have happened would have been that the population would be worm-free.

Not only has the MHRA failed to approve ivermectin, despite the rapid approval of several experimental therapies, the MHRA has also been stating in communications that using ivermectin could be dangerous.

This is a table from the WHO's vigiaccess.org pharmacovigilance database as of today:

Data retrieved from Vigiaccess.org (24.6.2021)			
Medicine	Year reporting started	Deaths	ADR reports
Ivermectin	1992	20	5,484
Remdesivir	2020	534	6,707
Covid-19 vaccine	2020	6,667	1,198,200

Clearly, the new treatments approved under EUAs appear far more dangerous.

Which brings me to my next point: I have independently analysed the Yellow Card Data on the government's website and submitted an urgent preliminary report to Dr June Raine, head of the MHRA. In the report I conclude that an urgent cessation of vaccine programme is needed. "The MHRA now has more than enough evidence on the Yellow Card system to declare the Covid-19 vaccines unsafe for use in humans. Preparation should be made to scale up humanitarian efforts to assist those harmed by the Covid-19 vaccines and to anticipate and ameliorate medium to longer-term effects. As the mechanism for harms from the vaccines appears to be similar to Covid-19 itself, this includes engaging with numerous international doctors and scientists with expertise in successfully treating Covid-19."

My work on the Yellow Card data is continuing and an updated report should be ready by the end of next week. I have not received a reply from Dr Raine.

As a professional in the medical field I feel it is incumbent upon me to support Mark Sexton's assertions that the government of the United Kingdom must now be aware of the damage the vaccines are causing. These vaccines are still being evaluated in clinical trials that are due to be completed in 2023. As they are being rolled out ahead of the completion of these trials, extra-special vigilance needs to be paid to adverse drug reactions – and this pharmacovigilance needs to occur independently of the manufacturers and those with vested interests in the success of the vaccine programme.

Had ivermectin been employed against Covid-19 last year or, at the latest, upon receipt of my report on the 4th of January, many deaths and much suffering could have been avoided. In addition, a re-evaluation of the Emergency Use Authorisations of the vaccines and other novel therapies rushed through the approval process would have been required, as EUAs are only appropriate if there is no effective treatment for Covid-19.

I include in this email copies of the reports that I have sent to the relevant UK authorities, and other information that may be of interest. You will find further information on ivermectin at www. bird-group.org, a crowdfunded initiative that is supporting our efforts to get ivermectin into use in the UK.

I am willing to provide all of the evidence, correspondence with government, and my professional expertise and knowledge to form part of your criminal investigation into the Misconduct and Misfeasance in public office by members of Parliament. I am available via email as above or on xxxxx xxxxxx should you wish to discuss the content of this email.

Kind regards,

Dr Tess Lawrie

Director

C: EBMC Ltd /EbMCsquared CIC and BIRD Group

I cannot recall whether I received a brief acknowledgment from Superintendent Pete Hill regarding my submission, neither can I locate it in my inbox. Despite this, the *I Ching* offers an intriguing perspective on Superintendent Hill's potential mindset at the time, which may explain his response – or lack thereof. The insights suggest that the Superintendent may have been sympathetic to his retired colleague's case.

My co-authors comment, *He is oppressed by creeping vines. He moves uncertainly and says, "movement brings remorse". If one feels remorse over this and makes a start, good fortune comes.*[1] Thus Superintendent Hill, being described as being *oppressed by creeping vines*, was moving uncertainly, and experiencing a sense of paralysis: *movement brings remorse*, indicating a person caught between fear of taking decisive action and the regret of remaining inactive.

This is further explained as *A man is oppressed by bonds that can easily be broken. The distress is drawing to an end. But he is still resolute; he is still influenced by the previous condition and fears that he may have cause for regret if he makes a move. But as soon as he grasps the situation, changes this mental attitude, and makes a firm decision, he masters the oppression.*[2]

In essence, the Superintendent's hesitation seems not due to a lack of capability but rather a mental state of indecision. Had he adjusted his attitude and taken firm action, he could have gained mastery over the situation and been empowered to do the right thing – act for the people he had promised to serve once upon a time. It serves as a reminder that, even when the truth is clear, the courage to confront it head-on can be stifled by personal fears and external pressures – pressures which, once recognised, can be overcome with decisive action. Thus, the *I Ching*'s insights into Superintendent Hill's perspective

---

1   Hexagram 47, Exhaustion, line 6. From I Ching, by Richard Wilhelm, 3rd Ed. p.184-5.
2   Hexagram 47, Exhaustion, line 6. From I Ching, by Richard Wilhelm, 3rd Ed. p.184-5.

suggests that while the Metropolitan Police Superintendent may have been sympathetic to Sexton's case, he did not had the inner strength to do what was called for in the circumstances – his inability to act was rooted in internal conflict and fear of repercussions.

I wonder how many policemen and women's conduct during Covid-19 could be explained in the same way? If only they realised their collective power and remembered their undertaking to serve real people instead of corporations, what a benefit they could be in service to their fellow man against the dark forces pitted against us all.

It seems fitting to reflect on this wisdom by my ancient co-authors from the *Peace* hexagram at this point: *Everything on earth is subject to change. Prosperity is followed by decline: this is the eternal law on earth. Evil can indeed be held in check but not permanently abolished. It always returns. This conviction might induce melancholy, but it should not; it ought only to keep us from falling into illusion when good fortune comes to us. If we continue mindful of the danger, we remain persevering and make no mistakes. As long as a man's inner nature remains stronger and richer than anything offered by external fortune, as long as he remains inwardly superior to fate, fortune will not desert him.*[1]

This passage speaks to the cyclical nature of human affairs, where good and evil are in a constant and inevitable flux. It's a reminder that while we may triumph over evil in the moment, the struggle is never truly over. Police men and women, as a body, could have played a significant role in challenging the dark forces that sought to divide and control us during the corrupt Covid-19 agenda. But instead, many allowed fear and external pressure to suppress their moral compass. The lesson, as the *I Ching* suggests, is that because nothing stays the same we must remain vigilant and aligned with our inner strength, for it is only by staying true to ourselves that we can overcome external trials and be a force for good in the world.

---

[1] Hexagram 11, Peace, line 3. From I Ching, by Richard Wilhelm, 3rd Ed. p.50-1.

MOVE 36. Dr Andrew Hill's Review Take Two

Yes, there does seem to be a preponderance of Hills in this story! On July 6th, 2021, two weeks after our publication, Dr Andrew Hill finally published his ivermectin review in a journal called Open Forum Infectious Diseases. Now featuring a peer review and 10 authors instead of 40, on the back of our expert review, this came as no surprise. Though this was clearly an attempt to reclaim and control the ivermectin narrative, the review findings surprisingly concurred with ours – when given for moderate and severe Covid-19 symptoms, ivermectin reduced death by 56% in Hill's review. Out of 128 people who died, 3% of people on ivermectin died compared to 9% of those who did not. Additionally, ivermectin was linked to faster recovery and shorter hospital stays. Although still suggesting that their results "need to be validated in larger confirmatory trials" (which they most certainly did not!), it was a relief that the findings were positive. People could use their common sense now and decide for themselves whether taking a safe old medicine that reduced the risk of death from Covid-19 was a good idea or not. I wrote to Hill to thank him for this improved rendering of the evidence, even though he was still calling for more trials.

With Hill still a pawn in the globalist agenda in my opinion, did this represent a change of heart? My co-authors note approvingly, *Perseverence in such conduct will bring good fortune.*[1] Hill, though still under the influence of larger forces (evident in the call for more trials), had exhibited a degree of integrity in the findings this time, which contributed positively to the larger conversation.

There were, however, several curiosities associated with the paper. For example, the review had a new funder. Instead of Unitaid, which had funded the previous version with an "unlimited research grant" ostensibly on behalf of the WHO, this updated review – with similar

---

1   Hexagram 16, Enthusiasm, line 2. From I Ching, by Richard Wilhelm, 3rd Ed. p.70.

content as the original – was supported by a Texas-based group called The Rainwater Foundation (which also funded the TOGETHER Trial along with the BMGF). We wondered whether the change of funder was an attempt to distance the review from associations with organisations and individuals whose ties could be viewed as problematic, such as Prof. Andrew Owen, who ran Liverpool University's Centre of Excellence for Long-Acting Therapeutics (CELT), a beneficiary of Unitaid millions.

Not everyone was pleased with Hill's improved review though. After Dr Hill's review was published, a Dr David Boulware of the University of Minnesota was quoted in the press as saying: "Of course, rolling out vaccination as quickly and widespread as possible would negate the need to use ivermectin as a treatment," and, "So big picture, vaccines are the better solution."[1] The gist of his argument was: who needs safe and effective ivermectin when we have new and experimental Covid-19 vaccines?

It is difficult for ordinary human beings like me to comprehend what motivates scientists who pushed novel vaccines with full knowledge of their experimental design. Surely, one would have to feel very little empathy for one's fellow man?

The *I Ching's* advice, *Influence over others should not express itself as a conscious and willed effort to manipulate them,*[2] speaks directly to the ethical dimensions of such conduct. A strong push for experimental genetic vaccines and disregard for alternative treatments like ivermectin reflect a form of influence that is not rooted in open, unbiased dialogue but in a rigid, directed effort to sway others to his viewpoint, regardless of evidence to the contrary. True influence should come from wisdom and clarity, not from an agenda-driven desire to control outcomes. Thus, if such influence was driven by the

---

1   https://www.medpagetoday.com/special-reports/exclusives/93485
2   Hexagram 31, Influence, line 4. From I Ching, by Richard Wilhelm, 3rd Ed. p.124-5.

promotion of an agenda that benefitted the wider globalist effort at the expense of people's health, it speaks to a form of manipulation that is both misguided and ethically questionable.

What do my co-authors say about the inner world of individuals who seem to wish harm upon people? *When an individual discovers within himself the beginnings of alienation from others, of misanthropy and ill humour, he must set about dissolving these obstructions. He must rouse himself inwardly, hasten to that which supports him. Such support is never found in hatred, but always in a moderate and just judgement of men, linked with good will. If he regains this unobstructed outlook on humanity, while at the same time all saturnine ill humour is dissolved, all occasion for remorse disappears.*[1] Thus, the darkness of self-righteousness and single-mindedness may cloud the capacity of such individuals for empathy toward others, and so they judge others harshly. If they could transcend these inner barriers, they would find a more harmonious, compassionate connection with the people around them, and with the broader world at large.

MOVE 37. Mr Robert F. Kennedy Jr Wants to Know About Ivermectin

An extremely positive consequence of Dr Hill's new publication was that I became connected with Mr Robert F. Kennedy Jr by US paediatrician, Dr Meryl Nass, who worked with Kennedy's health advocacy organisation, Children's Health Defense (CHD). At the time I was only vaguely familiar with RFK Jr's efforts to hold the pharmaceutical industry to account on behalf of parents and their vaccine-injured children. However, like most of the world, I remained intrigued by the assassination of his uncle, US President John F. Kennedy in 1963. The undisclosed high-level involvement in President Kennedy's killing continued to conjure up unsettling

---

1   Hexagram 59, Dispersion, line 2. From I Ching, by Richard Wilhelm, 3rd Ed. p.229.

feelings in my heart, much like the death of Princess Diana in 1997.

A quick discussion with my co-authors suggests that JFK's relationship with the globalists was not a happy one. By way of description, the *I Ching* uses the metaphor of a young girl under the guidance of an older man who marries her. It was apparently common in ancient China that a man would have a chief wife, as well as a discreet younger woman who would fulfil certain other needs. *A girl who is taken into the family, but not as the chief wife, must behave with special caution and reserve. She must not take it upon herself to supplant the mistress of the house, for this would mean disorder and lead to untenable relationships.*[1] This suggests to me that JFK refused to kowtow to the globalists' guidance. When he started demonstrating independent leadership, distinct from those used to exerting control from the shadows, this had deadly consequences for him.

Albeit still subsumed by "conspiracy theory" rhetoric, the Kennedy name had considerable weight. Thus, it was our extreme good fortune that JFK's nephew, Robert F. Kennedy Jr, was engaging with interest on the ivermectin issue, and I was pleased to help him. *In times of prosperity every able man called to fill an office draws like-minded people along with him.*[2] Bobby Kennedy's dedication to exposing corporate malfeasance and standing up for the rights of those harmed by vaccines with CHD aligned perfectly with the work we were doing through EbMCsquared. His genuine concern for public health, coupled with his legal background and interests in holding Covid-19 culprits to account, made our collaboration in the second half of 2021 a powerful moment in the ongoing fight for truth and justice.

After explaining the situation with Dr Hill, how we had been let down in January 2021 when Hill published his problematic review, and what had transpired during the Zoom meeting we had together,

---

1   Hexagram 54, The Marrying Maiden, The Judgement. From I Ching, by Richard Wilhelm, 3rd Ed. p.209.

2   Hexagram 11, Peace, line 1. From I Ching, by Richard Wilhelm, 3rd Ed. p.49-50.

I met virtually with Kennedy and his legal team a few times. I found him to be affable and forthright with an air of serious intent. His team seemed like a nice bunch, and creative in the exploration of the options available for collaboration. I learned that CHD was preparing a lawsuit challenging the suppression of ivermectin and other repurposed medicines in the USA, and they were also in active discussions with several American state Attorney Generals. Our support in terms of expertise was requested, and we provided it freely.

My co-authors say of this supportive collaboration, *in times of mutual confidence, people of high rank come in close contact with the lowly quite simply and without boasting of their wealth. This is not due to the force of circumstances but corresponds with the inmost sentiment. The approach is made quite spontaneously, because it is based on inner conviction.*[1] In case you're in any doubt, I am the *lowly* referred to in this commentary, in an unlikely encounter with someone of *high rank* – Kennedy. It was true that there were great differences between us with regard to status and possession, yet I felt quite comfortable at all times during these respectful and productive discussions.

We sent over everything we had, including our evidence pack, gold standard ivermectin review article, as well as rebuttals published in defence of our paper. I also shared the recording of that January 2021 Lawrie-Hill Zoom meeting along with the transcript. The USA team were astonished that the moment exposing how the science on ivermectin had been corrupted had been captured on record. From their lawyers' perspective, Hill's reactions demonstrated so clearly his discomfort at the deceit. When Kennedy asked if he could publish the transcript of the meeting in his upcoming book *The Real Anthony Fauci*, I agreed. It was a relief to get the information into the public domain at last. *Here we are shown a truly modest union of high and low*

---

1   Hexagram 11, Peace, line 4. From I Ching, by Richard Wilhelm, 3rd Ed. p.51.

that brings happiness and blessings.[1]

Nevertheless, my openness was not without risk. Kennedy's team suggested I get legal advice and gave me the name of a "good lawyer" in the UK who deals with such matters. However, when I received the first bill for a brief consultation, I realised this was another area in which I would just need to trust that things would be okay in the end. The legal system with its extortionate costs was not for the defence of ordinary people like me. I would continue to accept that the pursuit of truth and justice required a leap of faith, even in the face of financial and professional risks. The cost of silence was far greater than the price of standing firm in the face of adversity, as the growing number of vaccine-injured people daily would remind me.

Thankfully, Kennedy would subsequently be a great spokesman for the case of ivermectin. Having a reach that we could only dream of, he would three years later go on the Joe Rogan Show, a popular US podcast, to highlight the high-level Covid-19 corruption, including why ivermectin had to be suppressed by dark forces trying to control the Covid-19 narrative. For millions of viewers, Kennedy would spell it out, "They had to discredit ivermectin because there is a federal law. The Federal Emergency Use Authorisation Statute says that you cannot issue an emergency use authorisation to a vaccine if there is an existing medication that has been approved for any purpose, that has been demonstrated that is effective against the target illness. So they had to destroy ivermectin and hydroxychloroquine and discredit it. And they had to tell everybody that it's not effective because if they had acknowledged that it was effective in anybody, the whole $200 billion dollar vaccine enterprise would have collapsed."[2]

Further to this, even more good work came from this collaboration. We learned from Kennedy's lawyers that the Nebraska Attorney

---

[1]   Hexagram 11, Peace, line 5. From I Ching, by Richard Wilhelm, 3rd Ed. p.51.

[2]   Joe Rogan and Robert F. Kennedy Jr interview 27th June 2024. www.youtube.com/watch?v=p6LJXPOv4SM

General was preparing to issue a formal opinion authorising doctors in the state to prescribe ivermectin and hydroxychloroquine for Covid-19, should they choose. My co-authors confirm the importance of such general efforts observing, *What has been spoiled through man's fault can be made good again through man's work.*[1] The 48-page opinion, which was published three months later in October 2021, included a detailed discussion of BIRD's work on ivermectin's effectiveness and safety. (Exhibit 21.)[2]

"Allowing physicians to consider these early treatments will free them to evaluate additional tools that could save lives, keep patients out of the hospital, and provide relief for our already strained healthcare system", the opinion by Nebraska Attorney General Douglas Peterson concluded. This was the first such opinion in the US and was a crucial milestone, with the potential for other states to follow Nebraska's lead, as well as the potential to influence policy in other countries.

Yet disappointingly and somewhat predictably, this landmark opinion was never raised in the popular and controlled legacy media. With hindsight, thus, one observes that the AG's opinion failed to change the stance of major health organisations or have much real-world impact. One can only speculate as to why this was the case. My co-authors suggest, *a man has a difficult and responsible task to which he is not adequate. Moreover, he does not devote himself to it with all his strength but goes about with inferior people; therefore the execution of the work fails. In this way he also incurs personal opprobrium.*[3]

Confucius says about this line: "weak character coupled with honoured place, meagre knowledge with large plans, limited powers with heavy responsibility, will seldom escape disaster."[4] In this context, the

---

1   Hexagram 18, Work on What Has Been Spoiled, The Judgement. From I Ching, by Richard Wilhelm, 3rd Ed. p.75-6.

2   Exhibit 21. Nebraska Attorney General's Opinion (14 October 2021).

3   Hexagram 50, The Cauldron, line 4. From I Ching, by Richard Wilhelm, 3rd Ed. p.196.

4   Hexagram 50, The Cauldron, line 4. From I Ching, by Richard Wilhelm, 3rd Ed. p.196.

failure to act on the Attorney General's opinion speaks to a deeper issue within our systems – those entrusted with leadership, despite their power or position, are only as effective as their moral integrity and willingness to follow through on difficult decisions. When these qualities are lacking, it's not just the individuals who fail, but society as a whole that suffers the consequences.

MOVE 38. The First Ever WORLD IVERMECTIN DAY is a Success!

The first ever World Ivermectin Day, held on 27th July 2021, was a critical moment for us, as well as a bold step. With censorship running high, it was an attempt to lead the narrative rather than play catch up with the fearmongering and propaganda of the criminal elites running the Covid-19 show. Announcing the event across all of our social media, to our partner organisations, supporters and colleagues worldwide, we asked people to send in their video presentations and testimonials of ivermectin studies and experiences.

The response was overwhelming. With the help of a creative young website developer from Canada, Devyn Brugge, who stepped in quickly to design a website and logo that captured the spirit of the event, Mark Lawrie's quick editing of the incoming material, and the help of a new administrative assistant, Zoe Strickland, we were good to go within three weeks with a 24-hour program of uplifting and exceptional content for World Ivermectin Day.

Daniel O'Connor from TrialSite News cross-posted the livestream, helping the cause tremendously, and FLCCC provided superb content too. Prof. Satoshi Ōmura, the co-discoverer of ivermectin and co-winner of the Nobel Prize for Medicine in 2015, from Kitasato University in Tokyo, sent a video in support. As a result of this extraordinary international effort, World Ivermectin Day went off without a hitch, streaming powerful content to a keen, global audience. In addition to the unique event showcasing real world ivermectin evidence and usefulness, it also brought together supporters from all over the world, sending a clear message to friend and foe alike of perseverance and unity, and determination to stand up for the truth. Not only were we not going to let the dark forces keep us down – we would have some fun highlighting their fraud. One thing evil cannot abide is courage, laughter and unity.

Thus, World Ivermectin Day became more than just an event – it became a key part of an ongoing movement that demanded transparency, ethics and integrity, a statement against censorship and free speech. *Here at the highest stage of development all ornament is discarded. Form no longer conceals content but brings out its value to the full. Perfect grace consists not in exterior ornamentation of the substance, but in the simple fitness of its form.*[1] In this context, the *I Ching*'s idea of *perfect grace* is high praise for this novel endeavour of ours. The strength of our movement was not in flashy displays, but in the honest alignment of our actions with our purpose. Our cause spoke for itself because it was clear, simple, and true. As my co-authors suggest, when our purpose is clear and strong, we don't need any extra decoration or showmanship. What mattered most was the truth we were standing for, and the courage and unity with which we stood together to share it.

Looking back, that period was one where, often having to act on instinct, we relied heavily on creative, enthusiastic, and multitalented individuals to push the movement forward. It was also a time that required delicate navigation. Having worked independently for some time in E-BMC Ltd, outsourcing various projects as needed, I had seldom needed to coordinate a team. As the company director of EbMCsquared CIC, I took a different approach to leadership, partly due to our scant resources, partly because a different way of

---

1   Hexagram 22, Grace, line 6. From I Ching, by Richard Wilhelm, 3rd Ed. p.93.

organising was needed to accomplish our extraordinary task. Thus, in 2021, all paid team members, including myself, received the same hourly rate – £15 an hour. I experimented with other ways of doing away with hierarchy too, and this approach was not without its challenges. Occasionally, egos clashed, and we had to fall back on more traditional frameworks until we had worked through the issues.

About Brugge, the talented Canadian website developer, my co-authors comment, *When a spring gushes forth, it does not know at first where it will go. But its steady flow fills up the deep places blocking its progress, and success is attained. Water, by nature, must flow on.*[1] Brugge seemed as pleased to find us as we were to find him. Like a spring, he brought a vibrant and spontaneous force to the group and, just as a young spring doesn't initially know its path but eventually fills up the deep places and overcomes obstacles, Brugge's involvement gave EbMCsquared a crucial creative momentum that we needed.

Like many fellow Canadians, Brugge was deeply affected by the troubling and authoritarian measures being implemented by Prime Minister Justin Trudeau. This political and social climate, heavy with fear, control, and division, no doubt led to a sense of despair, especially for a sensitive and aware young man, such as Brugge, who might have felt isolated or powerless in the face of it all. The *I Ching* comments about the situation *Religious forces are needed to overcome the egotism that divides men.*[2] To overcome the despair and alienation, something larger, something beyond the self, was needed to inspire action and guide young people like Brugge back towards hope and purpose. It suggests that our collective effort served to do this for him and others. *Religious forces* referred to here aren't a literal reference to religion, but rather to a higher, transcendent force for good that can

---

1   Hexagram 4, Youthful Folly. From I Ching, by Richard Wilhelm, 3rd Ed. p.21.
2   Hexagram 59, Dispersion, The Judgement. From I Ching, by Richard Wilhelm, 3rd Ed. p.227.

inspire unity, humility, and collective action, transcending individual egos and divisiveness.

Further about Brugge's approach, the *I Ching* remarks *An inexperienced person who seeks instruction in a childlike and unassuming way is on the right path, for the man devoid of arrogance who subordinates himself to his teacher will certainly be helped.*[1] With his naturally enthusiastic attitude, Brugge not only found his place within our EbMCsquared team but would become among the key architects of our future image. Following the success of World Ivermectin Day, Brugge would be tasked a more significant project, that of designing the website of the World Council for Health and finalising its iconic logo. More on this later.

Meanwhile, curious to know my co-authors' reflections on Canada PM Justin Trudeau, I asked for commentary. As elected leader of arguably the most civilised country in the world, Trudeau was playing a significant role in the Covid-19 drama in 2021. A puppet of the World Economic Forum (WEF), Trudeau betrayed Canada's men, women and children, mandating the dangerous genetic vaccines and leading other anti-human elements of the globalist agenda, seemingly without a glimmer of remorse.

Trudeau's willingness to align with globalist forces against his own people is what was on the mind of my co-authors too. Though groomed for the role, my co-authors' commentary suggests he might not have realised what he was getting into when he surrendered his agency to globalist forces.

The maiden is powerful. One should not marry such a maiden.[...] The inferior thing seems so harmless and inviting that a man delights in it; it looks so small and weak that he imagines he may dally with it and come to no harm.[2] But Trudeau married the maiden. The result was

---

1   Hexagram 4, Youthful Folly, line 5. From I Ching, by Richard Wilhelm, 3rd Ed. p.23.
2   Hexagram 44, Coming to Meet, The Judgement. From I Ching, by Richard Wilhelm, 3rd Ed. p.171.

that his allegiances and the corrupt system in which he had chosen to operate from thereon controlled him. *The ruler is overshadowed by a party that has usurped power. If a man at such a time were to try to take energetic measures, he would encounter only mistrust and envy, which would probably prohibit all movement.*[1]

In addition, the *I Ching* further notes about Trudeau's role, *Lines are coming. Blessings and fame draw near. Good fortune.*[2] This line speaks to the suggestion that Trudeau's "lines" were scripted. *The ruler is modest and therefore open to the counsel of able men. Thus he is surrounded by men who suggest to him the line of action.*[3] Performing his *lines* well increased the *blessings* (power) he received from his *rulers*.

My co-authors warn against the arrogance that comes with such *blessings*. Their final words on Trudeau reflect the downfall of someone who overestimated their position of power or influence. *His house is in a state of abundance. He screens off his family. He peers through the gate and no longer perceives anyone. For three years he sees nothing. Misfortune.*[4]

This describes a man who because of his arrogance and obstinacy attains the opposite of what he strives for. He seeks abundance and splendour for his dwelling. He wishes at all odds to be master of his house, which so alienates his family that in the end he finds himself completely isolated.[5] Trudeau's overreliance on his *ruler* and disregard for the wellbeing of the Canadian people would no doubt have significant consequences for him.

MOVE 39. Tedros & Gates Threaten Further Pandemonium

To ensure the world was kept in fear, two major representatives of the globalist agenda, Dr Tedros Adhanom Ghebreyesus of the WHO

---

1   Hexagram 55, Abundance, line 2. From I Ching, by Richard Wilhelm, 3rd Ed. p.214-5.
2   Hexagram 55, Abundance, line 5. From I Ching, by Richard Wilhelm, 3rd Ed. p.215-6.
3   Hexagram 55, Abundance, line 5. From I Ching, by Richard Wilhelm, 3rd Ed. p.215-6.
4   Hexagram 55, Abundance, line 6. From I Ching, by Richard Wilhelm, 3rd Ed. p.216.
5   Hexagram 55, Abundance, line 6. From I Ching, by Richard Wilhelm, 3rd Ed. p.216.

and Mr Bill Gates, continued to sound alarm bells about more global health crises that would allegedly necessitate the deployment of more vaccines. The idea of a Marburg pandemic was, to my knowledge, first proposed as the "next pandemic" by the Gates-funded and significant WHO funder GAVI, in April 2021.[1] Then, in August 2021, Tedros (apparently the correct name for reference, as opposed to Ghebreyesus)[2] made an unwarranted official announcement, declaring a Marburg virus outbreak based on a handful of cases in Equatorial Guinea.[3] Marburg was a virus most people hadn't even heard of before. The sudden focus on a rare haemorrhagic disease that was still extremely obscure was absurd. Yet the manoeuvres of mankind's foes were certainly worth paying heed to, as their bioweapon capabilities were extensive.

The WHO's awareness-raising on Marburg was not made in isolation. It was paralleled by comments made by Mr Gates in several media appearances about the likelihood of further pandemics. In one particular appearance with the US Chamber of Commerce on 23rd June 2021, accompanied by his wife, Melinda, Bill Gates warned that the "next pandemic" would be more contagious and deadlier, with even more catastrophic consequences than Covid-19.[4] What stood out in this appearance by the Gates couple was not just their words, but the way they delivered them. Both Bill and Melinda wore eerie, knowing smiles that did not match the gravity of what they were communicating. In fact, It appeared less like a warning and more like a chilling prediction, one they could not hide their excitement about! It continues to be so strange to me that Gates, the man who

1   Vaccines Work. The Next Pandemic: Marburg? https://www.gavi.org/vaccineswork/next-pandemic/marburg

2   https://en.wikipedia.org/wiki/Tedros_Adhanom_Ghebreyesus

3   WHO announcement on Marburg, 11 August 2021: https://www.youtube.com/watch?v=0zoqPEnF3B0

4   US Chamber of Commerce interview with Bill and Melinda Gates: https://www.youtube.com/watch?v=fWQ2DsHWrQE

once confessed to making $20 for every $1 invested in vaccines, had any credibility at all when it came to predicting pandemics or calling for more vaccines.

From our perspective, it certainly looked like there might be another orchestrated event on the horizon, potentially a haemorrhagic fever "pandemic". Whilst Tedros and Gates were sounding alarms about Marburg and pandemics, in August 2021 the UK government announced that a Marburg virus vaccine was already in the process of development in partnership with the University of Oxford. The announcement was made in a press release from the UK government allegedly as part of their broader efforts to prepare for future infectious disease threats. With fewer than 500 cases ever reported, a Marburg outbreak was hardly realistic, let alone imminent – so why were Oxford University, GSK and Janssen Pharmaceuticals, and other UK government partners, investing extensive resources in Marburg vaccines for this incredibly rare pathogen?

The Marburg vaccine developed and manufactured at Oxford University used the same platform technology as for the Oxford-AstraZeneca Covid-19 vaccine, a chimpanzee adenovirus vector, ChAdOx1. This is the AstraZeneca Covid-19 vaccine product that was paused or restricted in various countries due to excessive ADRs, particularly thrombotic reactions. In collaboration with the US's NIH and NIAID, two other platforms for Marburg vaccines were tested in hamsters, including a replicon-based RNA platform, and findings on all three were published in 2024 prior to initiating human clinical trials.[1] At the time of writing this, Oxford's clinical trials in humans were well underway.[2]

This alignment, where vaccines for rare infectious diseases like

1   O'Donnell, et al, 2021. Vaccine Platform Comparison: Protective Efficacy against Lethal Marburg Virus Challenge in the Hamster Model. doi.org/10.3390/ijms25158516

2   www.oxfordmail.co.uk/news/24445345.oxford-university-scientists-testing-marburg-virus-vaccine/

Marburg were being developed just as predictions about the next pandemic surfaced, did not raise many eyebrows among everyday people, who were in a state of numbness, fear and compliance. However, it raised ours. The WHO had identified Marburg vaccines as a priority for research and development and, in the UK, the "Health Security" Agency (formerly Public Health England) had classified it as a high-consequence infectious disease. When the global health establishment starts preparing for threats that are not immediately on the horizon, the people of the world need a robust and long-term strategy.

Who pays for all of these novel vaccines? one might wonder. Well, in the case of the Oxford Marburg virus vaccine, its development was funded by the UK Vaccine Network (a DHSC project),[1] which was funded by UK Aid, which was funded by the UK government, which is funded by the UK taxpayer. A Marburg virus vaccine is not the only gene-based vaccine in development for haemorrhagic fever viruses either. There are several, all being funded with taxpayer money.[2]

With regard to WHO's vested interest in vaccines and pandemics, I had been raising awareness of the WHO's ACT Accelerator fund (ACT stands for Access to Covid-19 Tools) in all presentations on ivermectin, which clearly showed that the business of pandemics was a racket – there was no incentive to treat Covid-19 symptoms when there was so much money to be made from these new kinds of gene-based vaccines. The ACT Accelerator Fund was designed to speed up the development and distribution of the experimental Covid-19 shots, diagnostics, and treatments, of course heavily backed by significant partners, including the BMFG, GAVI, and CEPI (Coalition for Epidemic Preparedness Innovations).[3] Thus, Covid-19 was a multi-billion-dollar industry for all concerned, including the WHO.

1   The Vaccine Network. www.gov.uk/government/groups/uk-vaccines-network.

2   www.gov.uk/government/groups/uk-vaccines-network. Projects funded by DHSC through the UK Vaccine Network.

3   https://www.who.int/initiatives/act-accelerator/about

Pandemics were no longer just a public health crisis, if they ever were. they were a way to generate staggering profits, with the added benefits of power and control.

As mentioned, the WHO's ACT Accelerator budgetary aim for Covid-19 in 2020 was set at an astonishing $31.3 billion – a sum intended to be raised largely through country partners and, hence, taxpayer contributions from people like you and me. It's not difficult to imagine how this figure could multiply with additional "pandemics" like a "Marburg pandemic". In fact, the "next pandemic" declared unilaterally by Tedros was a "monkeypox pandemic" on 22 July 2022. Without any evidence of such, his declaration, overruling the majority vote of his expert WHO committee, fell rather flat, was widely ignored, and then without further ado or apology seemed to disappear from collective memory entirely.

On the subject of individuals like the WHO's Director General, whose actions during the Covid-19 chapter facilitated mass democide, I asked my co-authors for commentary. What makes them tick, I wondered? Was it just about power and control? *Going quickly when one's tasks are finished is without blame. But one must reflect on how much one may decrease others.*[1] The *I Ching's* wisdom reminds us that life is not just about finishing tasks for one's employers efficiently, but about considering the harm we cause in the process, especially when those actions, like this index case, lead to mass suffering and harm! Clearly, during the Covid-19 chapter, many could have benefited from this particular teaching, not least those administering the shots without questioning whether they might be complicit in causing harm.

My co-authors continue *Someone does indeed increase him. Ten pairs of tortoises cannot oppose it. Supreme good fortune.*[2] This suggests that Tedros' position and perspective was considerably dependent on

---

1   Hexagram 41, Decrease, line 5. From I Ching, by Richard Wilhelm, 3rd Ed. p.161.
2   Hexagram 41, Decrease, line 1. From I Ching, by Richard Wilhelm, 3rd Ed. p.159-60.

other powerful parties, and that his rise to power within the WHO at the expense of exploiting or diminishing men, women and children was ordained by these more powerful others.

Exploring this concept further, one wondered whether his role was indeed pre-determined in a greater cosmic story and might even have served a higher purpose, like the story in the Bible's Book of Revelation, for instance. Jamaica's legendary Bob Marley in *Redemption Song* sang the words, "We've got to fulfil The Book", with reference to the Book of Revelation, which is full of dragons and beasts that do eventually get their comeuppance.

The line *Someone does indeed increase him* might thus suggest that Tedros' rise to power, though seemingly driven by manipulation and control, may have been intended as a sort of catalyst for awakening or necessary change by dispassionate cosmic forces outside our awareness, albeit through a period of immense suffering. An epic tale about the triumph of good over evil requires convincing villains.

Indeed, the *ten pairs of tortoises cannot oppose it* phrase emphasises the unstoppable nature of Tedros' meteoric rise in public awareness. When the need for great change was being expressed and instigated in different ways, including our grassroots efforts, might my co-authors be suggesting that it was Tedros' fate to play this horrid role to shake mankind into looking through the veil? To encourage us to seek a deeper awareness? Whether Tedros himself was aware of this potential dimension to his actions, which would contribute to galvanising a portion of mankind to work on what had been spoiled, is uncertain. There certainly is a cosmic irony in this interpretation, if the forces of darkness can propel a necessary and positive awakening, despite the individual's own blindness to a higher good. It invites the question: can we learn from the harm inflicted by such figures, and use it as fuel to change the course of the future?

MOVE 40. A People's Health Organisation Is Urgently Needed

They might not be happy to hear it, but Tedros and Gates' actions certainly did act as fuel for positive change. Following the obvious collusion between them and governments on the Marburg threat, it had become clear that we could wait no longer – a powerful new grassroots organisation was urgently needed to stand up, fight, and create for the survival of mankind against the overwhelming odds. It was imperative. Due to the limitations of our platform, supporters, and audience, BIRD was not authoritative enough – the "B" stood for British – and we could not fight all aspects of the global agenda as BIRD. Even if we tagged the word 'International' as a suffix, we needed to be able to speak freely about the dangers of the Covid-19 shots. We needed an international platform that could compete with other 'global' organisations – from the grassroots up, not top down. We needed to attract further international reinforcements to support our tired troops. And we needed our voices to be heard by men, women and children with the gravitas we deserved.

Thus, talks to create the World Council for Health WCH began in earnest. As a 'world' organisation we needed world representation. Dr Jennifer Hibberd reached out to her fellow Canadian Karen McKenna, who provided administrative support to the World Doctors Alliance, and Dr Tracy Chandler of New Zealand Doctors Speaking Out on Science (NZDSOS), who joined the early Steering Group. Conversations were held with BIRD's partner organisations and individuals with whom we had been cooperating to determine who was 'in' and who was 'out', which was largely based on their stance on the Covid-19 vaccines and their willingness to take a risk. Some, like the FLCCC, held back at first but later joined. It was a risky undertaking, no doubt; putting all eggs in one basket had never been a good strategy...until perhaps this pivotal moment in our human

story. By the time of our launch two months later, we would have a steering committee of ten, with a robust hidden team of strategists. Meanwhile, Devyn Brugge put creative suggestions forward for a World Council for Health website.

Lest the reader perceives those of us who put our hands up to form the World Council for Health as something special, let me emphasise that we were just ordinary people. In fact, like the scruffy contingent in the *Message from our Mother*, limited by a lost tribe,[1] none were perfect, all bore the wounds of past traumas and held perspectives tainted by glaring blind spots. However, we held the space for you through this initiative, bound by the shared knowledge of the dangers at hand, and that you would have done the same had you our insights.

My co-authors advise *In times of prosperity it is important above all to possess enough greatness of soul to bear with imperfect people. For in the hands of a great master no material is unproductive; he can find use for everything. But this generosity is by no means laxity or weakness. It is during times of prosperity especially that we must always be ready to risk even dangerous undertakings, such as the crossing of a river, if they are necessary.* [2]

Coming from varied walks of life: scientists, doctors, activists, and a preponderance of mothers, we each had our own story, our own journey. None of us could claim to have the perfect solution, nor were we immune to the conflicts and struggles that would inevitably arise in our efforts. My co-authors explain here that in times of collaboration it is important to exercise generosity and patience with others. It's easy to forget that creativity often comes from the most unlikely sources, and working through challenges catalysed by imperfections often yields great value.

1　Message from our Mother is on page 17
2　Hexagram 11, Peace, line 2. From I Ching, by Richard Wilhelm, 3rd Ed. p.50.

The *I Ching* also warns of the dangers of complacency with such an undertaking, explaining *So too we must not neglect what is distant but must attend scrupulously to everything. Factionalism and the dominance of cliques are especially to be avoided. Even if people of like mind come forward together, they ought not to form a faction by holding together for mutual advantage; instead, each man should do his duty. These are four ways in which one can overcome the hidden danger of a gradual slackening that always lurks in any time of peace. And that is how one finds the middle way for action.[1]*

When things seem to be going well, and equally when trouble brews, it's easy to fall into the trap of factionalism and division, of clinging to personal advantage or the comfort of acquaintances rather than seeking the common good. But our work to activate and further the World Council for Health required the opposite: we had to transcend the temptation to form exclusive circles or cliques. It was not about finding a way to elevate ourselves or gain favour, it was about standing firm against the globalists, persevering with creative solutions, and taking risks when the stakes were highest. We would need to critically appraise ourselves regularly, and be ready to entertain other perspectives.

Crucially, as relative strangers, we would also need to trust one another. We had to learn quickly what was important and how to get along together. We had no choice but do so, humanity was in grave danger from out-of-control megalomaniacs. The way things were going, the survival of mankind might well end up depending on our perseverance, humility and our unity.

---

1   Hexagram 11, Peace, line 2. From I Ching, by Richard Wilhelm, 3rd Ed. p.50.

Chapter 8

Retreat

Mountain under heaven: the image of RETREAT.
Thus the superior man keeps the inferior man at a distance,
Not angrily but with reserve.[1]

The mountain rises up under heaven, but owing to its nature it
finally comes to a stop. Heaven on the other hand retreats upwards
before it into the distance and remains out of reach. This symbolises
the behaviour of the superior man towards a climbing inferior; he
retreats into his own thoughts as the inferior man comes forward.
He does not hate him, for hatred is a form of subjective involvement
by which we are bound to the hated object. The superior man shows
strength (heaven) in that he brings the inferior man to a standstill
(mountain) by his dignified reserve.[2]

EbMCsquared's gold standard ivermectin publication and the urgent
vaccine harms report to the MHRA made a significant dent in the

---

1   Hexagram 33, Retreat, The Image. From I Ching, by Richard Wilhelm, 3rd Ed. p.130.
2   Hexagram 33, Retreat, The Image. From I Ching, by Richard Wilhelm, 3rd Ed. p.130.

globalist narrative, which left hired hands scurrying to conduct new offensives against us. Thus, following a couple of weeks of relative peace, we came under heavy fire.

The first offensive came in the form of an article in *The Guardian*, announcing that a key study in favour of ivermectin for Covid-19 had been withdrawn. Quoting a London medical student and a couple of seemingly random individuals from Australia, the implication suggested by these "experts" was that this rendered the body of evidence in favour of ivermectin null and void.

The second offensive came from the FDA, supported by the director of the US National Institute of Allergy and Infectious Diseases (NIAID), Dr Anthony Fauci. Fauci was a strong advocate of the competing drug Remdesivir and the deadly Covid-19 shots. He was also a key architect of the Covid-19 scam.

The third offensive was via Gates' farcical TOGETHER Trial. The trial's predictably negative ivermectin results were expediently published with fanfare in the tabloid press by its investigators without peer review in an attempt to hamstring BIRD's international health advocacy efforts.

At this stage, we were pretty exhausted and had no choice but to preserve and restore our energy. Of this time, my co-authors observe: *The wall of the town sinks back into the moat from which it was dug. The hour of doom is at hand. When matters have come to this pass, we should submit to fate and not try to stave it off by violent resistance. The one recourse left us is to hold our own within our intimate circle. Should we persevere in trying to resist the evil in the usual way, our collapse would only be more complete, and humiliation would be the result.*[1]

Thus, we focused on holding the fort *with dignified reserve*, getting medical help to many who needed it, and continuing preparations behind the scenes towards a new grassroots international health

---

1   Hexagram 11, Peace, line 6. From I Ching, by Richard Wilhelm, 3rd Ed. p.52.

organisation. We knew that while the battle raged on, we were not fighting it alone. Whilst we may not have been able to counter their attacks effectively, not least, because the dark forces controlled the mainstream and social media, the unstoppable flow of Covid-19 vaccine harms was trickling into broader awareness. In addition, the groundswell of personal testimonies from doctors and the public about ivermectin steadily confirmed for many that something in the official approach to Covid-19 was very wrong, even if they could not put their finger on it.

Though the volume of stories was hard to ignore, with the so-called authorities sticking strongly to their false narrative, and the power of the media behind them, it remained a very confusing time for many. Yet, every individual who shared their story on social media, every doctor who stood up in defiance, contributed to something bigger, something that could not be silenced by the powerful few.

MOVE 41. The Elgazzar Strike

After the publication of our powerful review in the *American Journal of Therapeutics*, we were expecting attacks and sure as anything they came. The first strike occurred when an individual by the name of Mr Jack Lawrence, allegedly a London medical student who had never published anything in a scientific journal in his life, "discovered" that an Egyptian study included in our review had "ethical concerns". The story, published within ten days of our article, was broken by a reporter called Ms Melissa Davey in *The Guardian* newspaper. It was entitled "Huge study supporting ivermectin as Covid treatment withdrawn over ethical concerns" and essentially accused the principal author, Prof. Elgazzar, and his co-authors of fraud.[1]

The pre-print article of the Elgazzar study was taken down, not

---

1   https://www.theguardian.com/science/2021/jul/16/huge-study-supporting-ivermectin-as-
     covid-treatment-withdrawn-over-ethical-concerns

withdrawn, concurrently with *The Guardian*'s "exposé". "Medical student" Lawrence said he "discovered" multiple inconsistencies in the study's raw data, including falsified patient records. When tasked with "a simple university assignment", he had instead done "a comprehensive investigation" into this Egyptian study. Two unknown so-called experts from Australia, "data analyst" Mr Gideon Meyerowitz-Katz and "researcher" Dr Kyle Sheldrick, were invited by reporter Davey to weigh in, making authoritative statements such as the data was "just totally faked". Going by the Twitter handle of Chief Health Nerd, Meyerowitz-Katz claimed that excluding Elgazzar's study completely changed the results and that it could be "the most consequential medical fraud ever committed". The irony was galling if one allowed it to be.

Seemingly not forewarned by his controllers, even Dr Andrew Hill seemed taken by surprise with this Guardian offensive. In a somewhat endearing display of naivety, Hill's initial response to the Elgazzar study "withdrawal" was to deny that removing these data made any difference to the evidence he found in favour of ivermectin in his recently published review. Writing to Australian colleagues who were also BIRD members, upon their inquiry, he confirmed what we too had found: "We ran the meta-analysis with the Elgazzar study removed and it did not change the overall conclusions. The results are in the Appendix to our paper."

In a further email on the matter that was kindly shared with me by Australia's Prof. Wendy Hoy, Hill responded off the bat:

"I don't believe that all the trials of ivermectin are unreliable. We have a wide range of clinical trials in many countries. It would be hard to see how they could have colluded to provide the current results. Many of these research groups did not know each other when the research programme was started. Across the trials, we are seeing stronger treatment effects for higher doses and effects on a range of endpoints."

On the face of it, it seemed to me that Dr Hill did not quite grasp the objective of his deployers, to destroy ivermectin as a credible option for Covid-19 in favour of experimental vaccines and other novel and expensive new drugs, and his own role in their theatre. Thus, Hill stuck to his guns for a day or two before hastily correcting his perspective to align with new instructions, which became: ivermectin studies could no longer be trusted, so he would have to withdraw his ivermectin review too. And, indeed, this was what happened. Our review, on the other hand, stayed in place. Despite a barrage of criticisms and attempts to discredit it, we held firm with rebuttals in defence of our work.

The question still remains, though: was the Elgazzar study fraudulent? With limited information coming from Prof. Elgazzar himself, and given that he was not a native English speaker, the flaws in his study's reporting were notable. This had prompted us to conduct additional sensitivity analyses in our review to determine if removing the study would significantly affect our results. It did not. Coming under attack following the *Guardian* "news", Bryant led a defence of our review in this regard. (Exhibit 22.)[1] However, in the chaotic landscape of Covid, where multiple narrative threads were at play and deception seemed to be a constant, it was entirely possible that the trial had been intentionally manipulated. For this reason, we maintained a healthy scepticism and continued to investigate further. The experimental shot promoter and oral ivermectin foe, Bill Gates, certainly seemed very interested in ivermectin – as long-acting injections, not in its traditional low-cost oral formulation. Could Elgazzar

---

1   Exhibit 22. Bryant et al response on the Elgazzar withdrawal in American Journal of
     Therapeutics (2021).

be another hired hand in the intended slow reveal of these novel ivermectin formulations, potentially scheduled to appear sometime in
the future, yet also available to implode and create confusion at any
time if need be? It had certainly crossed our minds.

My co-authors describe the situation in which Prof. Elgazzar
found himself suddenly during Covid-19 was that of *a rather vertical ascent – direct rise from obscurity and loneliness to power and
influence.*[1] They go on to say that *When a man's attitude of mind is so
modest that this expresses itself in his outward behaviour, it is a source
of good fortune to him. For the possibility of exerting a lasting influence
arises of itself and no one can interfere.*[2]

Thus, my co-authors are suggesting that it was good intentions
that drove Elgazzar to offer his medical knowledge and scientific findings to benefit others, especially the Western world, during a time of
crisis. After coming under heavy criticism, perhaps, as a modest man,
he realised that he was up against powerful forces beyond his control
and decided to step back. By doing so, he may have recognised his
own limitations and chose to focus on where he could make a real difference, leaving the larger, more political battles to those with more
power. In this sense, he may have simply backed away from the spotlight, quietly retreating from the noise to attend to the more pressing
matters at hand – helping his patients – his unquestionable calling
in a health crisis, rather than becoming embroiled in a struggle he
couldn't win with antagonistic hidden forces.

With an opportunity to further reflect on the role of miscella-
neous reporters who promulgated the fraudulent Covid-19 narrative,
I also sought my co-authors' insights on Ms Davey. The act of writing
the article may have been a small one, but its effects were extensive, an
effective strike against the fight for truth, undeniably. My co-authors

---

1   Hexagram 46, Pushing Upwards, The Judgement. From I Ching, by Richard Wilhelm, 3rd Ed
    p.178.
2   Hexagram 15, Modesty, line 2. From I Ching, by Richard Wilhelm, 3rd Ed. p.65.

observe that her influence through the *Guardian* article was by means of *friendly persuasion* – manipulative jargon was all our antagonists had to deploy against us at this stage – noting that *The time has not yet come for sweeping measures*[1]. Further insights were revealed by Davey's website where this young Australian woman declared that she was on extended leave, working with the WHO in Copenhagen "in the areas of intelligence and compliance". This suggests that Davey might have been part of a more intricate, behind-the-scenes operation to control public perception.

My co-authors remark in regard to our approach to Ms Davey: *A boar's tusk is in itself dangerous but if the bull's nature is altered, the tusk is no longer a menace. Thus also where men are concerned, wild force should not be combatted directly; instead, its roots should be eradicated.*[2] These insights suggest that tackling her article directly would have been a waste of our energy – as we deduced at the time. A broader, more strategic approach to addressing the outputs of chaos agents, like Ms Davey, individuals whose actions contribute to larger patterns of confusion or misinformation, was likely to be more productive than rushing to oppose their written missives.

MOVE 42. Ambushed by *Rebel Wisdom*

Mr David Fuller, known for his work as a producer, director of documentaries, writer, and journalist with a history at the BBC, described himself as a "sense-maker" in his podcast *Rebel Wisdom*. The show focused on philosophical and cultural topics, and I often found his selection of guests thought-provoking. Prior to the Covid-19 chapter and this personal experience, I had a great deal of respect for his work.

Thus, when Fuller invited me for an interview on ivermectin,

1　Hexagram 9, The Taming Power of the Small, The Judgement. From I Ching, by Richard Wilhelm, 3rd Ed. p.40-1.

2　Hexagram 26, The Taming Power of the Great, line 5. From I Ching, by Richard Wilhelm, 3rd Ed. p.106.

inspired by *The Guardian* "exposé", I was excited. I thought this would be a perfect opportunity to set the record straight for his intelligent, "sense-making" audience. After all, using ivermectin for early Covid symptoms based on the evidence was simply "common sense." I approached the interview in good faith, eager to share this important information.

However, instead of airing our conversation as a stand-alone interview, Fuller intercut it with interviews from two other individuals: Dr Graham Walker, a young doctor from the US with no expertise in ivermectin whatsoever, and Mr Gideon Meyerowitz-Katz, one of Ms Davey's "experts". A junior PhD student at the University of Wollongong, Australia, allegedly specialising in chronic disease and diabetes – Meyerowitz-Katz hardly had the qualifications of a senior epidemiologist or an experienced academic. In fact, his bio on the American Council on Science and Health, an organisation funded by industry giants like American Petroleum, Bayer, and General Electric, described him as an "aspiring researcher"; not surprisingly, his publications seemed more aligned with corporate interests than with scientific integrity.

Unfortunately, I was not given the chance to respond to the spliced-in inaccuracies by Walker and Meyerowitz-Katz, and what should have been a serious conversation about saving lives using common sense was reduced to a pseudo-intellectual circus. In his quest for sense-making, Fuller did not seem to realise that I had put everything on the line to bring this information to the public – my career, income and reputation. And it was not only me who would bear the consequences, but the superb efforts of EbMCsquared team and the entire BIRD group. Not least, his audience were people we wanted on our side. Each one of them was a potential collaborator in the quest for the truth.

Meyerowitz-Katz was given full airtime to make sweeping claims, like "there is no mortality benefit for ivermectin," with no opportunity for me to correct him. Meanwhile, my years of experience were diminished by two individuals with little relevant expertise. When I finally saw the show, I was appalled. Engaging in this important topic in such a thoughtless and superficial way felt like an ambush, and afterwards I began to question Fuller's true intentions. Was he simply blinded by the implications of an effective treatment being suppressed, as so many others were? Was he afraid of being called "anti-vax"? Or was he swayed by outside influences, perhaps his BBC colleagues, who shaped his "sense-making" more than our rigorous research?

The feedback in the comments section confirmed what I had already suspected: many viewers saw right through Fuller's misguided approach. Like me, they were disappointed by how Fuller allowed an important conversation to be distorted. Here are some of the comments below the video entitled *Ivermectin, For and Against, with Tess Lawrie, Graham Walker & Gideon Meyerowitz-Katz*, which was posted on July 25th, 2021:

@Specialsausse: Scepticism is not evidence. "It doesn't ring true to me" and " it just doesn't make sense to me" are not arguments. Lawrie was the only scientifically minded person among the panel. The fact that she's also the only one that stands to lose anything for her position lends weight to her position as well.

@pergamX: This is hardly the way to make sense of all this, since guests never have a chance to refute each other's arguments and get into the weeds. The ER doc is a junior and very manipulative – the way he introduced himself into the conversation – he gave way too many qualifications as per why he is unbiased... The other junior is trying to reduce the discussion to statistical significance. The whole thing is laid out wrong, since the debate is, and always has been, about precautionary principle, i.e. use the drug while waiting large trial data vs. sit on the fence until the data is here.

@maxilopez1596: A few thoughts: 1: why is the burden of proof of efficacy so high for ivermectin, but so low for vaccination? 2: why are safely concerns so high for ivermectin, but so low for vaccination? 3: If there is indeed insufficient evidence that ivermectin is effective, why then at least haven't we had more clinical trials? At a fraction of the cost of other measures. We're a year and a half into the pandemic at this stage. 4: Many doctors around the world aren't allowed to prescribe Ivermectin, so we don't really know how many of those would if they could.

@palmer1979tube: Video does not consist of actual simultaneous interviews, so none of the participants actively respond to each other. It is particularly unfair to Tess Lawrie, who cannot respond to the accusations made by the two critical participants.

@andthensome512: My 60 year old buddy had a pretty bad case and got prescribed Ivermectin about 9 days in. Within 2 days his fever broke and he was feeling much better.

@playonwords55: This guy who isn't treating patients with IVM is saying that the doctor who is treating patients with IVM is wrong about his observational results. You can't make this shit up.

@stevewoodmansee5268: When assessing opinion, I find it useful when experts disclose their, and their spouses, funding sources.

@freedomishealthy1086: Let's face it, there is a reason that you can't find doctors with the prestige and intelligence of Tess Laurie to speak against Ivermectin. She outclasses these guys like a mile.

@Mikepereich: I think it's safe to assume that the folks who are sceptical of ivermectin seem to not apply that amount of scepticism to the vaccine trials.

@BM-je2se: The journalist guy asked good questions and Tess was great, but the two young guys really had no business being interviewed. If you want a real debate for or against Iver, get doctors who have used Iver on their patients and end up either for or against it. My guess is that you will have trouble finding the latter.

@woodyouwoodyou: This is tantamount to someone standing on a beach watching someone drown, so caught up in their analysis they're frozen, this drug has already been proven safe, so what are you waiting for.

@mniman7022: Very poor arguments from Dr Walker. Completely derailed an important conversation with emotional blather and opinionated nonsense.

@andyjoed: This isn't a debate. These are separate interviews. Why can't these people debate each other. What is the wedge that is preventing anyone from actually debating this stuff with each other. It's maddening.

@reddevil00745able: I love how he tries pushing Tess into saying censorship is good in certain situations. Omg!! Thug live moment!! You go Tess. Free speech all the way. People need to be able to make up their own minds. What a novel idea.

@irenamagdalena6807: I don't understand something here if ivermectin is not harmful and I want it, even assuming it will not help
me, what is the problem to give it to me? Why it is squashed at all
costs? Why it is taken off the shelf? Why, why, why....

@johncrab67: Tess Lawrie is the only good part of these three separate interviews.

Many thanks to the individuals who took the time to air their views in
the comments section. And there were many, many more comments
like these. Needless to say, like most interviews I did on You Tube
about ivermectin in 2021, the *Rebel Wisdom* episode on ivermectin
"sense-making" was removed from You Tube within a week or two.
Fuller seemed surprised; after all, hadn't he appropriately rubbished
ivermectin? He appealed and managed to get it reinstated!

My co-authors' perspective on this "ambush" is interesting. About
Fuller's predicament, they say, *You hold together with the wrong people.*[1] Perhaps Fuller, by aligning himself with those who did not
belong to the sphere of ethical discourse on health and science, risked
being drawn into false intimacy. *We are often among people who do not
belong to our own sphere. In that case we must beware of being drawn
into false intimacy through force of habit. Needless to say, this would
have evil consequences. Maintaining sociability without intimacy is the
only right attitude towards such people, because otherwise we should not
be free to enter into relationship with people of our own kind later on.*
[2] Had Fuller, by associating with those who shared his intellectual
curiosities without any moral responsibility, been led astray? How
had he sourced his "experts" I wondered?

As my co-authors recommend, for a man in Fuller's influential

---

1   Hexagram 8, Holding Together, line 3. From I Ching, by Richard Wilhelm, 3rd Ed. p.38.
2   Hexagram 8, Holding Together, line 3. From I Ching, by Richard Wilhelm, 3rd Ed. p.38.

position, *the mind should be kept humble and free, so that it may remain receptive to good advice. People soon give up counselling a man who thinks that he knows everything better than anyone else.*[1]

This episode was a painful reminder of how easily meaningful discourse can be derailed by ego and a misguided sense of authority. Despite the opportunity to truly engage in an open, honest dialogue about ivermectin and its potential role in saving lives, Fuller allowed his own biases and superficial act of "sense-making" to take precedence. There is, no doubt, a lesson in this for us all.

MOVE 43. TOGETHER Trial Publishes in the Tabloid Press

The TOGETHER trial's findings were published in the media on August 6th, 2021, before any formal scientific review or publication had taken place, reported by major outlets such as *The Globe and Mail*, Reuters, and other news agencies. This pre-emptive release in the media, coming before the study was published in a peer-reviewed journal, was irregular, as the results were not yet available for independent scientific scrutiny.

This was a clear sign to us of desperation, as the corporate establishment, with all its resources, scrambled to undermine the growing momentum behind ivermectin for Covid-19. The trial itself was fundamentally flawed – its dose was too small, the treatment was too short, and it began too late in the course of the illness. Despite these major deficiencies, the trial still showed a signal of benefit, though not statistically significant due to its underpowered design. But that did not matter; the narrative had already been set: ivermectin did not work.

What made matters worse was the early knowledge of the trial's outcome. Millionaire technology entrepreneur, Steve Kirsch, had

---

[1]   Hexagram 31, Influence, The Image. From I Ching, by Richard Wilhelm, 3rd Ed. p.123.

already informed me of the (negative) findings months before the public announcement, which I had found hard to believe at the time. When I asked how he could be so certain, Kirsch had chuckled, "I just asked Ed Mills on the phone what they found, and he told me."

Dr Edward Mills, as principal investigator of TOGETHER from McMaster University, should have remained blinded to the results, yet there he was, sharing the findings with affluent allies before they had been officially analysed. By the time the trial's ivermectin findings were published in the press, there was no way for us to intervene. Notably, fluvoxamine, the SSRI drug favoured and promoted by Kirsch as a Covid-19 treatment, the drug he had asked me to conduct a systematic review on earlier in the year, performed very well in the TOGETHER Trial.

About the curious relationship between Mills and Kirsch, where, upon a telephone call from Kirsch, Mills "spills the beans", my co-authors use the following metaphor: *On the earth is water: the image of HOLDING TOGETHER. Thus the kings of antiquity bestowed the different states as fiefs and cultivated friendly relations with the feudal Lords.*[1] This paternal relationship between king and vassals in ancient China demonstrates how individuals create bonds through shared interests. In this case, Mills and Kirsch's common interests seemed to take precedence over Mills' duty to maintain trial integrity, creating an unspoken alliance that ultimately undermined the ethical standards that should have guided the TOGETHER trial. In their choice of image, my co-authors demonstrate humour and irony too – the TOGETHER trial narrative was *HOLDING TOGETHER* not by scientific rigour or transparency, but by these very shared interests!

Again, the question arises, why would a scientist engage in such unscientific and disreputable activities? My co-authors observe that Mills' success was assured by his association with powerful people

---

[1]   Hexagram 8, Holding Together, The Image. From I Ching, by Richard Wilhelm, 3rd Ed. p.37.

and was well rewarded. *PUSHING UPWARD has supreme success. He need not be afraid to do this, because success is assured.*[1] In terms of Mills' conduct, my co-authors observe that *the best water is only a potentiality for refreshment.*[2] It was not that Mills did not know how to conduct ethical research, perhaps he simply chose not to drink from the clear well of good clinical and research practice principles?

With high-level hands like Mills quoted in the media, and no scientific data to scrutinise, we independent scientists had nothing with which to challenge their unsubstantiated claims. The message from the propaganda machine was clear: ivermectin did not work, and that's all most people would ever hear.

What was even more frustrating was that we had to wait months for the formal publication while the mainstream media continued to push the anti-ivermectin narrative. Meanwhile, several independent scientists like those at c19ivm.org uncovered what we already knew: the trial was riddled with conflicts of interest and inaccuracies. "Extreme COI, impossible data, blinding broken, randomisation/ blinding failure, uncorrected errors, protocol violations, no response from authors, refusal to release data", the c19ivm.org team concluded.[3] Despite these flaws, the establishment insisted that TOGETHER was the largest and highest quality ivermectin study ever conducted.

At this point, the BIRD team found itself burned out and exhausted from the relentless barrage of attacks coming from all directions. Gates and his cronies were targeting ivermectin with everything they had, wielding their influence across every media outlet and scientific publication. Thankfully, some determined journalists and scientists, including Alexandros Merinos, Eva Tallaksen, and Phil Harper, stepped in to unravel the web of lies. They began

---

1   Hexagram 46, Pushing Upwards, The Judgement. From I Ching, by Richard Wilhelm, 3rd Ed. p.178.

2   Hexagram 48, The Well, line 5. From I Ching, by Richard Wilhelm, 3rd Ed. p.188.

3   The TOGETHER Trial critique. https://c19ivm.org/meta.html #togetherivm

pushing back against the narrative, challenging the disinformation head-on, albeit in the alternative media outlets that had a limited reach.

Meanwhile, our tenacious Dr Fordham mustered efforts to finish drafting a paper on the remarkable data collected by US geriatrician Dr David Chesler, whose clinical experience during the early months of the Covid crisis demonstrated that ivermectin, when combined with zinc and doxycycline, dramatically reduced Covid-19 transmission and death rates among elderly residents at four independent nursing homes in the US. This was not an isolated finding either. Dr Chesler's data echoed the successes of other frontline doctors: Dr Jackie Stone in Zimbabwe, Prof. Thomas Borody in Australia, Dr Sabine Hazan in the US, and Prof. Femi Babalola in Nigeria, all of whom had used a similar approach. The incredibly low Covid-19 rates in Uttar Pradesh, India, had also been attributed to this combination therapy, which had been widely deployed by the Uttar Pradesh authorities.

The formal publication of the TOGETHER trial, detailing its dodgy methods and findings, was later published in *The Lancet Regional Health – Americas*, on March 30, 2022. Ironically, Mills himself later admitted that the study showed a "clear signal" that ivermectin worked, if only more patients had been included. International scientists submitted requests to obtain the data for independent analysis. However, despite the data being declared open source on a Gates-funded platform called ICODA, the TOGETHER Trial data were never made available, at least, not by the time of writing. This refusal to release the data, combined with glaring inconsistencies, only served to strengthen the case that this trial was never about finding the truth; rather, it was about suppressing a treatment that did not fit the narrative.

About Mr Gates, my co-authors suggest, *If we wish to know what anyone is like, we have only to observe on whom he bestows his care and what side of his own nature he cultivates and nourishes.*[1] Despite Gates' apparent involvement in an anti-human agenda, I've often felt sympathy for him. He seems to have drawn the short straw in this cosmic theatre. Growing up in the household of a eugenicist, he was likely exposed to a worldview that devalued human life, which could only have made for a tormented inner world.

With so much going for him, my co-authors poignantly remark he *let [his] magic tortoise go. The magic tortoise is a creature possessed of such supernatural powers that it lives on air and needs no earthly nourishment. The image means that a man fitted by nature and position to live freely and independently renounces this self-reliance and instead looks with envy and discontent at others who are outwardly in better circumstances. But such base envy only arises derision and contempt in those others. This has bad results.*[2]

Gates' life had been so blessed with good fortune, accumulating extraordinary material wealth and influence, but instead of using his good fortune to nourish others, he used it against us, without realising that no amount of material goods and power can ever satisfy the needs of one's soul. As such, my co-authors' observation is astute: Gates' good fortune has led to misfortune, not only for himself but for all people and the earth too.

Nevertheless, even for Bill Gates, my ancient co-authors suggest that redemption is possible if he were to use his power and influence to nourish others and the earth instead of whatever else it is he has set his mind and money to do. Genuinely helping other people could *bring general happiness for him and for all others.*[3]

---

1   Hexagram 27, The Corners of the Mouth, The Judgement. From I Ching, by Richard Wilhelm, 3rd Ed. p.107-8.

2   Hexagram 27, The Corners of the Mouth, line 1. From I Ching, by Richard Wilhelm, 3rd Ed. p.108-9.

3   Hexagram 27, The Corners of the Mouth, line 6. From I Ching, by Richard Wilhelm, 3rd Ed. p.110-1.

Finally, the *I Ching* reminds us, in relation to Gates, of the generous spirit of our Mother: *The earth in its devotion carries all things, good and evil, without exception.*[1]

MOVE 44. You're Not a Horse, Y'all

On August 29, 2021, at the same time that Pfizer's genetic injection was given full US authorisation based on fraudulent data,[2] the FDA announced that Americans must stop taking ivermectin. The intensive propaganda campaign designed to ridicule people making their own common sense health decisions was held together by the following vulgar FDA tweet: "You are not a horse, you are not a cow. Seriously, y'all. Stop it."

The UK's *Guardian* newspaper led with an article entitled "Agency issues message after misinformation about ivermectin, a medicine used to deworm livestock, spreads on social media."

"Ahead of full US authorisation of the Pfizer coronavirus vaccine, the federal Food and Drug Administration (FDA) had a simple message for Americans contemplating using ivermectin, a medicine used to deworm livestock, instead of getting a Covid shot"[3], the Guardian article began. It went on to include authority figure quotes urging people not to seek Covid treatment outside of recognised channels, and the accompanying FDA fact sheet included a long list of scary side effects that one might have with ivermectin. All the while, the experimental Covid vaccines and other novel experimental drugs had rapidly been authorised without reference to their very, very scary side effects – like myocarditis, blood clots in the brain, and sudden death.

Ignoring all the data on adverse reactions to the Covid-19 vaccines,

---

1   Hexagram 2, The Receptive, The Image. From I Ching, by Richard Wilhelm, 3rd Ed. p.13.
2   Covid-19: Researcher blows the whistle on data integrity issues in Pfizer's vaccine trial. BMJ 2021;375:n2635.
3   https://www.theguardian.com/us-news/2021/aug/23/fda-horse-message-ivermectin-covid-coronavirus

"at least one person had been hospitalised" after taking ivermectin, the captured media reported. Information about this one case could not be independently verified. Another argument put forward by the FDA in the press as a reason not to use ivermectin was, believe it or not, that animals needed it, and shortages were being reported in veterinary supplies!

The "You are not a horse" tweet quickly became the second most shared in the FDA's history. However, the FDA was later forced to remove this tweet and other related posts through a legal settlement with three courageous doctors, Drs Mary Talley Bowden, Paul Marik, and Robert Apter, who sued the FDA for interfering with their ability to prescribe ivermectin and harming their reputations.

Dr Anthony Fauci, head of NIAID chimed in during a live CNN interview with a further alarmist message about ivermectin: "Don't do it; there's no evidence whatsoever that it works and it could potentially have toxicity." Fauci is the notorious topic of a book by Robert F. Kennedy Jr, entitled *The Real Anthony Fauci*. If you haven't yet read it, I strongly recommend you do. The man's capacity for evil had no bounds.

My co-authors confirm that Fauci was a key architect of the Covid crisis, with a deep interest in keeping the anti-ivermectin narrative going for as long as possible, but his approach was not sustainable – the truth would out eventually. *Under certain conditions, intimidation without gentleness may achieve something momentarily, but not for all time.*[1] Fauci's reign would end but not before he had caused unprecedented harm.

They also comment that Fauci was part of a much bigger circle. *Lakes resting one on the other: the image of THE JOYOUS. Thus the superior man joins with his friends for discussion and practise.*[2] Yet, there

---

1   Hexagram 58, The Joyous, The Judgement. From I Ching, by Richard Wilhelm, 3rd Ed. p.224.
2   Hexagram 58, The Joyous, The Image. From I Ching, by Richard Wilhelm, 3rd Ed. p.224.

remained something ponderous and melancholy about him, thus this additional insight, that *There is always something ponderous and one sided about the learning of the self-taught,*[1] rings true. In mid-2021, Fauci was in considerable trouble. His orderly plan, involving genetic injections and other experimental drugs, was at risk of being unravelled by ivermectin advocates. Not only that, but he was also soon to be exposed as complicit in a long-standing evil agenda – as described in *The Real Anthony Fauci* – to interfere with mankind.. *While the strong, loyal man is striving eagerly and in good faith to create order, he meets the ringleader of the disorder, as if by accident, and seizes him.*[2] Perhaps the strong man is Robert F. Kennedy Jr in this context?

But in abolishing abuses one must not be too hasty. This would turn out badly because the abuses have been in existence so long.[3] The core message of this commentary is about concealment and suppression of the truth, but it also carries an underlying warning about the dangers of allowing something unjust to remain hidden for too long. Ultimately, it reminds us that truth cannot remain hidden forever, and those complicit in the long-standing deception must eventually face consequences. His having received a presidential pardon by Joe Biden before stepping down as US President, my co-authors seem to be warning against letting Fauci off the hook too easily.

MOVE 45. Focusing on What is Important: Helping People
With limited support available for people suffering from Covid-19 symptoms and emails pouring in daily, it became clear that we needed to get tangible help to people. Thus, in August 2021, we quickly launched an online Covid Care Clinic, offering free support from a handful of ethical British doctors to the public. While we weren't

---

1   Hexagram 58, The Joyous, The Image. From I Ching, by Richard Wilhelm, 3rd Ed. p.224-5.
2   Hexagram 36, Darkening of the Light, line 3. From I Ching, by Richard Wilhelm, 3rd Ed. p.141.
3   Hexagram 36, Darkening of the Light, line 3. From I Ching, by Richard Wilhelm, 3rd Ed. p.141.

able to supply ivermectin, there were several effective protocols available at the time to manage symptoms that extended beyond ivermectin alone. In addition, many people were able to make their own arrangements to obtain it.

Passionate about helping people, lovely Linda Rae, whom I had never met in person, took on the role of administrator, and a small group of dedicated doctors, including an infectious diseases specialist from Scotland, worked ambitiously to provide a seven-day-a-week service. Linda had worked in the NHS as an occupational therapist but when Covid-19 was launched she had seen the situation with a clarity denied to most. Inspired by BIRD's work, she had very quickly found her focus, stepping away from her former role to volunteer her multiple talents to the cause. *When one sees the way ahead thus clearly, free of all doubt, a cheerful mood sets in, and one chooses what is right without further thought. Such a clear path ahead always leads to the good.*[1]

Our intention had been to expand the service. However, the huge need, our dedication, and the value we provided was not enough to keep it going. Relying on donations to run, the service was not sustainable in the long term. However, in 2021, many people were helped and healed through this online service, and the feedback was overwhelmingly positive. One particularly grateful and modest individual whose health had been restored was so moved by the advice and support he received that he donated a one-off sum to cover the cost of a doctor's salary for a month. *The ruler is modest and therefore open to the counsel of able men. Thus he is surrounded by men who suggest to him the lines of action.* (He was a good patient and followed doctor's advice!) *This brings blessing, fame, and good fortune to him and all the people.*[2] It was generous gestures such as these that allowed us to continue providing this welcome care for a little longer; by his

---

1   Hexagram 33, Retreat, line 6. From I Ching, by Richard Wilhelm, 3rd Ed. p.132.

2   Hexagram 55, Abundance, line 5, From I Ching, by Richard Wilhelm, 3rd Ed. p.216.

paying it forward, he enabled others to benefit from this vital service. If only our example could have inspired GP surgeries to do the same, the Covid-19 chapter in the UK would have quickly come to an end.

I was often asked and indeed wondered: why did doctors in particular, my colleagues and some former friends, continue to inject the public with those unsafe experimental vaccine products? Had they not sought to look at the scientific literature? They would have found no solid evidence to support this novel biotechnology. Had they not wondered what the long-term effects of a gene-based vaccine might be in the body? Immunology 101 would have raised serious concerns about the risks of such an approach, particularly the possibility that the novel genetic material could integrate into the human genome. Had they not considered the kind of adverse reactions that could occur, from turning the bodies of men, women, and soon children, into spike protein factories? It seemed impossible that they had not, and yet they persisted with injecting the Covid-19 vaccines.

I found the insights of my co-authors illuminating on this matter. Commenting about this peculiar situation, they wrote that *Heaven and earth are out of communion and all things are benumbed. What is above has no relation to what is below, and on earth confusion and disorder prevail. [...] The way of inferior people is in ascent; the way of superior people is on the decline. But the superior people do not allow themselves to be turned from their principles. If the possibility of exerting influence is closed to them, they nevertheless remain faithful in their principles and withdraw into seclusion.*[1] Thus, it is possible that some doctors felt the situation was hopeless and withdrew, perhaps even resigned from their practices. Conversely, for others who followed the instruction *of inferior people* (the authorities controlled by dark agendas), it most likely required a compromise of their principles.

There are many ways in which a compromise in principles can

---

1   Hexagram 12, Standstill, The Judgement. From I Ching, by Richard Wilhelm, 3rd Ed. p.52-3.

be induced, not least by fear, and I do believe that a fear of getting Covid-19 – and dying – was a big driver for health professionals on the frontline to do as they were told. In addition, I believe that this fear of death was instilled in them and exacerbated through the official 'no-reply' directives that they found in their professional inboxes daily. The intensive masking, hand washing, gloving up and so on, with instructions to do so at every turn, was ubiquitous in both primary care and hospital settings. Failure to do so, especially to refuse the shots, came with stern reprisals.

However, my co-authors elaborate another reason for compromising one's principles – money: *Thus the superior man falls back upon his inner worth in order to escape the difficulties. He does not permit himself to be honoured with revenue.*[1] This information suggests that the doctors who followed the directives without questioning may also have been dazzled by the rewards offered to them. They were tempted, seduced by the system, and may have rationalised their actions by convincing themselves that they were simply doing what they were told by a higher authority – and it was an emergency after all. The rewards for compliance were great: financial incentives and career security. It was nevertheless surprising to me that those who took oaths to heal people would allow the allure of such offers to so easily cloud their moral compass.

---

1   Hexagram 12, Standstill, The Image. From I Ching, by Richard Wilhelm, 3rd Ed. p.53.

Chapter 9

Fellowship With Men

FELLOWSHIP WITH MEN in the open.
Success.
It furthers one to cross the great water.
The perseverance of the superior man furthers.[1]

True fellowship among men must be based upon a concern that is universal. It is not the private interests of the individual that create lasting fellowship among men, but rather the goals of humanity. That is why it is said that fellowship with men in the open succeeds. If unity of this kind prevails, even difficult and dangerous tasks, such as crossing the great water, can be accomplished. But in order to bring about this sort of fellowship, a persevering and enlightened leader is needed – a man with clear, convincing, and inspiring aims and the strength to carry them out.[2]

---

1   Hexagram 13, Fellowship with Men, The Judgement. From I Ching, by Richard Wilhelm, 3rd Ed. p.56-7.

2   Hexagram 13, Fellowship with Men, The Judgement. From I Ching, by Richard Wilhelm, 3rd Ed. p.56-7.

After the hammering we received following our robust scientific publication and the Yellow Card report on Covid-19 vaccine harms, help came from all over the world. It was as if our efforts, and the predicament of steadfastly standing for the truth, confronting the corrupt system, enduring their malicious hired hands, had finally been noticed. Suddenly, scientists, lawyers, and journalists rose to openly support our work. They used our findings in their own diverse efforts, amplifying them across various platforms and professions. It was a moment of profound solidarity, and for the first time in what felt like a long and lonely battle, we began to see that unity around a common concern was indeed possible, and ivermectin was central to this.

Whether it was our perseverance that inspired others, or whether it was the sheer weight of evidence that revealed the disrespect, deceit, and vulgarity of the "health security" agencies and their sociopathic think tanks, one could not be sure. But it did not matter. What mattered was that people were stepping forward, contributing to a countermovement that was slowly but surely gaining momentum. Real or imagined, it felt as though BIRD was at the heart of it all. And in that moment, there was hope. Hope that, despite the crushing odds, humanity was waking up.

In this chapter, you'll read about some of the many remarkable individuals who joined us openly in this fight for truth, including a curious journalist at last daring to ask the right questions. Distinguished scientists and doctors, once too quiet, rallied around, adding their expertise to ivermectin's evidence base. I share the remarkable legal challenge of the Indian Bar Association who sued the WHO's Chief Scientist, Dr Swaminathan, as well as US courts making landmark decisions that shifted the balance. Lastly, I reveal how Dr Fordham, a discerning voice for truth amidst the contrived chaos, doggedly sought answers from his British parliamentary representative, demanding accountability.

These are the stories of fellowship, of men and women openly united not just by ideals, but by a commitment to truth in the face of overwhelming opposition. About my personal development, my co-authors' remark: *Dragon appearing in the field. It furthers one to see the great man. Here the effects of the light giving power begin to manifest themselves. In terms of human affairs, this means that the great man makes his appearance in his chosen field of activity. As yet he has no commanding position but is still with his peers. However, what distinguishes him from the others is his seriousness of purpose, his unqualified reliability, and the influence he exists on his environment without conscious effort. Such a man is destined to gain great influence and to set the world in order. Therefore it is favourable to see him.*[1]

MOVE 46. A Curious Journalist at Last

It was an absolute delight to find a series of persistent requests from a Phil Harper, BAFTA award-winning Director & Producer, and Specialist in VR/immersive/360/digital formats, whatever these technical sounding skills were, in my LinkedIn inbox in late June. I seldom checked LinkedIn. "Hi Tess, I've just discovered your work on the Yellow Card system. I'm interested to talk with you, since this clearly looks to be in the public interest," his message read.

Harper turned out to be the kind of guy who needed to get to the bottom of things for his own peace of mind. He did not cope well with uncertainty; when he had a question, he needed to know the answer. My co-authors agree that this attribute was key to Harper's tenacity and truly admirable: being able to discriminate is *the backbone of morality. Unlimited possibilities are not suited to man; If they existed, his life would dissolve in the boundless.*[2]

An investigative journalist and documentary filmmaker living

---

1   Hexagram 1, The Creative, line 2. From I Ching, by Richard Wilhelm, 3rd Ed. p.8.

2   Hexagram 60, Limitation, The Image. From I Ching, by Richard Wilhelm, 3rd Ed. p.232.

in India at the time, what prompted Harper to reach out to me was a mainstream media story about Christian Eriksen, a professional Danish footballer, who suffered a heart attack on the pitch during a game against Finland in Copenhagen. Harper told me, "He's 29 and basically dropped dead on the pitch. They defibrillated him, performed CPR, and he came back. There was some speculation he had had the vaccine three weeks prior. At first, the BBC were reporting he had had it – now that story seems to have disappeared, and the football association are putting out press releases which do not mention it... They're now saying he did not have the vaccine."

The metaphor of a footballer receiving a yellow card is hard to ignore. Eriksen had in many ways been fortunate to receive a "yellow card" when, from the distressing footage displayed live on television, he clearly might have received a "red card" instead. In the aftermath of Eriksen's collapse, the press quickly stepped in to assure the public that the vaccine was not to blame. To make this point clear, it was emphasised that both the Italian and Spanish teams had already been vaccinated. The suggestion, perhaps, was that the possibility of other players being at risk was too disturbing for the average football fan to even consider. As such, any link between Eriksen's cardiac arrest and the Covid vaccine was swiftly dismissed.

During my subsequent Zoom conversation with Harper, we discussed the Yellow Card report and I introduced him to the story of ivermectin. To my surprise, Harper was incredulous. But my incredulity trumped his – it was the Covid vaccine report that had led him to us, not our work on ivermectin! There was something refreshingly genuine and unguarded about Harper's approach. He was the perfect person to investigate the Dr Andrew Hill saga because he came from a place of curiosity and trust in government. Notably, while he could conceive of scientific misconduct, like the majority of folk he struggled even more to comprehend the idea of hostile authorities deliberately suppressing the truth.

His investigation, once published on his Substack "The Digger", was illuminating for all involved, especially me.[1] I was astonished by what he had uncovered and how clearly he articulated it. The fresh perspective he brought to the story was dramatic, particularly regarding the conflicts of interest surrounding those who sought to discredit ivermectin. One revelation, in particular, stunned me: A Prof. Andrew Owen, a colleague of Hill's at the University of Liverpool, had connections that raised serious ethical questions.

Prof. Andrew Owen was the Director of the Centre of Excellence in Long-acting Therapeutics (CELT) at the University of Liverpool. As the principal investigator for the LONGEVITY project, Owen had been funded by Unitaid to develop long-acting drugs for malaria and other infections. In addition to this, he had worked on the NIH-funded Long-acting/Extended-release Antiretroviral Resource Program (LEAP). Owen was also a co-founder and CSO for Tandem Nano Ltd., a company focused on drug delivery, and had been heavily involved in evaluating novel antivirals for Covid-19. Despite being invested in competing drug development, Owen sat on the UK's Covid Therapeutics Advisory Panel (CTAP)!

Harper's findings suggested that Prof. Owen probably influenced the conclusions of the paper on ivermectin's efficacy as a Covid-19 treatment, authored by Dr Hill. Owen was not listed as an author. However, Owen's digital fingerprint appeared in the metadata of the pre-print version of Hill's original paper, raising serious questions about whether he had meddled with the conclusions on behalf of his funder or for his own financial gain – to benefit from his private, corporate, and academic interests in competing drugs. Either way, combined with the report of forensic communications specialist, Mr

---

1   https://philharper.substack.com/p/professor-tied-to-altered-andrew?

Lyndon Alexander,[1] it implied scientific misconduct.

On the risk/benefit assessment for emergency use of ivermectin, Alexander noted: "The continuing failure of Dr Hill and his co-authors to offer any conclusions on the risk/benefit implications of the use of ivermectin defies a clinical or scientific explanation." About Dr Hill's ethical position, the forensic communications specialist concluded: "Dr Hill has never explained his conduct in allowing interference in his Preprint Paper, but the unavoidable conclusion is that Dr Hill did not have the strength of character or ethical commitment to present conclusions that he believed were correct, based on the 'best evidence' available to him at the time."

I learnt from Liverpool University's official response to a complaint of scientific misconduct lodged against Dr Hill by the French civic organisation Bon Sens, that Hill was in fact an Honorary Research Fellow in the Pharmacology Department, involved in industry-sponsored HIV research, NIAID Dr Fauci's favourite research topic, since the early 1990s. Hill's work had generally focused on antiretroviral drugs, and according to his biography he was an advisor to the Clinton Foundation and the BMGF.

"Honorary" positions are not accompanied by remuneration by the university. Thus, the report notes that for his HIV work, "Dr Hill was employed by a major pharmaceutical company. The post has been renewed regularly since then." (Exhibit 23.)[2] It was no surprise to me to read Hill's remuneration during his research career came in whole or part from the pharmaceutical industry, not from the university. The panel that evaluated the complaint, however, "did not find any evidence of misconduct in research which warrants a Formal Investigation."

The realisation that such potential conflicts of interest could exist

---

1   Exhibit 6. Forensic Analysis of Dr Hill's pre-print, commissioned by Bon Sens.
2   Exhibit 23. Liverpool University's Report. (September 2021).

so openly was hard to fathom. Had everything in so-called academia been reduced to money?

Harper's reveal of Prof. Owen's digital fingerprint on the Hill preprint was the final nail in the coffin for any credibility and authority Hill might have had regarding ivermectin. Meanwhile, about Owen's involvement, my co-authors are clear: *When the time for return has come, a man should not take shelter in trivial excuses, but should look within and examine himself. And if he has done something wrong he should make a noble hearted resolve to confess his fault. No one will regret having taken this road.*[1] However, *If a man misses the right time for return, he meets with misfortune. This misfortune has its inner cause in a wrong attitude towards the world...What is pictured here is blind obstinacy and the judgement that is visited upon it.*[2] Whilst an apology was due, it sounded like we should not hold our breath.

Harper's meticulous investigation into the corrupted Hill manuscript was nothing short of groundbreaking, and I hoped that his work would serve as an enduring example of true journalism, one that could inspire other journalists who colluded directly or indirectly with the globalist media empire to follow his lead.

In tandem with Harper, data analyst Alexandros Marinos made complementary and highly enlightening revelations, adding depth to the Hill investigation and ongoing exposé. I was so grateful that these guys did not let the matter rest. Approvingly, my co-authors remark of the continuing collective efforts, *Thus we do not simply abandon the field to the opponent; we make it difficult for him to advance by showing perseverance in single acts of resistance.*[3] Together, we had made it clear that we – scientists, journalists, doctors, and others – would doggedly uncover truths and hold the prevailing powers and their corrupt office bearers to account.

---

1   Hexagram 24, The Turning Point, line 5. From I Ching, by Richard Wilhelm, 3rd Ed. p.99-100.

2   Hexagram 24, The Turning Point, line 6. From I Ching, by Richard Wilhelm, 3rd Ed. p.100.

3   Hexagram 33, Retreat, The Judgement. From I Ching, by Richard Wilhelm, 3rd Ed. p.130-1.

On the matter of the footballer, Eriksen went to ground and never spoke openly about his near-death experience to my knowledge. It is well-known that professional football players are owned, traded and sold, so this is not surprising. Albeit well-paid, professional football is about as overt as a system of slavery can be. Thus, we never learnt whether Eriksen was prevented from telling his side of the story.

A formal statement from Inter Milan's director, Giuseppe Marotta, clarified that despite online rumours and misinformation, there was no evidence linking Eriksen's collapse to a Covid-19 vaccine, with Marotta explicitly stating that Eriksen had neither been vaccinated nor contracted Covid-19. It could not have been an easy time for Eriksen. If he entertained the possibility that the Covid vaccine was as the root of his collapse, when his career was dependent on physical fitness, the worry for his family, as well as his fellow professional footballers would have been extreme. With the best care at hand, incentives highlighting the path of least disruption might have seemed the best option for Eriksen at the time.

Following the reflections above, an intriguing conversation occurred with my co-authors about Eriksen's role. They describe the professional footballer's circumstances as *conditioned and unfree[…]*, highlighting the need to cultivate *in himself an attitude of compliance and voluntary dependence.*[1] They also draw attention to the likelihood that Eriksen was indeed someone who could shed light on the issues with the Covid vaccines by virtue of his character and position of influence: *The image of fire. Thus, the great man, by perpetuating this brightness, illumines the full quarters of the world.*[2]

Given his chosen career, the commitment it takes to make it, and the fact that he had recovered and was back on the pitch a year later signed with Manchester United, I was not surprised to learn from my

---

1   Hexagram 30, The Clinging, The Judgement. From I Ching, by Richard Wilhelm, 3rd Ed.
      p.119.

2   Hexagram 30, The Clinging, The Image. From I Ching, by Richard Wilhelm, 3rd Ed. p.119.

co-authors that Eriksen was a man of action, represented by a *Dragon appearing in the field. In terms of human affairs, this means that the great man makes his appearance in his chosen field of activity. As yet he has no commanding position but is still with his peers. However what distinguishes him from the others is his seriousness of purpose, his unqualified reliability, and the influence he exerts on his environment without conscious effect. Such a man is destined to gain great influence and to set the world in order. Therefore it is favourable to see him.*[1]

Was I being urged to reach out to Eriksen more than three years later to find out what had actually transpired? Fitted with an Implantable Cardioverter Defibrillator (ICD) device, intended to prevent fatal cardiac arrests by discharging a jolt to restore regular heart rhythm, Eriksen's inspiring return to professional football was a testament to his resilience and determination. My co-authors go on to suggest *his influence spreads and becomes visible throughout the whole world.*[2] Would his story be more than about his personal triumph? Could it have a transformative impact on the world? Well, we would just have to wait and see.

MOVE 47. Distinguished Scientists & Doctors Rally Round

During the period surrounding the publication of our review, a deluge of competing ivermectin reviews flooded the academic landscape, each aimed at confusing and disorienting the public. The barrage of nitpicking our review and cherry-picking data for theirs was overwhelming. For our small rebuttal team led by Dr Fordham, supported by our loyal and creative BIRD administrators, Rob Trup and Linda Rae, keeping pace with the seemingly limitless resources of our detractors became a gruelling task. Each new review felt like

---

1   Hexagram 1, The Creative, line 2. From I Ching, by Richard Wilhelm, 3rd Ed. p.8.
2   Hexagram 1, The Creative, line 5. From I Ching, by Richard Wilhelm, 3rd Ed. p.9.

another battle in an exhausting war of attrition. Despite these challenges, a growing sense of solidarity emerged around our efforts, even as occasional troublemakers attempted to infiltrate our ranks. In the midst of the confusion, the integrity of our work was obvious.

Out of the many ivermectin reviews, however, one particular review by Roman et al., published unashamedly by Editor-in-Chief Dr Robert T. Schooley of *Clinical Infectious Diseases*, stood out as a glaring example of scientific malpractice.[1] This study was marred by gross falsification of source data, highly selective inclusion of studies, and a blatant cherry-picking of data from those included. The conclusions drawn did not align with the evidence presented. In a further twist of irony, the authors, who were clearly engaged in distorting the evidence, had the audacity to claim that there was a "misinformation infodemic" surrounding ivermectin, accusing others of manipulating data for political gain! This was both ironic and infuriating given their own flagrant misrepresentation of the facts.

Led by Dr Fordham, we swiftly issued a formal letter of concern, requesting the retraction of the paper. The letter, signed by 40 international doctors and scientists, highlighted the numerous flaws in Roman's analysis and called on the journal to account for publishing such a defective review. (Exhibit 24).[2] The solidarity of professionals from around the world challenging this erroneous paper reflected the growing resolve of ethical doctors and scientists to unite against corruption. Despite our compelling scholarly demand, Dr Schooley remained unmoved, and the problematic paper by Roman et al. remained published, a stark testament to the decay of academic science.

Similarly, Cochrane finally produced its ivermectin review. Its authors, Popp et al., did not take a pragmatic approach like most other existing reviews, which compared ivermectin versus no ivermectin

---

1   Roman et al (2021). doi.org/10.1093/cid/ciab591
2   Exhibit 24. Retraction demand by Fordham et al (2021).

for Covid symptoms.[1] Instead, they used a granular approach similar to that of the WHO and Roman et al., where they excluded most studies and dissected out the remainder into assorted categories rendering meta-analysis futile. (Exhibit 25).[2] In short, the review did not appear to be geared towards addressing the research issue or attempting to adequately answer the question at hand, which was did ivermectin help people with Covid-19? Thus, like the Roman review, Popp et al predictably found no evidence in favour of ivermectin and, as a result, added nothing to the evidence base.

Prof. Paul Garner, Cochrane Infectious Diseases Group's Co-ordinating Editor, was quoted as saying about the review: "The hype around ivermectin is driven by some studies where the effect size for ivermectin is frankly not credible, and this has driven the conclusions in other reviews. The study with a huge effect has now been retracted as fake. Careful appraisal is the cornerstone of Cochrane's work, and with such extreme public demands for a drug to work during the pandemic, it remains vital that we hold onto our scientific principles to guide care."[3]

Outraging those trying to get this useful and inexpensive medicine approved, the Cochrane review by Popp et al. muddied the waters for everyone eagerly watching this space. In other words, it did just what it seemed intended to do. As a result, many energetically stepped forward to counter this pseudo-scientific yet impactful counter move facilitated by Cochrane against ivermectin.

The anonymous ivmmeta.com[4] platform proved to be an indispensable resource, gathering and compiling ivermectin studies from around the world with exceptional diligence. In the midst of our battle against misinformation with limited resources, this data

1   Popp et al (2021). www.cochrane.org/CD015017/
2   Exhibit 25. Fordham et al. Use and Abuse of Systematic Reviews (2021).
3   https://cidg.cochrane.org/news/new-cochrane-review-ivermectin-preventing-and-treating-covid-19
4   https://c19ivm.org/meta.html

repository provided a rock-solid foundation of up-to-date research, consistently offering insights that others had overlooked. Yet, despite the invaluable nature of their work, it was a personal regret that the individuals behind this mammoth effort chose to remain anonymous, withholding the recognition they truly deserved.

My co-authors suggest that the motivation behind c19ivm.org was rooted in a clear-sighted understanding of the big picture, an understanding unclouded by illusion or false optimism. *Firm as a rock. Not a whole day. Perseverance brings good fortune. This describes a person who does not allow himself to be misled by any illusions. While others are letting themselves be dazzled by enthusiasm, he recognises with perfect clarity the first signs of the time. Thus he neither flatters those above nor neglects those beneath him; he is as firm as a rock. When the first sign of discord appears, he knows the right moment for withdrawing and does not delay even for a day. Perseverance and such conduct will bring good fortune.*[1]

The unwavering focus and strategic discretion of the individuals behind c19ivm.org reflect the qualities of individuals who are not swayed by external pressures or the enthusiasm of the crowd. *Like a rock*, they recognised the truth of the times and, when the moment for action arose, acted without hesitation; they did what was right with strength and resolve. Their persistence and integrity in the face of adversity resonate with the wisdom of knowing when to stand firm and when to retreat, without falling into common traps or drawing unnecessary fire, ensuring the continued success of their efforts. We will be forever grateful to these individuals for their anonymous support of BIRD's efforts and their role in the collective fight to save humanity.

Additionally, we were fortunate to receive critical support from Professors Norman Fenton and Martin Neil at Queen Mary University of London. As Director of the Risk and Information

---

[1] Hexagram 16, Enthusiasm, line 2. From I Ching, by Richard Wilhelm, 3rd Ed. p.69.

Management Research Group and a Professor in Computer Science and Statistics, respectively, Fenton and Neil were experts in data analysis. They informed us that they had conducted a Bayesian analysis on a relevant subset of the studies included in our review. Their findings strongly supported our conclusions, adding significant academic weight to our argument. The paper they published, titled "Bayesian Meta-Analysis of Ivermectin Effectiveness in Treating Covid-19 Disease,"[1] was a highly erudite analysis that not only validated our claims about the corrupted Roman et al. paper, but also bolstered the credibility of ivermectin as a viable Covid treatment.

Times of growth are beset with difficulties. They resemble a first birth...Thus, it is very important not to remain alone; in order to overcome the chaos he needs helpers.[2] And excellent help had arrived!

Given their prestigious positions within established academia, their endorsement was both reassuring and invaluable. The support from Fenton and Neil represented a significant shift, aligning us with experts whose endorsement added both credibility and momentum. Following their paper, with its provenance from Queen Mary University of London, it felt like a breakthrough was imminent, and that we might soon see the tide turn in our favour.

Clinical colleagues from other countries shared their findings too. Dr Fernando Valerio from Honduras, where ivermectin was deployed early, presented clinical data in a scientific paper that concluded that "Decreases in Covid-19 case fatality rates in Honduras were associated with both the initial publication of a multi-drug Covid-19 therapeutic protocol and a subsequent outreach program."[3] Results with similar protocols were published by Dr Sabine Hazan in the USA, Prof. Thomas Borody in Australia, and Dr Jackie Stone in Zimbabwe.

---

1 www.researchgate.net/publication/353195913_Bayesian_Meta_Analysis_of_Ivermectin_ Effectiveness_in_Treating_Covid-19_Disease

2 Hexagram 3, Difficulty at the Beginning, The Judgement. From I Ching, by Richard Wilhelm, 3rd Ed. p.16-7.

3 Ontai et al. doi.org/10.23880/eij-16000217

Dr Jackie Stone's experience and efforts during the Covid era had weight and influence. One of her most significant contributions in August 2021 was the publication of a landmark article, "Changes in SpO2 on Room Air for 34 Severe COVID-19 Patients after Ivermectin-Based Combination Treatment: 62% Normalization within 24 Hours."[1] This study demonstrated that ivermectin significantly improved oxygen saturation within 24 hours of the first dose, an effect that was hard to dismiss from any clinician's perspective. Her paper, based on a cohort of her patients, became a critical resource in understanding the effect that ivermectin induced in respiratory symptoms attributed to severe Covid-19.

In Zimbabwe's resource-poor setting, where Dr Stone had only 17 intensive care beds at her disposal, her well-documented clinical expertise in treating severely ill Covid patients at home became invaluable. At a time when fear and uncertainty gripped the world, and people with Covid symptoms were told to stay home until they turned blue, Stone successfully reduced suffering and death by utilising safe, inexpensive options, especially ivermectin. *The root of all influence lies in one's own inner being: given true and vigorous expression in word and deed, its effect is great. The effect is but the reflection of something that emanates from one's own heart.*[2] Dedicated to helping people, she made it a priority to share her findings with the broader medical community, and her voice was authoritative, clear and credible.

Together with Dr Martin Gill, an ear, nose, and throat surgeon in South Africa, Stone developed an effective Covid-19 treatment protocol based on their frontline experience. The treatment protocol included ivermectin, doxycycline, zinc, vitamin C, vitamin D, aspirin, and colloidal silver, combined with melatonin and quercetin

---

1   Stone et al. doi.org/10.3390/biologics2030015
2   Hexagram 61, Inner Truth, line 2. From I Ching, by Richard Wilhelm, 3rd Ed. p.237.

if available. Dr Stone passionately advocated for early intervention, something she had long practiced in treating malaria and other serious infections. "We always treat early, we don't wait for people to get seriously sick," she said many times in interviews. In addition, with years of experience treating HIV, Dr Stone also understood the need for combination therapies to combat rapidly replicating and mutating viruses. She knew that zinc, silver, and zinc ionophores had antiviral properties. But Stone made it clear that when she began treating Covid-19 patients with ivermectin in August 2020, she saw death rates drop virtually overnight!

Dr Stone's success brought her significant hardship. Instead of being celebrated for her contributions, she faced the grim prospect of a custodial sentence for simply doing what she knew was best for her patients – treating them early. The Zimbabwe Medical Council charged her with criminal offenses for what essentially amounted to upholding her Hippocratic Oath. As a result, she faced the very real threat of losing her medical license and was confronted with a potential $100,000 fine or five years in prison for prescribing ivermectin.

With such high stakes related to her actions, Stone, my co-authors note was *inevitably tossed to and fro between joy and sorrow*.[1] Her commitment to healing and standing by her patients' side brought her moments of deep fulfilment, but the constant professional and personal battles took their toll. The external pressures from the corporate medical establishment, the constant threats, and the lack of support from her peers chipped away at her resolve. It was extremely sad news for everyone who knew her when Dr Stone took her life three years later, exhausted and depressed following years of relentless attacks from the corporate machine. Ultimately, the tension between her inner truth and the overwhelming forces against her became too much to bear, leaving her spirit drained by a battle she felt she could not win.

---

[1]   Hexagram 61, Inner truth, line 3. From I Ching, by Richard Wilhelm, 3rd Ed. p.238.

MOVE 48. India Sues the WHO, and Other Notable Legal Actions

When the Covid scam began, ivermectin was already a widely used medicine in India, primarily for treating parasitic diseases; thus, it was quickly adopted as a go-to treatment for symptoms attributed to Covid-19. In Uttar Pradesh, the government distributed home-based kits containing 12mg ivermectin tablets to its population of 237 million, which resulted in impressively low Covid-19 rates – far lower than countries like the US, which relied on expensive and novel drug cocktails but claimed much higher infection rates. Despite this success, in May 2021, the WHO's chief scientist, Dr Soumya Swaminathan, publicly recommended against using ivermectin for treating Covid-19, except in clinical trials, in response to its escalating use in India. Citing Merck's statement that there was no evidence to support its use, her authoritative statements even led to ivermectin being removed from existing effective treatment protocols in India in some instances. As previously noted, Merck, a pharmaceutical company with vested interests in developing costly Covid-19 vaccines and novel therapeutics, was hardly a neutral authority. The WHO's Chief Scientist citing Merck should have been quite an embarrassment for the WHO, but such blatant lies and collusion were the norm during Covid.

In response, Adv. Dipali Ohja and the Indian Bar Association (IBA) launched a legal challenge against Dr Swaminathan. (Exhibit 26).[1] Using evidence from BIRD, the FLCCC, and Doctors for Life in Brazil, the IBA sent a 50-page, 8-part legal notice, accusing Dr Swaminathan of running a disinformation campaign by deliberately suppressing ivermectin's effectiveness for Covid-19. The notice highlighted her public statements, including a May 2021 tweet where she reinforced the WHO's position against ivermectin and her

---

1　　Exhibit 26. Indian Bar Association Legal Notice (25 May 2021).

comments in an interview dismissing the drug's effectiveness, and flagrantly contradicting the evidence of independent expert groups like BIRD and the FLCCC. Instead, she promoted masks as the "only vaccine" in the absence of other options.

The case filed by the IBA against Dr Soumya Swaminathan attracted significant attention, particularly from Indian news outlets and alternative media platforms like RFK Jr.'s Children's Health Defense. While the mainstream media largely ignored it and the WHO downplayed its importance, the case was a major boost for grassroots advocates like us. It demonstrated that even a small, determined individual – a petite and feisty Indian lawyer – could challenge powerful global institutions using the same weapon they wielded: ink on paper. Advocate Ohja's legal approach against the Covid agenda was arguably more impactful than any we had witnessed to date, especially as it struck at culpable individuals, as well as a key organisation in the chain of the globalists' command.

Identifying the individual responsible for an action or omission and holding them to account, Ohja's approach is well worth noting. Legal actions against organisations and corporations are likely to be onerous, resource intensive, and protracted. However, the globalists cannot carry out their agenda without the willing participation of order followers. In fact, they are powerless without compliant minions. Those facilitating atrocities directly or indirectly on behalf of their official masters, in this case the WHO, for the globalist elites, are often unaware that they are personally liable for their conduct under the law as living men and women and cannot shift the blame onto their employers. In addition, WHO privileges and immunity are meaningless if the organisation's core objective, which, for the WHO, is the attainment by all peoples of the highest possible level of health, can be shown to be compromised by their official policies and recommendations, as with what happened during the Covid-19 chapter. At the end of the day, however, the human being alone is responsible for their conduct on this earth.

For many Indians, the Swaminathan incident represented a deep betrayal. How could a senior Indian doctor, a woman and mother, employed by the WHO, side with the globalists in actions that would bring harm upon her own people, including children? My co-authors say *a man of dark nature is in a position of authority and brings harm to the wise and able man.*[1] To me this seems an apt assessment of the situation. Dr Swaminathan was someone trusted by the Indian public to represent their welfare through her role at the WHO and she was caught out acting with questionable morals and integrity. Why? *Order within the family depends on the character of the master of the house.*[2] If the character of the leader is flawed or corrupt, the nation and its people suffer as a consequence. This certainly rings true. Dr Swaminathan, as a trusted figure and Indian leader, was expected to put the welfare of her people first; instead, in the opinion of many of her countrymen, she led them directly into harms' way, into disorder and confusion.

However, my co-authors' input could also be interpreted in another way. They might be suggesting that Swaminathan's conduct was informed by the master of her house, the WHO's General – was she just doing his bidding? This begs another question. Was it simply a coincidence that she was called upon to deliver the WHO message to Indians not to use ivermectin, or was she deliberately deployed by her employer to beguile her countrymen, because they would be inclined to listen and to trust her due to her Indian heritage?

Swaminathan's response to the IBA indictment was swift. She deleted the dishonest tweet of May 2021. About this my co-authors note, *in the face of a superior enemy* (which Adv. Ohja clearly was),

---

[1]   Hexagram 36, Darkening of the Light. From I Ching, by Richard Wilhelm, 3rd Ed. p.139.

[2]   Hexagram 37, The Family, line 6. From I Ching, by Richard Wilhelm, 3rd Ed. p.147.

with whom it would be hopeless to engage in battle, an orderly retreat is the only correct procedure, because it will save the army from defeat and disintegration.[1] The WHO and Swaminathan knew they would lose against the formidable diminutive Ohja. She had the power of Truth on her side.

About Adv. Ohja, my co-authors comment, *Both thunder and lightning come, the image of ABUNDANCE. Thus the superior man decides lawsuits and carries out punishments.*[2] All the corrupt WHO could do in the face of Ohja's abundant greatness and clarity was retreat and use the age-old tactic of the oppressor to obstruct justice – delay. Nevertheless, it is likely that Swaminathan's role in spreading disinformation about ivermectin and the experimental Covid vaccines could lead to further legal actions if ever she were to enter India, so abhorrent was her conduct to many.

Adv. Ohja was not to be easily deterred by court delays and obfuscations. On a mission to save India from Gates and other globalists, she and the IBA escalated their efforts. Their next legal move was to sue India's Health Minister, Mr Mansukh Mandaviya, for the harmful Covid-19 policies implemented in the country. This new case called for the removal of individuals within India's Covid Task Force who were connected to organisations like the BMGF, the Rockefeller Foundation, and Program for Appropriate Technology in Health (PATH; funded by both afore mentioned organisations), alleging that these individuals were promoting policies driven by the financial interests of vaccine manufacturers.

Notably, Bill Gates' history in India has been marked by unethical conduct, particularly in relation to vaccines. The most notorious of these incidents occurred during the trials of the Human Papillomavirus (HPV) vaccine in the mid-2000s. In these trials, conducted by

---

1   Hexagram 7, The Army, line 4. From I Ching, by Richard Wilhelm, 3rd Ed. p.34.
2   Hexagram 55, Abundance, The Image. From I Ching, by Richard Wilhelm, 3rd Ed. p.213-4.

the Indian Council of Medical Research (ICMR) and the BMGF in collaboration with local health bodies, hundreds of young girls, mostly from poor rural areas, were enrolled without proper informed consent. Many suffered severe side effects, including deaths, after receiving the trial vaccine. Just like with the Covid-19 vaccines, the parents were not informed of the potential risks. Gates' involvement in vaccine-related issues in India would continue to be the subject of various legal actions, highlighting the ongoing controversy surrounding his influence in the country's public health policies. Adv. Ohja and the IBA efforts to hold Covid culprits to account was admirable and inspiring.

In addition to these and the legal efforts of Robert F. Kennedy Jr.'s Children's Health Defense, our work also supported other actions by individuals and organisations in countries including Malaysia, the UK and South Africa. In the UK, a judicial review of the MHRA's failure to approve ivermectin for Covid-19 was sought by a private individual with BIRD's support, and in the USA, lawyer Ralph Lorigo took hospitals to court on behalf of the families of seriously ill patients to demand access to effective treatment.

Like Ohja, Ralph Lorigo was dynamite. "On your side and in your court", his website proclaimed, and this certainly rang true when it came to ivermectin – he was on our side. Lorigo was a powerful weapon against corrupt institutions withholding ivermectin from severely ill patients. I lost count of the cases he won, but Dr Pierre Kory kept count. In Kory's 2024 book *The War on Ivermectin*, Kory recorded that Lorigo won 40 cases and lost 40 cases. Out of the 40 cases where the judge ruled in favour of the patient being given ivermectin, 38 of the patients survived; of those where the judge ruled in favour of the hospital, allegedly only two survived. An isolated US voice from a profession for which I was developing an unhealthy cynicism (after repeated efforts to garner interest in the case of ivermectin, and the hefty costs involved), as had occurred with Adv.

Dipali Ohja, I developed a great respect for Lorigo.

Illustrating this, my co-authors say *Deliver yourself from your great toe. Then the companion comes, And him you can trust.*[1] One's *great toe* in this line represents the idea of my holding a certain view about lawyers that needed shedding. *For otherwise the friends who share his views, on whom he could really rely and together with whom he could accomplish something, mistrust him and stay away.*[2]

There were good lawyers fighting for people's rights and the truth. Lorigo's unwavering commitment to his clients, even when it meant standing alone against a powerful system, helped me move beyond my doubt and cynicism of the legal profession. Legal efforts were an essential part of our advocacy. Lorigo emerged as that trusted fellow warrior, one who could be relied upon in the fight for truth and healing. *The army needs perseverance And a strong man.*[3] In the US, Lorigo was the man.

MOVE 49. Dr Fordham Seeks Answers from His Parliamentary Representative

Physicist and cancer survivor Dr Edmund Fordham, who had previously run as an independent candidate in the South East Cambridgeshire constituency, had a clearer understanding of the roles and responsibilities of parliamentary representatives than most. In 2021, driven by his growing concerns about the lack of early treatment for Covid-19, particularly the potential of ivermectin, and the fact that NICE had blatantly ignored its own rubric on evidence-based medicine in a pandemic scenario, he sought to bring these issues to the attention of his parliamentary representative, Conservative MP Mrs Lucy Frazer. In a well-crafted letter to Frazer, Fordham requested that a meeting with the newly appointed Health

---

1   Hexagram 40, Deliverance, line 4. From I Ching, by Richard Wilhelm, 3rd Ed. p.156-7.

2   Hexagram 40, Deliverance, line 4. From I Ching, by Richard Wilhelm, 3rd Ed. p.156-7.

3   Hexagram 7, The Army, The Judgement. From I Ching, by Richard Wilhelm, 3rd Ed. p.32.

Secretary, Mr Sajid Javid, be facilitated. Given Frazer's background as a barrister, Fordham's carefully reasoned arguments should have made perfect sense to her.

Here is Fordham's letter.

Re: Solution to the Covid-19 pandemic: ivermectin. Request for meeting between Sajid Javid and principals of the British Ivermectin Recommendation Development (BiRD) panel

Dear Mrs Frazer

As you know, I have been researching repurposed drugs for covid-19 since writing on 3 April 2020 on the subject. My letter was ignored by HMG for months before extracting a response regarding the Therapeutics Taskforce, which is staffed, as we now know from FoIA requests, by precisely zero doctors or medical researchers. This total deficit of essential skill sets explains part of HMG's open disregard of off-the-shelf medicines for treating Covid-19, though thousands of doctors worldwide have been doing just that since the start of the pandemic, with what is now a long list of successful off-the-shelf therapeutics. The UK's attitude has been shameful, amounting to deliberate withholding of potentially life-saving medicines from sick people, in open reversal of the NHS's mission. Recent meta-analysis of ivermectin in Covid-19: Since January, I have been working with Dr Tess Lawrie MB BCh PhD and other principals of BiRD on a detailed systematic review of available clinical trials of ivermectin for the treatment and prevention of Covid-19. On 17 June this culminated in the publication of our paper: "Ivermectin for Prevention and Treatment of Covid-19 infection", in the American Journal of Therapeutics copy enclosed. In just 10 days this has achieved over 18,000 PDF downloads. It is ranked by "Altmetric" research statistics as 1st in 181,242 recent papers, and 59th in all 18,041,393 research papers ever tracked.[1] Earlier versions of this meta-analysis were presented on 20 February to the BiRD panel of medical doctors, scientists and other stakeholders, in a formal Evidence to Decision (EtD) framework, with the panel voting: "ivermectin should be adopted to reduce morbidity and mortality associated with Covid-19 infection and to prevent Covid-19 infection among those at higher risk."

Request for meeting with Mr Sajid Javid: With the recent change in Secretary of State I am requesting an urgent meeting with the principals of the British Ivermectin Recommendation Development (BiRD) panel. Mr Javid has publicly stated his ambition "to get the country back to normal". We can provide Mr Javid with a complete solution, available immediately. Multiple (documented) approaches to HMG have been ignored, while the loss of thousands of lives continued. Mr Javid has an opportunity to remedy this disgraceful record. Importance of ivermectin for public policy: The importance of cheap, safe and simple therapeutics in treating, and preventing, Covid-19 can hardly be over-stated. Virtually all "Non-Pharmaceutical Interventions" (NPIs) are redundant. The country can be set back on the road to economic recovery forthwith. Treatment is not just a matter of saving the severely ill. Early (i.e. within 3-4 days) treatment should be in the hands of GPs for outpatient treatment. The spectre of "hospital overload" then evaporates. Prophylaxis of contacts will stop community transmission, or genuine outbreaks in institutions. Ivermectin is used in nursing homes, where patients up to the age of 106 have been successfully treated. It can be used for international travel, as I have used it myself, though "immunocompromised" from my medical history. A clear and simple policy

---

1   By 2024, our published ivermectin review was ranked 8th out of more than 26 million tracked scientific articles. At the time of writing, however, the Altmeter metrics had been removed from the online version of the article, in what appeared to be an attempt to reduce awareness of our article's scientific importance and ranking.

of: "Treat the disease, isolate only the sick, and prophylax the vulnerable" is obviously feasible. Ivermectin stands out from all other repurposed medicines as effective at all stages of the Covid-19 illness. Its effectiveness in prophylaxis is proven, for high-exposure workers, the vulnerable, and household contacts of confirmed cases. It beggars belief that the importance of this medicine has been ignored. Safety and Status of ivermectin: Ivermectin is a WHO "Essential Medicine". These are the "safe and effective" medicines "that every healthcare system should have" – but the NHS does not. It has been used worldwide in well over 3.8 billion doses with a negligible rate of "serious adverse events". Its success in treating "river blindness" (onchocerciasis) won the 2015 Nobel Prize for its discoverers. Yet this "Essential Medicine" is unlicensed in the UK.

Efficacy of ivermectin: This is now beyond any serious doubt. Our meta-analysis was inspired by a "narrative" review by Dr Pierre Kory MD et alia, of the "Front-Line Covid Critical Care" (FLCCC) alliance of US intensive care specialists who see the toughest covid-19 cases. Their "MATH+" treatment protocol far surpasses the deplorable record of the NHS in discharging their patients safely.

Kory et al. did not however perform a meta-analysis, which is what our paper supplies. Meta-analyses are the highest quality of evidence for medical regulators, such as our own MHRA. Dr Lawrie and her consultancy E-BMC Ltd are world-class experts. We restricted our meta-analysis, deliberately, to so-called Randomised Controlled Trials (RCTs), simply because regulatory agencies typically disregard anything else. No less than 24 such RCTs are now available. The better-quality observational trials typically confirm the results of the RCTs, whether in severe hospitalised illness, or in prophylaxis.

The current attitude of the WHO – recommending ivermectin only in clinical trials – is a contrivance indefensible on the facts.

The important clinical trials have already been done. Ivermectin in treatment of covid-19: Kory et al. noted that ivermectin is the sole therapeutic effective at all stages of the complex clinical course of Covid-19, from the early "viremic" stages through the "pulmonary" stage and in intensive care. It should not be thought of as the sole medicine and no clinicians using it in treatment regard it thus. It is used in combination with vitamins and mineral supplements, other anti-viral medications, and anti-inflammatory and anti-coagulant medications when needed. Importantly for the NHS, it is eminently suitable for home care by GPs.

Ivermectin in prevention of covid-19: Over 6 clinical trials (three of them RCTs) over thousands of participants demonstrate ivermectin's effectiveness as a prophylactic, for high-exposure healthcare workers, and for household contacts of known cases. Some trials achieved total protection (zero infections). The reproduction number (the famous "R") for household transmission drops to around 0.3 – well below propagating level – when contacts take ivermectin prophylaxis. Periodic ivermectin plus vitamin and mineral supplements therefore provides a public health effect identical to vaccination, at a fraction of the cost, and a safety profile established over billions of doses.

Existing initiatives: The Prime Minister's "Antivirals Taskforce" has been ridiculed as "landing from another planet and having absolutely no clue of what he is talking about" because the declared objectives of "antiviral treatments ready for autumn 2021" already exist, available now, with unrivalled safety data and effectiveness demonstrated to the highest standards of rigour. The Antivirals Taskforce is truly redundant; its mission is already accomplished. Similarly, the announcement of an ivermectin "arm" in the PRIN-CIPLE trial is (i) unethical per the Helsinki Declaration since basic effectiveness is already known, and (ii) scientifically barren, because the genuine research questions (dose, frequency, adjunct medications) are absent from the protocol. We are happy to engage with the PRINCIPLE PI's to advise.

Conclusions: This cheap and safe medicine has already been demonstrated over two dozen RCTs and a meta-analysis. In a rational world this would be more than sufficient evidence for the MHRA. Dexamethasone, hailed as a major advance in the RECOVERY trial (though saving only a proportion of the most severely ill) was adopted after just one RCT. "Moderate certainty" evidence in two dozen (24) RCTs has always been more than sufficient evidence for licensing new medicines; further obstruction can only be for discreditable reasons. I look forward to an urgent appointment with Mr Javid, to brief him on the latest evidence, with Dr Lawrie and the principals of BiRD.

Yours sincerely

Edmund Fordham MA PhD CPhys CEng FInstP EurIng

On 21 July 2021, Mrs Lucy Frazer QC confirmed that she had written to Mr Sajid Javid, forwarding Fordham's request for a meeting "in respect of [his] detailed research into the efficacy of ivermectin for Covid-19." However, much to Fordham's frustration, there was no response – nothing at all. This lack of action was particularly irksome to him, as he believed there was a professional responsibility to at least acknowledge and respond to such a request from his Conservative Party colleague.

After following up with no result from MP Lucy Frazer, Fordham eventually submitted a Freedom of Information request to the Department of Health and Social Care, seeking clarity on what had happened after Frazer sent on his letter to Javid requesting a meeting. To his astonishment, there was no record of Frazer ever corresponding with Javid in this regard.

So what actually happened? According to my co-authors, *whereas an inferior man revels in power when he comes into possession of it, the superior man never makes this mistake.*[1] This is a key distinction in the context of the Covid chapter, where it became evident that many politicians had become a law unto themselves, seemingly unaccountable to their constituencies. How many of their own rules were broken? How many letters went unanswered? The sheer scale of neglect and arrogance was staggering. It was as if they were drunk with their own power, forgetful of their primary responsibility, which was to serve the people in their constituencies.

In Frazer's case, if she had indeed failed to forward the letter while assuring Fordham that she had, this would seem to corroborate the notion that Frazer lied to him. It was a breach of trust – a clear example of political evasion. The sense Fordham had through this unsatisfactory experience was that perhaps Whitehall had sent a clear directive to parliamentarians: "Don't talk about ivermectin, it mustn't exist." Such a command would have been in line with the political climate of the time, where certain truths were actively suppressed for reasons of control and narrative. This was the feeling Fordham took from his interactions with MP Frazer, who seemed less a representative of the people and more an instrument of political expediency.

In a broader sense, Fordham's struggle highlights how many in positions of power have lost sight of their duty to engage meaningfully with those they are meant to serve. They have lost sight of their *Fellowship with Men.* Caught up in a secretive game played behind closed doors, rather than treating their constituents with respect and openness, they treat them with disdain, evasion, or even outright dishonesty. This failure to engage in genuine fellowship is symptomatic of a larger political culture in which leaders grow more concerned with preserving their own power than with fostering the kind of

---

1   Hexagram 34, The Power of the Great, line 3. From I Ching, by Richard Wilhelm, 3rd Ed. p.134-5.

meaningful connection that leads to real service and action.

However, *greatness and justice must be indissolubly united*,[1] otherwise power is *mere force*. This is a lesson that had clearly been lost on many of those in the halls of power at the time. Power, in the absence of responsibility and fairness, becomes nothing more than coercion, an abuse of authority. It was time that political representatives understood this fact. The public did not simply need leadership; they needed accountable, transparent, and just leadership.

My co-authors liken Frazer's behaviour to that of a goat, which in ancient China was symbolised as possessing *hardness outwardly, and weakness within*.[2] The image of the goat is significant. It suggests an external facade of stubbornness and belligerence, but with little internal fortitude or integrity. The co-authors suggest that politicians like Frazer could stand to learn from this. *One can relinquish a belligerent, stubborn way of acting, and in doing so, will not have to regret it*.[3] Losing the goat with ease would be associated with no remorse, a lesson in letting go of hard-headedness and embracing honesty and clarity instead. It is a reminder that power can be wielded with grace, without the need for deceit or force, and that humility and transparency are integral to true strength as a leader.

Fordham's actions, on the other hand, reflect a kind of integrity that is crucial to true fellowship with others. In contrast to Frazer's evasive behaviour, Fordham's insistence on justice, truth, and accountability sets him apart as someone who values true fellowship. Not merely as an exchange of favours or power, Fordham sought a deeper connection based on mutual respect and the wellbeing of his fellow man. As such, he represents the type of leader that understands

---

1   Hexagram 34, The Power of the Great, The Judgement. From I Ching, by Richard Wilhelm, 3rd Ed. p.133.

2   Hexagram 34, The Power of the Great, line 5. From I Ching, by Richard Wilhelm, 3rd Ed. p.135.

3   Hexagram 34, The Power of the Great, line 5. From I Ching, by Richard Wilhelm, 3rd Ed. p.135.

fellowship as a bond based on responsibility and the willingness to engage with others honestly and openly.

About this situation, my wise co-authors conclude, *Truth and strength must dwell in the heart, while gentleness reveals itself in social intercourse. In this way one assumes the right attitude towards God and man and achieves something. Under certain conditions, intimidation without gentleness may achieve something momentarily, but not for all time. When, on the other hand, the hearts of men are won by friendliness, they are led to take all hardships upon themselves willingly, and if need be will not shun death itself, so great is the power of joy over men.*[1]

---

1   Hexagram 58, The Joyous, The Judgement. From I Ching, by Richard Wilhelm, 3rd Ed. p.224.

Chapter 10

Gathering Together

Over the earth, the lake:
The image of GATHERING TOGETHER.
Thus the superior man renews his weapons
In order to meet the unforeseen.[1]

If the water in the lake gathers until it rises above the earth, there is danger of a breakthrough. Precautions must be taken to prevent this. Similarly where men gather together in great numbers, strife is likely to arise; where possessions are collected, robbery is likely to occur. Thus in the time of GATHERING TOGETHER we must arm promptly to ward off the unexpected. Human woes usually come as a result of unexpected events against which we are not fore-armed. If we are prepared, they can be prevented.[2]

As the growing movement around ivermectin gathered force, it was

---

[1] Hexagram 45, Gathering Together, The Image. From I Ching, by Richard Wilhelm, 3rd Ed. p.175.

[2] Hexagram 45, Gathering Together, The Image. From I Ching, by Richard Wilhelm, 3rd Ed. p.175.

not just the scientific community that began to take notice. It was as if a dam had broken, and a flood of unexpected and often unwelcomed forces surged forth. As my co-authors wisely warn, the surge of attention around ivermectin brought with it new challenges – and the threats from those who sought to maintain control over the fake narrative.

This pressure was felt acutely when an opinion piece on ivermectin appeared in *Nature Medicine*, one of the world's most prestigious medical journals. The piece, written with dubious intent, was a clear example of the forces being gathered against ivermectin's growing support.

Another significant gathering took place with a certain influential Conservative Party politician by the name of Sir Graham Brady at Birdcage Walk in Westminster, London. Experts from across the world came together, in person and virtually, to convey the seriousness of the issues with the Covid-19 genetic injections, the withholding of ivermectin and other early treatments, and the inappropriateness of PCR tests for disease diagnosis. The *human woe* associated with this meeting was the palpable disappointment in the outcome for all involved.

In this chapter, I also tell the story of my first-ever invited lecture in my hometown, at Bath Royal Literary and Scientific Institute (BRLSI), where for two centuries scientists have gathered for philosophical discourse and cutting-edge research. Ill-prepared for the hostility from certain quarters, I upset their establishment views on Covid-19 vaccines by calling them gene therapies, which had unhappy consequences.

The last gathering discussed in this chapter covers the explosive moment when Joe Rogan openly admitted to taking ivermectin. This served to gather groups both for and against ivermectin in an open, albeit power-skewed, battle for control of the narrative manifest in an aggressive media storm.

Many of our relationships with organisations and individuals were consolidating at this time. Yet it was interesting to observe and explore those that never developed or remained fragile. *Hold to him outwardly also. Perseverance brings good fortune. Here the relations with a man who is the centre of union are well established. Then we may, and indeed we should, show our attachment openly. But we must remain constant and not allow ourselves to be led astray.*[1] This comment by my co-authors was equally applicable to those willing and unwilling to openly associate with us, as it was to our approach to new associations – how did one know whom to trust?

MOVE 50. Hired Hands Get Busy

Following the concerted efforts of diverse doctor and scientist groups, a remorseless band of hired hands were quickly deployed on an ivermectin opinion piece that was published in the highly ranked medical journal *Nature Medicine* within weeks of our primary publication and rebuttals. Mr Jack Lawrence, the third-year "medical student" of *The Guardian* article fame, was given first author credit on this paper, much to his jubilation, which he shared unstintingly on Twitter. Of course, publishing one's first publication in a top medical journal was surreal – it did not happen. In a normal world, especially such baseless opinion pieces, written by unqualified individuals who dismissed the work of thousands of highly qualified medical experts, would never make it into a prestigious publication. But clearly, we weren't in a normal world anymore.

Lawrence, a blogger writing about Covid-19 'misinformation' in 2020, also operated with the pseudonym "Ivor Mectin" on Twitter, and was certainly no medical expert. A quick check revealed that he was actually a third-year *bio*medical student at St. George's,

---

1   Hexagram 8, Holding Together, line 4. From I Ching, by Richard Wilhelm, 3rd Ed. p.38.

University of London, not even a *medical* student as *The Guardian* article had stated, clearly in an effort to give more credence to his back story. Thus, his interest in ivermectin did not stem from first-hand experience with Covid-19 patients in hospital wards. His real back story, it seemed, was far more obscure. Deploying Lawrence as first author on a hit piece on ivermectin certainly suggested the ivermectin antagonists were having to scrape the barrel.

On Twitter, his 'Ivor Mectin" pseudonym sarcastically claimed to have a significant relationship with Bill Gates, stating that he worked for "Bill Gates Moon Laboratory". Under his real name on Twitter, he wrote on September 23, 2021: "I've been smiling all day but also at a loss for words. My first published academic article came out today and it's in *Nature Medicine*! It's a piece co-authored with [Meyerowitz-Katz and Sheldrick's Twitter handles] and I still can't believe it's real!" As much as Lawrence was amazed and thrilled to see his hit piece on ivermectin published in *Nature Medicine*, nothing surprised us about the lengths to which dark forces would go to maintain the narrative that ivermectin was dangerous and unproven!

Enquiring about young Lawrence's motives, my co-authors describe his situation as *Youthful Folly. In the time of youth, folly is not an evil. One may succeed in spite of it, provided one finds an experienced teacher and has the right attitude towards him. Without this modesty and this interest there is no guarantee that he has the necessary receptivity, which should express itself in respectful acceptance of the teacher. This is the reason why the teacher must wait to be sought out instead of offering himself. Only thus can the instruction take place at the right time and in the right way.*[1]

This generous and wise perspective suggests to me that perhaps young Lawrence did not think things through fully. Perhaps he was

---

1   Hexagram 4, Youthful Folly, The Judgement. From I Ching, by Richard Wilhelm, 3rd Ed. p.20-1.

approached with a deceitful proposition by powerful figures, either directly or indirectly, and took it on carelessly or even playfully, unaware of the full consequences of his actions. It could have simply been about the easy money and status...this might be a temptation for many a young man with university debts and lowly prospects. My co-authors remind us through Lawrence's example, that *Nature attains what is right for all without artifice or special intentions. Man achieves the height of wisdom when all that he does is as self-evident as what nature does.*[1] This suggests that true wisdom lies in acting with integrity, guided by a deeper understanding, rather than pursuing personal gain or fleeting rewards, no matter the external pressures.

Further, my co-authors suggest an internal struggle may have occurred subsequently within Lawrence regarding his actions. *Dragons fight in the meadow. Their blood is black and yellow. [...] when black and yellow blood flow, it is a sign that in this unnatural contest both primal powers suffer injury.*[2] Perhaps Lawrence will eventually come forward to explain what transpired, shedding light on the arrangement that compromised his integrity, and how he found himself entangled with his Australian counterparts in this regrettable misconduct.

Mr Gideon Meyerowitz-Katz and Dr Kyle Sheldrick, one listed second and the other last (most senior) on the *Nature Medicine* opinion piece, were among Lawrence's co-authors. Presented in the British media again as an ivermectin "expert", Australian Meyerowitz-Katz, unsurprisingly, was not the senior academic as portrayed. Notably, his academic trajectory really only got going with Covid-19. With several of Meyerowitz-Katz's publications funded by the Australian government, his articles directly supported the government's draconian Covid-19 measures. Despite his opinion frequently

---

1   Hexagram 2, The Receptive, line 2. From I Ching, by Richard Wilhelm, 3rd Ed. p.13-4.
2   Hexagram 2, The Receptive, line 6. From I Ching, by Richard Wilhelm, 3rd Ed. p.15.

contradicting respected experts such as Prof. John Ioannidis, a seasoned epidemiologist at Stanford University, he was inexplicably given space in high-ranked journals.

As noted in Chapter 8, Meyerowitz-Katz was an "aspiring researcher" aligned with industry interests. Despite this modest label, he loudly voiced his anti-ivermectin opinions on Twitter, positioning himself as a self-proclaimed expert with a special knack for "debunking junk science." To reinforce his persona, he wore a T-shirt emblazoned with the bold statement: *"TRUST ME, I AM AN EPIDEMIOLOGIST."* Quite the declaration for someone still in the early stages of his PhD.

My co-authors observed about Meyerowitz-Katz that *By growing used to what is dangerous, a man can easily allow it to become part of him. He is familiar with it and grows used to evil. With this he has lost the right way, and misfortune is the natural result.*[1] Meyerowitz-Katz, like others who had come to embrace the dangerous narrative he peddled, appeared to have traded his integrity for career advancement and alignment with powerful forces. In doing so, he may have irreversibly compromised his own judgement. Misfortune, indeed, seems a fitting outcome for those who consistently pursue personal gain at the expense of scientific honesty and the wellbeing of their fellow man.

My co-authors further highlight that for individuals like Meyerowitz-Katz, *Escape is out of the question,*[2] suggesting that once dangerous bedfellows have been chosen, it probably would not be easy to disengage from them. *When misled into action, [...] we should only bog down deeper in the danger; disagreeable as it may be to remain in such a situation, we must wait until a way out shows itself.*[3] This poignant observation emphasises how people who make strategic choices for

---

1   Hexagram 29, The Abysmal, line 1. From I Ching, by Richard Wilhelm, 3rd Ed. p.116.

2   Hexagram 29, The Abysmal, line 3. From I Ching, by Richard Wilhelm, 3rd Ed. p.116-7.

3   Hexagram 29, The Abysmal, line 3. From I Ching, by Richard Wilhelm, 3rd Ed. p.116-7.

personal or professional gain, while ignoring ethical considerations, can find themselves in increasingly difficult situations – ones that become harder to extricate themselves from over time.

Even more intriguing was the role played by Dr Kyle Sheldrick, who served as the senior corresponding author on the opinion piece. Despite his elevated position in this publication, Sheldrick was, in fact, only a PhD student at the University of New South Wales (UNSW), with a modest research portfolio comprising just 10 publications. While he held an undergraduate medical degree, his expertise lay in spinal research and MRI imaging, not in the clinical evaluation of drug efficacy or the nuanced interpretation of clinical trial data.

Furthermore, his publications in recent years had focused on areas such as spinal surgery, not on infectious diseases, antiviral treatments or evidence synthesis. This presented a critical gap in his qualifications when it came to evaluating or commenting on ivermectin's use for treating Covid-19, and placed him worlds apart from the available clinical and research expertise on the subject.

Notably, however, Sheldrick was co-founder of a biotechnology company that benefited from significant Australian government grants. About this allegiance, my co-authors confirmed *when the right connection with distinguished people has been found, a certain loss naturally ensues,*[1] suggesting that his integrity had been compromised for this financial gain and power. Ultimately, in making decisions by these parameters, personal and ethical loss was inevitable. But Sheldrick may well have remained satisfied with the trade-off.

In essence, four of the five authors behind the opinion piece had no formal medical training whatsoever. The third and fourth authors, James Heathers and Nicholas Brown, who described themselves as a psychology graduate and a psychology postdoc, referred to their own

---

1   Hexagram 17, Following, line 3. From I Ching, by Richard Wilhelm, 3rd Ed. p.73.

work as the efforts of "data thugs."[1] Their self-styled monikers, such as Heathers' "journal ghoul", only added to the absurdity. This opinion piece, which sought to discredit ivermectin and those ethical and dedicated clinicians who tried to share their expertise with the world, stood on shaky ground, propped up by a team of unqualified authors with little to no scientific substance to lend credibility to their claims. However, they held the truth about ivermectin down for a period, supported by an army of Gates' "fact-checkers" and military hybrid warfare specialists.

The Egyptian Prof. Elgazzar, who published the "retracted" study on ivermectin for Covid-19, summed up his thoughts about this lot in an email:

> "I refused [to respond to] both Lawrence and Sheldrick for 2 reasons: Firstly, they are thinking our work is fraud to push us to give to them [our data] and this is an old childish game. Why they didn't do this [– ask for and examine the data –] with some studies like RECOVERY or PRINCIPLE? Why they didn't do this with remdesivir [an expensive drug with scant evidence of efficacy or safety in Covid-19]? The second reason [I refused is because] they think they are Gods over us they think they are superior to us. They think they are better than the reviewers. They think they are high and we are low. In my opinion I don't like to deal with the likes of them."

These words encapsulated the frustration and disdain felt by many genuine researchers towards this group, highlighting not only their lack of scientific integrity but also their arrogant dismissal of others' work. It underscored the toxic environment in which these

---

1   www.science.org/content/article/meet-data-thugs-out-expose-shoddy-and-questionable-research

self-styled "experts" operated, one where power and money, rather than evidence and ethics, dictated their actions.

MOVE 51. "Drinking Tea with the Devil" at Birdcage Walk

In September 2021, I was invited by retired police officer Mr Mark Sexton to join a group with complementary expertise for a meeting with a senior Conservative Party politician in a location on Birdcage Walk, Westminster, London. At the time, I was not politically informed, and the name Sir Graham Brady meant nothing to me. On September 21st, at 1pm, fourteen international experts – doctors, scientists, and lawyers – assembled for a 90-minute meeting with Brady. Experts, including the eminent US cardiologist Dr Peter McCullough, German microbiologist Dr Sucharit Bhakdi, and British physician Dr Stephen Frost, joined via Zoom. The odds of 14 experts to one politician, and very limited time, would in most circumstances have felt like an insult. Thus, I was drawn to deduce that this politician must be a very important one. It turned out he was. Wielding enormous influence, as Chair of the 1922 Committee, Brady had the power and influence that brought down prime ministers.

The context of this meeting was indeed fraught with difficulty. My co-authors elaborate, *if one is in the difficult and responsible position of counsellor to a powerful man, one should restrain him in such a way that right may prevail. Therein lies the danger so great that the threat of actual bloodshed may arise. Nonetheless, the power of disinterested truth is greater than all these obstacles. It carries such weight that the end is achieved, and all danger of bloodshed and all fear disappear.*[1] We, a body of professional people, had the rare opportunity to counsel this powerful figure to halt the vaccine rollout, which was causing

---

1   Hexagram 9, The Taming Power of the Small, line 4. From I Ching, by Richard Wilhelm, 3rd Ed. p.42.

significant harm – bloodshed, in fact. An influential individual who does not want to openly engage with the concerns of the people he is supposed to serve is a difficult one to counsel indeed.

The meeting location at Birdcage Walk felt symbolic, a container close to yet detached from the real seat of power in Parliament. The choice of venue seemed carefully orchestrated to create the illusion that our concerns were being addressed. No minutes were taken, and the meeting was not recorded to my knowledge. A barrister present had insisted that it be conducted under Chatham House rules. This was my first encounter with such a set of "rules", and it quickly became apparent that they were part of the boys' club framework. The notion left me feeling disgusted. There is no honour in being forced to hide one's words behind a veil of secrecy. If that's the case, then you are surely in the wrong company. My co-authors share my sentiment: *You hold together with the wrong people. We are often among people who do not belong to a sphere. In that case we must beware of being drawn into false intimacy through force of habit. Maintaining sociability with such people is the only right attitude, because otherwise we should not be free to enter relationships with people of our own kind later on.*[1]

That was what weighed most heavily on my mind during the meeting. Chatham House was an ideological "think tank" of the globalists – it made no sense that we were playing by their rules. What would people feel when they learned about a secret meeting had been held with a senior politician in which the dangers of the experimental Covid vaccines had been discussed, if nothing came out of it? The optics would be disastrous. It could make us look like collaborators, not advocates of the people. I felt deeply uncomfortable, unsure if I had declined to go along with these "rules", I would have been immediately ejected from the conversation. A stranger in a strange land, I reasoned it was better to know what was said, even if

---

[1]   Hexagram 8, Holding Together, line 3. From I Ching, by Richard Wilhelm, 3rd Ed. p.38.

it was under such a restrictive framework, than to risk being excluded from this crucial dialogue. This prudency was appropriate according to my co-authors: *misfortune may overtake the bird if it is heedless and imprudent when building its nest.*[1]

It was clear from this experience that Chatham House rules, rather than facilitating free speech, fostered a lack of responsibility, allowing corrupt politicians self-serving actions without the risk of exposure. Additionally, by demanding confidentiality, they prevented public scrutiny, which encouraged politicians to make secretive deals and engage in questionable activities without accountability. In the context of the meeting at Birdcage Walk, they facilitated the invalidation of a very significant meeting, one that would demonstrate serious complicity on the part of individuals in government, like Brady. It required that we *remain constant and not allow ourselves to be led astray*[2] in such company.

The meeting was a waste of significant resources, tying up international experts – several doctors who were treating Covid vaccine-injured people, including a world-renowned virologist, molecular biologist, and cardiologist, a barrister, two lawyers and a funeral director – for what ultimately turned out to be a futile discussion. PCR tests weren't fit for purpose, informed consent had been ignored, viable treatments were available but not used, and harmful experimental shots had been unleashed on the public, a tsunami of death and disease would follow, Brady was told. The many ways in which the Nuremberg Code was violated by the UK's official Coronavirus Act of 2020 was stressed. We made it clear, the genetic injections being rolled out in the guise of Covid-19 vaccines must be stopped.

Brady listened about the harm, injury, and death the injections were causing, and heard our demands that the Covid-19 vaccine

---

1   Hexagram 56, The Wanderer, line 6. From I Ching, by Richard Wilhelm, 3rd Ed. p.219.
2   Hexagram 8, Holding Together, line 4. From I Ching, by Richard Wilhelm, 3rd Ed. p.38.

rollout be stopped, or paused at the very least. However, he appeared largely unmoved, his response scripted, as if he had been told to meet us only to placate our concerns, not out of genuine interest in resolving anything. He was impatient for the meeting to be brought to a close. I handed him a pack with the evidence on ivermectin – as well as our Yellow Card report – upon his prompt and hasty departure, which left us still all seated at the table somewhat bemused, if not deflated.

A hurriedly agreed outcome, the crumb bestowed on us by this publicly paid official who claimed there was little he could do, was: if we drafted some questions illustrating our concerns, he would endeavour to raise them in Parliament.

Sexton walked Brady back to Parliament, and when he returned, he recounted the conversation he'd had with him. He said "I told Brady that if the general public ever found out that the government was aware of the harm the vaccines were causing and had done nothing to stop it, there would be riots in the streets."

Brady's response was casual: "We thought that would've happened by now," he said. Such nonchalance expressed his relief. We had been too polite. He had expected more of a grilling. We had chosen to tell him what he already knew, rather than interrogate him.

After the meeting with Brady, Dr Stephen Frost, founder of a group called Doctors for Covid Ethics, and others spent days meticulously crafting 67 crucial questions addressing the key concerns with the Covid-19 response. Sexton personally sent the questions to Brady via his personal assistant. Whilst she promptly acknowledged receipt and confirmed that Graham Brady had received them, despite all the time and effort invested by so many professionals, Sexton never heard back from Brady himself. Sexton followed up several times, hoping for a response, but nothing materialised. The 67 questions and our combined expertise were effectively ignored.

There was no evidence that Brady ever did anything. He allowed the experimental injections to continue without lifting a finger to stop them, including the injecting of children. Sexton subsequently laid a complaint against Brady with the police of misconduct in public office, but as he expected, nothing was done. Misconduct in public office occurs when a public official wilfully neglects their duties and abuses the public's trust, without reasonable excuse or justification. Malfeasance in public office happens when a public official knowingly and wilfully acts in a way that causes harm, injury, or financial loss to a third party, understanding their actions are likely to cause such harm. Brady could not pretend he hadn't heard the facts, and yet he ignored them, and hid this from parliament and the public – it is likely that both applied to Brady.

A week later, the meeting was allegedly "leaked" to the press. Painted in a highly derogatory light, *The Independent* described our group as "anti-vaxxers," labelling the reputable doctors, scientists, and lawyers involved as individuals spreading false claims about the pandemic and vaccines. The article framed Brady's attendance as an attempt to listen to opposing views without endorsing them. The expertise we brought to the table was ignored, and we were dismissed as fringe voices.

An excerpt from the brief article in *The Independent* (30th September 2021) read:

"Anti-vaxxers are said to have met Tory MP Sir Graham Brady last week in a meeting where they called on the Covid vaccine rollout to be suspended. A group claimed they met with a senior Tory MP last Tuesday, during which they criticised the current vaccination programme – which is estimated to have saved hundreds of thousands of lives so far. The anti-vaxxers have made false claims against the Covid pandemic and vaccines in the past, including denying the existence of a pandemic and that vaccines are dangerous.

Mark Sexton, who has spoken at anti-lockdown protests, posted a video claiming he was among those who met with Sir Graham Brady on September 21. He said it was put to the MP that the Covid vaccine rollout should be paused urgently and should not be given to children. One of the meeting's participants, undertaker John O'Looney, confirmed the MP was Sir Graham Brady, who heads the Conservative Party's 1922 Committee.

According to *The Times*, Sir Graham would not confirm whether the meeting took place. He said he supported vaccines and that listening to views 'does not amount to an endorsement', the newspaper reported."

Some in the group were angry at Brady's disinterest. Not only was it an opportunity to waste our time, but it was also an opportunity to see how much we knew and to gauge the strength of our convictions. Frost, who had experienced these sorts of fruitless meetings before, likened it to "Drinking tea with the Devil." As an ethical doctor, Frost had good reason to feel impatient and frustrated – people were being harmed in real-time, and there were no signs that government officials, like Brady, were planning to act with integrity. Frost was tired of waiting.

O'Looney wrote in the email correspondence that ensued subsequently among the group: "The very best part of that meeting was meeting you guys and hugging you all, but any hopes I had for a 'miracle' evaporated pretty quickly simply watching Sir Graham and his body language. Brady was not genuinely interested in what we were saying. The meeting felt like a formality, designed to placate us while the powers that be continued with their agenda."

O'Looney was eager to share the contents of the meeting with the public and frustrated with the lack of follow-up action. His perspective resonated with me; an upside to the meeting was being around the table with like-minded professionals, sharing our different areas of expertise, and comparing notes. It felt like we were cementing the pieces of the puzzle together, not only for Brady, in case he did not already know, but for one another.

As the Covid scandal progressed, O'Looney, who as a funeral director was noting the most extraordinary, calamari-like clots in the cadavers, never gave up taking every opportunity to share what he knew with the public and came across as a wholly authentic human being. My co-authors concur that O'Looney was a rare individual of integrity. *A man who is able to awaken enthusiasm through his own sureness and freedom from hesitation. He attracts people because he has no doubts and is wholly sincere.*[1]

Weeks passed after the submission of the written material and Sexton was unable to make direct contact with Brady. Upon prompting, Sexton eventually received an email from Brady's PA some weeks later, promising an update from Brady, but nothing was ever received. My co-authors highlight that Sexton's role in public life was akin to *the faithful steward whose measures further the general welfare. The whole family can trust him, because love governs their intercourse. His character of itself exercises the right influence.*[2] Despite Sexton's efforts to orchestrate the event and his hope for a positive result, it had led to nothing tangible.

Whilst some of the group approved of sending formal Notices of Liability to Brady and other co-conspirators to demand the immediate suspension of the gene-based vaccines, believing they were complicit in crimes like mass murder, sterilisation, violations of the Nuremberg Code, and psychological torture, others were against this course of action. Lawyer Mr Philip Hyland, an employment lawyer

---

1   Hexagram 16, Enthusiasm, line 4. From I Ching, by Richard Wilhelm, 3rd Ed. p.70-1.
2   Hexagram 37, The Family, line 4. From I Ching, by Richard Wilhelm, 3rd Ed. p.146.

who had been called upon to defend ethical doctors and care workers alike from unlawful Covid-19 responses, stood firm on the point that Brady as a paid public official had a moral duty to act on the information received.

The barrister who had been adamantly in favour of adhering to Chatham House rules argued that Brady, as a "backbench MP," had no legal responsibilities, and that presenting him with such a notice would only antagonise him, thereby damaging any prospect of him becoming an ally. The barrister's perspective, though perhaps well-intentioned, seemed to dominate, undermining any unity of purpose that might have been possible among our diverse group of relative strangers. I was surprised by his reluctance to challenge Brady, whose true intentions seemed very dubious.

On this situation, my co-authors submit: *Game is in the field – it has left its usual haunts in the forest and is devastating the fields. This points to an enemy invasion.*[1] The metaphor speaks to an unsettling disruption, a force coming from an unexpected direction, scattering what might have been a more cohesive effort. Proactive steps that could have resulted from our encounter with Brady were, for all intents and purposes, scuppered. Frankly, the idea of Brady ever aligning with us, given all that had transpired, required more than a stretch of the imagination; it seemed an exercise in denial. After everything we had witnessed, the barrister's insistence on framing Brady as a potential ally felt less like pragmatic diplomacy to me and more like a refusal to acknowledge his complicity.

Much later, in July 2023, Brady was interviewed by journalist Lee Hall on *British Thought Leaders*.[2] In the interview Brady admitted "we knew that the level of [Covid-19] infections in the UK were falling before the lockdowns started", "the public were taken for a

---

1   Hexagram 7, The Army, line 5. From I Ching, by Richard Wilhelm, 3rd Ed. p.34-5.
2   https://www.youtube.com/watch?v=o7HB_iXZlII

ride" and "the science was never settled and eminent scientists were silenced who had different views". Well, *he* certainly knew. We had told him of the impending tsunami of death and disease from the Covid-19 vaccines in no uncertain terms. There could be no plausible deniability for Brady.

In hindsight, the decision to send Brady to meet with us was a clear signal that, despite our limited influence, the dark forces feared us and what we represented – the voice of the people. This incident also confirmed, I believe, for the wider group of participants, the fundamental futility of secretive institutions like Chatham House. I had little doubt that these organisations were never meant to serve the people; rather, they existed solely to perpetuate the power of a select group, a globalist boys' club designed to keep its illegitimate clique in control. The infestation of cronyism in government, like the dying taps of a death watch beetle in an old house, was apparent. Brady's feigned nonchalance, when he suggested they had expected riots, made it clear they knew their days were numbered. Their system, like they themselves, had long since outlived any meaningful purpose.

MOVE 52. Hullabaloo at the BRLSI

By September 2021, I had spoken at various public events, most of which were online. There was a certain courage in this, and I had presentation slides to back me up if I faltered, as I certainly was no expert in public speaking. However, it is one thing making an appearance in a distant land and place, doing so in one's hometown felt entirely different. What if I made a fool of myself? As most would wish, in my hometown, I wanted to be able to walk down the street without a care.

That said, in May 2021, I had responded to a request to speak in person at a rally in Bristol, a neighbouring city about 45 minutes' drive from where I lived in Bath. Having never spoken publicly before, I was filled with both excitement and trepidation. For this event I had written a speech, and to help myself, I wrote key points on my hand, having no idea how others manage without such prompts. I've never been able to memorise speeches word for word, and at school and university, I would work up quite a sweat and get flustered speaking in front of the class.

At that time of the rally, few doctors in the UK were speaking up, and the urgency and despondency of the moment demanded that I do so. As I stood on that village green in front of a few hundred people on a cloudy day, under a small gazebo with a generator humming nearby, the sense that this reality was a kind of theatre was hard to shake. I shared my background as a doctor and researcher, spoke about ivermectin, and reassured the crowd not to be afraid. I likened our uncertain situation to labour pains – unpredictable and potentially messy, but ultimately leading to a positive outcome – birth.

And then, I sang. I had woken up that morning with *Three Little Birds* by Bob Marley in my head but had no intention of singing it. I could do many things, but singing was not one of them. Yet, when I stood there, facing the crowd, it just felt right. With the line, "Don't worry about a thing, because every little thing is gonna be alright," I offered a simple message of hope. I encouraged the crowd to sing along, and I think many were surprised to see such vulnerability coupled with fearlessness in such uncertain times. Of course, the fact that the song includes birds was spot on as BIRD's representative!

Around the village green that Saturday afternoon, police vans and officers in riot gear surrounded a peaceful crowd of men and women, with a few babies and children scattered in between. All they wanted was to learn more about how to protect their families. After the event, I spoke to a group of bored officers and handed them some leaflets on ivermectin. Upon hearing my credentials, they took the leaflets with interest.

Despite my nerves and the lingering self-reproach from the sing-along, the experience in Bristol, though nerve-wracking, felt a world away from Bath. Bath, a more parochial and conservative town, had no rallies to speak of; everyone obediently followed the status quo. So, it came as a pleasant surprise when I received an invitation to speak at the Bath Royal Literary and Scientific Institute (BRLSI) in August.

The invitation came from none other than the Convenor for Science and Medicine at the BRLSI, Mr Tim Hooker. It was more than I could have hoped for – especially from an institution like this. Superseding the Bath Philosophy Society, the BRLSI was founded in 1824 with the aim of promoting and advancing science, literature, and art in Bath.

With the UK's intellectual establishment feigning oblivion – looking everywhere but at the truth – the essence of British pantomime was reigning at the time. That they might be interested in hearing my perspective on Covid-19 felt almost too good to believe. Rapidly being framed as a scientific pariah by the establishment, I took the invitation to be both a challenge and a glimmer of hope. Would the BRLSI be a home for free thinkers as it was originally intended? I would do a good job with my presentation, and then wait and see!

The date for the event was set for September 30th, well ahead of time. However, a week or so before the talk, I received this notification from Mr Hooker:

"I should let you know that BRLSI will adhere to their strict policy of asking attendees to wear a face mask (speakers exempted), even though that requirement cannot be enforced. I hasten to add that is not my regulation but a BRLSI regulation which I have strenuously resisted."

The tone was courteous if not somewhat embarrassed. It did not bode well for a free-thinking institution, nor for what I would be sharing with its audience. Ticket sales had been extremely modest, it was unlikely to be a full house, or even half a house, so they need not worry about transmission on account of there being a crowd! I was grateful to Mr Hooker for giving me the heads up though...

It is important that there should be men who mediate between leaders and followers. These should be disinterested people, especially in times of increase, since the benefit is to spread from the leader to the people. [...] This sort of intermediary, who also exercises a good influence on the leader, is especially important.[1]

Hooker knew it did not look good and I appreciated his honesty; it served to warn me in advance about potential difficulties. Clearly he was not aligned with the herd, and was doing me a great service by dint of the unexpected invitation to speak to the BRLSI members. I let Mr Hooker know that I believed people should have the freedom to make their own choices with regard to wearing masks on the night. For the record, I wrote that there was limited evidence supporting the effectiveness of mask-wearing, and an increasing body of research suggesting that it may actually be harmful.

The BRLSI building itself is a landmark on Bath's Queen Square, with a massive stone obelisk standing proudly in the square in front. It was my first time in the main hall, situated on the first floor of its historic Georgian building. What a beautiful and elegant venue, reminiscent of the drawing rooms in Jane Austen novels. The presence of illustrious philosophers and writers from centuries past seemed to echo in the air, and I felt both humbled and honoured to be standing in a space that had once hosted so many creative thinkers.

As the evening unfolded, the turnout was modest, no more than 25 in the audience, scattered across a set of around 50 chairs laid out

---

1   Hexagram 42, Increase, line 4. From I Ching, by Richard Wilhelm, 3rd Ed. p.164.

on the carpet. The room was well-lit, though the screen was far too small for the presentation to be truly effective. Still, I was warmly welcomed by Mr Hooker and introduced to several attendees, most of whom were elderly women. I'd say the average age in the room was probably about 65, potentially the benefactors of this apparently struggling institution. It was quite a cold and windy night, so I was really grateful that they'd all bothered to turn up. A few who had been wearing masks removed them with relief upon seeing that I was not wearing one and greeted me with smiling faces. A man who I was told would be responsible for overseeing the live Zoom transmission, introduced as a fellow doctor, Dr Manford, kept his firmly in place, however. There was some fussing over the technical aspects, and as a result, we started a little later than the scheduled 7pm time.

The lecture was called "Covid-19 and the State of Evidence-Based Medicine". I had prepared a comprehensive slide deck, hoping to walk the audience through my professional experience, the suppression of ivermectin, and the risks associated with the new types of genetic vaccines. My goal was not to offer medical advice, but to lay out the facts clearly and concisely, inspiring those present to take control of their own health and question the official narratives they had been fed by the authorities. In this small group, with time limited, I hoped to convey the conflicts of interest in relation to the Covid policies and their implications.

The audience seemed truly engaged, their faces attentive and curious as I shared the evidence and my insights. But just as I was nearing the end of my presentation, an unexpected voice suddenly erupted into the room. At first, I was confused, not knowing where it was coming from. It became clear when the voice continued that it was coming from the Zoom feed. The virtual interrupter stated that what I was saying was false and, what I remember most were the words, "You should be ashamed!" I was as much taken aback by the provenance of the dissident voice as the personal attack itself – surely it was convenors' role to mute virtual attendees?

But the shock did not stop there. Hooker's co-convenor Dr Manford, who allowed my faceless accuser to finish his outburst without interruption, then accused me of deliberately speaking too long to avoid answering any questions! It was evident he was upset, though I had been oblivious to any tension building. Perhaps there had been a private Zoom chat going on behind the scenes, but I hadn't been privy to it. As for the time, I hadn't been keeping track; I thought everything was going smoothly, especially considering the engaged expressions on the faces of the audience. Eyes glaring above his face mask, Dr Manford's loathing was directed at me.

What had had the potential to be a promising exchange of ideas was suddenly derailed by this hostility. I had never been involved in any interaction like it. Perhaps I had been too opinionated? I am a reasonable human being, open to the notion that there is a lot I don't know and that I may even be wrong about certain things I think I do know. Why not wait until I had ended to have a cordial discussion? If time was short, we could arrange a follow up meeting?

Hooker reminded his co-convenor of his responsibility to mute virtual attendees, as the elders frowned and hushed him. Of the incident, my co-authors remark metaphorically *Here the Lord of Light is in a subordinate place and is wounded by the Lord of Darkness. But the injury is not fatal; It is only a hindrance. The wounded man gives no thought to himself; he thinks only of saving others who are also in danger. Fearful he tries with all his strength to save all that can be saved. There is good fortune in this acting according to duty.*[1] Regaining my flow, I finished quickly and answered a few questions from the floor before Manford declared the event closed and stormed off down the stairs.

---

[1]   Hexagram 36, Darkening of the Light, line 2. From I Ching, by Richard Wilhelm, 3rd Ed.
      p.141.

Tim Hooker and his wife Lee invited me and my partner for a drink at the adjacent Francis Hotel afterwards. Though all were visibly shaken by the incident, we couldn't help but smile a little at the absurdity of it all. What a hullabaloo! But we also agreed – it was not over nothing. The truth about ivermectin and the genetic Covid-19 vaccines, especially for those who place blind faith in "the science," was deeply uncomfortable.

Sadly, the incident revealed to me that the BRLSI was no longer the place of intellectual significance it once was. What had once been a home for free thinkers and philosophers now seemed to serve as little more than a sanctuary for establishment views – merely an ornament to philosophy. Again, my co-authors observations are astute, and highlight the importance of critical contemplation in changing times: *By contemplating the forms existing in the heavens, we come to understand time and its changing demands. Through contemplation of the forms existing in human society, it becomes possible to shape the world.*[1] Philosophy was no longer valued at the BRLSI, which needed to change with the times.

The hostility of those two individuals – one virtual, one physical, both faceless – played on my mind, however, and was only partially assuaged by Hooker's reassuring email:

Let me immediately congratulate you on your superb lecture at BRLSI on Thursday evening and say how much your in-house audience appreciated every word you said. The thoroughness of your preparation, the detail of information and the clarity of your calm, authoritative presentation were a model of professionalism and held everyone in rapt attention. I cannot thank you enough for explaining so clearly the present clinical situation regarding Covid-19 and directing everyone's attention to the need for an open-minded

---

[1]   Hexagram 22, The Judgement. From I Ching, by Richard Wilhelm, 3rd Ed. p.90-1.

balance within the media between reporting on evidential scientific data and non-scientific policy. Regrettably, as you would expect, I understand that some members of the virtual audience were of a closed mind and behaved disrespectfully. Indeed, a group of elderly ladies within our (physically present) audience felt you had been unfairly targeted by the aggressive male zoom attendee who broke through your talk so rudely. They immediately voiced their opinion that you had been targeted because you are female, intelligent and strong. They have a point!

In fact, a dear friend of mine, Mrs Chrissy Philp, who was also a benefactor of the BRLSI, had been part of the virtual audience. She alerted me and all to this fact during the Zoom set-up phase with an excited greeting. As a scientist, astrologer and wise elder, Chrissy Philp was well aware of the prevailing patriarchal scientism within her beloved institute. An as yet undiscovered genius in my opinion, Chrissy had completed an extraordinary treatise about a cosmic blueprint of the brain decades earlier, which showed how our brains are, practically speaking, receivers for frequencies generated by the ever-changing cosmos. Integrating physics, psychology, astrology, metaphor, and *I Ching* code, Chrissy's complex theory, embracing science and wisdom, aligned with Professor Stephen Hawking's – that we live in a holographic universe – and her treatise proved it.

Yet in this world of patriarchal reductionist science, her theory was dismissed without due consideration. Accepting of her fate, Chrissy knew that she was regarded as little more than an eccentric old woman by her male counterparts at the BRLSI, her genius overshadowed by their didactic worldview. She could do nothing but *quietly let nature take its course.[1]* The universe had its own plan, and pushed her around by her own admission. In good humour, Chrissy

---

[1]   Hexagram 25, The Unexpected, line 5. From I Ching, by Richard Wilhelm, 3rd Ed. p.103.

had resigned herself to the fact that her work would be discovered posthumously. Nevertheless, Chrissy continued to donate funds generously to the BRLSI regardless, and on one occasion, she even gifted a treasure trove of important books. To her horror, however, instead of preserving them for posterity, the institute sold them off!

Fortuitously for me, as you will remember, it was Chrissy Philp who introduced me to my co-authors, Richard Wilhelm's translation of the *I Ching*, in January 2020. This was not the only wisdom she shared that resonated. Chrissy's cosmic blueprint theory made immediate sense to me, and I was eager to share it with others. However, I soon realised that she was right, it was inaccessible to most people for the time being. As regards the *I Ching*, I remained fascinated, got acquainted with it better, and the rest is both history and mystery, as evidenced by this book.

Getting back to the incident at the BRLSI itself, my co-authors' final word was that I was right to be unsettled by the experience, and yet was required to persevere: *this provides a teaching for those who cannot leave their posts in times of darkness. In order to escape danger, they need invincible perseverance of spirit and redoubled caution in their dealings with the world.*[1] The unpleasantness and hostility were far from over, as I would come to realise in due course...

MOVE 53. Shock and Horror: Joe Rogan Takes Ivermectin

Joe Rogan, the popular US podcast host with millions of followers, publicly disclosed in September 2021 that he took ivermectin as part of his treatment for Covid-19. As someone who was not afraid to tackle controversial topics, Rogan's decision to openly discuss his use of ivermectin sparked immediate backlash. Picked up by CNN and the BBC, the controversy was intensified, and Rogan was accused

---

1   Hexagram 36, Darkening of the Light, line 5. From I Ching, by Richard Wilhelm, 3rd Ed. p.142.

of promoting misinformation, calling his decision to use "folk remedies" like ivermectin irresponsible and potentially dangerous. However, the fact that Rogan admitted to throwing the kitchen sink at it when he became symptomatic did not exactly help ivermectin's case, it just added to the controversy.

As someone who had followed Rogan intermittently and appreciated his boundary-pushing stance, I was keenly aware of his impact, and I and the team had reached out to him a couple of times in 2021, hoping to get an opportunity to speak about ivermectin and the vaccines on his influential platform. Unfortunately, an invitation was not forthcoming. As with Russell Brand, the fact that Rogan never interviewed me, convenor of the BIRD group, and co-author of a highly ranked scientific review on ivermectin, did make me wonder though. Was Rogan's intention to raise awareness of ivermectin's usefulness to his audience, or was there something more personal or agenda-driven at play?

Maybe it was as simple as the fact that I was a woman, and Rogan, being a manly man, preferred his frank chats with men, that prevented a conversation with me. Or maybe it was because I was British, and he preferred interviewing Americans. Perhaps he perceived me as somewhat insignificant, yet BIRD's efforts could have helped him out. Was it possible that a podcast host of his worldly perspective had never heard of us, who knew? I was not offended in the least, but disappointed that his popular platform, which seemed to be trying to counter official narratives, was inexplicably out of our reach.

My co-authors observe, *He hides weapons in the thicket; he climbs the high hill in front of it. For three years he does not rise up.*[1] This suggests to me that secrecy, and hidden agendas, may have been at the heart of the situation surrounding Rogan's disclosure on ivermectin. The lines evoke the idea of someone preparing for a longer-term

---

[1] Hexagram 13, Fellowship with Men, line 3. From I Ching, by Richard Wilhelm, 3rd Ed. p.58.

strategy, not immediately revealing their full intentions. My co-authors go on to say that there were *obstacles standing in the way of fellowship with others.*[1] I suppose they mean me and BIRD in this context. The nagging doubts remained about why he chose to add to the ivermectin controversy in my opinion, rather than helping to settle it. Perhaps it all boiled down to trust, or a lack of it, all round.

Man has received from heaven a nature innately good, to guide him in all his movements. By devotion to this divine spirit within himself, he attains an unsullied innocence that leads him to do right with instinctive sureness and without any ulterior thought of reward and personal advantage. This instinctive certainty brings about supreme success and "furthers through perseverance". However, not everything instinctive is nature in this higher sense of the word, but only that which is right and in accord with the will of heaven. Without this quality of rightness, an unreflecting, instinctive way of acting brings only misfortune. Confucius says about this: "He who departs from innocence, what does he come to? Heaven's will and blessing do not go with his deeds."[2]

The BBC was quick to ridicule Rogan's stance. Using polarising language in a six-minute "report"on the 16th September 2021 that framed ivermectin's use primarily for animals, Ros Atkins, a BBC news anchor, quoted pejoratively to BBC viewers, "Anti-vaxxers started imploring each other to go to pet stores, claiming the horse and people ivermectin were the same.[3] They started sharing tips on how to eat the gel kind. They started hoarding it. The gel kind being equine paste dewormer, which comes in an apple flavour." Atkins' sneering delivery was intended to evoke images of misguided and irresponsible behaviour, corroborating the false narrative that ivermectin was a dangerous, animal-only medicine. His emphasis on ivermectin's use in the US also subtly diverted people from the truth

---

1   Hexagram 13, Fellowship with Men, line 3. From I Ching, by Richard Wilhelm, 3rd Ed. p.58.

2   Hexagram 25, Innocence, The Judgement. From I Ching, by Richard Wilhelm, 3rd Ed. p.101.

3   https://bird-group.org/bbc-misleading-repor/

– that ivermectin was being used to treat Covid-19 symptoms, by those who knew it worked, in the UK and worldwide.

Largely drawing on the then-debunked press release from the USA, the BBC coverage frequently referenced livestock (horses, cows, and other animals!), which appeared many times throughout the report. Words like 'goo', 'de-wormer', and 'paste' were included to evoke a sense of repulsion at the thought of using ivermectin.

With over four billion doses administered globally, Atkins brushed over the fact that ivermectin has been safely used in humans for decades and had proved safer than common over-the-counter medications like aspirin. This critical omission, clearly an intentional oversight, furthered the biased portrayal of the drug. If one were to follow Atkins' line of reasoning, it would imply that people should also avoid common, life-saving medicines like aspirin and antibiotics simply because they have veterinary counterparts – an absurd and illogical conclusion.

Atkins' claim that "there is no data for ivermectin for Covid-19" was presented as an undeniable fact, yet this was categorically false. In reality, there was a wealth of data supporting ivermectin's use at the time – 64 studies, of which 45 had undergone peer review.[1] These studies, involving over 26,500 participants, consistently demonstrated the drug's potential in reducing Covid-19-related mortality and transmission. Furthermore, there were at least seven meta-analyses, where data from different studies were pooled, from credible international researchers reinforcing these findings.

The sheer ignorance and manipulation of the facts were hard to stomach. As an experienced scientist, hearing this deliberate misrepresentation of the facts was upsetting. However, one of the more egregious aspects of the BBC report was Atkins' disrespectful and derogatory reference to my FLCCC colleagues Dr Pierre Kory and

---

1   c19ivm.org

Dr Paul Marik. To witness this BBC ignoramus, who held so much influence over public opinion, not only steering people away from a potential treatment that could help save lives, but casting aspersions on those who were actually doing so, was deeply infuriating.

What would make people like Ros Atkins do such a thing? *Keeping his jaw still. The words have order. Remorse disappears.*[1] My co-authors suggest that Atkins might have had to suppress any inner conflict or remorse about the narrative he was pushing. Interestingly, this was the same observation my co-authors made about *Daily Mail* reporter, David Rose, in Chapter 2. There must have been consequences to these mainstream media employees questioning the larger agenda. "If you refuse to deliver the headline, someone else will!" perhaps.

With Atkins' employer, the BBC, being one of the main propaganda mouthpieces of the globalists' Covid-19 agenda, prioritising compliance over personal reflection was probably necessary for Atkins to keep his job. My co-authors reflect, *On the mountain, a tree: the image of DEVELOPMENT. Thus the superior man abides in dignity and virtue, in order to improve the mores.*[2] *The tree on the mountain is visible from afar, and its development influences the landscape of the entire region. It does not shoot up like a swamp plant; Its growth proceeds gradually. No sudden influence or awakening is of lasting effect. Progress must be quite gradual, and in order to obtain such progress in public opinion and in the morals of the people, it is necessary for the personality to acquire influence and weight. This comes about through careful and constant work on one's own moral development.*[3]

This is as much a reflection on the need for moral development as an observation of the fact that we had much work to do to acquire

---

1   Hexagram 52, Keeping Still, Mountain, line 5. From I Ching, by Richard Wilhelm, 3rd Ed. p.203.

2   Hexagram 53, Development, The Image. From I Ching, by Richard Wilhelm, 3rd Ed. p.205.

3   Hexagram 53, Development, The Image. From I Ching, by Richard Wilhelm, 3rd Ed. p.205.

sufficient influence and weight to counter the damage being done by individuals like Atkins and propaganda mouthpieces like the BBC. Developing the required influence would take time. Thus, it was necessary for me, BIRD and the EbMCsquared team to have perseverance, *for perseverance alone prevents slow progress from dwindling to nothing.*[1]

---

1   Hexagram 53, Development, The Judgement. From I Ching, by Richard Wilhelm, 3rd Ed. p.205.

Chapter 11

Possession In Great Measure

He makes a difference
Between himself and his neighbour.
No blame.[1]

This characterises the position of a man placed among rich and pow-
erful neighbours. It is a dangerous position. He must look neither to
the right nor the left, and must shun envy and the temptation to vie
with others. In this way he remains free of mistakes. Another gen-
erally accepted translation of the line is as follows: He does not rely
on his abundance. No blame. This would mean that the individual
avoids mistakes because he possesses as if he possessed nothing.[2]

Taking the plunge with only modest support and lots of silent
opposition and incredulity, we officially launched World Council
for Health (WCH) on 22nd September 2021. Looking back, it was

---

1   Hexagram 14, Possession in Great Measure, line 4. From I Ching, by Richard Wilhelm, 3rd Ed.
     p.62.
2   Hexagram 14, Possession in Great Measure, line 6. From I Ching, by Richard Wilhelm, 3rd Ed.
     p.62.

an unbelievably bold step, given our resources totalling a handful of courageous individuals, but the positive energy and potential were palpable. At the time, BIRD was already walking a tightrope in its health advocacy mission, with mainstream propagandists eager to slander us as "anti-vaxxers." Many fellow ivermectin advocates, hesitant to speak out against the experimental vaccines, were starting to distance themselves from those of us who did, and yet the need to do so was ever pressing.

Thus, launching WCH gave us a fresh platform to advance our mission and solidify our influence and credibility. Becoming the first organisation to publicly challenge the dangerous Covid-19 vaccines, using science as well as good common sense to back our position, our authentic voices resonated deeply with our supporters – it showed that we would not stand by and wait for others to agree to what urgently needed saying loud and clear. Following the launch, we were flooded with applications to volunteer, mostly from women, whose skills, willingness to help wherever needed, and collaborative spirits were Heaven-sent. In an austere and deceitful information landscape, our weekly live-streamed meetings, in which the truth was frankly spoken and uncertainties acknowledged, were welcomed.

Shortly after the launch, *An unexpected evil came accidentally from without*.[1] I personally fell ill with symptoms of Covid-19. As someone who rarely gets sick, this experience was enlightening. My symptoms, initially flu-like, quickly worsened so that, by day four, I realised that without intervention my recovery would be prolonged. At that point, I began ivermectin combination therapy, and by day seven, I was almost back to normal. Although it took longer for my sense of smell and taste to return, the rapid recovery

---

[1] Hexagram 25, Innocence, line 5. From I Ching, by Richard Wilhelm, 3rd Ed. p.103.

after starting ivermectin-based treatment, after nine months of advocating for it based on the evidence and clinical experience of others, was gratifying.

A similarly gratifying incident occurred a couple of weeks later, when I was contacted by a husband seeking ivermectin for his wife who was in the intensive care unit of a Devon hospital. In this restrictive setting, we had to devise an unusual plan to get it to her, thereby managing to save her life. This was also a stark reminder of the absurd lengths people were forced to go to in order to access a safe and effective treatment during Covid-19 times.

Lastly discussed in this chapter is how, in November 2021, our newly established world authority became the first organisation to formally issue a 'Cease and Desist' notice, demanding a halt to the genetic Covid-19 vaccines. As the global pressure to push Covid-19 vaccinations intensified, this unprecedented action was pivotal in cementing WCH's reputation as an organisation that stands for people, not governments.

Here the small, weak, and evil elements are about to take their departure, while the great, strong, and good elements are moving up. This brings good fortune and success.[1] Thus, this chapter highlights our increasing power in the face of overwhelming opposition, through our collective courage, action, and defiance. From the successful launch of WCH to the brave actions taken to save lives worldwide, we began to show that our movement was not only growing but gaining significant influence. The Cease and Desist Notice sent a clear message to the globalists, corrupt governments, and the WHO: the fight for truth, health sovereignty, and justice had only just begun. And at its core stood a new peoples' health organisation, the World Council for Health.

---

1   Hexagram 11 Peace, The Judgement. From I Ching, by Richard Wilhelm, 3rd Ed. p.49.

MOVE 54. There's a Better Way! World Council for Health is Officially Launched

The Covid-19 chapter marked a frightening time in history, with censorship and widespread human rights violations carried out by the very authorities meant to protect us. It took a great deal of courage to be part of a new health organisation that appeared to be taking on the likes of the WHO. Doctors, scientists, and lawyers around the world were being vilified for speaking out against the official narrative, with many, like Dr Jackie Stone from Zimbabwe, facing prison for upholding her Hippocratic Oath. Our goal in creating the World Council for Health was not just to create a trusted body to offer unbiased evidence-based health guidance, but also to protect individuals and partner organisations that stood for health, choice, and human rights.

In several countries, draconian measures meant individuals couldn't show their faces or publicly align with organisations. Many people also struggled to accept the reality of the situation, feeling powerless in the face of overwhelming forces. There was real fear; people worried about losing their jobs, their income, if they took a public stance. So, building an international steering group to represent the organisation took effort. With the combined efforts of Dr Jennifer Hibberd from Canada, Shabnam Palesa Mohamed from South Africa, and me, we pulled together an amazing and diverse team of doctors, dentists, scientists, and lawyers, including Dr Mark Trozzi (Canada), Dr Tracy Chandler (New Zealand), Dr Naseeba Kathrada, (South Africa), Karen McKenna, Canada, Dr Zac Cox (UK), Dr Maria Hubmer-Mogg (Austria) and Anna De Buisseret (UK). Though some would drop away soon, and others later, their willingness to be named in connection with our new initiative made the press release harder to ignore. Our goal was to challenge the powers that should not be, and launching with a steering group of ten, comprising eight women and two men had impact.

While these brave individuals were intended to be our front-facing team, we also had a dedicated behind-the-scenes group, also mostly volunteers, who helped guide strategy and offer support. One of these individuals was a young mother, Emma Sron, from the USA, who brought a multitude of talents and experience garnered in working with other nonprofit organisations. Emma would later become a key member of our Steering Group and coordinate the WCH Mind Health Committee. In addition, Emma brought much enthusiasm, freshness and creativity, as well as the necessary technical and social media skills, that were needed to reach our audience.

Together we were determined to make sure WCH would not become just another bureaucratic organisation with corporate ties or big donors. Instead, we designed it to be transparent and inclusive, funded by our activities and grassroots supporters, offering practical advice that respected people's right to make their own health choices. We knew the globalists would likely target us and try to discredit our efforts. So, we made sure not to make this easy for them. Great change had arrived, a war had been declared on mankind (though many were unaware of this fact), and we needed a wartime strategy.

World Council for Health, though but a raft in 2021, was intended from its humble beginning to be the vessel to carry us safely across the waters to a better world. A rousing motto would be needed!

"There's a better way!" emerged easily, just slipping out without much effort at all. The volunteer who came up with it during a team brainstorming session had extensive professional experience at McKinsey & Company, the billion-dollar global management consulting firm founded in 1926 and headquartered in New York City. With hindsight, it was a beautiful irony that someone who had worked for this company, known for its use of deception and propaganda on behalf of exploitative corporate clients, had contributed something of great value: a motto that would guide us, unify the scattered peoples of the world, and inspire a movement that would carry mankind toward a brighter future. There's a better way for a better world, after all.

At our launch on 22ⁿᵈ September 2021, we brought together over 45 health and advocacy organisations into the WCH coalition. Many of BIRD's partners joined us, and we actively reached out to other groups across various sectors – health, science, law, policing, media, and more. We would continue to gather as many groups as we could, many of them fledgling, knowing that together we were stronger.

We launched with a beautiful website, designed by Brugge, whose enthusiasm and creativity also helped bring together our ideas for the logo, which would become iconic. The heart and the hand were proposed by Shabnam, the pink apple by me, and by the time Brugge assembled it all, we also had a healthy pair of lungs encapsulated too. The apple stood for wholesomeness (as opposed to the bitten apple of Apple Corporation!), the lungs symbolised the importance of our breath as the basis of human life), and the heart on the hand represented standing up and taking responsibility for our health and conduct.

In addition to the release of an at-home Covid care guide, offering a range of options to prevent and treat Covid-19 based on sound scientific principles and holistic approaches, the launch was coupled with weekly live-streamed, health-focused meetings, which we called General Assemblies. At a time when intimidation and secrecy were how the globalists played the game, we were determined to show that mankind would not be subjugated by fear. We hoped that this demonstration of courage would inspire others.

He is blessed by heaven. Good fortune. Nothing that does not further.[1] *Confucius says of this line: to bless means to help. Heaven helps*

---

[1]   Hexagram 14, Possession in Great Measure, line 6. From I Ching, by Richard Wilhelm, 3rd Ed. p.62.

the man who is devoted; men help the man who is true. He who walks in truth and is devoted in his thinking, and furthermore reveres the worthy, is blessed by heaven. He has good fortune, and there is nothing that would not further.[1]

MOVE 55. Covid-19 Vaccination Must Stop: WCH's Cease and Desist Notice

At the end of 2021, the WHO and complicit governments had ramped up their vaccine propaganda, polarising people and communities around the world with terms like "conspiracy theorists" and "anti-vaxxers", and authorising the dangerous shots for children and pregnant women, despite mounting evidence that they did not work and were unsafe. My co-authors confirm that this was a period of *Darkening of the Light. In adversity it furthers one to be persevering. One must not unresistingly let himself be swept along by unfavourable circumstances, nor permit his steadfastness to be shaken. He can avoid this by maintaining his inner light, while remaining outwardly yielding and tractable.[2]*

This certainly seems like an accurate assessment of the situation. The light of truth was obscured by falsehoods and manipulation, due to the rise of individuals in power who did not serve the collective good. *Wise and able* men bringing the truth were silenced and discredited and great harm was inflicted upon mankind as a whole, including the vulnerable, pregnant women, as well as children who were being vaccinated in their schools without parental-informed consent. People of *dark nature,*[3] like Dr Tedros Adhanom Ghebreyesus, Mr Bill Gates, Dr Anthony Fauci, Mr Matt Hancock, Dr Janet Woodcock, and many

---

1   Hexagram 14, Possession in Great Measure, line 6. From I Ching, by Richard Wilhelm, 3rd Ed. p.62-3.

2   Hexagram 36, Darkening of the Light, The Judgement. From I Ching, by Richard Wilhelm, 3rd Ed. p.140.

3   Hexagram 36, Darkening of the Light, The Judgement. From I Ching, by Richard Wilhelm, 3rd Ed. p.139.

others, through their actions, distorted truth, misled the public, and undermined the wisdom of those who could help.

Since we, in the form of the WCH, were now a health "authority", not appointed by a country or industry corporation but emerged from the grassroots and self-declared, we were much better positioned to counter the globalists' deadly narrative. We quickly set to work on our most important task – stopping the Covid-19 injections. WCH's Law and Activism Committee, led by Shabnam Palesa Mohamed, with clarity and greatness, drafted a "Cease and Desist Notice of Liability," calling for an immediate halt to the Covid-19 vaccines:[1]

29 November 2021

DECLARATION, CEASE AND DESIST AND NOTICE OF LIABILITY

WORLD COUNCIL FOR HEALTH CALLS FOR AN IMMEDIATE STOP TO THE COVID-19 EXPERIMENTAL "VACCINES"

CONSENSUS OF WORLD'S FOREMOST EXPERTS

Globally renowned experts, including Dr. Paul Alexander, Dr. Byram Bridle, Dr. Geert Vanden Bossche, Prof. Dolores Cahill, and Drs. Sucharit Bhakdi, Ryan Cole, Richard Fleming, Robert W. Malone, Peter McCullough, Mark Trozzi, Michael Yeadon, Wolfgang Wodarg, and Vladimir Zelenko, among many others, consistently warn the world about the adverse effects resulting from Covid-19 experimental injections; they also warn about their long-term effects, which cannot be known at this time since most clinical trials will be not completed

---

1   Some of the website links in this document may no longer be active.

until 2023, and some as late as 2025.

In June 2021, Dr. Tess Lawrie, co-founder of the World Council for Health and member of the Council's Steering Committee, courageously described the global crisis and called for urgent action: "*There is now more than enough evidence on the [UK] Yellow Card system to declare the COVID-19 vaccines unsafe for use in humans. Preparation should be made to scale up humanitarian efforts to assist those harmed by the COVID-19 vaccines and to anticipate and ameliorate medium to longer-term effects.*"

A. DECLARATION

The World Council for Health declares that it is time to put an end to this humanitarian crisis. Further, the Council also declares that any direct or indirect involvement in the manufacturing, distribution, administration and promotion of these injections violates basic principles of common law, constitutional law and natural justice, as well as the Nuremberg Code, the Helsinki Declaration, and other international treaties.

B. UNCENSORED FACTS

We now know that children are over one hundred times more likely to die from these experimental injections than Covid-19. Injected athletes, globally, are collapsing before our very eyes. In spite of the fact that reporting systems are limited and passive, millions of adverse effects have been recorded, which include death, paralysis, blood clots, strokes, myocarditis, pericarditis, heart attacks, spontaneous miscarriage, chronic fatigue and extreme depression.

See: https://coronavirus-yellowcard.mhra.gov.uk/

See: https://vaers.hhs.gov/

See: https://www.ema.europa.eu/en/human-regulatory/research-development/pharmacovigilance/eudravigilance

See: http://www.vigiaccess.org/ (search covid-19 vaccine)

C. VICTIM TESTIMONIES

The World Council for Health acknowledges and respects the experiences and testimony of the victims of this worldwide medical experiment. We also declare and confirm that safe, effective and affordable treatments for Covid-19 exist and should be made available to all who need them.

See: https://www.wewanttobeheard.com/

See: https://nomoresilence.world/

See: https://www.vaxtestimonies.org/en/

D. NOT SAFE, NOT EFFECTIVE

Recent studies confirm the risks associated with Covid-19 experimental injections. Emerging research establishes that the injections are neither safe nor effective, and, in fact, are toxic. While some of the known ingredients of the injections cause biological harm, it is even more concerning that the unknown and undisclosed ingredients may present an even greater threat to human health.

E. CEASE AND DESIST

The World Council for Health is ethically and lawfully bound to issue this Declaration, demanding that governments and corporations cease and desist from direct or indirect participation in the manufacturing, distribution, administration or promotion of Covid-19 experimental injections.

The Council declares that every living man and woman has a moral and legal duty to take immediate and decisive action to halt this unprecedented medical experiment, which continues to cause unnecessary and immeasurable harm.

F. NOTICE OF LIABILITY

The right of bodily integrity and the right to informed consent are inalienable and universal human rights, which have been trampled by government mandates and corporate imperatives. Thus, the World Council for Health declares that any person or organisation directly or indirectly participating in the manufacturing, distribution, administration or promotion of Covid-19 experimental biologics will be held liable for the violation of principles of justice grounded in civil, criminal, constitutional and natural law, as well as international treaties.

Signed: World Council for Health Steering Committee

About this significant but simple piece of work, my co-authors comment, *the neighbour in the east who slaughters an ox does not attain as much real happiness as the neighbour in the west with his small offering.*[1] My co-authors elaborate that this means *a simple sacrifice offered with real piety holds a greater blessing than an impressive service without warmth.*[2] In this context, the *I Ching* is speaking about the importance of sincerity over grandeur. The *slaughtering of an ox* symbolises a grand gesture, but the *small offering* in the west represents a humble, heartfelt action. Though our courage was boundless, our resources were limited. Our Cease and Desist Notice might have seemed small and insignificant compared to the vast global machine we were up against, but it was prepared with genuine care and dedication to the truth and human wellbeing. It was the simplicity of our approach, rooted in authenticity, courage and integrity, that would ultimately bear greater significance in the eyes of the world.

We were united on this action. The great sense of relief among our allies was palpable, even among those not yet willing to speak out

---

1   Hexagram 63, After Completion, line 5. From I Ching, by Richard Wilhelm, 3rd Ed. p.247-8.
2   Hexagram 63, After Completion, line 5. From I Ching, by Richard Wilhelm, 3rd Ed. p.247-8.

openly against the experimental vaccines. What needed to be said had finally been spoken aloud and firmly. It was as though a collective weight had been lifted, a collective breath exhaled. Mankind now had an unapologetic defender, and we were it. We stood as the voice of reason and integrity in a time when silence or compliance had become the norm. For those who had been quietly suffering under the weight of uncertainty and fear, our stance brought not only clarity but also courage. It was not just about taking action, it was about embodying a truth that many had been too fearful to express, and that, in itself, was a powerful form of resistance.

Around this time, Dr Robert Malone, a United States medical doctor and biochemist, also expressed concerns about the Covid-19 vaccines, primarily regarding their use in children and young adults. In December 2021, when our notice was published, Dr Malone highlighted in media interviews that he was an inventor of the mRNA technology. While expressing concerns about the lack of long-term safety data on the Covid vaccines, and questioning whether a global, mass vaccination campaign during a pandemic was appropriate, he still had a faith in the mRNA vaccine technology for reasons I couldn't fathom.

When it came to these Covid-19 genetic products, there was no question in my mind, they were a gamble for all who took them. A cursory search of the existing scientific literature showed this unequivocally. mRNA products were originally developed as gene therapy, to be given to sick people as treatment, not as a traditional vaccine, which is intended to prevent disease among the well. As genetic (GMO) vaccines, they had failed to be shown as safe in animal experiments preceding the global deployment in human beings.

Thus, in December 2021, I found myself deeply disappointed with Dr Malone's failure to unequivocally urge people and governments to halt the Covid-19 vaccines. If the inventor of the mRNA technology had come forward with a clear, strong message saying, "Stop the shots. I invented this technology, and I know it's not suitable for this application. It's too risky and could potentially make you ill, die, or alter your human genome," my guess is that people would have listened.

My co-authors share this reflection about Malone's role: *It lends grace to the beard on his chin.*[1] *The beard is not an independent thing; it moves only with the chin. The image, therefore, means that form is to be considered only as a result and attribute of content. The beard is a superfluous ornament. To devote care to it for its own sake, without regard for the inner content of which it is an ornament, would bespeak a certain vanity*[2]. Might Malone's perspective on mRNA vaccines have been clouded by vanity because of his role as inventor, I wondered?

As Steve Bannon remarked about Dr Robert Malone during his *War Room* podcast in September 2021, "You're hearing it from an individual who invented the mRNA [vaccine] and has dedicated his life to vaccines. He's the opposite of an anti-vaxxer!" Yet, despite these qualifications, Malone's message remained frustratingly mild. I understand that researchers tend to have faith in their creations, especially when there is significant financial investment and a global market at stake. So I wondered whether there was a degree of wishful thinking involved in Malone's stance, a belief that most people would be okay, but that children should never have been part of the equation. That Dr Malone took a shot for the team seems testament to this.

The perspective that Malone frequently shared was that the Pfizer and Moderna vaccines might worsen Covid-19 infections, which was certainly true; taking poisonous shots repeatedly would make any disease worse, as well as create new ones. Malone maintained a

---

1   Hexagram 22, Grace, line 2. From I Ching, by Richard Wilhelm, 3rd Ed. p.92.

2   Hexagram 22, Grace, line 2. From I Ching, by Richard Wilhelm, 3rd Ed. p.92.

position of "following the science," waiting for studies on the safety or not of the Covid shots to be published, and then adjusting his commentary accordingly. This made no sense to me. We don't give poison and then wait to see what the science reveals. We simply don't administer the poison in the first place!

Even after contracting "long Covid" as a result of, or despite his vaccination, Malone continued to advise about the pros and cons of getting a Covid-19 shot, as if any pros existed. "You shouldn't have to take the vaccine if you've recovered from natural infection," Malone told a group of impressionable children on a beach in Hawaii during an awkward recorded gathering with his wife, Dr Jill Malone. I found this advice to children in December 2021 extraordinary, as well as confusing. "You shouldn't have to take it, full stop," I would have made clear.

Nevertheless, when our Cease and Desist Notice to stop the Covid-19 inoculations was published, Malone was still recommending the shots, albeit (only) for those at the highest risk of Covid-19. I watched his interviews on prominent media platforms, silently urging him to speak up, that these injections were not just ineffective, but life-threateningly dangerous, that they should never be recommended for anyone, not men, women, boys or girls, and especially *not* those at highest risk of Covid-19 who were at greatest risk of vaccine harm too.

Needless to say, Malone's Substack articles, under the banner *"Who is Robert Malone?"*, raised that precise question for me every time his media emails arrived in my inbox, or I heard him speaking in the numerous interviews he gave on the subject of the Covid-19 shots. Who was Robert Malone?

My co-authors share this perspective. *The situation is not unfavourable; there is a prospect of ultimate success, but there are still obstacles in the way, and we can merely take preparatory measures. Only through*

the small means of friendly persuasion can we exert any influence. The
time has not yet come for sweeping measures. However, we may be able,
to a limited extent, to act as a restraining and subduing influence. To
carry out our purpose we need firm determination within and gentle-
ness and adaptability in external relations.[1]

If the inventor of mRNA was not screaming "STOP THE
SHOTS!", then perhaps the concerns raised by others, including the
World Council for Health, were not that serious? Perhaps it was still
a matter of weighing the pros and cons, as Dr Malone suggested? My
concern was that, lulled into a false sense of security, people might
have felt "Don't worry, Dr Malone's the expert. He'll let us know if
there's anything serious to worry about."

Grace in hills and gardens. The role of silk is meagre and small.
Humiliation, but in the end, good fortune.[2]

Despite my disappointment that Dr Robert Malone did not
speak up loud and clear about the dangers of mRNA biotechnology
in 2021, his role, like the grace of silk referred to by my co-authors,
might have been small in terms of a direct impact on protecting
people from the genetic Covid-19 injections, but was not without significance. He helped wake people up, albeit at a slow and measured
pace. My co-authors suggest that, whilst displaying a keen desire to
be part of a solution, his contribution to the collective effort may
have been limited by his values, the position he chose to occupy, and
the acquaintances he chose to keep. However, despite misgivings, we
developed a cordial relationship in due course.

Women often play a pivotal, unseen, role behind the scenes,
propelling the actions and decisions of seemingly powerful men.
This dynamic is hinted at by my co-authors in further commentary.
Someone does indeed increase him; ten pairs of tortoises cannot oppose

---

1   Hexagram 9, The Taming Power of the Small, The Judgement. From I Ching, by Richard
     Wilhelm, 3rd Ed. p.40-1.
2   Hexagram 22, Grace, line 5. From I Ching, by Richard Wilhelm, 3rd Ed. p.93.

it,[1] I wondered whether this was a reference to Dr Jill Malone. While not publicly in the spotlight, she appeared to play a significant role in shaping and guiding her husband's actions. *He brings increase to no one. Someone even strikes him. He does not keep his heart constantly steady. Misfortune.*[2] As a quiet yet powerful influencer, perhaps she increased her husband's success through her wisdom and careful direction, helping him to avoid pitfalls, navigate complex situations, and protecting him from attacks?

With regard to the Covid-19 vaccines, I had not yet sought my co-authors insights', thus at this juncture I thought to inquire. *Innocent action brings misfortune. Nothing furthers.*[3] This response confirms that they are definitely best avoided. In addition, it highlights that the majority of the public were innocent to the vaccine contents and effects, as well as the potential consequences – misfortune. They describe our WCH predicament, *where everywhere superior men are held in restraint by inferior men. When one has something to say, It is not believed.*[4]

Finally, they represent the outcome of taking the Covid shot by the image of an empty lake. *There is no water in the lake. The IMAGE of exhaustion. Thus the superior man stakes his life On following his will.*[5] To me, this suggests what I know to be true, that people took their lives in their hands by taking the shots. *When the water has flowed out below, the lake must dry up and become exhausted. This symbolises an adverse fate in human life. In such times there is nothing a man can do but acquiesce in the fate and remain true to himself. This concerns the deepest stratum of his being, for this alone is superior to all external fate.*[6]

There is a lot to reflect on in this commentary from my co-authors.

1   Hexagram 42, Increase, line 2. From I Ching, by Richard Wilhelm, 3rd Ed. p.163.
2   Hexagram 42, Increase, line 6. From I Ching, by Richard Wilhelm, 3rd Ed. p.165.
3   Hexagram 25, Innocence, line 6. From I Ching, by Richard Wilhelm, 3rd Ed. p.103.
4   Hexagram 47, Exhaustion, The Judgement. From I Ching, by Richard Wilhelm, 3rd Ed. p.181.
5   Hexagram 47, Exhaustion, The Image. From I Ching, by Richard Wilhelm, 3rd Ed. p.182.
6   Hexagram 47, Exhaustion, The Image. From I Ching, by Richard Wilhelm, 3rd Ed. p.182.

What I would like to draw attention to is the positive aspect – that remaining true to ourselves is *superior to all external fate*. No matter what is in those shots, no matter what has been done to us as individuals and mankind as a whole, we can defy it by seeking and adhering to our inner truth. Through self-mastery, one can heal, my co-authors are saying.

I asked for elaboration on the dangers, and my co-authors explained, *The king offers him Mount Ch'i. Good fortune. No blame.*[1] [...] *This indicates a stage in which pushing upward attains its goal* [...] and *a significance that endures beyond time.*[2]

Chi is a term for energy or life force, and many modern-day thinkers have suggested that the nefarious intention of those pushing the Covid-19 vaccines is to separate mankind from our life force, spirit, or God. In the context of the emerging evidence that the human genome may be irreversibly changed by these genetic products, there may be a scientific basis for such theories. There are many things we do not yet grasp about the human experience and our present situation.

Great change is an inevitable part of our existence and this happens on individual, seasonal and cosmic scales. Our ancestors were far more aware of this than modern-day folk caught up in a material world. Certainly, the method and purpose of all great change need not necessarily be understood at the time. The main thing, according to the *I Ching,* is that the *dedicated man embodies an enduring meaning in his way of life,* like *heavenly bodies exemplify duration. They move in their fixed orbits, and because of this their light-giving power endures.*[3]

Might my co-authors be suggesting that the Covid-19 vaccines were part of the mechanics of the great change cycle being experienced, from dark to more light, which was inevitable given how dark

---

1   Hexagram 46, Pushing Upwards, line 4. From I Ching, by Richard Wilhelm, 3rd Ed. p.180.

2   Hexagram 46, Pushing Upwards, line 4. From I Ching, by Richard Wilhelm, 3rd Ed. p.180.

3   Hexagram 32, The Judgement. From I Ching, by Richard Wilhelm, 3rd Ed. p.127.

things had become?

They leave us with the image of DURATION: thunder and wind. *Thunder rolls, and the wind blows; both are examples of extreme mobility and are seemingly the very opposite of duration, but the laws governing their appearance and subsidence, their coming and going, endure. In the same way the independence of the superior man is not based on rigidity and immobility of character. He always keeps abreast of the time and changes with it. What endures is the unswerving directive, the inner law of his being, which determines all his actions.* [1]

MOVE 56. Ivermectin Chocolate Smugglers Save Carol's Life

On Sunday 21st November 2021 I received a text message from a desperate husband, Mike Hayes. His wife, Carol, had reached out to her local GP practice for a repeat prescription of her asthma inhaler after she had been feeling unwell and short of breath for a few days. The practice nurse insisted on seeing her in person and by the time they had arrived at the practice, Carol was so short of breath that she could barely manage the steps on her own. When the nurse finally saw her, she was freezing cold and her oxygen levels were at 94% saturation, but her chest was clear of infection.

Asthma was the diagnosis, and the nurse prescribed steroids in addition to the inhaler. Whilst administering to Carol, the nurse asked if Carol was Covid-vaccinated. This is when things began to take an unsettling turn. When Carol explained that she was not, the nurse became visibly upset, telling Carol that she had put her – the nurse – in a vulnerable position! The nurse disappeared and returned to inform the worried couple that Carol would need to be transferred to the hospital immediately for further treatment and possible ventilation. This suggestion was met with firm resistance from Carol and

---

[1]   Hexagram 32, The Image. From I Ching, by Richard Wilhelm, 3rd Ed. p.127.

Mike, who were well-aware that peoples' rights were being violated in UK hospitals. As a loving and capable husband, Mike was quite sure he could give Carol the best care at home. However, their rejection of the ventilation idea clearly irritated the medical staff.

After some back-and-forth, during which time Carol felt increasingly unwell, the couple were told to go to North Devon Hospital in Barnstable, but with specific Covid-era instructions: Mike would not be allowed to enter the hospital with Carol. Carol was to be dropped off at the entrance alone.

This notion felt dehumanising, and when they arrived at the hospital, things only escalated. Despite Carol being extremely unwell, she was forced to wait outside in the cold winter rain – Mike obviously waited with her. The receptionist and some staff even questioned whether Carol had Covid, shouting across the waiting room, apparently to reduce their risk of exposure. Mike refused to leave Carol's side and, when they were eventually let in, Carol was tested for Covid-19, and the PCR test results came back positive.

When the doctor arrived, he declared she had Covid-19 pneumonia and insisted that Carol would need to be admitted and placed on a ventilator. Convinced that her asthma was at the root of the problem, Carol and Mike stood firm in their refusal. They had already made it clear that they did not want a ventilator; Carol had a signed document stating her wishes to avoid that option. Mike, beside himself at the thought of leaving Carol there alone and with the possibility of having her wishes violated, was despatched from the ICU and told he would not be able to visit his wife.

At home, Mike Hayes prepared a bag with ivermectin, vitamin C, D and zinc and delivered it to the reception of the hospital. By the time the bag reached Carol, the ivermectin had been removed from it without any discussion. In normal circumstances, this would be called theft, but these were not normal circumstances – human rights could be violated for the "greater good".

Meanwhile, in contact with Carol via her phone, Mike could see that her condition was deteriorating. Despairing and brainstorming his options, on Sunday 21st November, Mike, whom I did not yet know, reached out to me via Telegram. His message said:

Hi Tess, I'm desperately seeking help for my wife who's in the hospital and they won't give her the ivermectin that I have sourced. I have managed finally today to get them to give her Vitamin C, D and Zinc. They have been pushing for the ventilator, which we have managed somehow to keep off so far. Carol is on oxygen in the ICU, but really wants out. She has been given 'DEXAMETHASONE' to which I have suggested 'Methylprednisolone' but with no uptake. Is there anyone you know of that can help put pressure on them or help me explain in better terms a treatment? I know this is a big reach out and ask. I'm just firing everywhere for help.

Thank you

Michael Hayes

What hospital is she in and how far are you from Bath? Was my response, followed by:

I don't know where you are but if possible you could collect some meds from me?

It turned out to be more than a three-hour drive for Mike to me. Carol had in the meantime been told by her apparently heartless medical team that she was dying and should say "goodbye" to her family. Shortly after Mike arrived at my office that Sunday afternoon, Carol video-called him to say her goodbyes. Ashen-faced, receiving face-mask oxygen and struggling to talk, I could see for myself that she was hanging on by a thread. Mike was heartbroken. My co-authors comment about this moment, *Misfortune had reached its peak: it can no longer be warded off.* [1]

It has never ceased to amaze me that, in this situation where they had declared death inevitable, the medical staff of North Devon Hospital withheld an extremely safe medicine like ivermectin from Carol, violating not only a dying individual's right to choose, but violating basic common sense. In such a dire situation, they would not even let her give it a go. *The real nature of man is likewise originally good, but it becomes clouded by contact with earthly things and therefore needs purification before it can shine forth in its native clarity.* [2]

Whilst it seemed Carol had lost all hope, after seeing Mike together with me and hearing that I had some ivermectin for her, there was a glimmer of light. She told Mike she would hang on. I felt a great affinity for this courageous pair and very much wanted to see Carol well and home safe and sound. Whilst I made it clear to them both that I was no longer a clinically practising doctor, I could certainly help them in my capacity as their new friend. I gave Mike a few strips of ivermectin from my personal supply, as well as some additional nutritional supplements to use as he saw fit.

With his own ivermectin having been confiscated by the hospital staff, Mike was notably concerned about how to get the ivermectin to Carol. I suggested he might try smuggling the tablets in food, within a small yogurt pot perhaps. Together, with Carol still on the call, we discussed a few alternatives, and Mike left in a better state than he had arrived, fortified with some ivermectin, a big hug, and something resembling a plan.

When I arrived back home I relayed the story to my man, who creatively suggested Mike try to conceal the ivermectin in a chocolate bar. The paradox of what is called 'healthcare' is that the National

---

1   Hexagram 23, Splitting Apart, line 4. From I Ching, by Richard Wilhelm, 3rd Ed. p.95-6.
2   Hexagram 35: Progress, The Image. From I Ching, by Richard Wilhelm, 3rd Ed. p.137.

Health Service has no objection to unhealthy foodstuffs being given to patients, so there was little chance that a chocolate bar would be withheld! I immediately texted this suggestion on to Mike who thought it was a brilliant idea. Though he was prohibited from seeing her, Carol would most likely be allowed a gift of chocolate from him.

Mike bought a large slab of chocolate and, as soon as he arrived home, he opened it carefully, scraped out little cavities in the chocolate, sunk in the 12 mg ivermectin tablets into each piece, melted chocolate to cover the tablets over, and sealed it carefully again. Then he raced back to the hospital, handed over the ivermectin chocolate to the staff at the front desk, and reluctantly left. It was a tense time waiting to hear whether Carol had received the package without interference experienced before. Mike's heart sang when he heard from Carol the next day. The mission had been successful! She had received the ivermectin and had managed to eat a couple of squares of the ivermectin chocolate without arousing suspicion.

By the afternoon, Carol, who had previously been on oxygen support at 100%, was sustaining her oxygen saturation levels without nasal cannulas. The doctor on his rounds seemed confused, asking the nurse if the oxygen saturation monitor was broken. By the evening, Carol was so much better that she was moved from the ICU back to a general ward. By the 25th November, three days after receiving ivermectin on her 'death-bed', Carol made the decision to discharge herself from the hospital, fully recovering at home under Mike's tender love and care.

I cannot fully express how Carol's rapid recovery with ivermectin impacted me. Not only was it a wonderful testament to ivermectin's effectiveness, but it was also a testament to the triumph of a woman's spirit and a man's willingness to go to the ends of the earth for the woman he loves. In addition, coming at the end of what had been a gruelling year, this experience with Carol and Mike Hayes affirmed to me that battling the official insanity was well worth it. In many ways, helping them felt like the most meaningful thing I had done all year – beyond paperwork, beyond the countless meetings, beyond the social media forays, and beyond the emails from faceless officials with no last names, like Brian, Anne, Lesley, and John. I had actually managed to help two people, and likely saved a life.

Doing the right thing had been intuitive and effortless, I had been able to help without even trying. It had simply involved acting on one's conscience and not fearing the consequences from powers that should not be. Knowing that Carol was home safe and Mike was by her side gave me a profound sense of pleasure. It was just the nourishment that my spirit needed to persevere in this battle for mankind with a renewed sense of purpose.

Of course, the absurdity of the situation still makes me chuckle: A doctor had to arrange to smuggle a safe, old 'deworming' pill into a hospital – in chocolate, no less – for a terminally ill patient, even though the NHS prescribed ivermectin to terminally ill cancer patients on steroids to prevent them from getting worms. No doubt Obelix from the French comic book Asterix would have said: "These Romans are crazy!"

MOVE 57. A Tribute to Mothers and Warriors

Notable during the Covid years were the many "talking heads," influential podcast hosts and their guests, most of whom were men. In contrast, most of the grassroots freedom activists and health advocates were women – middle-aged, like me, and older. As for our own men, dazed, confused and disempowered, it was as if they had handed over their agency and suspended their decision-making faculties to hang on the words of podcasters and newsmen, watching and worrying instead of doing. As if hot air ever solved anything.

Meanwhile, women saw the writing on the wall and were the ones prepared to take action. Community meetings to which I was invited to speak were mostly populated by mothers and grandmothers. Likewise, it was no surprise to me that the original World Council for Health steering group was predominantly made up of women, as were the volunteers who enthusiastically stepped forward to assist us.

I explored this apparent idiosyncrasy, women being the predominant warriors in the health freedom movement in 2021, with my co-authors, who offered some really interesting insights and provided two key observations. Firstly, although women may have had less overt power than men, they still held significant influence within their families and over the men in their lives. Women had to rely on these more subtle forms of influence to bring about change.

The metaphor used by my co-authors compares this situation to a concubine being given a place in the family. By virtue of her status, she needs to be modest and reserved, or like a "lame man." *A girl entering a family with the consent of the wife will not rank outwardly as the equal of the latter but will withdraw modestly into the background. However, if she understands how to fit herself into the pattern of things, her position will be entirely satisfactory, and she will feel sheltered in the love of the husband to whom she bears children. The same meaning is brought out in the relationships between officials. A man may enjoy the personal friendship of a prince and be taken into his confidence. Outwardly this man must keep tactfully in the background behind the official ministers of state, but, although he is hampered by this status, as if he were lame, he can nevertheless accomplish something through the kindliness of his nature.[1]*

However, the Covid-19 chapter highlighted the disappointment of many gentle women with the compliance and lack of resistance to the Covid agenda shown by men. A democide was taking place. Children were being harmed. Where were our strong warriors and

---

1   Hexagram 54, The Marrying Maiden, line 1. From I Ching, by Richard Wilhelm, 3rd Ed. p.210.

protectors? Despite the disappointment in their partners, they remained true to their intuitive beliefs about what was going on and did their best to act on those beliefs by attending community meetings and engaging in small acts of resistance. The second observation from my co-authors speaks to this act of loyalty to their inner wisdom. *Here the situation is that of a girl married to a man who has disappointed her. Man and wife ought to work together like a pair of eyes. Here the girl is left behind in loneliness; the man of her choice either has become unfaithful or has died. But she does not lose the inner light of loyalty. Though the other eye is gone she maintains her loyalty even in loneliness.[1]*

This is not to say that there were not many husbands in the same predicament, estranged from their wives due to their differing perspectives on Covid-19 and what should be done about the injections, but I asked my co-authors specifically about the preponderance of women I saw at the community meetings. The relatively fewer men who attended these meetings often remarked about this preponderance too. My co-authors' metaphor here suggests that even in the absence of support from those who should be allies, the women's sense of loyalty and conviction did not waver. Despite the disappointment and isolation, their faith remained steadfast. Though the *other eye*, representing the traditional protectors, was absent or compromised, their inner light of loyalty and determination drove women to keep pushing forward for the truth. This feminine resilience, loyalty and conviction would become the driving force behind the co-creation of a better world for our children.

I felt a deep affinity for these women warriors, their gentle voices unheard by their families, husbands, sons and daughters, yet filled with power and passion. Often the collective wisdom in the community hall was as palpable and overwhelming as the sorrow and

---

1   Hexagram 54, The Marrying Maiden, line 2. From I Ching, by Richard Wilhelm, 3rd Ed. p.211.

impotence we felt in the face of the harm being inflicted upon our children, our men, and our communities.

But with WCH, there was also a powerful sense of women coming together with newfound enthusiasm, as if they were sensing the moment had finally arrived. We would no longer tolerate the nonsense imposed by a cruel, patriarchal system, obsessed with rules and regulations that had tried to control us with ink on paper but ending up destroying everything, like reckless and ill-informed schoolboys. Women volunteers from all walks of life stepped forward to support our initiatives, offering their skills in areas ranging from editing and graphics to event organisation, amplifying the strength of our message.

It furthers one to install helpers and set armies marching.[1] The time of enthusiasm derives from the fact that there is at hand an eminent man who is in sympathy with the spirit of the people and acts in accord with it. Hence he finds universal and willing obedience...It is enthusiasm that enables us to install helpers for the completion of an undertaking without fear of secret opposition. It is enthusiasm too that can unify mass movements, as in war, so that they achieve victory.[2] The WCH team became the rallying point, a symbol of hope and action, and the catalyst for the collective energy of many wise women, as well as some strong men, that would drive *a better way* forward. Without the time given freely by so many, World Council for Health and the better way movement would not be what it is today.

Meanwhile, on board the World Council for Health's Steering Group in 2021 was at least one very strong man – emergency physician Dr Mark Trozzi! Prior to the formation of WCH, I knew little about this powerful Canadian warrior, who had been fighting corrupt Canadian authorities seemingly single-handedly, and shouting from the rooftops about the dangers of the Covid shots in efforts to

---

1   Hexagram 16, Enthusiasm, The Judgement. From I Ching, by Richard Wilhelm, 3rd Ed. p.67-8.

2   Hexagram 16, Enthusiasm, The Judgement. From I Ching, by Richard Wilhelm, 3rd Ed. p.67-8.

warn his fellow Canadians, since the start of the Covid-19 hoax.

Shooting from the hip and not mincing his words, many associated with us might have considered Dr Trozzi, feisty at 5 foot 8 with Italian ancestry, a liability in the subtle game we were playing to win the public's trust. The globalists would readily label him an "anti-vaxxer." Equally, he may have had reservations about joining us, a new and risky association. Thankfully, this was not the case! My co-authors highlight why. Dr Trozzi, not only an incredible doctor but also father of five and a grandfather, had realised that fighting single-handed only gets one so far. For the sort of battle we were in, companionship was essential. *Going leads to obstructions, coming leads to union.[1] This describes a situation that cannot be managed single handed. In such a case the direct way is not the shortest. If a person were to forge ahead on his own strength and without the necessary preparations, he would not find the support he needs and would realise too late that he had been mistaken in his calculations, in as much as the conditions on which he hoped he could rely would prove to be inadequate. In this case it is better, therefore, to hold back for the time being and to gather together trustworthy companions who can be counted upon for help in overcoming the obstructions.[2]*

The wisdom in this line from my co-authors underscores the importance of strategic collaboration in the face of adversity. It highlights the truth that strength lies in unity, and rushing ahead without solid support can lead to failure. Whilst others may have been afraid of collaborating with us, Dr Mark Trozzi recognised the need to build a coalition of reliable allies, ensuring that the battle would be fought with the collective strength of many. He listened to his intuition, and allowed his heart to lead him, stepping into fellowship with strangers around the world in trust. Implicit in our relationship, my co-authors explain, is that *the strong man takes a position inferior*

---

1   Hexagram 39, Obstruction, line 4. From I Ching, by Richard Wilhelm, 3rd Ed. p.153.
2   Hexagram 39, Obstruction, line 4. From I Ching, by Richard Wilhelm, 3rd Ed. p.153.

to that of the weak girl and shows consideration for her. This attraction between affinities is a general law of nature. Heaven and earth attract each other and thus all creatures come into being.[1]

What really struck me once I got to know Dr Mark Trozzi was how such an accomplished, strong man could be so humble. During these times of arrogance and ignorance, such humility was an anomaly. There was no display of ego from him when I suggested he rephrase certain sentiments in support of our goal of reaching alienated people. My co-authors also observed this willingness to compromise, noting it as a key element in how to influence others. *A lake on the mountain: The image of influence. Thus the superior man encourages people to approach him By his readiness to receive them.[...] The image counsels that the mind should be kept humble and free, so that it may remain receptive to good advice.*[2]

This concept from the *I Ching* reminds us how one should always remain open to wisdom and input, no matter the external strength or position one holds, because *People soon give up counselling a man who thinks he knows everything better than anyone else.*[3] This speaks to the importance of maintaining a learning attitude, regardless of achievements or authority, and recognising that arrogance can close the door to valuable guidance and personal growth. It was in this spirit of humility that Dr Trozzi's actions spoke louder than any words, creating an example for us all in how true strength is often coupled with the ability to listen and learn. Dr Trozzi wanted to save as many lives as possible. An ethical doctor through and through, nothing was going to stop him. I am deeply grateful for his warrior spirit, sense of humour, and fellowship over the past years!

1　Hexagram 31, Influence, The Judgement. From I Ching, by Richard Wilhelm, 3rd Ed. p.122.

2　Hexagram 31, Influence, The Image. From I Ching, by Richard Wilhelm, 3rd Ed. p.123.

3　Hexagram 31, Influence, The Image. From I Ching, by Richard Wilhelm, 3rd Ed. p.123.

Chapter 12

Splitting Apart

SPLITTING APART. It does not further one
To go anywhere.[1]

This pictures a time when inferior people are pushing forward and are about to crowd out the few remaining strong and superior men. Under these circumstances, which are due to the time, it is not favourable for the superior man to undertake anything.[2]

As 2021 came to a close, amidst the fearmongering about new Covid-19 variants and the targeted push to get people "boosted," it became increasingly clear how fragile unity within the freedom movement was, and how easily things could unravel. For me personally, as new WHO contracts were offered, as much a testament to how much my work was valued, as it was to how insular WHO staff were, oblivious to my new role, it was time for closure on the WHO. For almost

---

[1]   Hexagram 23, Splitting Apart, The Judgement. From I Ching, by Richard Wilhelm, 3rd Ed. p.94.
[2]   Hexagram 23, Splitting Apart, The Judgement. From I Ching, by Richard Wilhelm, 3rd Ed. p.94.

ten years, the WHO and NHS-based Cochrane Review groups had been my biggest clients. For the same reason I had declined further Cochrane contracts, I closed the chapter on the WHO for good that December, turning my back on my old world of evidence synthesis and guideline methodology. WCH was but a seedling, nonetheless I did not hesitate to burn the bridge and step firmly into the unknown to help to establish this new peoples' organisation. A great sadness, however, was the rapid disintegration of former work relationships, not least because I was too busy to nourish them.

Oxford's Principle Trial investigators resurfaced declaring mid-December they had run out of ivermectin so were pausing the ivermectin arm of the trial. Not only was the informed public astounded that a well-funded international trial should be put on hold due to ivermectin supply issues, we were too. We made attempts to hold them accountable, requesting the individual patient data they had collected thus far. However, with no response and lacking the resources to challenge them, plus many pots on the boil, we finally chose to walk away from this distraction.

I sent one final letter to Dr Andrew Hill, urging him to come clean about his corrupted ivermectin pre-print paper. Unfortunately, this too was met with silence. After making a short documentary entitled *A Letter to Dr Andrew Hill*, I let go of the hope that he would ever tell us what really happened between him and those who did not want ivermectin evidence to see the light of day.

Meanwhile, emails had been flooding in regarding independent findings from researchers in Spain, Chile and beyond that graphene had been found in various Covid-19 vaccine brands. This raised even more serious questions about what might really be hidden in those poisonous little vials, and spoke to possible mechanisms of harm, as well as intended functionality. We felt compelled to investigate further, which we did through EbMCsquared, hoping to end the speculation. But this episode only highlighted how fragile the movement was, and how easily we could be divided over such unsettling discoveries.

Finally, toward the end of a thirteen-month cycle, with the relentless push for dangerous vaccines aimed at faithful congregations worldwide, I was forced to confront my growing disbelief at the ongoing betrayal of mankind by organised religion. This was starkly epitomised by the actions of Anglican Archbishop Justin Welby. On national and international news broadcasts, as well as in the press, Welby claimed that Jesus would want people to take the experimental Covid-19 vaccines. Horrified by his actions, this made me ponder what the Covid-19 chapter had exposed about organised religion.

My co-authors use a metaphor about a magic tortoise to describe this phase of our advocacy. *You let your magic tortoise go. The magic tortoise is a creature possessed of such supernatural powers that it lives on air and needs no earthly nourishment. The image means that a man fitted by nature and position to live freely and independently renounces this self-reliance and instead looks with envy and discontent at others who are outwardly in better circumstances. But such base envy only arouses derision and contempt in those others. This has bad results.*[1]

The story of the tortoise speaks here to the struggle of maintaining personal and collective direction and autonomy when surrounded by so many distractions, in an increasingly totalitarian world intent on disrupting our mission. Ultimately, the tortoise symbolises the ideal of living freely and independently, something that both I and others in the freedom movement were striving for, but during this phase, our survival and cohesion was constantly tested against the weight of external influences.

---

1   Hexagram 27, The Corners of the Mouth, From I Ching, by Richard Wilhelm, 3rd Ed. p.109.

MOVE 58. PRINCIPLE Trial Has Supply Issues

After everything we had been through with the PRINCIPLE Trial – countless emails to Oxford University's Professor Chris Butler and his team, attempting to pry answers from them about their protocol, recruitment strategy, analysis plan, and results, FLCCC/BIRD joint letters of concern, freedom of information (FOI) requests – we were exasperated to hear, in mid-December 2021, the trial announce that the ivermectin arm was "currently paused due to temporary supply issues."

It seemed absurd. This is a medicine that people were freely ordering on the internet, usually without a doctor's prescription because it's safer than aspirin and Tylenol, yet a trial being run by one of the world's most prestigious universities couldn't seem to secure enough of it. How is that even possible? Of course, the website did not bother explaining what caused this so-called "temporary supply issue."

However, with no details, a series of false starts, and a highly dubious protocol, it seemed to many to be a fabrication. It was no surprise that they were eager to ditch ivermectin. The investigator team had been fending off increasing scrutiny and tough questions from scientists and the public alike, and perhaps they just reached a point where it seemed easier to quietly close the trial's ivermectin arm and hope no one would notice or care. People, like a man by the name of John Crawley, tried to hold investigators to account. They shared their correspondence with us that revealed a blanket response to their reasonable questions: "Your questions cannot be answered as they are subject to University research confidentiality".

Such efforts of individuals like Crawley, challenging false narratives and captured science, were crucial to our cause. Their vigilance and tenacity played a key role in our larger, somewhat vulnerable efforts to hold powerful institutions like Oxford University, recipients of large corporate grants, accountable. My co-authors reflect on such human relationships: *Affection as the essential principle of relatedness is of the greatest importance in all relationships in the world. For the union of heaven and earth is the origin of the whole of nature. Among human beings likewise, spontaneous affection is the all-inclusive principle of union.*[1] Although I had never met most of the individuals behind the numerous emails and efforts, I felt a tremendous affection for them. Likewise, they expressed their deep gratitude for the work we were doing. In the end, it was this shared sense of purpose and respect that united us, often across great distances, strengthening the power we wielded together. People Power.

The fact that the PRINCIPLE investigators couldn't keep a simple supply of ivermectin on hand said everything about where their priorities really lay. Merck, the original ivermectin manufacturer, did not directly comment on the December supply issue, and did not step in to help the poor Oxford team out either, but they did manage to issue a statement saying they had "concluded that the probability of ivermectin providing a potentially safe and efficacious treatment option for SARS-CoV-2 infection is low."

Given Oxford University's esteemed status, and the media's collusion, exposing the misdeeds related to the PRINCIPLE Trial was an uphill battle (no pun intended this time). A strategic approach was needed. We wrote to Professor Butler again, requesting their de-identified interim trial data to facilitate the conduct of a meta-analysis (analysis involving data pooling) of individual patient data (IPD). Receiving no reply from Butler, we did not pursue it further, rather, we directed our energy once more towards where we could make a difference. *Whereas an inferior man revels in power when he comes into possession of it, the superior man never makes this*

---

[1]   Hexagram 54, The Marrying Maiden, The Judgement. From I Ching, by Richard Wilhelm, 3rd Ed. p. 209.

mistake. He is conscious at all times of the danger of pushing ahead regardless of circumstances, and therefore renounces in good time the empty display of force.[1]

MOVE 59. My Last Letter to Dr Andrew Hill

When I first connected with Dr Andrew Hill, I genuinely hoped we shared a common goal: to use the evidence we had to save lives, particularly by advocating for ivermectin as a safe, affordable, and effective treatment for Covid-19. I thought we could work together, combining our efforts in support of what the FLCCC with Dr Pierre Kory and Dr Paul Marik had started, to make a real difference. Frankly, we could have ended the Covid-19 health crisis before the vaccines were given emergency use authorisation. But our initial unity of purpose was shown to be an illusion when Hill chose to publish his corrupted paper before we could publish our robust systematic review. His conclusions, far from supporting our cause, undermined the very message we were trying to send to the world. His decision had devastating consequences, not only for our ivermectin advocacy but for people's health at large.

My grandmother witnessed medical malpractice, as well as a doctor's indifference, which almost led to the death of my father as a young boy. She saw the harm done and had no patience for the drunken doctor's feeble excuses. She spoke her mind, human being to human being, and obtained a sincere apology from the man, who in essence had got his priorities jumbled and simply not put his heart to the matter. With this in mind, in January 2022, I wrote Dr Hill another email.

---

1   Hexagram 34, The Power of the Great, line 3. From I Ching, by Richard Wilhelm, 3rd Ed. p. 135.

Dear Andy,

It is approximately one year since I shared with you my rapid review of the evidence on ivermectin for covid, one year since my video address to Prime Minister Boris Johnson advising him that we had a safe and effective medicine to beat the pandemic, and one year since you and I met to discuss working together to get ivermectin approved as soon as possible. Early in January 2021, we shared data and agreed that ivermectin looked like a cheap, safe and effective way to end the pandemic and that it needed to be rolled out as soon as possible.

We agreed that working together would facilitate this and you joined our strong author team preparing to conduct a Cochrane systematic review. Before we could collaborate, however, you published your paper as a pre-print.

I will never forget reading your paper for the first time. You reported that ivermectin was associated with reduced inflammatory markers and faster viral clearance, that ivermectin showed "significantly shorter duration of hospitalisation compared with control", and "in moderate or severe infection, there was a 75% reduction in deaths with favourable clinical recovery and reduced hospitalisation". At a time when hospitals were overflowing, people were being locked down to prevent viral transmission and the death count was rising, here we had a safe, established off-patent medicine that could reduce hospitalisation, viral transmission and deaths. Yet, your conclusions were, "Ivermectin should be validated in larger, appropriately controlled randomised trials before the results are sufficient for review by regulatory authorities".

On the 17th of January 2021, I wrote to you asking you to retract your paper, saying that it would cause immeasurable harm. We met on Zoom the next day. Your manuscript appeared rushed and its methodology was sub-standard – I made no bones about what I thought about it. I was not the only one alarmed by the poor quality and conclusions of your paper. Dr Kory and Dr Marik wrote to you and asked you to make corrections.

An independent forensic communications consultant has since confirmed that there were two or three other voices in your paper. These unacknowledged authors contrived to manipulate the wording to undermine the positive findings on ivermectin. Why did you let them write your conclusions? You criticise studies from other countries for not being peer-reviewed or published, the irony being that your manuscript was neither peer-reviewed nor published at the time, despite having a profound impact on people's lives. Indeed, when we sent our own comprehensive review on ivermectin to UK authorities, we were told that Dr Andrew Hill's review says that the evidence on ivermectin is insufficient and that more trials are needed.

There was much at stake in January 2021 when you put your paper on ResearchSquare.com as a pre-print – both in human lives and in profits. Billions had been spent on PCR tests, PPE equipment, and developing covid drugs and new gene-based vaccines. With safe, effective early covid treatment, none of the investments in novel drugs nor the restrictions on our liberty were necessary. We both know that the evidence on ivermectin extends way beyond randomised control trials. Real world data, plus all those conversations we have had with doctors at the frontline who are using ivermectin, leave no doubt that ivermectin is a useful medicine to prevent and treat Covid-19.

Are you so sure you're right and all these doctors are wrong? What happened to the scientist who stated in December 2020, "Difficult to see how bias assessment could change such consistent treatment effects..."; and in February 2021, "Ivermectin causes faster viral clearance. Mass vaccination plus ivermectin treatment for anyone testing positive is the way forwards"?

Why have you now allied yourself with those who seem to have a

mission to undermine ivermectin studies? And at the very least, why
have you not spoken up when the media and the authorities have
dismissed ivermectin as a horse dewormer?

In my opinion, your pre-print paper published on the 18th of
January did three things: it was instrumental in restricting ivermectin's use; it led to the discrediting and censoring of doctors recommending it; and it facilitated the emergency use authorisation of
the experimental gene-based Covid vaccines. With effective Covid
treatments, the authorities would not have been able to authorise
these new and experimental drugs without better safety data; and,
in my opinion, the public would never have acquiesced to the experimental gene-based therapies had they been made aware that covid
was treatable with safe, established medicines.

The profits reaped by your sponsor have been enormous. The cost
in both nation economies and human lives has been devastating. If
there was a point when we could have averted the oncoming iat-
rogenic humanitarian crisis, in my opinion, it was that Zoom call.
Together, you and I could have saved millions of lives and so much
suffering. If only you had made a different choice. If only you had
done the right thing.

I ask you now to make that difficult choice, to do what is in the
best interests of your friends and countrymen, to do what is in the
best interests of humanity at large. Help to expose the corruption
of science by coming forward to explain the pressure you have been
under to undermine the evidence on ivermectin. Explain the delicate situation you were in in January 2021, and name the people who
influenced you to change your conclusions. Only then, can we start
to ameliorate the harm done.

Please do the right thing now, Andy.

Yours Sincerely,

Tess

I never received a response. My co-authors comment about this effort, *He holds him fast with yellow ox hide. No one can tear him loose.*[1] *Yellow is the colour of the middle. It indicates that which is correct and in line with duty. Ox hide is strong and not to be torn. While the superior men retreat and the inferior press after them, the inferior man represented here holds on so firmly and tightly to the superior man that the latter cannot shake him off. And because he is in quest of what is right and so strong in purpose, he reaches his goal. Thus the line confirms what is said in the Judgement: "in what is small" – here equivalent to "in the inferior man" – "perseverance furthers."*

My co-authors' observation, that I did not want to let Dr Hill off the hook, resonates. It was a challenge for me that I could not change Hill's mind. He was not a "bad man" in the sense that he was not cruel or malicious, or even intentionally harmful, yet the consequences of his actions in my opinion were undeniable. Indifference can be as dangerous as cruelty, and even those with good intentions can make devastating choices.

It was hard to accept that I could not effectively convey the impact of Hill's conduct to the man. In some strange way, I felt responsible for not being able to convince him to do what I considered to be the right thing. With hindsight, such feelings were undoubtedly misplaced. His published email address was "microhaart@", not bighaart@ or bravehaart@; thus, perhaps Hill already knew that an inability to empathise with others was his Achilles heel.

Dismayed by Hill's continued lack of accountability, we decided, as a last attempt to reach him, to follow up with a video of the letter appeal. To our gratification, the 20-minute documentary entitled *A Letter to Dr Andrew Hill,* produced by Oracle Films and directed by Mark Lawrie, was widely watched and shared.[2] It would continue to

---

1   Hexagram 33, Retreat, line 2. From I Ching, by Richard Wilhelm, 3rd Ed.p.131.
2   www.Lawriefiles.com.

resurface over the years, remaining a powerful tool in the awakening of many. Ivermectin was the key to the Covid-19 Pandora's box, and, once people watched this documentary, it was clear that there was no going back.

Thus, with hindsight, I had to concede there was some "good" in Dr Hill's role. While I believed the choices he made led to harm, his actions also sparked something greater – a wake-up call. His decision to publish that paper, flawed as it was, compounded by the interference of his associates, became a turning point. It was how I began this chapter of my life and, indeed, this book. His actions catalysed BIRD, which led to the World Council for Health, pointed us toward a multitude of revelations, and, in the end, helped to expose a simple yet profound truth: great change was needed. Through his missteps, others were able to see the bigger picture more clearly. Though his complicity and indifference were evident, anyone exposed to the evidence of Hill's misconduct could see that there had to be a better way for our world. Our actions and our inactions have consequences. The *better way* lay in each one of us taking personal responsibility for our conduct.

MOVE 60. Personal Closure on the WHO

When I first joined the World Health Organization as an external consultant, I was full of idealism, believing that working within the UN system was the best way to create real change and make a difference. Having lived most of my life in South Africa, I was passionate about improving health for people in developing countries, women and children in particular. It felt an honour to contribute to the work of this international organisation, and I was hopeful that by doing so I would be making a great difference to the lives of many people. My work was contract-based, and I travelled to Geneva as needed, thus I never lived in Geneva, nor was I an integral part of the permanent teams that hired me. I was also never subject to the internal politics that clearly existed, which in the latter years of my association with the WHO included unhappy discourse around pay cuts. I was fortunate that I never made Geneva my permanent home. Life in Geneva for WHO and UN employees, I learned, was gruelling, particularly for employees who weren't Swiss, which were most people.

During my time in association with the WHO, I was fortunate to have worked with many intelligent, dedicated and inspiring people who had arrived in Geneva from all corners of the world. Most, like myself, had aspired to work at the WHO because they saw it as the place to make a real impact. The prestige of the organisation was immense, and people worked incredibly hard to secure their roles within the system. Once you were in, the pressure to fit in and succeed was relentless.

Both work and living were high-stakes games, and the competition was fierce. The work itself was demanding, with long hours and constant pressure. The cost of living was astronomical, and securing accommodation in Geneva was always a struggle. I heard some had to wait years to find a suitable apartment. Those who settled there had to fully commit to the authoritarian system, as remaining in Switzerland and staying within the UN structures required relentless effort, political manoeuvring, ongoing applications, and up-to-date documentation. It was an environment where fitting in, working hard, and adhering to the narrative were crucial. Separated from common sense and traditional family wisdom that guides people in their home settings, which for some may even have included the Turkish divination method of reading coffee cups, a sense of pious self-importance often became an unfortunate but inevitable characteristic. It created the perfect breeding ground for a committed workforce, ready to spring into action at the first declaration of a global "pandemic".

WHO project leaders became increasingly pressured to attract grants for their departments, which also brought additional kudos. Thus, the organisational outputs became shaped by financial interests, in favour of agendas aligned with its largest donors. My concerns first arose as a methodologist on the WHO Antenatal Care guideline, originally published in 2016, specifically with regard to the recommendation on micronutrient supplementation during pregnancy. Funded primarily by USAID and BMGF, within the ANC guideline we had published a recommendation against replacing effective iron and folic acid supplementation programmes with multiple micronutrient (MMN) supplements, which were significantly more costly for countries and associated with various other issues, including difficulty ensuring manufacturing quality and standards. However, Gates and USAID lobbyists pushed relentlessly for the WHO team responsible to revisit this recommendation, criticising the existing recommendation in various scientific articles in high-impact journals.

At the time, I wondered why they were so eager to get these supplements into women around the world, without good evidence on benefits and risks. Nevertheless, in 2018, the WHO recommendation was revisited and altered to accommodate MMN supplement programmes in developing countries under research conditions. The situation left me with a deep sense of unease. It felt like we had been manipulated to change the 2016 recommendation and that there was more at play than the health and wellbeing of pregnant women. This is the incident that led to my first doubts about the integrity of the WHO. What was the motivation of those pushing so hard to gain access to women's bodies with a new pill, the ingredients of which would be difficult to monitor and standardise? Might the MMN supplement programme be part of a larger globalist depopulation agenda?

With regard to Covid-19, however, a factor that I feel played a significant role in keeping WHO employees ignorant of the true science was their institutionalised isolation. Whilst spoon-fed the official narrative, working from home helped to ensure that employees were kept in the dark. Like many, most welcomed working from home, saving on transport costs, enjoying a more comfortable setting, and having extra time with family. However, this isolation removed the possibility of spontaneous conversations in the corridors, and over lunch, where ideas and doubts might have been shared or eaves-dropped – the latter being unavoidable in the busy cafeterias.

Constantly reminded of the central position the WHO now occupied in shaping the global response to the Covid-19 pandemic that they had declared, the WHO staff most likely felt the gravitas of their roles. The organisation's influence had suddenly expanded beyond developing countries. Even the US and European countries, which had previously ignored WHO guidance, were now following it. In this atmosphere, by reinforcing the sense that they were part of something monumentally important, and in attracting great funding too, staff were thoroughly brainwashed into believing the Covid narrative. Thus, as their perceived status grew, so did their blindness to the underlying issues.

I am not making excuses for WHO staff, who some might judge harshly as being complicit in a democide. The question naturally arises: Were they victims or conspirators? I asked my co-authors for their wisdom on this matter, gathering that they have a wealth of all human experience to draw on. Their answer was unequivocal. They were well-intentioned, just like us, and seeking to do the best for mankind. *True fellowship among men must be based upon a concern that is universal. It is not the private interests of the individual that create lasting fellowship among men, but rather the goals of humanity.*[1]

Thus, they remind us that being part of a collective, especially a

---

1   Hexagram 13, Fellowship of Men, The Judgement. From I Ching, by Richard Wilhelm, 3rd Ed. p.56.

powerful institution like the WHO, can often blur the lines of individual responsibility. These employees, much like any of us working within large systems, might have started out with noble intentions, believing that their work would help solve global health crises and improve the lives of millions. They, too, wanted to make a difference. But the issue arises when the collective – the WHO, in this instance – becomes a force that shapes their actions and perceptions in ways they may not fully comprehend. In this case, the WHO, an institution built on the ideals of health for all, became caught up in an agenda that many employees did not question. They were swept up in the tide of information, trusting the authority of their organisation, assuming it was acting in the best interests of the world. They did what they were told, believing that the directives were for the "greater good".

My co-authors offer further insight and caution about the situation at the WHO: *But in order to bring about this sort of fellowship, a persevering and enlightened leader is needed – a man with clear, convincing, and inspiring aims and the strength to carry them out.* [1]

The leader of the WHO, Dr Tedros Adhanom Ghebreyesus, was not a medical doctor. He held a PhD for a study about the effects of dams on malaria transmission in Tigray, Ethiopia. Minister of Health for Ethiopia's coalition government between 2005 and 2012, Tedros "formed relationships with figures and organisations including former American president Bill Clinton, his Clinton Foundation and the Bill & Melinda Gates Foundation." [2] Thereafter, he became Minister of Foreign Affairs until 2016, and Director-General of the WHO in 2017.

It is reasonable to question whether a man like Tedros truly resonated in the hearts of WHO employees as *a persevering and enlightened leader – a man with clear, convincing and inspiring aims*, particularly

---

1   Hexagram 13, Fellowship of Men, The Judgement. From I Ching, by Richard Wilhelm, 3rd Ed. p.56.
2   https://en.wikipedia.org/wiki/Tedros_Adhanom_Ghebreyesus

as Tedros is also a former leading figure of the Tigray People's Liberation Front (TPLF), which was designated as a terrorist organisation by the U.S. until 2014. The TPLF is known to have engaged in brutal conflict including mass killings in Ethiopia for decades.[1] Despite this, it formed part of the coalition government of the Ethiopian People's Revolutionary Democratic Front from 1991 to 2018. According to analysts, the TPLF continues to terrorise people and be a threat to peace in countries in the Horn of Africa to date.[2]

Does Tedros remember Ethiopian Emperor Haile Selassie I, I wonder? How different our world might look today if the WHO leader had an iota of Selassie's character and integrity (although individuals like Tedros might be easily replaceable). A great, much loved and respected leader, Emperor Haile Selassie I lived in exile in my home town of Bath, England, between 1936 and 1941 during Italy's invasion and attempted colonisation of Ethiopia. It's an interesting synchronicity, given that Emperor Selassie I, in my opinion, would no doubt be Tedros' nemesis were he alive today.

In distinct contrast to Tedros, over his lifetime, Emperor Haile Selassie I became internationally renowned as an advocate for African unity and world peace. A speech he made to the United Nations in 1963 remains more significant today than ever. In the profound address to this already captured international body, Selassie said, "Until the philosophy that holds one race superior and another inferior is finally discredited and abandoned, until the colour of a man's skin is no more significant than the colour of his eyes, until the basic human rights are guaranteed to all without regard to race – until that day, the dream of lasting peace and world citizenship and the rule of international morality will remain but a fleeting illusion, to be pursued but never attained. Until bigotry, prejudice, malicious

---

1   www.uscis.gov/sites/default/files/document/legal-docs/2014_Implementation_of_New_
    Discretionary_Exemption_for_Activities_or_Associations_Relating_to_TPLF.pdf
2   www.america-times.com/tplf-terrorism-threat-to-regional-peace-and-stability/

and inhuman self-interest have been replaced by understanding, tolerance and goodwill, until all Africans stand and speak as free beings – equal in the eyes of all men, as they are in the eyes of heaven – until that day, the African continent will not know peace."[1]

It is poignant to note how much Ethiopians, Africans, and, indeed, all the world's people have suffered since Emperor Haile Selassie I made this heartfelt speech. It's is also a stark reminder of how long global institutions have been failing us, and how long dark forces have been dividing, ruling and warring against us.

To get back to my co-authors' comments on the WHO employees, acknowledging the importance of unity and collective effort, they highlight that fellowship can lead to unintentional complicity if one is not careful. This is not to say that individuals at the WHO were intentionally part of a malevolent plan, but rather that the structure itself created an environment where critical questioning was either suppressed or overlooked. In many ways, they may have been victims of their own fellowship, caught within a system that prioritised uniformity of thought over individual discernment.

True community is about valuing individuality, mutual respect, personal responsibility, freedom of expression and transparency. For those within the WHO, as much as for those of us looking from the outside, understanding the ethical boundaries of our collective actions is vital. In the end, we must all ask ourselves: are we truly working together for the good of mankind, or have the ethical lines of our collective been blurred? It is important not to excuse or condemn blindly, but to recognise the complexities within these obsolete systems that no longer serve humanity.

Thus, as my co-authors point out, the WHO staff were well-intentioned, trying to do what they believed was best for the world. But, as the situation unfolded, their fellowship within the WHO's

---

[1]   https://digitallibrary.un.org/record/731800/files/A_PV-1229-EN.pdf

overarching structure may have clouded their ability to question, to resist, and to see the deeper implications of the decisions being made under their watch. It is a sobering reminder that, in any large organisation or collective, the line between being a victim of circumstance and a perpetrator of harm can become tragically thin.

When it came to their own health too, tragically most WHO colleagues simply went along with the Covid-19 vaccination programme. Proof that they had taken the Covid shots became a requirement for entering the WHO premises, even though such mandates were unlawful and violated inalienable human rights. The irony was not lost on me: the WHO, an institution purporting to uphold human rights, was now imposing conditions that directly contradicted the values it claimed to champion. Yet, the employees, many acquaintances of mine, so conditioned to following instructions and authority, did not seem to notice or question that their rights were being infringed upon.

I couldn't help but wonder if the Covid-19 vaccines administered to WHO staff in Geneva were different from those given to the general population. Might they have been given special batch of vaccines more innocuous than those given to the general population to ensure their compliance and shield them from the consequences of the WHO's Covid recommendations? At the time of writing, there was no way of knowing.

Shortly after releasing the Yellow Card report in June 2021, I had an opportunity to discuss the findings with a couple of WHO colleagues during an online meeting for normative work. In sharing the conclusion that the experimental Covid vaccines were not safe for use in humans, I was met with a response of complete disbelief. In them, I sensed a determination to feel relevant during this perceived global crisis, alongside an arrogance and complacency in the belief that the WHO should be in charge of "The Science."

"What will the world do without the WHO if there's another pandemic?" one former colleague asked of me when I remarked that not everyone in the world was happy with the WHO and that some, like the WCH, even called for its dismantling. It seemed to me that WHO employees had been made to feel indispensable by their boss and associated hierarchy, and they naturally believed it.

Thus, realising there was no way to make an impact within my WHO circle of acquaintances, I retired my independent company from WHO contracts. Having allocated most of the Evidence-based Medicine Consultancy's Ltd contractual obligations to my freelance colleagues that year, once these were completed my obligations were over. In December 2021, I gently informed my regular WHO team, with whom I had a respectful and enjoyable working relationship, that I could no longer take on new contracts with the organisation. With one colleague, whom I considered a friend, I explained that I could not continue working for an institution complicit in so much harm due to its Covid policies. She was seemingly unaware of the purpose behind the activation of the World Council for Health, which directly challenged the WHO's authority.

My co-authors observe in hindsight that *In a struggle with an enemy of superior strength, retreat is no disgrace. Timely withdrawal prevents bad consequences. If, out of a full sense of honour, a man allowed himself to be tempted into an unequal conflict, he would be drawing down disaster upon himself. In such a case a wise and conciliatory attitude benefits the whole community, which will then not be drawn into the conflict*. I did not wish to cause my former colleagues any trouble either. Nevertheless, I was sad that no further questions were asked, and how easy it was to be separated from once agreeable, heart-centred people, our former bond rendered seemingly insignificant.

Separation was a sign of the times. About what transpired, my

---

1   Hexagram 6, Conflict, line 2. From I Ching, by Richard Wilhelm, 3rd Ed. p.30.

co-authors reflect: *Heaven and earth are out of communion and all things are benumbed. What is above has no relation to what is below, and on earth confusion and disorder prevail. The dark power is within, the light power is without. Weaknesses within, harshness without. Within are the inferior, and without are the superior. The way of inferior people is on the ascent; the way of superior people is on the decline. But the superior people do not allow themselves to be turned from their principles. If the possibility of exerting influence is closed to them, they nevertheless remain faithful to their principles and withdraw into seclusion.*[1]

MOVE 61. The Graphene Conundrum

In the latter half of 2021, a wave of alarming information began to surface that would drastically shift the landscape of the Covid-19 narrative. We were bombarded with emails detailing a shocking revelation: graphene oxide (GO) was allegedly present in the Covid-19 vaccines. These claims were initially presented by a Spanish research team, La Quinta Columna, who, in June 2021, publicly released their findings. Their research, later reported by Dr Ariyana Love in *Global Research*, asserted that GO nanoparticles were present in all the major vaccine brands, including AstraZeneca, Pfizer, Moderna, Sinovac, Janssen, and Johnson & Johnson. The idea that such a toxic substance could be intentionally introduced into millions of people raised grave concerns among scientists, researchers, and the general public alike. The original finding came from Dr Pablo Campra at the University of Almeria. In July 2021, Dr Campra used Transmission Electron Microscopy (TEM) to identify what he believed were GO flakes within the Pfizer vaccine. His detection techniques included infrared spectroscopy and optical microscopy, both of which lent support to his claims.

---

[1]   Hexagram 12, Standstill. The Judgement. From I Ching, by Richard Wilhelm, 3rd Ed. p.52.

Numerous independent efforts to uncover the truth about what was really inside the Covid-19 injections followed. A secretive group known as The Scientist Club undertook their own analysis of several vaccine brands, and their findings concurred with Campra; carbon-based graphene sheets and GO nanoparticles were found within the vaccines they studied. Dr Campra expanded his testing, announcing in a report that, using Raman Spectroscopy, he had again identified graphene and GO in another eight vials. This method, which analyses molecular vibrations, further corroborated the growing suspicion that GO may indeed be a core component of these unsafe products.

Other researchers, like Dr Antonietta Gatti from Italy, found graphene in the vaccines too, as well as in PCR test kits and face masks. A striking revelation came from whistleblower Karen Kingston, a former Pfizer employee, who shared that GO had been deliberately hidden under the guise of trade secrets, explaining why it was not listed in the vaccine patent filings. She claimed that this omission was intentional. Kingston, like many of the scientists conducting investigations into the Covid-19 injection ingredients, seemed to be living in fear, anticipating serious consequences for this reveal.

However, the most chilling revelation came from Dr Andreas Noack, an Austrian scientist and expert in activated carbon and graphene. In a critical video released in November 2021,[1] he explained that the frequency bands detected by Dr Campra pointed to graphene hydroxide (GHO), a highly stable, razor-sharp material at the nanoscale. Dr Noack warned that these "nano-razorblades", when injected into the body, could cause severe damage to vital organs like the heart, brain, and cardiovascular system, shredding blood vessels. The danger lay in their invisibility; these particles were virtually undetectable with traditional toxicological methods, making them a

---

[1]   https://www.bitchute.com/embed/Ervbi96YgrzG/

silent and highly effective bioweapon.

There certainly was a basis for serious concern but it was difficult to know what to do with this information in December 2021. A search of the literature indicated that GO was being investigated for its potential use in mRNA gene therapy and vaccine delivery, due to its capacity to enhance binding efficiency, stability, and cellular uptake, especially when combined with materials like chitosan, a substance found in the exoskeletons of crustaceans (e.g., shrimp and crabs) and the cell walls of fungi.[1]

If GO or GHO had been snuck into the novel Covid-19 vaccines, the non-biodegradable nature of these carbon substances could trigger inflammation, clump together in the body, interact with vital organs, and interfere with our genetic material. In addition, the risk of thrombosis highlighted in some studies seemed to corroborate Dr Noack's dire warning about cardiovascular side effects. Also considered a disposal risk to the environment, it's hard not to question why such toxic materials would ever be considered for use in health products of any sort, let alone injectable ones! The link in the footnotes will enable you to explore this fairly extensive body of research into GO and vaccine development yourself.

Tragically, within days of releasing his worrying video, Dr Noack died suspiciously. His wife claimed that Dr Noack, a middle-aged man, was killed for revealing this critical information, adding to the growing fears surrounding this particular line of investigation. Sadly, the revelation about potentially lethal graphene in the Covid-19 shots created division in the fragile freedom movement. Requiring costly expertise and equipment, and with the challenge of getting hold of the tightly controlled Covid vaccine vials, the findings continued to be very difficult to verify. Ideally, in a normal world where authorities were interested in not causing harm, we would have been able

---

1   www.pubmed.ncbi.nlm.nih.gov/?term=graphene+oxide+AND+vaccine

to openly question these things, assemble scientists from around the world to meet together, conduct the science independently and collaboratively, compare techniques, and discuss their findings. However, this was not the state of the world at the time.

Thus, EbMCsquared commissioned an independent analysis from a Cambridge group called UNIT. Dr Deepti Bisht of UNIT had expressed interest and capacity to do this via email correspondence, with the objective of independently identifying any undeclared ingredients in Covid-19 vaccines. It was a challenge to find some vials for UNIT to analyse. We eventually managed to source four – two Moderna, one AstraZeneca and one Pfizer vial – with the assistance of a hospital nurse and couple of retired policemen.

Unfortunately, access to the Cambridge-based laboratory was terminated part way through the UNIT investigation. However, when UNIT's interim and only report was published, acknowledging the limitations, the investigators' findings corroborated what other international researchers had found:

"In conclusion, it can be stated that the four samples of vaccines (Moderna 1, Modern 2, AstraZeneca, Pfizer) all contain significant amount of carbon composites, graphene compounds and iron oxide. These ingredients were undeclared by the manufacturers and are absent from the list of ingredients for the vaccines." (Exhibit 27.)[1]

Sadly, the report caused a schism with our dear ally, Dr Mike Yeadon, who had kindly supported our ivermectin cause in mid-2021 and had a growing influence. Yeadon hastened to distance himself from the UNIT commission, pre-emptively declaring to his large social media following that the detailed 48-page report was most likely "false research." I quickly put Mike in direct contact with UNIT so that he could receive clarification from scientist Dr Deepti Bisht and reconsider his public statements but he kept his distance.

---

1   Exhibit 27. UNIT report 02/2022.

Affording Dr Bisht the opportunity to defend UNIT's report, she responded in an email to me, which I forwarded to Mike:

When, I began the analysis, I had not hoped to find GO in it, despite the fact that I knew that GO was used in targeted therapies and also for military purposes. What I never expected was that the vials that were being rolled out to the general healthy population would have copious amounts of substance in it. In a nutshell, if these four vials represent the general composition of the entire roll-out, then there is not only reason to be alarmed, but reason to take immediate action.

As you rightly say, this is an interim report and it warrants further analysis focused on the Raman Spectrum supplemented either by SEM (scanning electron microscopy) or TEM (transmission electron microscopy, which Campra did). However, despite it being an interim report, one cannot refute the findings. Further work can only crystallise and fine tune the findings, it would not 'unfind' them.

To my knowledge, Mike did not respond directly to Bisht, expressing a fear to me that the issue being discovered by international scientists independently may be "enemy action, designed to distract us." Thus, a lid was put on any constructive scientific discussions about how to further address and elucidate the graphene issue, relegating it to the realms of a "conspiracy theory" once more. The conundrum of whether graphene was consistently present in the shots, along with its type, risks, and intended purpose, became an issue that we could no longer openly discuss lest it cause further division in an easily fractured movement. To the gratitude of many including me, Dr Yeadon continued to speak out very strongly against the experimental Covid-19 vaccines, as well as the broader globalist agenda.

However, a niggling worry remained. It is legitimate to question any figure who has worked closely with large corporations or organisations, like Mike, Dr Malone, and me – how does their history and investment inform their present stance, especially when it involves controversy? Thus, let me state here that I have no financial interests in the pharmaceutical industry, no investment portfolio, and no grants from individuals with industry ties, foundations or organisations; I have no competing interests when it comes to my work on ivermectin, vaccines or any other drugs. In addition, I no longer have a relationship with the WHO and the Cochrane Collaboration. My work and income from these organisations ended in December 2021 when I made a conscious choice to separate from them, in good standing.

It seemed unlikely that Mike would hold shares in Pfizer and other mRNA gene therapy manufacturers in 2021, being among the first to sound the alarm on their dangers, and given his adamant position against the Covid-19 shots. However, a former chief scientist and vice-president of the allergy and respiratory research division at Pfizer, Mike was also the co-founder and former CEO of the biotechnology company Ziarco, which sold for in excess of £300 million in 2017 to Novartis AG. Of course, ivermectin, emerging also as an inexpensive treatment for various cancers, would represent serious commercial competition to Novartis AG, for example, which had several novel cancer drugs in development.

My co-authors describe Yeadon's relationship with his former industry as that of "waiting for rain". *There is nothing to do but to wait until the rain falls,*[1] they say, highlighting that obedience is required in successful unions between parties of different rank, in the following metaphor: *The sovereign gives his daughter in marriage. This brings blessing and supreme good fortune. By his decree the imperial princesses, although higher in rank than their husbands, had to obey them like all other wives. Here too we are shown a truly modest union of high and low*

---

1   Hexagram 5, The Image. From I Ching, by Richard Wilhelm, 3rd Ed. p.25.

that brings happiness and blessings.[1]

In this metaphor about marriage, my co-authors suggest that Yeadon's relationship with his former industry, which had brought him *supreme good fortune*, needed to be handled with care and humility during the Covid-19 crisis, acknowledging its complexity. In 2021, in addition to having cancer drugs in the pipeline, Novartis AG was also actively involved in manufacturing the Covid-19 mRNA products, including the Pfizer-BioNTech Covid-19 vaccine. This seems a delicate situation, for sure.

I have often wondered what correspondence and conversations Yeadon might have had with his former industry colleagues about the dangers of this biotechnology. Perhaps one day Mike and I will have this much overdue in-real-life conversation. It would be great to get together and discuss this, as well as points of current scientific debate.

The lesson to us all here is that it is not only our past affiliations that shape our present, but the way we navigate the inevitable tension between loyalty, ambition, and truth in a world where corporate interests and personal convictions often collide. Furthermore, it raises interesting questions, such as, what establishes our integrity in a movement demanding honest, independent thought and authentic action? What establishes our credibility in a movement seeking the truth?

MOVE 62. Would Jesus approve?

One of the most troubling occurrences during Covid-19 was the apparent collusion of organised religion with the supranational military-industrial-banking complex to induce compliance with unlawful, unscientific, and downright harmful Covid-19 policies. Religious beliefs were not only used as a tool to manipulate people

---

1   Hexagram 11, Peace, line 5. From I Ching, by Richard Wilhelm, 3rd Ed. p.51.

into following political decrees, but also as a vehicle to propagate fear.

The speed at which churches closed their doors while big business continued to trade was anathema to many people. When places of worship did eventually open, congregants were subjected to various fear-driven measures. Sanitising rituals were demanded upon entry, social distancing was enforced with tape and stickers, and various longstanding religious practices were modified or curtailed. One particularly discordant image shared on social media showed priests in the USA using toy guns to conduct baptisms. Even singing in church was deemed dangerous. As such, it was either done through face masks or prohibited entirely. Those who did not comply with these pious political directives were often vilified, prevented from attending services, and risked being cast out of their congregations. Fear of exclusion kept many reluctantly compliant. My elderly parents, for instance, frequently remarked on how ridiculous, uncomfortable, and dehumanising the measures were, how difficult it was to breathe, let alone sing, with a mask on, and how going to church simply was not the same anymore.

Why were we urged to put our faith in "The Science" rather than in God during the Covid-19 chapter? The former Archbishop of Canterbury, Justin Welby, might know the answer to these questions. Since 2013, Welby had led the worldwide body of Anglican Christian churches. The Anglican Communion website claimed that in the UK he was regarded as the nation's senior Christian and spiritual voice. With responsibility for over 13,000 parishes and millions of Christians across 165 countries, his leadership was far-reaching. On 21st December 2021, shortly after our Cease and Desist Notice was published, the UK's *Daily Mail* ran an article quoting the Archbishop.[1] At the time, there were well over two million reports of adverse

---

1 https://www.dailymail.co.uk/news/article-10334569/Archbishop-Canterbury-says-unvaccinated-immoral-love-neighbour.html. *The Independent, Washington Post*, BBC and other influential media also published Welby's statements

Covid-19 vaccine reactions, including thousands of deaths, reported to the WHO's pharmacovigilance database. On the UK's Yellow Card scheme, around 400,000 individual reports were logged, including approximately 2,000 fatalities.

The video of the Archbishop that accompanied the *Daily Mail* article chilled me to the bone. Welby urged people to get vaccinated, saying, "It's not about me and my rights. Now, obviously, there are some people who for health reasons can't go vaccinating – [that's a] different question. But it's not about me and my rights to choose, it's about how I love my neighbour. To love one another as Jesus said: Get vaccinated. Get boosted."

I was horrified. To my ear, it sounded as though Welby had been briefed to say these carefully chosen, guilt-invoking words. It seemed as if he had been called upon to deliver this message because of his immense influence as the leader of the Anglican Church. Extraordinarily, he stated that getting vaccinated (with an experimental genetic product that had not been proven safe in humans!) was a "moral issue". As my co-authors note, *Extraordinary measures should be resorted to only when all else fails.*[1] This certainly was an *extraordinary measure,* a seemingly desperate move to manipulate people with faith in Jesus to comply.

The leveraging of Jesus' goodwill, by a figure of worldwide Christian authority to gaslight the public should have been a matter of grave concern for all. A misuse of such power was sure to have serious consequences. Yet I heard none of the other Anglican ministers contradicting their leader, at least not publicly. Surely Jesus would never have promoted unsafe and experimental medical technologies that harm men, women, and children while lining the pockets of billionaires and corporations? To my mind, this stood in direct opposition

---

1   Hexagram 62, Preponderance of the Small, line 1. From I Ching, by Richard Wilhelm, 3rd Ed. p.241.

to everything Jesus stood for. Jesus stood for truth and justice, he defied banks and government, he healed with his hands, and he protected children. He fought against the same corrupt systems that continue to exploit us today.

In his media interview, the Archbishop mentioned that he had previously struggled with organising a conspiracy in the Anglican Church. His attempt at a joke perhaps, but it begged the question "How many conspiracies had there been, and why?" Three years later, it would be revealed that Welby had been involved in conspiring to cover up the horrific sexual abuse of more than 100 boys and young men by a church member. It was this, not the Covid-19 blasphemy, that led to his resignation in 2024.

For me, this betrayal by the leader of the Anglican church marked a significant milestone. It reminded me that Jesus did not belong to corporate institutions, Jesus belonged in our hearts. A better world was on the way, where evil would no longer be able to hide. It would no longer lurk in the shadows when we were done shining our lights. Remembering who we are as man-kind, innately courageous, compassionate, creative, life-loving, and kind to one another, it was time to trust in our collective power. Breathe. And, one. Two. Three – push!

Chapter 13

Retreat

Mountain under heaven: the image of RETREAT.
Thus the superior man keeps the inferior man at a distance,
Not angrily but with reserve.[1]

The mountain rises up under heaven, but owing to its nature it finally comes to a stop. Heaven on the other hand retreats upwards before it into the distance and remains out of reach. This symbolises the behaviour of the superior man towards a climbing inferior; he retreats into his own thoughts as the inferior man comes forward. He does not hate him, for hatred is a form of subjective involvement by which we are bound to the hated object. The superior man shows strength (heaven) in that he brings the inferior man to a standstill (mountain) by his dignified reserve.[2]

In addition to a love for mathematics, I learned two important lessons from my father. One, hiking South Africa's Drakensberg Mountains

---

1   Hexagram 33, Retreat, The Image. From I Ching, by Richard Wilhelm, 3rd Ed. p.130.
2   Hexagram 33, Retreat, The Image. From I Ching, by Richard Wilhelm, 3rd Ed. p.130.

together in my childhood taught me how to persevere when there is no end in sight. The other, through the application of his swift and arbitrary spanking, taught me the necessity to retreat with dignified reserve. Great strides were made through EbMCsquared CIC in practical terms over the preceding months with BIRD's work advocating for ivermectin and the strong launch of the World Council for Health; thus, by early 2022, the darkness was pushing strongly back. With its tentacles reaching into government departments, international agencies, hospitals, schools, and homes, the intensity of attacks on those advocating for health, choice, and human rights increased. Censorship and hate speech against ethical scientists, doctors, and lawyers escalated in the media, labelling us as "anti-vaxxers" and "conspiracy theorists". On prime time television, politicians, media personalities, and celebrities discussed whether we should be forcibly vaccinated, fined, or locked up.

The public too suffered a barrage of fearmongering. The so-called 'Omicron' variant, an anagram of "moronic", had arrived in the UK at the end of November 2021, allegedly introduced from South Africa by a couple of English travellers. The public, held captive by the ongoing chaos, hurried to stand in line for Covid-19 boosters. Misinformation, propagated by government machinery and corporate media, reigned supreme, and jobsworths carried out their policing without hesitation. Increasingly, diverse professionals fighting for truth and justice fell prey to corporate-controlled professional bodies. Needless to say, they came for me too. On account of my independence and good standing with professional bodies and commissioning officers, with no superior to pay homage to other than my own conscience, I refused to be an easy catch.

As the cycle of intense activity over thirteen months, with its successes and failures, drew to a close, it also brought into our EbMCsquared fold a remarkable woman, mother, and natural law expert, Karen-Ruth Skölmli.

MOVE 63. Under Investigation by the General Medical Council

A year after it had all begun with ivermectin, Dr Andrew Hill, and BIRD, I was notified by Mr Guy Pitchon, an "investigating officer" from the General Medical Council (GMC), that I was under investigation due to the academic lecture I had given in September 2021 in my hometown, at the BRLSI. Aside from the extraordinary interruption from a virtual attendee, and a certain medical professional whose face I never saw because he wore a mask throughout the lecture and had stormed out, I had felt that the lecture had gone reasonably well. Afterwards, men and women had smiled and thanked me for my presentation, some even venturing to shake my hand in defiance of the prevailing fear of "catching Covid-19".

Mr Hooker, the convener, afterwards confirmed my perception via email: "Once again, thank you so much for presenting such a magnificent talk to our audience. It has stimulated lively debate, predictably ruffled a few feathers amongst the 'closed-minded' but thankfully thrilled others who greatly appreciated hearing facts that are not being exposed by mainstream media."

Despite this very positive response from Hooker, danger was lurking in the heart of his co-convener, who seemed particularly aggrieved by my statement that the Covid-19 vaccines were not normal vaccines, but rather gene therapies. I was only too aware that there had been some fallout following my talk, as the video had never been published on the BRLSI YouTube channel as was usual for such lectures. I had requested a copy for my own records, but weeks passed without receiving it. Eventually, Hooker conveyed the disheartening news that the BRLSI would not release it to me (or him), even though I held the intellectual copyright to the material. Horrified by his organisation's decision, Hooker told me that, in his 17 years of association with the BRLSI, this had never happened before.

I received this earnest email from him on 15th November, 2021:

"I have been on the point of writing to you about the video recording of your excellent talk but I'm afraid the news is not good. After your talk, I was plunged into battling with BRLSI over a couple of complaints they had received over your references to Big Pharma. Whereas your physical audience was most appreciative of your talk it seems that some comments from the virtual chat room were distinctly hostile. Indeed, I was even criticised for supporting your talk in my vote of thanks and I was called to an informal 'tribunal' to justify my position. I think they were rather dumbfounded by my response that I would always support evidence-based Science, and most especially from a scientist of your international standing and recognition. Nevertheless, I was never allowed to see the video recording or any of the comments from the chat room, favourable or otherwise. However, I had not anticipated that the whole recording would be censored in its entirety and not made available for viewing on the BRLSI YouTube channel. Accordingly, I have resigned my position of Convenor for Science and Medicine at BRLSI and terminated my seventeen years of association and support for what used to be such a noble Institution.

I addressed my letter of resignation to all subject convenors at BRLSI, some of whom also held positions of Management and Directorship, expressing that it is utterly untenable for any Scientific Institution to bow to political propaganda and to fail to uphold the high standards of rigorous, peer-reviewed, evidence-based Science. Furthermore, I underlined that my complaint of the aggressive behaviour towards you breached the BRLSI's Code of Conduct but in this I received no support."

I was extremely saddened by this turn of events. I had hoped that such circumstances would not have negative consequences for Mr Hooker, whom, through our communications over the preceding three months, I had come to greatly like and respect. His integrity and commitment to science had been evident, and it pained me to see him caught in the middle of such a troubling situation. My wise co-authors retrospectively share my dismay, pointing out that those in high places, like Hooker, *through renunciation, should bring increase to those below. By neglecting this duty and helping no one, they, in turn, lose the furthering influence of others and soon find themselves alone. In this way, they invite attacks.*[1] It was regrettable that Mr Hooker might have lost friends and acquaintances through his resignation, which was brought on by my controversial lecture. And, not least, that he had lost faith in the BRLSI: "Such a shame that BRLSI is no longer worthy of being considered a scientific institution," he wrote on a separate occasion. Hooker might have wondered, had he remained, could he have had a positive effect on the crusty, outdated institution in due course? I hoped he did not miss it too much.

The BRLSI, a valuable and beautiful historic place once used to meet with friends and share ideas, was now left to its own devices, no doubt with certain truculent and closed-minded members ruminating. Though I too hoped that Mr Hooker's renunciation would achieve its goal: to provoke some internal reflection and perhaps even remorse within the BRLSI leadership and wider community. Positive change could yet emerge from this difficult experience.

But not for me at the time. The letter from the GMC's Mr Pitchon advised as follows:

What we're investigating

On the basis of the information currently available, we've identified

---

[1]   Hexagram 42, Increase, line 6. From I Ching, by Richard Wilhelm, 3rd Ed. p.165.

some areas of good medical practice that have been called into question. We need to find out more information to see if this is correct and, if so, whether your fitness to practise medicine is potentially impaired. In particular:

You gave a talk at Bath Royal Literary and Scientific Institution on 30 September 2021, during which you allegedly made inaccurate and/or misleading comments about Covid-19 and the Covid-19 vaccines including, but not limited to, misrepresenting data on adverse effects, and calling the vaccine a 'gene therapy'.

My co-authors observe of Mr Pitchon that *going quickly when one's tasks are finished, is without blame. But one must reflect on how much one may decrease others.*[1] Did people like Pitchon, in their zeal to fulfil their duties as 'Investigating Officers' ever pause to consider the harm their investigations into ethical doctors were causing, not only to those they investigated on behalf of their superiors but to mankind as a whole? Their own families too, if Covid-19 vaccinated and 'boosted', were likely to have been harmed by the very system I and other ethical doctors were challenging – a corrupt pharmaceutical industry at best, a war on mankind at worst. Are my ancient co-authors alluding to the modern-day concept of a "jobsworth" I wondered?

But perhaps there was no 'zeal' involved at all. It was just a job to pay the bills, so that one could get on with and afford what one considered to be *life* – the things that bring personal satisfaction or comfort, perhaps a hobby or sport one loves, a wife, a son, or the pursuit of personal goals. This mindset, however, overlooks the deeper truth: every moment of our lives requires attention. We cannot afford to live on autopilot, allowing routine and material pursuits to take precedence without considering the broader consequences of our actions.

---

1   Hexagram 41, Decrease, line 1. From I Ching, by Richard Wilhelm, 3rd Ed. p.159.

The central theme of my co-authors' wisdom in this case is how a dramatic *shift of wealth* can occur through the actions of individuals who prioritise their job duties over common sense, follow orders without questioning them, and turn a blind eye to the impact of their actions. These actions, during the Covid chapter in particular, brought a decrease in prosperity for the people, favouring government and 'elite' interests. *A decrease in the prosperity of the people in favour of government is an out-and-out decrease,*[1] the *I Ching* confirms. This underscores the real danger of blindly following orders, without considering the broader consequences for society.

During the Covid-19 chapter, people lost their health, jobs, sovereignty, and community. This *out-and-out decrease* is particularly poignant to the case of those health professionals who received income boosts from Big Pharma and government for administering vaccinations, bringing tremendous harm to those who trusted them, their patients – men, women and children.

Similarly, those like Pitchon, investing their valuable time in the artificial, corporate world of government with its punitive and arbitrary Covid rules and regulations, were empowered to bring harm upon individual servants of the people: doctors like me. *The man in a superior position who is thus aided must weigh carefully how much he can accept without doing the helpful servant or friend real harm.*[2] Such individuals *in a superior position* should pause to reflect on whether their work is causing harm to others who are working for the good. If, by following orders, they are enabling harm to be done in the name of authority or convenience, they must ask themselves: What is the true cost of blindly obeying a superior?

And if, by chance, they come to realise they are simply following orders, my co-authors indicate with wisdom refined through

---

1 Hexagram 41, Decrease. From I Ching, by Richard Wilhelm, 3rd Ed. p.158.
2 Hexagram 41, Decrease line 1. From I Ching, by Richard Wilhelm, 3rd Ed. p.160.

millennia, this needs to stop: *He who throws himself away in order to do the bidding of a superior diminishes his own position without thereby giving lasting benefit to the other. This is wrong.*[1] Self-sacrifice, though one may not see it as thus, for the sole purpose of obedience does not lead to true service or progress. In fact, it weakens the human being who submits, and ultimately offers no real benefit to the person in the superior position either.

The cover letter from Mr Pitchon recommended I obtain legal counsel, which I duly did, enlisting the steadfast support of Mr Philip Hyland. *One must join forces with friends of like mind and put himself under the leadership of a man equal to the situation: then one will succeed in removing obstacles.*[2]

Hyland was no stranger to the GMC's overreach, having already represented three other doctors who prioritised treating their patients ethically, rather than adhering to politically driven orders. Of Hyland, my co-authors observe: *When a man has withdrawn from the world, its tumult often becomes unbearable to him. There are many people who, in noble pride, hold themselves aloof from all that is low and rebuff it brusquely whenever it comes to meet them. Such persons are reproached for being proud and distant, but since active duties no longer hold them to the world, this does not greatly matter. They know how to bear the dislike of the masses with composure.*[3]

Hyland, committed to the concept and administration of justice come hell or high water, would not care what Pitchon or the GMC lawyer that was subsequently assigned to the case thought of him. An ordinary man disillusioned with his profession, Hyland was one of the few lawyers who had observed how, during Covid-19, official policies and regulatory bodies violated the very principles the legal system should uphold. Laws and regulations, fines and punishment,

---

1 Hexagram 41, Decrease line 2. From I Ching, by Richard Wilhelm, 3rd Ed. p.160.
2 Hexagram 39, Obstruction, The Judgement. From I Ching, by Richard Wilhelm, 3rd Ed. p.151.
3 Hexagram 44, Coming to Meet, line 6. From I Ching, by Richard Wilhelm, 3rd Ed. p.173.

had facilitated and even protected criminality. Hyland carried on regardless, a lone warrior of the law, intent on justice for the people. Of Hyland's approach, my co-authors approve: *"The perseverance of the solitary man furthers."* His profession was in disarray, but Hyland did not allow it to defeat him.

"Who the hell do the GMC think they are, giving themselves jurisdiction to police academic talks?" was Hyland's first response upon my telling him about the investigation. "A robust response is required. It's censorship and abuse of power!"

Indeed, who watches the watchdogs? Interfering in academic discussions certainly represented a dangerous overreach into areas where the GMC had no authority. Perhaps, had the GMC activities been monitored by doctors and the public, or been comprised of health professionals themselves, instead of managers and officers, it may not have betrayed those it was meant to serve. Unfortunately we, the people, were responsible for this sorry state of affairs. As pointed out by my co-authors, our indifference had facilitated it. *The inferior man rises only because the superior man does not regard him as dangerous and so lends him power. If he were resisted from the first, he could never gain influence.*[1]

The accompanying transcript of my lecture that Pitchon attached, for which I had been previously unable to obtain a recording, included the words of the online dissenter that, at the time of the unexpected outburst, I had barely grasped. The transcript confirmed his low opinion of me: "As a supposed expert in evidence-based medicine, you do not have a very good understanding in that case, and you should be ashamed of yourself for what you have done today." Upon request, Pitchon also furnished us with the video recording of my offending lecture, previously denied to both Hooker and me by the BRLSI.

---

1   Hexagram 44, Coming to Meet, The Judgement. From I Ching, by Richard Wilhelm, 3rd Ed. p.171.

What had provoked the GMC complaint? It's one thing to feel uncomfortable or be aggrieved by the words of others, but to seek to impair or remove their livelihood because one holds a different view is quite another thing altogether. My shock at revisiting this matter through a GMC investigation deepened when I saw the lengths that had been gone to by my antagonists at the BRLSI. Of course, Mr Hooker would never have agreed to be named in such a complaint. To avoid this obstacle, the BRLSI host named in the transcript had been mis-identified. Instead of Mr Hooker, his convenor role was attributed to a Professor whom I hadn't met. While I was not sure whether the Professor, whom I understood was a linguist, had been at the event at all, he certainly played no vocal part in it. Thus, it seemed the name was changed in order to conceal the fact that the action against me was not sanctioned by all involved.

I wrote back to Mr Pitchon, querying why an academic lecture was being investigated by the General Medical Council. I was, after all, both a medical doctor and a scientist, with a medical degree and a PhD. Surely, as a PhD scientist, if not as a doctor, I was free to share my scientific work and perspective?

Pitchon responded: "In your lecture you rely on your GMC registration to underpin the relevance of your findings, and it is this that contributed to the concerns meeting the threshold for investigation."

Sadly, this was an out-and-out lie. In the transcript that he had sent me of my lecture, I had not at any stage mentioned my GMC registration to the audience. Indeed, my work as an international scientist and guideline methodologist did not depend on it; it was not even stated on my curriculum vitae. I wrote back to Pitchon: "Could you point out to me where I have relied on my GMC registration to underpin the relevance of my findings please? I don't recall this."

Pitchon then surprised me with an apology – and a fresh tack:

Dear Dr Lawrie

I apologise for my error.

You are correct in saying that you didn't rely on your GMC registration in your lecture.

The reference relates to the written evidence submission that you sent to the *parliamentary select committee* which reads:

'I am the Director of the Evidence-based Medicine Consultancy Ltd in Bath, United Kingdom. I have a medical degree (MBBCh) and a Doctorate in Philosophy (PhD) from the University of the Witwatersrand in Johannesburg, South Africa. Whilst I have practiced clinical Medicine in both the United Kingdom and South Africa, I now perform non-clinical research work only. My United Kingdom General Medical Council registration number is 3634680.

As the director of E-BMC Ltd, which I established in 2013, I am committed to improving the quality of healthcare globally through rigorous research. My research expertise is drawn from experience in both developing and developed countries, which uniquely positions me to evaluate and design research for a variety of healthcare settings. As a result, I am a frequent member of Technical Teams responsible for developing international clinical practice guidelines and am currently employed as the Guideline Methodologist on two World Health Organization (WHO) clinical practice guidelines due to be published in 2021.'

To clarify, the primary concern being investigated relates to the content of the lecture, and whether the findings and conclusions you make are reasonable, and not misleading, and in line with Good Medical Practice guidance. As I explained, the next step will be for the GMC to appoint an expert to review that content. I'm sorry for any confusion caused.

Pitchon's curious email, referencing my private parliamentary submission to the Department of Health and Social Care Chairman Mr Jeremy Hunt in March 2021, which I had understood had not travelled further than Hunt's inbox, had nothing at all to do with the matter in question, my academic lecture at the BRLSI. How could the GMC relate a confidential Submission to Parliament, where I declare my GMC registration as a non-clinical doctor as a statement of fact, to an invited lecture given in a local scientific institution nine months later? Being my first encounter ever with my professional body in 30 or so years, I was bemused.

But to my lawyer, Mr Philip Hyland, it was like a red rag to a bull. "They are really scraping the barrel," Hyland wrote, incensed about the breach of parliamentary privilege, undertaking to send them a letter asking what exactly they were investigating.

He holds him fast with yellow ox hide. No one can tear him loose. Yellow is the colour of the middle. It indicates that which is correct and in line with duty. Ox hide is strong and not to be torn. While the superior men (those in high position) *retreat and the inferior* (us in this case) *press after them, the inferior man represented here holds on so firmly and tightly to the superior men that the latter cannot shake him off.[1]*

Pitchon misspelled Hyland's name in the return correspondence, for which Hyland promptly reprimanded him, whilst also informing the GMC investigation officer that a complaint had been lodged with the Metropolitan Police, regarding serious misconduct of certain government officials in public office with regard to the roll-out of experimental Covid-19 vaccines. The complaint included the GMC's harassment of doctors and their abuse of power against those providing evidence-based opinions that did not align with the official narrative. In addition he wrote:

---

1   Hexagram 33 Retreat, line 2. From I Ching, by Richard Wilhelm, 3rd Ed. p.131.

"Investigating Tess for giving a talk, then shifting the focus of the investigation to what evidence she gave to a Parliamentary Select Committee is absurd. The GMC should know that evidence provided to a Parliamentary Select Committee is covered by privilege. The reason we're in this mess is that two safe and effective therapeutics were deliberately suppressed. That issue is also under investigation by the Police, and Tess's evidence is part of the Ivermectin strand.

It is imperative you answer the following questions:

1. Could you explain why the focus of investigation changed from a lecture to evidence supplied to a select committee?

2. Could you set out in full how giving evidence to a select committee comes within the GMC's jurisdiction?

3. Do you also accept that there is a body of medical opinion that supports the use of ivermectin?

4. Do you accept there is clinical data that supports the use of ivermectin?

5. Do you accept according to the WHO database ivermectin has a far better safety profile than the SARS coV2 injections?

6. Do you accept that the issue of criminality surrounding the suppression of safer and more effective therapeutics was set out in Robert F Kennedy's book on Fauci and included a section on ivermectin?

7. Do you accept that the Metropolitan Police have a crime recorded as committed by the GMC in relation to how the GMC has treated Doctors who have questioned the narrative? The crime being abuse of public office and serious misconduct in public office?

8. Do you accept that evidence is still being collected on the reported crime?

9. Do you accept that Doctors have a duty to speak out when they

have evidence based concerns relating to patient safety and the conduct of regulators, the government and the civil service?

10. Do you accept that Dr White [also "under investigation" for speaking out against Covid policies] is recorded as being a victim of the crime and myself being accorded the status of informant?

Could you come back to me as soon as possible as your actions are causing avoidable distress to Dr Lawrie. If you feel unable to answer these questions without incriminating yourself then you may need to take independent legal advice on your position.

Time would prove that Hyland had the endurance necessary to hold the guilty to account. *Duration is a state whose movement is not worn down by hindrances.*[1] Hyland would face many hindrances, but he remained undeterred. So focused was he on doing what was right and just that he would shrug off every obstacle. *"Duration"* was at the core of his character, and it would see him through. An admirable example of a human being and I was privileged to have him on my side.

We would hear no more about the investigation from Mr Pitchon and the GMC until two years later. "The case examiners have concluded this case with no further action," we were informed. It had all just been about intimidation. The letter dated January 20th, 2023, included the following summary:

Background

The GMC received a complaint that Dr Lawrie gave a lecture titled 'Covid-19 and the State of Evidence-Based Medicine' (the Lecture), which was recorded on zoom, at the Bath Royal Literary and Scientific Institution (the Institution) on 30 September 2021, in

---

[1] Hexagram 32, Duration, The Judgement. From I Ching, by Richard Wilhelm, 3rd Ed. p.126.

which she denied the safety of Covid-19 vaccines and spread misinformation about Covid-19 treatments. The Institution is an independent charity which promotes science, literature and art to the City of Bath, tickets for its lectures can be bought by both member and non-members of the Institution. Based on the information provided, the GMC opened an investigation into allegations that Dr Lawrie made inaccurate and/or misleading comments about Covid-19 and Covid-19 vaccines.

During the investigation the GMC obtained a video copy and transcript of the Lecture. During the initial part of the Lecture Dr Lawrie presented her views on the evidence on ivermectin as a treatment for Covid-19, later in her lecture Dr Lawrie presented her views on vaccines.

It was established during the GMC investigation that the advertisement for the Lecture stated that Dr Lawrie was an external consultant to the World Health Organization, a clinical practice guideline expert, and that she was Director of the Evidence-Based Medicine Consultancy Ltd and EbMCsquared CIC. The EbMCsquared CIC website states that it was established by Dr Lawrie as a 'a non-profit company, in March 2021, in response to the tremendous need for independent and objective health care research and provision, arising out of the Covid-19 health emergency.'

On 10 February 2022, Dr Lawrie's representatives submitted that "taken at its highest there is a substantial body of medical opinion that supports what Doctor Lawrie is saying."

Reasons for our decision

As case examiners we must decide whether there is a realistic prospect of establishing that a doctor's fitness to practise is currently impaired to a degree justifying action on his or her registration.

This test has two parts.

1. We must decide if the allegations are serious enough to warrant action on the doctor's registration.

2. We must also consider whether the allegations are capable of proof to the required standard, namely that it is more likely than not that the alleged events occurred.

In making decisions, we should have regard to the GMC's objectives. These are to protect, promote and maintain the health and safety of the public; promote and maintain public confidence in the profession; and promote and maintain proper standards and conduct for members of the profession.

Doctors are entitled to hold and express personal views, however they also have an overriding duty to patients and to uphold the public's confidence in the profession. In the absence of expert or other evidence capable of proving that Dr Lawrie's conduct was such that public confidence in the medical profession would be undermined, or that it risked the health, safety and well-being of the public, or that it undermined proper standards and conduct for members of the profession, we agree that there is no realistic prospect of establishing evidentially that Dr Lawrie's fitness to practise is impaired to a degree justifying action on her registration.

Conclusion

For the reasons given above, we have decided to close the case with no action.

A few words on the complaint itself are necessary. The claim was that I had misrepresented data on adverse effects of Covid-19 vaccines, and called them gene therapies. With regard to the former, I had indeed presented adverse effects data. But these were not sucked out of thin air, or even calculated, they were taken from the WHO's Vigibase pharmacovigilance database. I had referenced the data two weeks before my BRLSI lecture and, at this time, there were 1,904,499 adverse drug reaction reports attributed to the Covid-19 shots on the WHO database, and 10,046 deaths. Accrued in just 9 months of the vaccine roll-out, the word "unprecedented" doesn't quite cover the shocking nature of these data. Such data are estimated to be but a small fraction of the true number of adverse reactions, the majority not being recorded or reported.

With regard to whether or not the Covid-19 vaccines were gene therapies might be considered debatable. They were definitely gene products (GMO products to be precise) but the word "therapy" implies a treatment, which they were not. Thus, gene biotechnology may be a more appropriate term for the Covid-19 injections, which certainly should never have been called vaccines. Using official diagrams, I had explained to the BRLSI audience how these mRNA (Pfizer and Moderna) and DNA vaccines (AstraZeneca) were supposed to work: they contain a genetic "recipe" that uses the machinery of our cells to make "spike proteins". In this way, they turn the cells in our bodies into spike protein factories. Such foreign proteins trigger an immune response to get rid of them. One of many problems with this novel technology was the fact that there was no off-switch.

At the time, what we did not yet know, and what independent scientists like Kevin McKernan have since revealed, is that the Pfizer, Moderna and other "Covid-19 vaccine" products contained plasmid DNA in large quantities. Plasmid DNA is a small circular DNA molecule capable of replicating independently. As used in the Covid-19 manufacturing process, plasmid DNA was derived from E. coli bacteria. The process involved inserting the desired gene sequence, the coronavirus spike protein gene, into the plasmids, transforming them into E. coli cells, and amplifying the plasmids through bacterial replication. Though the plasmids are supposed to be enzymatically removed after producing the mRNA coding for the spike protein, the high levels and consistency in which they could be found in the Covid-19 vaccine vials suggested that its presence was more than inadvertent DNA contamination but, rather, that it was an inherent quality of the final product disseminated. Though genetic integration of the Covid-19 vaccine genetic material was certainly a strong possibility based on the fundaments of these GMO products, I did not tell the BRLSI audience this because it had not been proven in September 2021.

I would later write to the CEO of the GMC, Mr Charlie Massey, that the GMC was in breach of its obligations to doctors and the public and, accordingly, I was withholding my fees. (Exhibit 28.)[1] *Voluntary retreat brings good fortune to the superior man.*[2] No response from the GMC's CEO was very forthcoming. I decided that I would no longer be associated with this corrupted institution. In clear conscience I could not put my fees towards their tacit support of organised criminal activities, persecuting doctors and not protecting patients from the experimental genetic injections, on behalf of the globalists and government. As the ancient and wise agree, *The situation is unequivocal. Inner detachment has become an established fact, and we are at liberty to depart.*[3]

As for the actions and inactions of those simply following orders like Pitchon, *To render true service of lasting value to another, one must serve him without relinquishing oneself.*[4] This is the essence of responsible action. True service involves contributing meaningfully without losing one's sense of self, one's agency, integrity, and personal responsibility. By acknowledging our roles in the larger system of harm and exploitation, we can begin to confront the ignorance that

---

1   Exhibit 28. Letter to Mr Charlie Massey, CEO of the General Medical Council.
2   Hexagram 33, Retreat, Line 4. From I Ching, by Richard Wilhelm, 3rd Ed. p.132.
3   Hexagram 33 Retreat, line 6. From I Ching, by Richard Wilhelm, 3rd Ed. p.132.
4   Hexagram 41 Decrease, line 2. From I Ching, by Richard Wilhelm, 3rd Ed. p.160.

perpetuates mankind's captivity and end it. Acknowledging our complicity brings hope. Through awareness and reflection, we possess the power to change, not only mastering ourselves but bringing benefit to others.

MOVE 64. Health Sovereignty Becomes Our Mission

Few would have heard of Karen-Ruth Skölmli in 2021, though she is undoubtedly a foundation stone of World Council for Health and the better way movement. In seeking legal counsel about the GMC inquiry, a couple I knew had put Ruth's name forward to me, though she declined the case, feeling that her expertise in this area was lacking. Instead, Ruth's journey with us began as a volunteer at EbMCsquared CIC in January 2022. It is often said that the true measure of a person's life is the impact they leave behind, the wisdom they impart, and the legacy they leave for others to follow. Ruth, a beacon of sovereignty and justice, was a testament to human value.

Very soon it was clear that she held the missing piece of the puzzle, the knowledge of what it meant to be a sovereign being and why this was important to our initiative to counter the globalists. Determined to teach us how to reclaim our sovereignty, inalienable rights, and personal autonomy from corporate entities, Ruth knew this was essential for us to be able to empower others effectively to do so too.

At the time I met Ruth, it seemed like the word "sovereign" was more often used in association with gold coins or the Queen, it sounded so archaic to my modern ear. Once I had learnt what it really meant, I wondered whether it had been deliberately hidden from us. Ruth's humble teachings centred on one profound truth: that sovereignty was the inherent authority we possess over ourselves, and this was not to be a mere concept but a lived reality. We were the authors of our own stories; nobody had authority over us.

Quietly livid at the destruction wreaked upon mankind by

indifferent and corrupt authorities, Ruth's teachings entitled *Sovereign Natural Empowerment* were a call to action. One could not be sovereign and remain a slave. Firm and consistent action was required to liberate ourselves.

Ruth taught the difference between the legal system, which is based on merchant law, the law of the sea and of pirates, and natural law, the law of man, heaven and earth. Legal systems depended on black ink, reams of paper, clauses, and tricksy semantics. Natural law, she explained, is simple: it is the principle of acting in honour and causing no harm. Thus, being sovereign meant acting on one's conscience, not blindly taking orders from others, nor wilfully harming anyone, protecting your own territory (your body), and working in harmony with nature.

Ruth, who would humbly refer to herself as a "nobody" was anything but. She emphasised the importance of recognising one's power and personal responsibility to all who would listen. It was our responsibility as individuals and communities to hold corporations – the dead entities with no moral obligations to people, God or the universe – accountable. This was a lesson that echoed through our conversations, and it was her gentle and firm commitment to holding the powers that should not be accountable, and empowering others, that drew me and many others to her firm yet shy persona.

Sovereignty encapsulates the fact that all individuals are born equal, with an inherent authority over themselves. There are no conditions attached to our existence. Natural law affords us inalienable rights to food, shelter, travel and the liberty to do what we wish as long as we don't hurt others. These rights cannot be taken away by government, which, in natural law, is below us on the rungs of influence. Government is there to serve us, not the other way around. Nevertheless, the idea of sovereignty flies in the face of the conventional societal frameworks, which have been attempting to make us submit to the whims of external or corporate power for centuries. Escalating in the last century, we have been unwittingly born amidst government and societal expectations that we would receive scheduled vaccinations, attend school brain-washing, prepare to earn a "living", get a mortgage, be taxed to the hilt, and prepare to die, with the ever-increasing pressure to pay bills at every turn.

Thus, Ruth highlighted that sovereignty is not just a passive concept but one that demands active engagement. This idea ties directly into the broader concept of justice and accountability, and aligns with my co-authors' efforts to draw our attention to how our correct conduct on this earth is important. They remind us, *in a resolute struggle of the good against evil, there are however, definite rules that must not be disregarded if it is to succeed. First, resolution must be based on a union of strength and friendliness. Second, a compromise with evil is not possible; evil must under all circumstances be openly discredited. Nor must our passions and shortcomings be glossed over. Third, the struggle must not be carried out directly by force. If evil is branded it thinks of weapons, and if we do it the favour of fighting against it blow for blow, we lose in the end because thus we ourselves get entangled in hatred and passion. Therefore it is important to begin at home, to be on guard in our own persons against the faults we have branded.*[1] To beat the globalists we needed to master ourselves. It was Ruth's clarity that provided this breakthrough.

Self-mastery, and learning to stand firm and say "No" would become central to our mission to counter the *evil*. As Ruth so poignantly put it, the right to be free is not just a personal right; it is a collective one. By reclaiming our sovereignty, we collectively weaken the globalists' grip and begin to co-create a better way. Thus, we had a duty to actively

---

1   Hexagram 43, Breakthrough, The Judgement. From I Ching, by Richard Wilhelm, 3rd Ed. p.166-7.

claim it. *The best way to fight evil is to make energetic progress in the good.*[1]

I had been intimidated at the thought of building a new world health organisation, but here was Ruth saying we needed to build a new world, no less! It certainly was a daunting task at first.

It took a while to fully grasp the implications of the concept. Ruth would sometimes get frustrated with us. Had her wisdom fallen on fallow soil? She was on her own mission to make a difference fighting injustice, were we the correct fellows for her? *In friendships and close relationships an individual must make a careful choice. He surrounds himself either with good or bad company; He cannot have both at once. If he throws himself away on unworthy friends he loses connection with people of intellectual power who could further him in the good.*[2] Fortunately for us, Ruth found a home for her pioneering ideas and was grateful for our openness and interest in learning from her.

There was the birth certificate fraud, the council tax fraud, the income tax fraud, the electricity fraud, the parking fine fraud. The deceptions she revealed to us were at first incomprehensible. Surely she must be mistaken. Then little by little, the evidence piled up until it was undeniable. What I had thought was a relatively recent globalist agenda to enslave mankind had been going on for centuries.

What does one do with such revelations? Indeed, how does one build a better world and set oneself free in practice?

Ruth's teachings were a call to courage. One of the key barriers to the realisation of true sovereignty is fear. The fear of repercussions, whether legal, financial, or social, often keeps people in line. Sovereignty, she said, is the ability to act according to what one knows is right, without the fear of retribution or punishment. When individuals recognise their sovereignty, and begin to act accordingly, they free themselves from the paralysing grip of fear.

---

1   Hexagram 43, Breakthrough, The Judgement. From I Ching, by Richard Wilhelm, 3rd Ed. p.167.

2   Hexagram 17, Following, line 2. From I Ching, by Richard Wilhelm, 3rd Ed. p.73.

My co-authors note the profundity of the process. *When the right connection with distinguished people has been found, a certain loss naturally ensues. A man must part company with the inferior and superficial.*[1] Claiming sovereignty means that one no longer does things because one "ought to", "should do", "must do" or because others tell you to. Superficial relationships and rituals are likely to fall away as one becomes more connected with the true meaning of life and our purpose here on Earth. One parts company with fear too, for this is an inferior state of being that keeps us in a cycle of victimhood, disassociated from our innate power and creativity. Losing one's fear is the first step towards real liberty and the realisation of one's true potential as a sovereign human being.

Determined to step into her own power, Ruth practised what she preached on many an occasion. Despite being naturally timid, and nervous about public speaking, she would challenge unlawful council actions, including taxes and parking fines, bravely representing herself in local courts on her own.

Our WCH mission was to empower people to take back control of their health. To do this, people needed trustworthy information free from vested interests, they needed choices, and they needed to be empowered to make them. Informed choices serve us better than uninformed ones. Asserting one's choice during Covid-19 had been discouraged, as had truth seeking. In addition, people were forced, manipulated, and tricked into doing things that harmed themselves and their families. Being sovereign does not mean being healthy, but it certainly does mean taking ownership of one's actions and inactions. Thus, educating on the relationship between health, choice and sovereignty had to be integral to our mission.

To choose how we live, what we put into our bodies, and whose advice we trust, we would need great and systemic change. Thus

---

1   Hexagram 17, Following, line 3. From I Ching, by Richard Wilhelm, 3rd Ed. p.73.

"health sovereignty" became our winning strategy to counter the globalists' "health security" agenda, which sought to strip away our rights for a dystopian "greater good." Health sovereignty became the WCH mission and the better way movement in a nutshell. And it fit WCH's pre-designed logo perfectly. With the simple WCH logo, health was represented by the wholesome apple and lungs, whereas the essence of sovereignty was perfectly represented by the symbol of the heart on the raised open palm of a hand.

Ruth's ability to simplify the complexities of natural law and make it accessible to everyone was one of her greatest gifts. A contributor to WCH's better way Charter, which was finalised by the team after the first better way Conference in 2022, Ruth's legacy would live on in these seven principles:

1. We act in honour and do no harm.
2. We are free beings with free will.
3. We are part of nature.
4. We are spiritual and need a life of meaning and purpose.
5. We thrive together.
6. We value different perspectives.
7. We use technology with discernment.

Underpinning the principles of the better way Charter is the courage not to tolerate the violation of inalienable rights, nor profit, power and influence coming before the wellbeing of people and the Earth.

Ruth crossed the great waters on 24th January 2024. Not one to be forced to do anything she did not choose to do, I trust she got home safely. Undoubtedly, she has left behind a powerful legacy.

Her wisdom remains a foundation stone of WCH and the growing better way movement. A wise, gentle, and firm guide, Ruth embodied the very principles she taught. Despite the brief time of our acquaintance, her impact on defining the WCH mission was remarkable. We are honoured to carry her message of sovereignty, self-empowerment, justice and accountability. Armed with the better way Charter, an iconic symbol, and a winning strategy, this is the way WCH would help birth a better world, with many friends all around the world, co-creating.

There are people who dispense blessings to the whole world. Every increase in power that comes to them benefits the whole of mankind and therefore does not bring decrease to others. Through perseverance and zealous work a man wins success and finds helpers as they are needed. But what he accomplishes is not a limited private advantage; it is a public good and available to everyone.[1] Thank you, Ruth, and the *I Ching* for taking the time to put us on the right path. Though truth, justice, self-mastery and, ultimately, our own sovereignty, there is a better way, indeed!

---

[1]   Hexagram 41 Decrease, line 6. From I Ching, by Richard Wilhelm, 3rd Ed. p.161.

Epilogue

Before I started writing *Game of Trust* I asked my prospective co-author collective, the Richard Wilhelm translation of the *I Ching*, if it would like to work together with me on this task, wondering whether it would be appropriate to use this esteemed old book in this way. I did not wish to offend the ancient oracle, which I considered, and had used for a few years as, a complementary decision-making tool. I also did this because Carl Jung had done it in Zurich in 1949 when writing the foreword to the Wilhelm-Baynes English translation. Enquiring of the *I Ching* as if it were a person, Jung sounded out its perspective on its own predicament back then. Carl Jung's idea that synchronicity, rather than pure causality, governs our lives more often than not, I believe was informed by his years of practice using the *I Ching*. For my purposes, I regarded the Wilhelm version of the *I Ching* as a collective work rather than the creation of a single author, recognising the many individuals who had shaped and refined it into the edition that found me in 2020.

The *I Ching* shared, in response to my enquiry, that it considered my proposition to be an educational experience – mutually beneficial, I believe. The judgement on the situation came from Hexagram 27, *The Corners* of the *Mouth (Providing Nourishment),* which in its commentary states, *The great man fosters and takes care of superior men, in order to take care of all men through them.*[1] Thus, not only

---

1   Hexagram 27, The Corners of the Mouth, The Judgement. From I Ching, by Richard Wilhelm, 3rd Ed. p.108.

would I be educated and nourished by the experience but, it being the *great man*, the *I Ching* hoped through participating and educating me that its wisdom would reach and nourish others.

Having been developed thousands of years earlier for the specific purpose of partnering mankind, it had found itself regrettably abandoned. *A one-eyed man who is able to see. The perseverance of a solitary man furthers.*[1] It went on to elaborate on its relationship with us. *Here the situation is that of a girl married to a man who has disappointed her. Man and wife ought to work together like a pair of eyes. Here the girl is left behind in loneliness; the man of her choice either has become unfaithful or has died. But she does not lose the inner light of loyalty. Though the other eye is gone, she maintains her loyalty even in loneliness.*[2] Needless to say, the *I Ching* was disappointed that its marriage with mankind had broken down. It had been patiently waiting for an opportunity to rekindle the relationship, and it hadn't lost trust that we would yet return for guidance and nourishment.

It continued to explain with respect to my proposition to collaborate, *The marrying maiden draws out the allotted time. A late marriage comes in due course. The girl is virtuous.*[3] *She does not wish to throw herself away, and allows the customary time for marriage to slip by. However, there is no harm in this; she is rewarded for her purity and, even though belatedly, finds the husband intended for her.*[4]

Thus it seemed to be telling me that it had been waiting for me and, like most mature suitors who draw the unexpected affection of a beautiful and intelligent woman, I was determined to make a good *husband*. I felt honoured to be given the job, despite apprehensions about revealing this super-esoteric experiment, in a world that tries to describe everything through a reductionist version of science.

---

1   Hexagram 54, The Marrying Maiden, line 2. From I Ching, by Richard Wilhelm, 3rd Ed. p.211.
2   Hexagram 54, The Marrying Maiden, line 2. From I Ching, by Richard Wilhelm, 3rd Ed. p.211.
3   Hexagram 54, The Marrying Maiden, line 4. From I Ching, by Richard Wilhelm, 3rd Ed. p.211.
4   Hexagram 54, The Marrying Maiden, line 4. From I Ching, by Richard Wilhelm, 3rd Ed. p.211.

As this was a prospective experiment, I did not know whether my hypothesis, that the *I Ching* would provide relevant and inquiry-specific responses that added helpful insights retrospectively, would be self-evident. But obviously I hoped it might. All scientists believe in their theories. We are inherently biased, which is why objective verification is ideal in any experiment.

I decided on 13 chapters, roughly correlating to a 13-month cycle commencing in January 2021 and ending in January 2022. The method I used to develop the story arc was this: I invited my co-authors to identify the chapter themes; they would also be consulted on specific incidents and events, as well as for insights into individual perspectives. In addition to writing about my own perceived and lived experiences, I would throw the coins, interpret and integrate the results from my co-authors' commentary in the context of the specific inquiries. It would be left to me to decide how consistent and resonant my co-authors' observations were with the context described.

Thus, keeping in mind what I intended to cover, I determined each chapter theme by throwing three coins. I used three copper 2-pence pieces because I favour the size of these robust and earthy coins. For heads, there are various busts of Elizabeth II, whereas the tails bear an image of a fleur-de-lis with "TWO PENCE" written in capital letters and numerals. A count of three is allocated to the coins showing heads, and a count of two to the coins showing tails. Throwing three coins can therefore add up to a count of six, seven, eight, or nine.

The coins are thrown six times for each enquiry. I noted down the total count for each throw in a notebook I dedicated to this task, from the bottom up, as is customary.

Even numbers are represented by a broken line (yin), and odd numbers are represented by a solid line (yang). A seven will always represent a solid line, and an eight will always represent a broken line. However, six and nine are mutable and can change to the alternative type of line.

Thus, six throws yield six numbers, which are represented by lines, solid or broken, to form what is called a hexagram, an image with six horizontal lines placed one above the other. There are 64 hexagrams in the *I Ching*, each bearing six lines, making a total of 384 lines, which each represent a unique observation.

Upon receiving the theme of the titles in this way, I set about drafting the chapters. However, when I reached Chapter 6, I felt the need to outline the remaining part of the book. It was at this point where I threw coins for Chapters 7, 8 and 9 sequentially, to get a sense of the dramatic arc my co-authors were envisioning. It fit well with my storyline. Thus I repeated this process for the remaining Chapters 10 to 13 in one sitting.

As mentioned above, in addition to these broad thematic strokes, I invited my co-authors to comment on particular communications, incidents, and individuals where I felt their wise insights could bring forward deeper understanding of situations or behaviours from which lessons could be gleaned. The richness of the experience in 2021, when the landscape changed on a daily basis and so many individuals contributed to both progress and hindrance, meant that it was not possible to interrogate all details, actions or reactions. My intention, therefore, through 64 "moves" was to examine conduct that was representative of different predispositions and perspectives, that would resonate more widely and produce learning for all.

In total, during the writing and research conducted for this book, I threw the coins over 110 times between November 2024 and April 2025, recording all results in a notebook. Once the enquiry was commenced, all primary hexagrams apart from six were included in the narrative. For the six omitted, it was because the lines of enquiry were subsequently superfluous, not because I found my co-authors' observations to be irrelevant.

I would also like to clarify that my intention was not to expose or judge individuals. Rather, it was to highlight that there is a long-standing, objective code of human conduct that ensures the health and wellbeing of mankind as well as all living creatures on Earth. This code is based on an organic system of yin and yang, open and closed, dark and light, entropy and energy; principles we have forgotten. Comprehending them now may help to ensure our own safe passage, as well as the survival of our species.

Whilst this account was never intended to be a comprehensive catalogue of 2021 Covid-19 intrigue, I trust it offers a glimpse into the great deception that occurred at a time when unprecedented darkness engulfed our world. In addition, I trust it highlights the tremendous collaborative grassroots efforts that led to the birth of a worldwide grassroots movement dedicated to co-creating a better world based on ethical principles.

Thus, in these final pages of this book, I invite the reader to step back and reflect on the broader experiment that underpins the narrative. It's an experiment conducted not in the conventional sense of a controlled trial, but in the experiential exploration of a mystical, ancient practice verified against the human psyche and intuition. Just as my writer's journey, which began as a search for clarity in the midst of chaos, ultimately reveals itself as a profound and ongoing enquiry into human conduct and the nature of consciousness, so too, my better way journey, which began by taking a stand against tyranny, required trusting that everything will be alright in the end.

In the practice of throwing three coins six times, the chance of throwing a hexagram with only sevens and eights (all unchanging lines) is approximately 17.8%. Such hexagrams with no changing lines provide a *Judgement* on a situation, and an *Image* to accompany it, consisting of combinations of two of the following: earth, mountain, water, heaven, fire, lake, thunder, wind. Thus, a hexagram with no changing lines describes a broad theme related to one of 64 different *I Ching* themes or situations, rather than a specific observation or piece of advice, which is elucidated through changing lines only. Hexagrams with changing lines (sixes and nines) mutate to form a second hexagram and, in this occurrence, two hexagrams are linked to the throw. The mutated hexagram represents a judgement on the change or situation produced by conduct observed or advised in the primary hexagram.

Since situation or changed hexagrams can be considered thematic, I postulated that if my co-authors were on the same page as me, and wanting to demonstrate that they too could be "statistically significant", one way of doing so might be to use situational hexagrams as chapter themes throughout, which would be an extremely rare occurrence, and might even convince the reductionist scientists that there is something to this ancient *I Ching* novelty!

I was thus excited after obtaining the first three hexagrams (Hexagrams 24, 62 ad 56) with no changing lines, and hoped that this pattern would continue. The low chance of throwing three hexagrams in a row like this (0.56%) immediately demonstrated to me that there was something much more mysterious at play. However, it was not going to be that easy to impress more doubtful scientists. To my subsequent disappointment, out of the 13 chapter hexagrams, only seven comprised unchanging lines (sevens and eights) only, as summarised below.

Chapter 1: Hexagram 24, The Turning Point.
Chapter 2: Hexagram 62, Preponderance of the Small.
Chapter 3: Hexagram 56, The Wanderer.
Chapter 4: Hexagram 15, Modesty. Lines 2 and 3 in Hexagram 7, The Army

Chapter 5: Hexagram 56, The Wanderer. Lines 4, 5, and 6 in
Hexagram 39, Obstruction.

Chapter 6: Hexagram 40, Deliverance.

Chapter 7: Hexagram 11, Peace.

Chapter 8: Hexagram 33, Retreat.

Chapter 9: Hexagram 13, Fellowship with Men. Line 2 in
Hexagram 1, The Creative.

Chapter 10: Hexagram 45, Gathering Together. Line 4 in
Hexagram 8, Holding Together.

Chapter 11: Hexagram 11, Peace. Lines 4 and 6 in Hexagram 14,
Possession in Great Measure.

Chapter 12: Hexagram 23, Splitting Apart. Line 1 in Hexagram 27,
The Corners of the Mouth.

Chapter 13: Hexagram 33, Retreat.

Notably, three key hexagrams of the 64 different overarching themes: The Wanderer (Hexagram 56), Peace (Hexagram 11), and Retreat (Hexagram 33) came up twice each in the 13 chapter choice throws, either as the judgement on the situation in general, or as the hexagrams with changing lines, offering more specific wisdom. The odds of this being due to chance are extremely low. These three themes resonated with me as the narrator of the story, reflecting a consistency in both my character and wanderer's predicament, as well as the ebb and flow of our actions and challenges – periods of peaceful activity, and periods of retreat. The likelihood of throwing Hexagram 40 (Deliverance) directly after Hexagram 39 (Obstruction) was also significant. Deliverance is the natural and sequential resolution following a period of difficulty, when the obstacles have been removed. Nevertheless, this exercise illustrates how incorrigible scientists, including me, can be in seeking through statistics a proof of significance even for mysterious things we do not yet understand. Our wise ancestors' eyes are probably rolling with wry amusement!

I chose to use the primary hexagrams, the ones with changing lines, for the titles of Chapters 4, 5 and 11. For Chapters 5 and 11, this was primarily because I had already drawn the resulting change hexagrams (Hexagrams 56 and 11) for Chapters 3 and 7, respectively, with no change. However, when it came to Hexagram 33, which was thrown twice too, neither throw produced changing lines. Thus, you may have noticed that there are two chapters with the title and theme of *Retreat*. This felt very appropriate, as the battle was not an even one and it was often prudent to conserve our forces for when we could make more impact. As with the repeated chapter title, we had no choice but to retreat more than once!

As for the observations and remarks of my co-authors obtained prospectively in relation to specific inquiries within each chapter, it too was not simply luck of the draw. Throughout the process, the comments and insights were pertinent, considered and inspiring without exception. As I reflected on various obstacles, decisions, and motivations of both powerful and ordinary figures, the *I Ching* became a mirror offering insight into the moral dimensions of those interactions.

When I set out to investigate the possibility that the *I Ching* could be used as a tool to reflect on past events, I had no way of knowing that it would work so well. The experiment could easily have had to be abandoned due to futility. However, with each new coin toss and its accompanying insights, I was drawn closer to my ancient companions and excited to share this unusual book and its mysterious process with you. My illuminating experience aligns with that of Carl Jung's, who in his theory of synchronicity concluded that meaningful coincidences, like rare events, suggest a correspondence between an individual's internal state and the external world. Whether my findings resonate independently, will be for the reader to determine.

On 3rd January 2025, more than halfway through the writing of this book, I checked in with my co-authors to ask whether they were happy with the format, progress and collaboration. Their verdict was *Possession in Great Measure, Supreme success.*[1] The accompanying commentary included the following: *The time is favourable, a time of strength within and clarity and culture without. Power is expressing itself in a graceful and controlled way.*[2] Additionally footnoted by Wilhelm, who was a Christian missionary, was the following: *The meaning of this hexagram parallels the saying of Jesus: "blessed are the meek for they shall inherit the earth."*[3]

The image accompanying the judgement was *Fire in heaven above: The image of POSSESSION IN GREAT MEASURE. Thus the superior man curbs evil and furthers the good. And thereby obeys the benevolent will of heaven.*[4] Thus, my co-authors seemed pleased with our work together shining a light into the darkness. *The sun brings both evil and good into the light of day. Man must combat and curb evil, and must favour and promote the good. Only in this way does he fulfil the benevolent will of God, who desires only good and not evil.*[5]

The changing lines of this inquiry were in Hexagram 59, Dispersion, which speaks to how *religious forces are needed to overcome the egotism that divides men,*[6] and that, if one wants to help dissolve the hardness of egotism, one needs to be *free of all selfish ulterior considerations* and *persevere in justice and steadfastness.*[7] Reminding us that *At*

---

1   Hexagram 14, Possession in Great Measure, The Judgement. From I Ching, by Richard Wilhelm, 3rd Ed. p.60.

2   Hexagram 14, Possession in Great Measure, The Judgement. From I Ching, by Richard Wilhelm, 3rd Ed. p.60.

3   Hexagram 14, Possession in Great Measure, The Judgement. From I Ching, by Richard Wilhelm, 3rd Ed. p.60.

4   Hexagram 14, Possession in Great Measure, The Image. From I Ching, by Richard Wilhelm, 3rd Ed. p.60.

5   Hexagram 14, Possession in Great Measure, The Image. From I Ching, by Richard Wilhelm, 3rd Ed. p.60.

6   Hexagram 59, Dispersion. The Judgement commentary. From I Ching, by Richard Wilhelm, 3rd Ed. p.227-8.

7   Hexagram 59, Dispersion. The Judgement commentary. From I Ching, by Richard Wilhelm, 3rd Ed. p.227-8.

such times when hidden divergences in temper make themselves felt and lead to mutual misunderstandings, we must take quick and vigorous action to dissolve the misunderstandings and mutual distrust.[1]

In general, they approved of my approach, which involved giving up the life I knew and stepping into the great unknown. *He dissolves his self. No remorse. Only on the basis of a great renunciation can he obtain the strength for great achievements. By setting his goal in a great task outside himself, he can attain this standpoint.*[2]

Partisanism was to be avoided. *Only by rising above party interests can we achieve something decisive.*[3]

They also confirmed that they see this work as a way to get mankind back on the right path, because a great idea can provide *a focal point for the organisation of recovery. Just as an illness reaches its crisis in a dissolving sweat, so a great and stimulating idea is a true salvation in times of general deadlock. It gives the people a rallying point – a man in a ruling position who can dispel misunderstandings.*[4] Personal responsibility, sovereignty, self-mastery, and creativity are essential for human survival and safe passage – a great idea, indeed!

Some readers may have found my use of ChatGPT as copyediting assistant discordant, or even distasteful, given the theme of ancient wisdom integral to this experiment. Indeed, embarking upon it I too wondered whether this would be a compromise of my dignity, as well as that of the *I Ching*'s. I therefore also inquired of my co-authors on January 3rd, 2025, once I had made the pragmatic decision to do so, what they "thought".

Their overall judgement of the situation was positive, that of an *INCREASE. It furthers one to undertake something. It furthers one to cross the great water.*[5] I was told that *A sacrifice of the higher element*

1 Hexagram 59, Dispersion, line 3. From I Ching, by Richard Wilhelm, 3rd Ed. p. 228.
2 Hexagram 59, Dispersion, line 3. From I Ching, by Richard Wilhelm, 3rd Ed. p. 229.
3 Hexagram 59. Dispersion, line 3. From I Ching, by Richard Wilhelm, 3rd Ed. p. 229.
4 Hexagram 59, Dispersion, line 5. From I Ching, by Richard Wilhelm, 3rd Ed. p. 230.
5 Hexagram 42, Increase, The Judgement. From I Ching, by Richard Wilhelm, 3rd Ed. p.162.

that produces an increase of the lower is called an out-and-out increase.[1]

It seems the *I Ching* was prepared to sacrifice its dignity *for the increase of those below* as this *is extremely valuable for the flowering of the commonwealth.*[2] It recognised that time was of the essence: *In times of progress and successful development it is necessary to work and make the best use of time.*[3] So right they were. I did not have a year to edit and nuance this text, I allocated five to six months to fit it in amongst my WCH work. But it was not only this factor that led to such pragmatism, as pointed out by my co-authors, it was that the times demanded we complete the book quickly. With our world changing at such a crazy pace, the novel ideas represented herein needed airing sooner rather than later. *The time of INCREASE does not endure, therefore it must be utilised while it lasts.*[4] I was instructed to seize the moment.

Nevertheless, a caution was added. I was not to compromise too much but, rather, to use ChatGPT with discernment lest *the spokes burst out of the wagon wheels*[5] or *I expose [myself] to personal rebuff.*[6] It certainly was a delicate balance. Upon writing the above in April 2025, I enquired again, had I achieved it?

My co-authors reminded me that *enthusiasm leads only to failure and humiliation if the time for achievement has not yet arrived. In such a time it is wise to spare ourselves the opprobrium of failure by holding back.*[7] However, they reassured me that despite *Treading upon the tail of the tiger. It does not bite the man. Success.*[8]

I was extremely relieved to read their further comment from line 5 in Hexagram 64: *Perseverance brings good fortune. No remorse. The*

---

1   Hexagram 42, Increase. From I Ching, by Richard Wilhelm, 3rd Ed. p.162.

2   Hexagram 42, Increase, The Judgement. From I Ching, by Richard Wilhelm, 3rd Ed. p.162.

3   Hexagram 42, Increase, The Judgement. From I Ching, by Richard Wilhelm, 3rd Ed. p.162.

4   Hexagram 42, Increase, The Judgement. From I Ching, by Richard Wilhelm, 3rd Ed. p.162.

5   Hexagram 9, The Taming Power of the Small, line 3. From I Ching, by Richard Wilhelm, 3rd Ed. p.42.

6   Hexagram 9, The Taming Power of the Small, line 2. From I Ching, by Richard Wilhelm, 3rd Ed. p.41-2.

7   Hexagram 64, Before Completion, line 1. From I Ching, by Richard Wilhelm, 3rd Ed. p.250.

8   Hexagram 10. Treading, The Judgement. From I Ching, by Richard Wilhelm, 3rd Ed. p.44.

light of the superior man is true. Good fortune.[1] In full elaboration, it reads: *The victory has been won. The power of steadfastness has not been rerouted. Everything has gone well. All misgivings have been overcome. The light of a superior personality shines forth anew and makes its influence felt among men who have faith in it and rally around it. The new time has arrived, and with it good fortune. And just as the sun shines forth in redoubled beauty after the rain, or as a forest grows more freshly from the charred ruins after a fire, so the new era appears all the more glorious in contrast with the misery of the old.*[2]

I have used this novel process to signpost people to WCH and a better way as much as to signpost them to the *I Ching*, of which I now have no doubt is a manual to human life prepared for us ages ago. Like our human path, the *I Ching* has been covered with dust through centuries of obfuscation, deception and neglect. Yet, it has been there all along, waiting for us to restore it to its rightful place. It served as the philosophical basis for Lao-Tse's teachings in the *Tao Te Ching* or Book of The Way). So too have Confucius, Carl Jung, and many other great thinkers and scholars been inspired by these ancient guidelines. If you are not yet acquainted, I hope *Game of Trust* will inspire you to explore the *I Ching* too.

By offering truthful perspectives on human conduct, the *I Ching* has taught me that trusting God is not just about surrendering to the flow of life, it involves active participation and better choices. Thus, in the face of uncertainty, I have found trust to be both a useful tool and a goal. Ultimately, for me personally, *Game of Trust* has been a living experiment in the act of trust itself.

But what else does this experiment suggest to me? It suggests that we might be living in a kind of simulation, much like a video game but with very real consequences.

---

1   Hexagram 64, Before Completion, line 5. From I Ching, by Richard Wilhelm, 3rd Ed. p.250.

2   Hexagram 64, Before Completion, line 5. From I Ching, by Richard Wilhelm, 3rd Ed. p.250.

The notion of this reality being a simulation, or simulacrum, as postulated by philosopher Howdie Mickoski,[1] is not a modern concept, it is integral to the *I Ching* itself. Indeed Richard Wilhelm notes in his introduction to the work that, *The second theme fundamental to the Book of Changes is its theory of ideas. The eight trigrams are images not so much of objects as of states of change. This view is associated with concepts expressed in the teachings of Lao-Tse, as also in those of Confucius, that every event in the visible world is the effect of an "image," that is, of an idea in the unseen world. Accordingly, everything that happens on earth is only a reproduction, as it were, of an event in a world beyond our sense perception; as regards its occurrence in time, it is later than the suprasensible event.*[2]

If our reality behaves like a video game, reproducing events beyond our sense perception, might we in our human form function here as a kind of avatar for a (our) greater awareness? In this case, might we be able to access direction from this greater awareness on the other side of the "computer screen" with the right manual, and/or an inner ability to tune in, so to speak? Such direction might not only give us a better understanding of the game we seem unwittingly engaged in, but also how to play it for the best results. Of course, unlike a video game, where nothing matters, everything we do or don't do in this reality, simulation or not, has very real consequences. In addition, we can choose to exit a video game we don't like, whereas we have to play this "game" whether we want to or not.

As in a video game, our conduct on Earth is integral to our performance and "success". "Conduct" is an interesting word. It means "behaviour" as well as "to transmit". As a word to define a new era where we remember that we are bioelectrical beings, that we comprise energy as well as matter, can connect with a deeper awareness, have

---

1   Exit the Cave and Escape the Cave are philosophical books by Howdie Mickoski
2   Introduction. From I Ching, by Richard Wilhelm, 3rd Ed. p.lvii.

ability to "receive" communications, and have ability to "transmit" good and bad energy to others, albeit by mysterious means currently not well understood, the word "conduct" seems highly appropriate.

With the belief that computer code is a relatively modern invention, you may be surprised to know that the *I Ching* inspired Leibniz, a German philosopher and mathematician in the 17th century, in his development of binary arithmetic that laid the foundations for modern computing. Computer programming would thus appear to be but a reduced version of the grand organic design as codified by the ancient *I Ching* scribes. Ironically, the proponents of artificial intelligence would have us believe that computer code is an advance on nature and can augment it. But AI, stuck with its zeros and ones, can only imitate. By contrast, the dynamics of change expressed in the *I Ching*, through yin and yang, entropy and energy, illustrate that human beings are capable of infinite creative potential.

If our human experiences can be defined by images codified in an old book, combined with a mysterious way of accessing them, whether they be mathematical, biological, or something yet to be fully understood, what does it mean for the self? It suggests our role far exceeds being mere avatars in a cosmic game; rather, it places us as creators of the very fabric of this existence. The *I Ching* thus seems both a key and a map to unlock our deeper awareness, as well as the manual to get us safely home as painlessly as possible.

To tap into our creativity and explore the truths of our existence, trusting in our inner goodness seems to be the ideal state. In my experience, as one takes those first steps in trust towards sovereignty, the veil between us and our deeper awareness becomes ever so slightly thinner. The more we develop self-awareness and master our ego, emotions and attachments, getting rid of that which no longer serves us, the easier it becomes to navigate what is true and what is fake.

Total transparency is where we're headed, it is part and parcel of our evolution. This is a terrifying concept for those oppressing us, as their wholesale deception will no longer be possible once we have remembered who we truly are and taken back our power.

I asked my co-authors whether they had any last words to add, having reached the end of this project together. I received a judgement that had already sprung to mind: *The Joyous. Success.*[1] They were pleased that we had persevered in the endeavour, and *now it was time for the superior man to join with his friends for discussion and practice.*[2] In part I felt that this was a reflection on what we had been doing, and that my new old friends were saying that they had enjoyed the process too. They further drew attention to the fact that learning should be a revitalising and cheerful process, *it is only through stimulating intercourse with congenial friends with whom one holds discussion and practices applications of the truth of life.*[3] It's time for us all to get together and talk about these novel concepts, I hope you will agree.

Speaking to the subject matter of the book itself, however, they used a military metaphor, cautioning against trying to engage with mankind's enemy without a coordinated approach. *An army must set foot in proper order. If the order is not good, misfortune threatens. At the beginning of a military enterprise, order is imperative. A just and valid cause must exist, and the obedience and coordination of the troops must be well organised, otherwise the result is inevitably failure.*[4] My co-authors clearly wished to draw our attention to the seriousness of our predicament. Unity and cooperation are essential to our survival against powerful anti-human forces. This message underscores the importance of our being aligned and prepared before taking action. It emphasises that efforts, no matter how well-intentioned, can fail if they are not structured and unified.

---

1   Hexagram 58, The Joyous, The Judgement. From I Ching, by Richard Wilhelm, 3rd Ed. p.224.
2   Hexagram 58, The Joyous, The Image. From I Ching, by Richard Wilhelm, 3rd Ed. p.224-5.
3   Hexagram 58, The Joyous, The Image. From I Ching, by Richard Wilhelm, 3rd Ed. p.224-5.
4   Hexagram 7, The Army, line 1. From I Ching, by Richard Wilhelm, 3rd Ed. p.33.

They further highlight that the odds are stacked against mankind at this juncture. *Unity and discipline will prove more effective than individual acts of bravery. In the face of a superior enemy with whom it would be hopeless to engage in battle, an orderly retreat is the only correct procedure, because it will save the army from defeat and disintegration.*[1] The metaphorical "army" must not rush into battle without the proper tools, strategies, and intelligence. This is not a time for reckless heroism, but for careful planning and mutual support. We should not be trying to take the dark forces head on. Rather, a focus on working together to organise and prepare for what is coming would yield better results.

It is by no means a sign of courage or strength to insist upon engaging in a hopeless struggle regardless of the circumstances.[2] By retreating, we preserve the strength and integrity of our team, giving us time to regroup and prepare for the next phase. This orderly retreat, then, becomes an act of wisdom.

Lastly, they warned, *Game is in the field – it has left its usual haunts in the forest and is devastating the fields. This points to an enemy invasion.*[3] This suggests that forces on the side of mankind have been infiltrated. Those with their anti-human agenda may strike from within as well as from without, so vigilance and strategy are crucial. *Energetic combat and punishment are here thoroughly justified, but they must not degenerate into a wild melee in which everyone fends for himself. Despite the greatest degree of perseverance and bravery, this would lead to misfortune. The army must be directed by an experienced leader. It is a matter of waging war, not of permitting the mob to slaughter all who fall into their hands; If they do, defeat will be the result, and despite all perseverance there is danger of misfortune.*[4]

Violence and war inspired by selfish motives are not winning

---

1   Hexagram 7, The Army, line 4. From I Ching, by Richard Wilhelm, 3rd Ed. p.34.
2   Hexagram 7, The Army, line 4. From I Ching, by Richard Wilhelm, 3rd Ed. p.34.
3   Hexagram 7, The Army, line 5. From I Ching, by Richard Wilhelm, 3rd Ed. p.35.
4   Hexagram 7, The Army, line 5. From I Ching, by Richard Wilhelm, 3rd Ed. p.35.

strategies. Rather, a better way strategy should be based on human creativity, sovereignty and unity. Thus, we need wise and ethical leaders and an organised approach to tackling the challenges ahead, recognising that international grassroots collaboration is essential as we actively work together to create a better world. *The best way to fight evil is to make energetic progress in the good.*[1]

Reflecting on Carl Jung's foreword more than 70 years ago, where the *I Ching* referred to itself as being neglected, abused and miscon-strued, waiting to be re-discovered, it has been an honour to have helped this ancient work resume its purpose, that of saving a per-ishing civilisation. In this game of trust, I trust, and hope you do too, that everything will be alright in the end. Nevertheless, during this great crossing, my and your active engagement and conduct is key.

Unlike all other *I Ching* contributions in this book, I choose to end with this wisdom, which I feel is pertinent to the information presented herein.

BREAK-THROUGH. One must resolutely make the matter known
At the court of the king.
It must be announced truthfully. Danger.
It is necessary to notify one's own city.
It does not further one to resort to arms.
It furthers one to undertake something.[2]

THE END

---

1   Hexagram 43, Break-through. The Judgement. From I Ching, by Richard Wilhelm, 3rd Ed. p.166.

2   Hexagram 43, Break-through. The Judgement. From I Ching, by Richard Wilhelm, 3rd Ed. p.166.

Online Exhibits and References

Note: Exhibits can be found at www.Lawriefiles.com.

Chapter 1

1. Exhibit 1: E-BMC Ltd.'s Urgent Rapid Review: Ivermectin reduces the risk of death from Covid-19 (4 January 2021).

2. Exhibit 2: E-BMC Ltd.'s Evidence-to-Decision Framework for the first online BIRD meeting (13 January 2021).

3. Exhibit 3. Dr Andrew Hill's first ResearchSquare pre-print (18 January 2021).

4. Exhibit 4: Press Release: "Effective treatment for Covid-19 has been right under our noses" (14 January 2021).

5. Exhibit 5: Dr Andrew Hill's presentation to the US National Institute for Health (6 January 2021).

6. Exhibit 6: Forensic Communications Assessment of Dr Hill's pre-print, commissioned by Bon Sens (6th October 2021).

7. Exhibit 7: Transcript of the Lawrie-Hill meeting (18 January 2021).

8. Exhibit 8: Dr Pierre Kory and Dr Paul Marik's email critique of the Hill review (21 January 2021).

9. Exhibit 9: Developing Global Norms for Sharing Data and Results During Public Health Emergencies. A deleted WHO document.

10. Kory et al, 2021. https://journals.lww.com/americantherapeutics/fulltext/2021/06000/review_of_the_emerging_evidence_demonstrating_the.4.aspx

Chapter 2

1. Exhibit 10. BIRD Proceedings and Recommendations on Ivermectin for Covid-19 (Final version:23 March 2021).

2. Exhibit 11. BIRD Proceedings and Recommendations on Ivermectin for Covid-19: Executive Summary. (Final version: 23 March 2021).

3. HPV vaccine safety: Cochrane launches urgent investigation into review after criticisms, The BMJ, August 2018, https://doi.org/10.1136/bmj.k3472.

4. HPV vaccine safety. https://pharmaceutical-journal.com/article/news/cochrane-launches-urgent-investigation-of-hpv-vaccine-review

5. https://www.trialsitenews.com/a/bird-evidence-to-decision-framework-meeting-for-ivermectins-efficacy

Chapter 3

1. Operation Warp Speed: Accelerated Covid-19 Vaccine Development Status and Efforts to Address Manufacturing Challenges. www.gao.gov/products/gao-21-319.

2. WHO Therapeutics and COVID-19. https://iris.who.int/bitstream/handle/10665/340374/WHO-2019-nCoV-therapeutics-2021.1-eng.pdf

Chapter 4

1. https://www.conservativewoman.co.uk/why-are-we-being-lied-to-about-covid-theres-no-good-reason/

Chapter 5

1. Exhibit 12. Lawrie Submission to British Parliament (24 March 2021).

2. Exhibit 13. Letter to PM Boris Johnson (19 April 2021).

3. Exhibit 14. YouTube's Misinformation Notice. (14 May 2021)

4. Exhibit 15. Seneff & Nigh. Worse than the disease? Reviewing some possible unintended consequences of the mRNA vaccines (2021).

5. Exhibit 16. Vimeo's account termination notice (13 May 2021).

6. Chaccour, Lines and Whitty. Effect of Ivermectin on Anopheles gambiae Mosquitoes Fed on Humans: The Potential of Oral Insecticides in Malaria Control (2010). doi.org/10.1086/653208.

Chapter 6

1. Exhibit 17. Urgent preliminary report of Yellow Card data up to 26 May 2021 (9 June 2021).

2. Exhibit 18. Dr June Raine's response (22 July 2021).

3. Exhibit 19. Bryant et al, Ivermectin for Prevention and Treatment of Covid-19 Infection: A Systematic Review, Meta-analysis, and Trial Sequential Analysis to Inform Clinical Guidelines. https://journals. lww.com/americantherapeutics/fulltext/2021/08000/ivermectin_for_ prevention_and_treatment_of.7.aspx (21st June 2021).

4. Exhibit 20. Example of a Joint Country Statement on ivermectin.

5. https://www.bmj.com/content/372/bmj.n810/rr-14 Dr Polykova's letter was removed by the BMJ allegedly for spreading misinformation. www.conservativewoman.co.uk/the-mhra-the-watchdog-covering-up-the-truth-about-vaccine-deaths-and-injuries/

6. From Watchdog to Enabler – Regulation in Covid and after. Dr June Raine. Oxford University Medic's Day, 5th March 2022. https://www. youtube.com/watch?v=xUQfzTqPUm4.

7. *The Guardian.* Doctors urged to be more vigilant over drug side effects. Sarah Boseley, 12th May, 2006.

8. https://www.clinicaltrialsarena.com/news/ivermectin-principle-trial-covid/?cf-view

Chapter 7

1. Exhibit 21. Nebraska's Attorney General Opinion (14 October 2021).

2. https://www.medpagetoday.com/special-reports/exclusives/93485.

3. Joe Rogan and Robert F. Kennedy Jr interview 27th June 2024. www. youtube.com/watch?v=p6LJXPOv4SM

4. Vaccines Work. The Next Pandemic: Marburg? https://www.gavi.org/vaccineswork/next-pandemic/marburg

5. https://en.wikipedia.org/wiki/Tedros_Adhanom_Ghebreyesus

6. WHO announcement on Marburg, 11 August 2021: https://www.youtube.com/watch?v=ozoqPEnF3Bo

7. US Chamber of Commerce interview: https://www.youtube.com/watch?v=fWQ2DsHWrQE

8. O'Donnell, et al, 2021. Vaccine Platform Comparison: Protective Efficacy against Lethal Marburg Virus Challenge in the Hamster Model. doi.org/10.3390/ijms25158516

9. www.oxfordmail.co.uk/news/24445345.oxford-university-scientists-testing-marburg-virus-vaccine/

10. WHO ACT-accelerator https://www.who.int/initiatives/act-accelerator/about

11. The Vaccine Network. www.gov.uk/government/groups/uk-vaccines-network.

12. www.gov.uk/government/groups/uk-vaccines-network. Projects funded by DHSC through the UK Vaccine Network.

Chapter 8

1. Exhibit 22. Bryant et al response on the Elgazzar withdrawal in *American Journal of Therapeutics*. https://journals.lww.com/americantherapeutics/fulltext/2022/08000/re__expression_of_concern_for_bryant_a,_lawrie_ta,.11.aspx

2. https://www.theguardian.com/science/2021/jul/16/huge-study-supporting-ivermectin-as-covid-treatment-withdrawn-over-ethical-concerns

3. The TOGETHER Trial critique. www.c19ivm.org/meta.html#togetherivm

4. Covid-19: Researcher blows the whistle on data integrity issues in Pfizer's vaccine trial. BMJ 2021;375:n2635.

Chapter 9

1. Exhibit 23. Liverpool University's Response Letter.
2. Exhibit 24. Retraction Demand by Fordham et al (2021).
3. Exhibit 25. Fordham et al. Use and Abuse of Systematic Reviews. (2021).
4. https://cidg.cochrane.org/news/new-cochrane-review-ivermectin-preventing-and-treating-covid-19
5. Exhibit 26. Indian Bar Association legal challenge (25 May 2021).
6. https://philharper.substack.com/p/professor-tied-to-altered-andrew?
7. Roman et al (2021). doi.org/10.1093/cid/ciab591.
8. Popp et al (2021). www.cochrane.org/CD015017/
9. www.researchgate.net/publication/353195913_Bayesian_Meta_Analysis_of_Ivermectin_Effectiveness_in_Treating_Covid-19_Disease
10. Ontai et al. doi.org/10.23880/eij-16000217
11. Stone et al. doi.org/10.3390/biologics2030015

Chapter 10

1. www.science.org/content/article/meet-data-thugs-out-expose-shoddy-and-questionable-research
2. Graham Brady interview on British Thought Leaders. https://www.youtube.com/watch?v=o7HB_iXZlII

Chapter 12

1. Exhibit 27. UNIT report 02/2022.
2. *A Letter to Dr Andrew Hill* documentary
3. https://en.wikipedia.org/wiki/Tedros_Adhanom_Ghebreyesus
4. www.uscis.gov/sites/default/files/document/legal-docs/2014_Implementation_of_New_Discretionary_Exemption_for_Activities_or_Associations_Relating_to_TPLF.pdf
5. www.america-times.com/tplf-terrorism-threat-to-regional-peace-and-stability/
6. www.pubmed.ncbi.nlm.nih.gov/?term=graphene+oxide+AND+vaccine

7. https://digitallibrary.un.org/record/731800/files/A_PV-1229-EN.pdf

Chapter 13

1. Exhibit 28. Letter to Mr Charlie Massey, CEO of the General Medical Council (2 October 2023).

Additional evidence, for example, the Medincell studies, can also be found at the online repository www.Lawriefiles.com.

Acknowledgements

I am humbled by, and deeply indebted to the late Richard Wilhelm, whose diligence and specialist knowledge made the *I Ching's* ancient wisdom accessible to Western audiences. So too, without Cary Baynes' meticulous rendering of Wilhelm's German translation into English, the wisdom of the *I Ching* would have remained out of my reach. Wilhelm and Baynes are thus among those whom I refer to as my "co-authors" in this book, which include the ancient Chinese sages Fu Hsi, King Wên, the Duke of Chou, and Confucius, whose careful, iterative considerations thousands of years ago have shaped and informed this investigation. Carl Jung's experiment with the *I Ching,* described in his engaging foreword in the Wilhelm-Carey edition, inspired and gave me the courage to conduct this *Game of Trust* experiment. I trust that the fruits of their collective and enduring efforts will now be appreciated by a new audience.

It has been an honour to get to know Chrissy Philp these past years, and witness a sage of the highest order at work in the world. Thank you for introducing me to the *I Ching* and inspiring me with your novel scientific theories.

In regard to the human drama at the heart of this story, one that is far from over, I extend heartfelt thanks to all who have played a positive role in this epic tale of good over evil.

In particular, my deepest gratitude goes to the gentle warriors at EbMCsquared CIC, whose unwavering integrity, creative energy, enthusiasm, and good humour have kept me on the path toward a better world.

I thank Vivienne Wallace, Pablo Lawrie, Francesca Havens, and Karen Harris for their careful proofreading, and ChatGPT for its copyediting assistance. Artist Jake Fern's portrait of me was a beautiful and timely gift, serving as an ideal front cover for this book.

I extend my greatest respect to Mark Lawrie, for his enduring support and for being a steadfast pillar of our mutual families—both biological and the EbMCsquared clan. His compassionate presence and brave heart has anchored us through each new challenge.

This work would not have been possible without my conscientious man, Daniel Rushforth, whose unwavering belief in its merit, and in me, enabled its completion.

Finally, to my dear children, Imogen, Pablo, and especially Grace: I am so very sorry for disrupting your lives when you needed a loving mother most, that I was not always there to guide you when you felt lost, cherish your spirit when you were down, and protect you from evil. Thank you for forgiving me. I dedicate this book to you.